ASIAN HISTORICAL DICTIONARIES
Edited by Jon Woronoff

Historical Dictionary
of
ISRAEL

by

BERNARD REICH

Asian Historical Dictionaries, No. 8

The Scarecrow Press, Inc.
Metuchen, N.J., & London
1992

British Library Cataloguing-in-publication data available

Library of Congress Cataloging-in-Publication Data

Reich, Bernard.
    Historical dictionary of Israel / by Bernard Reich.
      p.   cm. — (Asian historical dictionaries ; no. 8)
    Includes bibliographical references.
    ISBN 0-8108-2535-X (alk. paper)
    1. Israel—History—Dictionaries.   2. Israel—Politics and
government—Dictionaries. I. Title. II. Series.
DS126.5.R38   1992
956.94′003—dc20   92-5324

CONTENTS

EDITOR'S FOREWORD

Few countries have attracted more attention and aroused more controversy than Israel. An eternal hot point, it was born out of struggle and has waged several wars to survive. Domestically, it had to weld people of disparate backgrounds, and also different races and religions, into a modern state, a no less exacting challenge. Despite its diminutive size, it has played a notable role in international affairs, whether through development aid to the Third World or its influence on Middle Eastern events. Meanwhile, it has fashioned a unique society and created institutions like the kibbutz which intrigue outsiders.

Thus, unlike other volumes in the series of Asian Historical Dictionaries, the author's task is not to tell us more about a country that is poorly known. On Israel, plenty has been said and written. Indeed, some may feel that there is almost too much. So the author must primarily refresh our memories about crucial aspects and provide a handy reference to persons, places, and events. It is also indispensable to sift through the extensive literature, put the books in order, and point the reader toward more detailed information.

This has been done clearly, succinctly and comprehensively by Bernard Reich. As a leading specialist on Israel, he is familiar with the country which he visits regularly. He is also acquainted with the material and literature. Finally, as professor of political science at George Washington University, he has considerable experience in explaining Israel to others. In addition, he has himself contributed books and articles, including *The United States and Israel* and *Israeli National Security Policy*.

Jon Woronoff
Series Editor

ACKNOWLEDGMENTS

This dictionary was a difficult book to produce. The first problem was to select those terms for inclusion which were the most central for an understanding of Israel. There is so much to write about and so much has been written about this small country that the need to be concise posed the most difficult problem.

Many people were helpful in the preparation of the book and it would be impossible to name all of them. Some individuals were particularly helpful. Gladyce W. Ansell, Noah Dropkin, and Meyrav Wurmser, and some experts on Israel who prefer to remain unnamed, read earlier versions of the manuscript and made suggestions for improvement. As usual, Suzie provided the assistance essential to the timely completion of the work.

I alone bear responsibility for the final work.

Bernard Reich
Professor of Political Science
George Washington University
Washington, DC
October 1991

ABBREVIATIONS AND ACRONYMS

AMAN	Agaf Modiin (Intelligence Branch)
c.	*circa* (about)
CRM	Citizens' Rights and Peace Movement
DMC	Democratic Movement for Change
DMI	Director of Military Intelligence
GAHAL	Gush Herut Liberalim (Herut Liberal bloc)
HABAD	Hokhmah, Binah, Daat (wisdom, comprehension, knowledge)
HADASH	Hazit Demokratit Leshalom Uleshivyon (Democratic Front for Peace and Equality)
IAI	Israel Aircraft Industries
IDF	Israel Defense Forces
JNF	Jewish National Fund
LEHI	Lohamei Herut Yisrael (Fighters for the Freedom of Israel)
MAFDAL	Miflaga Datit Leumit (National Religious Party)
MAHAL	Mitnadvei Hutz Laeretz (foreign volunteers)
MAPAI	Mifleget Poalei Eretz Yisrael (Land of Israel Workers Party. Israel Workers Party)
MAPAM	Mifleget Poalim Hameuchedet (United Workers Party)
MK	Member of the Knesset
MOU	Memorandum of Understanding
NRP	National Religious Party
NUG	National Unity Government
PLO	Palestine Liberation Organization
q.v.	*quod vide* (which see)
SHABAK	Sherut Bitahon Klali, Shin Bet (General Security Services)

SHAI	Sherut Yediot (information service)
SHAS	Sephardi Torah Guardians
TAAS	Taasiya Tzvait (military industry)
TAMI	Tenuah Lemassoret Israel (Movement for Jewish Tradition)
UAR	United Arab Republic
UIA	United Israel Appeal
UJA	United Jewish Appeal
UNEF	United Nations Emergency Force
UNIFIL	United Nations Interim Force in Lebanon
UNSCOP	United Nations Special Committee on Palestine
UPA	United Palestine Appeal
WIZO	Women's International Zionist Organization
WZO	World Zionist Organization

CHRONOLOGY

Headings of relevant dictionary entries are in all capital letters here.

c.17th Century BC	The period of the Patriarchs of Judaism: ABRAHAM, Isaac, Jacob.
c.1250–1210 BC	The Exodus of the Jews from Egypt; wandering in the desert of SINAI and the conquest of CANAAN under Joshua.
c.1020–1004 BC	KING SAUL. Establishment of the Israelite kingdom.
c.1004–965 BC	KING DAVID. Consolidation and expansion of the kingdom.
c.965–928 BC	KING SOLOMON. The Temple is built in JERUSALEM.
c.928 BC	Division of the state and the establishment of Kingdoms of JUDAH and Israel.
c.722 BC	Assyrian conquest of SAMARIA, Kingdom of Israel; large number of Jews exiled.
c.586 BC	JERUSALEM is conquered and the Temple is destroyed. Mass deportation of Jews in the Babylonian captivity.
c.520–515 BC	The Temple is rebuilt.
c.167–160 BC	Hasmonean rebellion under Judah Maccabee.

164 BC	JERUSALEM is liberated and the Temple is rededicated.
37–4 BC	Reign of Herod.
c.19 BC	The Temple is rebuilt.
66 AD	Jewish revolt against Rome.
70	Siege of JERUSALEM. Destruction of the Temple by Romans. Direct Roman rule is imposed until 395.
73	Fall of MASSADA.
132–135	BAR KOCHBA WAR.
395–638	Byzantine rule.
638	Arab Muslim armies conquer JERUSALEM.
c. 636–1072	Arab rule.
1072–1099	Seljuq rule.
1099	JERUSALEM captured by the Crusaders.
1099–1291	Crusader rule with interruptions.
1187	JERUSALEM is captured by Saladin.
1291–1516	Mameluke rule.
1517–1917	Ottoman Turkish rule.
1878	PETAH TIKVA is founded.
1882–1903	First ALIYA.
1882	HIBBAT ZION MOVEMENT started. RISHON LEZION is founded.

1894	DREYFUS Trial in France.
1896	Publication of *DER JUDENSTAAT* by THEODOR HERZL.
1897	First (WORLD) ZIONIST CONGRESS is held in Basle, Switzerland. The WORLD ZIONIST ORGANIZATION is established.
1901	JEWISH NATIONAL FUND is established.
1904	HERZL dies.
1904–1914	Second ALIYA.
1909	The KIBBUTZ of DEGANIA is founded. TEL AVIV is established.
1917	The British army captures JERUSALEM.
November 2	The BALFOUR DECLARATION is issued.
1919–1923	Third ALIYA.
1920	The BRITISH MANDATE FOR PALESTINE is granted at San Remo although it is not formalized until 1922. HERBERT SAMUEL is appointed High Commissioner for PALESTINE. The HISTADRUT and HAGANA are founded.
1921	The MOSHAV of NAHALAL is founded.
1924–1931	Fourth ALIYA.
1925	HEBREW UNIVERSITY is inaugurated on MT. SCOPUS, JERUSALEM.
1929	Arab riots take place in JERUSALEM and massacres occur in HEBRON and SAFED.

1932–1938   Fifth ALIYA.

1935   The REVISIONIST movement, headed by
                          VLADIMIR ZEEV JABOTINSKY, se-
                          cedes from the WORLD ZIONIST
                          ORGANIZATION and establishes the
                          NEW ZIONIST ORGANIZATION.

1947   Great Britain turns the PALESTINE issue
                          over to the United Nations. The UNITED
                          NATIONS SPECIAL COMMITTEE ON
                          PALESTINE examines the problem and
                          recommends solutions.

    November 29   The United Nations General Assembly
                          adopts a resolution providing for an inde-
                          pendent Jewish state in PALESTINE to be
                          united economically with an independent
                          Arab state. An international regime is to be
                          established in JERUSALEM.

1948 May 14   Proclamation of the independence of the
                          State of Israel.

    May 15   The BRITISH MANDATE FOR PALES-
                          TINE is terminated; Arab armies of Egypt,
                          Iraq, Jordan, Lebanon, and Syria invade
                          and the first Arab-Israeli War (Israel's
                          WAR OF INDEPENDENCE) officially
                          begins. The United States and the Soviet
                          Union recognize Israel.

    June 11   The first truce in the Arab-Israeli hostilities
                          begins.

    July 8   The truce ends.

    July 18   The second truce begins.

    October 15   The truce ends.

1949 January 25   Election for the First KNESSET.

February 16 CHAIM WEIZMANN is elected the first PRESIDENT of Israel.

February 24 The ARMISTICE AGREEMENT with EGYPT is achieved.

March 8 The first session of the KNESSET begins in TEL AVIV.

March 10 The first regular GOVERNMENT is established under DAVID BEN-GURION as Prime Minister.

March 23 ARMISTICE AGREEMENT with Lebanon.

April 3 ARMISTICE AGREEMENT with Jordan.

May 11 Israel becomes a member of the United Nations.

July 20 ARMISTICE AGREEMENT with Syria.

September 12 Compulsory Education Law passed.

November 2 The WEIZMANN INSTITUTE OF SCIENCE is inaugurated.

December 13 A resolution to transfer the KNESSET and the GOVERNMENT to JERUSALEM is adopted.

December 26 The KNESSET session resumes in JERUSALEM.

1950 January Egyptians occupy the islands of TIRAN and Sanafir at the southern entrance to the GULF OF AQABA, thus blocking passage to the Israeli port of EILAT.

January 4 The KNESSET ratifies a GOVERNMENT statement opposing the internationalization of JERUSALEM.

June 13	The KNESSET adopts a resolution on the manner in which a CONSTITUTION for the state is to be devised.
July	Beginning of large-scale immigration to Israel from Iraq.
July 5	The LAW OF RETURN, confirming the right of every Jew to settle in Israel, is passed.
September 24	The airlift of Jews from Yemen to Israel is concluded.
1951 March	Israel launches a three-year plan to drain the HULEH swamps for irrigation and for generation of hydroelectric power.
July	The airlift of Jews from Iraq to Israel is completed.
July 20	King Abdullah of Jordan is assassinated, ostensibly because of negotiations with Israel.
July 30	Election for the Second KNESSET.
August 14	The 23rd (WORLD) ZIONIST CONGRESS opens in JERUSALEM.
August 20	The Second KNESSET opens.
September 1	The United Nations Security Council condemns Egyptian anti-Israel blockade in Suez Canal.
1952 November 9	President CHAIM WEIZMANN dies.
December 8	YITZHAK BEN ZVI is elected the second President of Israel.
1953 September 2	Israel initiates the second phase of the Jordan Development Plan.

October 14   ISRAEL DEFENSE FORCES (IDF) troops carry out a reprisal raid against the Jordanian village of Qibya.

1954 January   MOSHE SHARETT becomes Prime Minister.

June 2   HEBREW UNIVERSITY dedicates its new campus in JERUSALEM.

July 19   The Yarkon-Negev pipeline, to irrigate 25,000 acres in the NEGEV, is opened.

September 28   Egypt seizes the *Bat Galim,* an Israel-flag merchant vessel, at Suez when it attempts to transit the Suez Canal, and its crew is imprisoned.

October 12   Thirteen Jews are indicted in Egypt on charges of espionage.

1955 July 26   Election for the Third KNESSET.

August 15   The Third KNESSET opens. DAVID BEN-GURION becomes Prime Minister.

February   Egyptian fedayeen intensify operations against Israel.

September 27   Premier Gamal Abdul Nasser of Egypt signs an agreement with Czechoslovakia to obtain vast quantities of arms.

October 3   Czechoslovakia announces confirmation of an arms deal with Egypt. Later it is revealed to be a Soviet-Egyptian transaction.

1956 April 24   The 24th (WORLD) ZIONIST CONGRESS opens in JERUSALEM.

July 26   Egyptian President Gamal Abdul Nasser announces the nationalization of the Suez Canal Company.

October 29   Israel moves against Egyptian fedayeen bases and prepares for attack in the SINAI PENINSULA to eliminate commando bases.

November 5   France and the United Kingdom invade the Suez Canal Zone.

November 6   Israel announces acceptance of a ceasefire in the SINAI PENINSULA.

November 7   Egypt, France, and the United Kingdom accept the ceasefire.

December 22   Anglo-French troops complete their withdrawal from the Suez Canal Zone.

1957   Israel evacuates SINAI and the GAZA STRIP. The United Nations Emergency Force is established.

January 22   Israel evacuates all of SINAI except GAZA and SHARM EL-SHEIKH.

March 1   Israel agrees to evacuate GAZA and SHARM EL-SHEIKH.

March 8   UNEF forces take over from Israel the garrisoning of SHARM EL-SHEIKH and the administration of the GAZA STRIP.

March 25   The first large vessel arrives at the Israeli port of EILAT.

March 29   Convoy traffic resumes through the Suez Canal.

October 31   The Arid Zone Research Institute opens in BEERSHEVA.

1958 January 16 The BEERSHEVA-EILAT highway, Israel's "dry-land Suez Canal," opens.

December 4   The cornerstone of the new KNESSET building is laid.

1959 November 2   Election for the Fourth KNESSET.

November 18   Israeli Finance Minister LEVI ESHKOL announces that diversion of water from the JORDAN RIVER for irrigation purposes had become a priority project for Israel.

November 30   The Fourth KNESSET opens.

1960 February 1   Israeli and Syrian forces clash in the demilitarized zone.

March   Prime Minister BEN-GURION visits the United States and Great Britain.

March 11   TEL AVIV celebrates its jubilee.

April 26   Israel's National Water Council approves a plan for laying a giant conduit to carry water from the SEA OF GALILEE to southern Israel.

May 23   ADOLF EICHMANN is kidnapped from Argentina for trial in Israel.

1961 August 15   Election for the Fifth KNESSET.

April 11   The EICHMANN Trial opens in JERUSA-LEM.

July 5   Israel launches its first meteorological space rocket.

July 30   The cornerstone of the deep-sea port of ASHDOD is laid. The millionth immigrant since the establishment of the state arrives.

September 4   The Fifth KNESSET opens.

1962 May 31   ADOLF EICHMANN is executed.

June 30 Ten years of activities of the United States Operations Mission in Israel are completed, both governments agreeing that in view of Israel's progress, no special body is needed to administer US technical aid.

September 27 The Foreign Ministry announces that the United States has agreed to supply Israel with Hawk ground-to-air missiles for defense.

October 30 YITZHAK BEN ZVI is re-elected for a third term as PRESIDENT of Israel.

November 21 The new town of ARAD in the eastern NEGEV is officially inaugurated.

1963 March 20 The KNESSET calls upon the Bonn Government to terminate the activities of German scientists in Egypt.

April 18 Work begins on construction of Carmiel, a new town in GALILEE.

April 23 President YITZHAK BEN ZVI dies.

May 21 ZALMAN SHAZAR is elected by the KNESSET as Israel's third PRESIDENT.

June 16 DAVID BEN-GURION resigns from his post as Prime Minister and Minister of Defense.

June 26 A new government, with LEVI ESHKOL as Prime Minister, takes office.

July 11 *Shalom,* Israel's largest passenger liner, is launched in France.

October 21 Prime Minister LEVI ESHKOL announces far-reaching relaxations of military government restrictions on ARABS IN ISRAEL.

1964	January 1	YITZHAK RABIN becomes Chief of Staff of the ISRAEL DEFENSE FORCES.
	January 5	Pope Paul VI begins a pilgrimage to Christian holy sites in Israel.
1965	November 2	Election for the Sixth KNESSET.
	November 22	The Sixth KNESSET opens.
1966	November 12	An Israeli patrol car detonates a land mine near the Jordan frontier, killing three soldiers and injuring six. Israel complains to the United Nations Security Council.
	November 13	Israeli forces launch an attack on the Jordanian village of Samu.
1967	April 7	During an air clash six Syrian MIG 21s are shot down by Israeli planes.
	May 15	The United Arab Republic puts its forces on a state of alert and begins extensive redeployment of military units.
	May 18	The United Arab Republic asks the United Nations to remove UNEF from the Egypt-Israel armistice line and the United Nations complies. Israel announces that it is taking "appropriate measures" in response to the UAR build-up in the SINAI PENINSULA.
	May 22	UAR President Gamal Abdul Nasser announces an Egyptian blockade of the GULF OF AQABA, cutting off Israel's access to the Red Sea through the port of EILAT.
	May 24	Jordan announces it has given permission for Iraqi and Saudi Arabian forces to enter Jordan and that general mobilization in Jordan has been completed.

June 1	Prime Minister LEVI ESHKOL forms a broadly based "NATIONAL UNITY GOVERNMENT" in which former Chief of Staff MOSHE DAYAN becomes Minister of Defense.
June 5	Hostilities commence between Israel and the Arab states in the third Arab-Israeli (SIX DAY) WAR.
June 6	The UAR closes the Suez Canal to all shipping. The UAR breaks relations with the United States over allegations of US support for Israel in the war.
June 7	The Jordanian and Israeli Governments accept the United Nations call for a cease-fire. At the conclusion of hostilities, the Israelis had established themselves at the Jordan River and had control of the WEST BANK.
June 8	A ceasefire goes into effect between the UAR and Israel. Israeli forces had occupied the GAZA STRIP and the SINAI PENINSULA.
June 10	The USSR breaks diplomatic relations with Israel. Other Eastern European countries, except Rumania, subsequently follow suit.
June 11	A ceasefire goes into effect between Israel and Syria. The Israelis had penetrated beyond the former demarcation line, establishing themselves on the GOLAN HEIGHTS.
June 12	In a policy speech to parliament, Israeli Prime Minister LEVI ESHKOL declares that Israel could not return to the prewar situation and demands that the Arabs make peace with Israel.

June 28	The Israeli Minister of the Interior announces new municipal boundaries for JERUSALEM, in accordance with enabling legislation passed the previous day by the KNESSET; former Jordanian-held Jerusalem is included within the new municipal jurisdiction.
July 3	Israel announces a plan for the return of refugees from the 1967 war.
October 21	The Israeli destroyer *Eilat* is sunk by UAR patrol boats off the SINAI coast. In reprisal, on October 24, Israel shells Suez and its oil refineries.
November 22	UNITED NATIONS SECURITY COUNCIL RESOLUTION 242 is adopted.
1968 December 26	Arab fedayeen, who had just arrived from Beirut, attack an EL AL plane at Athens airport.
December 28	Israeli helicopter-borne commandos attack Beirut airport.
1969	The WAR OF ATTRITION (the fourth Arab-Israeli War) begins along the Suez Canal. LEVI ESHKOL dies; GOLDA MEIR becomes Prime Minister.
October	Election for the Seventh KNESSET.
1970 August	The WAR OF ATTRITION is ended by a cease-fire.
1973 April	EPHRAIM (KATCHALSKI) KATZIR is elected PRESIDENT.
October	The fifth Arab-Israeli (YOM KIPPUR) WAR.

November   The AGRANAT COMMISSION established.

December   Election for the Eighth KNESSET.

1974 January   EGYPT-ISRAEL DISENGAGEMENT AGREEMENT is signed.

April   GOLDA MEIR resigns; YITZHAK RABIN becomes Prime Minister.

May   Israel and SYRIA conclude a DISENGAGEMENT AGREEMENT.

1975   EGYPT and Israel sign a Disengagement agreement (SINAI II ACCORDS).

1976 July   Israeli commandos free hostages at ENTEBBE AIRPORT, Uganda.

1977 April   RABIN resigns as Prime Minister. SHIMON PERES is selected as LABOR PARTY leader.

May   Election for the Ninth KNESSET. LIKUD, under the leadership of MENACHEM BEGIN, emerges as the largest party.

June   BEGIN forms the government coalition with himself as Prime Minister.

November   President ANWAR SADAT of EGYPT announces to the Egyptian National Assembly his willingness to visit Israel to discuss peace; the Israeli KNESSET overwhelmingly approves an invitation to Sadat. Sadat arrives in JERUSALEM and addresses the Israeli Knesset. Negotiations begin.

December 13   The Cairo Conference opens.

December 25-26   The Ismailia Conference takes place.

1978		YITZHAK NAVON is elected PRESIDENT.
	March	Following an attack on an Israeli bus, Israel launches OPERATION LITANI against Palestinian bases in LEBANON.
	May	The UNITED STATES Congress approves a weapons package for Israel, Egypt, and Saudi Arabia.
	June	Israel completes the withdrawal of its armed forces and UNIFIL takes up positions in southern LEBANON.
	July 18–19	The Leeds Castle Conference takes place.
	September	SADAT, BEGIN, and CARTER meet at the Summit at Camp David, Maryland. The CAMP DAVID ACCORDS are signed on the 17th.
	October	Egypt and Israel begin peace negotiations at Blair House in Washington to implement the CAMP DAVID ACCORDS.
1979	March 26	The EGYPT-ISRAEL PEACE TREATY is signed in Washington.
	May 25	Israel begins withdrawal from the SINAI PENINSULA; Egypt and Israel begin discussion of autonomy issues.
1980	February	EGYPT and Israel exchange ambassadors.
	July 30	The KNESSET adopts a BASIC LAW reaffirming united JERUSALEM as Israel's capital.
1981	June	Israel destroys the Osirak nuclear reactor near Baghdad.
	June 30	Election for the Tenth KNESSET. LIKUD

secures the largest number of seats. A BEGIN coalition government secures a vote of confidence from the Knesset in August.

October 6 — President SADAT is assassinated.

November 30 — The UNITED STATES and Israel sign a MEMORANDUM OF UNDERSTANDING on Strategic Cooperation.

December — Israel extends its "law and jurisdiction" to the GOLAN HEIGHTS.

1982 April — Israel completes its withdrawal from the SINAI PENINSULA and returns it to Egypt.

June — WAR IN LEBANON (Operation Peace for Galilee). Israel launches an attempt to destroy PLO bases in LEBANON on June 6.

September 1 — UNITED STATES President Ronald Reagan outlines his "fresh start" initiative for peace in the Middle East.

September — Bashir Gemayel, president-elect of LEBANON, is assassinated. Massacres take place at the SABRA AND SHATILA REFUGEE CAMPS. The KAHAN COMMISSION is established to inquire into the massacres.

1983 February — The KAHAN COMMISSION reports its findings. ARIEL SHARON resigns as Defense Minister and is replaced by MOSHE ARENS.

March — CHAIM HERZOG is elected PRESIDENT.

May 17 — Israel and Lebanon sign an agreement concluded with the assistance of United

States Secretary of State George Shultz. Lebanon abrogates the agreement in March 1984.

September   MENACHEM BEGIN resigns as Prime Minister.

October   YITZHAK SHAMIR forms a new government and takes office as Prime Minister.

1984 July   Election for the Eleventh KNESSET.

September   A GOVERNMENT OF NATIONAL UNITY is formed with SHIMON PERES as Prime Minister and YITZHAK SHAMIR as alternate Prime Minister and Foreign Minister. The mass immigration of Ethiopian Jews (FALASHAS) to Israel in OPERATION MOSES takes place.

1985 July   The ISRAEL DEFENSE FORCES completes its withdrawal from LEBANON. A security zone is established in southern Lebanon.

September 11-12   Prime Minister SHIMON PERES and President Hosni Mubarak hold a summit meeting in Egypt.

1986 October   The NATIONAL UNITY GOVERNMENT ROTATION shifts SHAMIR to the position of Prime Minister and PERES to the post of Foreign Minister.

1987 December   An Arab uprising (INTIFADA) in the WEST BANK and the GAZA STRIP challenges Israel's authority in the territories.

1988   Israel launches a space satellite.

November   Election for the Twelfth KNESSET. The PALESTINE National Congress (PNC) meeting in Algiers declares an independent Palestinian state.

December 22   Prime Minister YITZHAK SHAMIR presents his coalition government to Parliament. It is approved by a vote of 84 to 19 with three abstentions.

1989 May 14   The CABINET formally approves an Arab-Israeli peace initiative.

November   Prime Minister SHAMIR visits the UNITED STATES and meets with President George Bush to discuss the peace process.

1990 March 13   Prime Minister YITZHAK SHAMIR dismisses Deputy Prime Minister SHIMON PERES and the other LABOR PARTY cabinet ministers resign.

March 15   The KNESSET passes a motion of no-confidence in the government led by YITZHAK SHAMIR by a vote of 60 to 55.

April 26   LABOR PARTY leader SHIMON PERES returns the mandate to form a government to President CHAIM HERZOG after failing in his efforts.

April 27   Acting Prime Minister YITZHAK SHAMIR accepts the mandate to form a new government.

June 11   The KNESSET approves YITZHAK SHAMIR's government composed of LIKUD and right-wing and religious parties.

September 30   Consular relations are reestablished between Israel and the SOVIET UNION.

November 5   RABBI MEIR KAHANE, leader of the KACH party, is assassinated in New York.

November 16   AGUDAT ISRAEL joins the coalition government of Prime Minister SHAMIR.

November 25   The cabinet approves Gen. EHUD BARAK to replace Lt. Gen. DAN SHOMRON as Chief of Staff of the IDF when Shomron's tenure ends in April 1991.

1991 February 3   REHAVAM ZEEVI of MOLEDET joins the CABINET as Minister Without Portfolio.

October 18   Israel and the SOVIET UNION restore diplomatic relations.

October 30   Peace conference organized by the United States and the SOVIET UNION meets in MADRID, Spain.

December 4–18   Peace talks between Israel and Arab delegations take place in Washington, DC. Numerous topics are on the agenda, with disagreement on where and when to reconvene a major issue.

1992 January 13   Negotiations between Israel and the Jordanian-Palestinian delegation resume in Washington.

January 28–29   Broader Middle Eastern regional issues are discussed at a conference convened in Moscow. States from both inside and outside of the Middle East meet to discuss regional issues such as economic development, arms control, water resources, and refugees.

TABLES

TABLE 1
PRESIDENTS

Chaim Weizmann	1948–1952
Yitzhak Ben Zvi	1952–1963
Shneur Zalman Shazar	1963–1973
Ephraim Katzir	1973–1978
Yitzhak Navon	1978–1983
Chaim Herzog	1983–

TABLE 2
PRIME MINISTERS

David Ben-Gurion	1948–1953
Moshe Sharett	1954–1955
David Ben-Gurion	1955–1963
Levi Eshkol	1963–1969
Golda Meir	1969–1974
Yitzhak Rabin	1974–1977
Menachem Begin	1977–1983
Yitzhak Shamir	1983–1984
Shimon Peres	1984–1986
Yitzhak Shamir	1986–

TABLE 3
MINISTERS OF FOREIGN AFFAIRS

Moshe Sharett	1948–1956
Golda Meir	1956–1966
Abba Eban	1966–1974
Yigal Allon	1974–1977
Moshe Dayan	1977–1979
Menachem Begin	1979–1980
Yitzhak Shamir	1980–1986
Shimon Peres	1986–1988
Moshe Arens	1988–1990
David Levy	1990–

TABLE 4
MINISTERS OF DEFENSE

David Ben-Gurion	1948–1954
Pinhas Lavon	1954–1955
David Ben-Gurion	1955–1963
Levi Eshkol	1963–1967
Moshe Dayan	1967–1974
Shimon Peres	1974–1977
Ezer Weizman	1977–1980
Menachem Begin	1980–1981
Ariel Sharon	1981–1983
Moshe Arens	1983–1984
Yitzhak Rabin	1984–1990
Moshe Arens	1990–

TABLE 5
MINISTERS OF FINANCE

Eliezer Kaplan	1948–1952
Levi Eshkol	1952–1963
Pinhas Sapir	1963–1968
Ze'ev Sharef	1968–1969
Pinhas Sapir	1969–1974
Yehoshua Rabinowitz	1974–1977
Simha Ehrlich	1977–1979
Yigael Hurvitz	1980–1981
Yoram Aridor	1981–1983
Yigal Cohen-Orgad	1983–1984
Yitzhak Moda'i	1984–1986
Moshe Nissim	1986–1988
Shimon Peres	1988–1990
Yitzhak Moda'i	1990–

TABLE 6
CHIEFS OF STAFF

Yaacov Dori	1948–1949
Yigael Yadin	1949–1952
Mordechai Makleff	1952–1953
Moshe Dayan	1953–1958
Chaim Laskov	1958–1961
Zvi Tsur	1961–1964
Yitzhak Rabin	1964–1968
Haim Bar Lev	1968–1972
David Elazar	1972–1974
Mordechai Gur	1974–1978
Raphael Eitan	1978–1983
Moshe Levy	1983–1987
Dan Shomron	1987–1991
Ehud Barak	1991–

TABLE 7
KNESSET
BEGINNING OF TERM

First Knesset	1949
Second Knesset	1951
Third Knesset	1955
Fourth Knesset	1959
Fifth Knesset	1961
Sixth Knesset	1965
Seventh Knesset	1969
Eighth Knesset	1973
Ninth Knesset	1977
Tenth Knesset	1981
Eleventh Knesset	1984
Twelfth Knesset	1988

TABLE 8
IMMIGRATION TO PALESTINE AND ISRAEL 1882–1989

YEAR(S)	IMMIGRATION
1882–1903	20,000–30,000
1904–1914	35,000–40,000
1919–1923	35,183
1924–1931	81,613
1932–1938	197,235
1939–1945	81,808
1946–1948, May 15	56,467
1948 (May 15–Dec 31)	101,819
1949	239,576
1950	170,215
1951	175,129
1952	24,369
1953	11,326
1954	18,370
1955	37,478
1956	56,234
1957	71,224
1958	27,082
1959	23,895
1960	24,510
1961	47,638
1962	61,328
1963	64,364
1964	54,716
1965	30,736
1966	15,730
1967	14,327
1968	20,544
1969	37,804
1970	36,750
1971	41,930
1972	55,888
1973	54,886
1974	31,981
1975	20,028
1976	19,754
1977	21,429
1978	26,394
1979	37,222

TABLE 8 *(continued)*

YEAR(S)	IMMIGRATION
1980	20,428
1981	12,599
1982	13,723
1983	16,906
1984	19,981
1985	10,642
1986	9,505
1987	12,965
1988	13,034
1989	24,050

Source: *Statistical Abstract of Israel 1988,* No. 39. Jerusalem: Central Bureau of Statistics, n.d., pages 157–158, and *Statistical Abstract of Israel 1990,* page 172.

TABLE 9
POPULATION AT END OF YEAR
(Thousands)

YEAR	JEWS	MOSLEMS	CHRIS-TIANS	DRUZE & OTHERS	TOTAL
1948	758.7	—————	156.0	—————	
1949	1013.9	111.5	34.0	14.5	1173.9
1950	1203.0	116.1	36.0	15.0	1370.1
1951	1404.4	118.9	39.0	15.5	1577.8
1952	1450.2	122.8	40.4	16.1	1629.5
1953	1483.6	127.6	41.4	16.8	1669.4
1954	1526.0	131.8	42.0	18.0	1717.8
1955	1590.5	136.3	43.3	19.0	1789.1
1956	1667.5	141.4	43.7	19.8	1872.4
1957	1762.8	146.8	45.8	20.5	1976.0
1958	1810.2	152.8	47.3	21.4	2031.7
1959	1858.8	159.2	48.3	22.3	2088.7
1960	1911.3	166.3	49.6	23.3	2150.4
1961	1981.7	179.4	51.3	26.3	2234.2
1962	2068.9	183.0	52.6	27.3	2331.8
1963	2155.6	192.2	53.9	28.5	2430.1
1964	2239.2	202.3	55.5	28.6	2525.6
1965	2299.1	212.4	57.1	29.8	2598.4
1966	2344.9	223.0	58.5	31.0	2657.4
1967	2383.6	289.6	71.0	32.1	2776.3
1968	2434.8	300.8	72.2	33.3	2841.1
1969	2506.8	314.5	73.5	34.6	2929.5
1970	2582.0	328.6	75.5	35.9	3022.1
1971	2662.0	344.0	77.3	37.3	3120.7
1972	2752.7	360.7	73.8	37.8	3225.0
1973	2845.0	377.2	76.7	39.3	3338.2
1974	2906.9	395.2	78.7	40.8	3421.6
1975	2959.4	411.4	80.2	42.2	3493.2
1976	3020.4	429.1	82.0	43.9	3575.4
1977	3077.3	446.5	83.8	45.6	3653.2
1978	3141.2	463.6	85.5	47.3	3737.6
1979	3218.4	481.2	87.6	49.0	3836.2
1980	3282.7	498.3	89.9	50.7	3921.7
1981	3320.3	513.7	91.5	52.3	3977.9
1982	3373.2	530.8	94.0	65.6	4063.6

TABLE 9 *(continued)*

YEAR	JEWS	MOSLEMS	CHRIS-TIANS	DRUZE & OTHERS	TOTAL
1983	3412.5	542.2	95.9	68.0	4118.6
1984	3471.7	559.7	98.2	70.0	4199.7
1985	3517.2	577.6	99.4	72.0	4266.2
1986	3561.4	595.0	100.9	74.0	4331.3
1987	3612.9	614.5	103.0	76.1	4406.5
1988	3659.0	634.6	105.0	78.1	4476.8
1989	3717.1	655.2	107.0	80.3	4559.6

Source: *Statistical Abstract of Israel 1988,* No. 39. Jerusalem: Central Bureau of Statistics, n.d., page 31, and *Statistical Abstract of Israel 1990,* page 38.

DECLARATION OF THE ESTABLISHMENT
OF THE STATE OF ISRAEL

ERETZ-ISRAEL [the Land of Israel] was the birthplace of the Jewish people. Here their spiritual, religious and political identity was shaped. Here they first attained to statehood, created cultural values of national and universal significance and gave to the world the eternal Book of Books.

After being forcibly exiled from their land, the people kept faith with it throughout their Dispersion and never ceased to pray and hope for their return to it and for the restoration in it of their political freedom.

Impelled by this historic and traditional attachment, Jews strove in every successive generation to re-establish themselves in their ancient homeland. In recent decades they returned in their masses. Pioneers, *ma'pilim* [immigrants coming to Eretz-Israel in defiance of restrictive legislation] and defenders, they made deserts bloom, revived the Hebrew language, built villages and towns, and created a thriving community, controlling its own economy and culture, loving peace but knowing how to defend itself, bringing the blessings of progress to all the country's inhabitants, and aspiring towards independent nationhood.

In the year 5657 (1897), at the summons of the spiritual father of the Jewish State, Theodor Herzl, the First Zionist Congress convened and proclaimed the right of the Jewish people to national rebirth in its own country.

This right was recognized in the Balfour Declaration of the 2nd November, 1917, and re-affirmed in the Mandate of the League of Nations which, in particular, gave international sanction to the historic connection between the Jewish people and Eretz-Israel and to the right of the Jewish people to rebuild its National Home.

The catastrophe which recently befell the Jewish people—the massacre of millions of Jews in Europe—was another clear demonstration of the urgency of solving the problem of its homelessness by re-establishing in Eretz-Israel the Jewish State, which would open the gates of the homeland wide to every Jew and confer upon the Jewish people the status of a fully-privileged member of the comity of nations.

Survivors of the Nazi holocaust in Europe, as well as Jews from other parts of the world, continued to migrate to Eretz-Israel, undaunted by difficulties, restrictions and dangers, and never ceased to assert their right to a life of dignity, freedom and honest toil in their national homeland.

In the Second World War, the Jewish community of this country contributed its full share to the struggle of the freedom- and peace-loving nations against the forces of Nazi wickedness and, by the blood of its soldiers and its war effort, gained the right to be reckoned among the peoples who founded the United Nations.

On the 29th November, 1947, the United Nations General Assembly passed a resolution calling for the establishment of a Jewish State in Eretz-Israel; the General Assembly required the inhabitants of Eretz-Israel to take such steps as were necessary on their part for the implementation of that resolution. This recognition by the United Nations of the right of the Jewish people to establish their State is irrevocable.

This right is the natural right of the Jewish people to be masters of their own fate, like all other nations, in their own sovereign State.

ACCORDINGLY WE, MEMBERS OF THE PEO-
PLE'S COUNCIL, REPRESENTATIVES OF THE
JEWISH COMMUNITY OF ERETZ-ISRAEL AND
OF THE ZIONIST MOVEMENT, ARE HERE AS-
SEMBLED ON THE DAY OF THE TERMINA-

TION OF THE BRITISH MANDATE OVER
ERETZ-ISRAEL AND, BY VIRTUE OF OUR NAT-
URAL AND HISTORIC RIGHT AND ON THE
STRENGTH OF THE RESOLUTION OF THE
UNITED NATIONS GENERAL ASSEMBLY,
HEREBY DECLARE THE ESTABLISHMENT OF
A JEWISH STATE IN ERETZ-ISRAEL, TO BE
KNOWN AS THE STATE OF ISRAEL.

WE DECLARE that, with effect from the moment of the termination of the Mandate, being tonight, the eve of Sabbath, the 5th Iyar, 5708 (14th May, 1948), until the establishment of the elected, regular authorities of the State in accordance with the Constitution which shall be adopted by the Elected Constituent Assembly not later than the 1st October, 1948, the People's Council shall act as a Provisional Council of State, and its executive organ, the People's Administration, shall be the Provisional Government of the Jewish State, to be called "Israel".

THE STATE OF ISRAEL will be open for Jewish immigration and for the Ingathering of the Exiles; it will foster the development of the country for the benefit of all inhabitants; it will be based on freedom, justice and peace as envisaged by the prophets of Israel; it will ensure complete equality of social and political rights to all its inhabitants irrespective of religion, race or sex; it will guarantee freedom of religion, conscience, language, education and culture; it will safeguard the Holy Places of all religions; and it will be faithful to the principles of the Charter of the United Nations.

THE STATE OF ISRAEL is prepared to cooperate with the agencies and representatives of the United Nations in implementing the resolution of the General Assembly of the 29th November, 1947, and will take steps to bring about the economic union of the whole of Eretz-Israel.

WE APPEAL to the United Nations to assist the Jewish people in the building–up of its State and to receive the State of Israel into the comity of nations.

WE APPEAL—in the very midst of the onslaught launched against us now for months—to the Arab inhabitants of the State of Israel to preserve peace and participate in the upbuilding of the State on the basis of full and equal citizenship and due representation in all its provisional and permanent institutions.

WE EXTEND our hand to all neighbouring states and their peoples in an offer of peace and good neighbourliness, and appeal to them to establish bonds of cooperation and mutual help with the sovereign Jewish people settled in its own land. The State of Israel is prepared to do its share in common effort for the advancement of the entire Middle East.

WE APPEAL to the Jewish people throughout the Diaspora to rally round the Jews of Eretz-Israel in the tasks of immigration and upbuilding and to stand by them in the great struggle for the realization of the age-old dream—the redemption of Israel.

PLACING OUR TRUST IN THE ALMIGHTY, WE AFFIX OUR SIGNATURES TO THIS PROCLAMATION AT THIS SESSION OF THE PROVISIONAL COUNCIL OF STATE, ON THE SOIL OF THE HOMELAND, IN THE CITY OF TEL-AVIV, ON THIS SABBATH EVE, THE 5TH DAY OF IYAR, 5708 (14 MAY, 1948).

The Declaration was published in Israel's *Official Gazette,* No. 1 of the 5th Iyar, 5708 (14th May, 1948).

INTRODUCTION

Israel is an independent Jewish state, small in size and population, located at the southwestern tip of Asia on the eastern shore of the Mediterranean Sea. It achieved independence in 1948. Since Biblical days, Jews of the Diaspora have hoped that they would return to Zion, the "promised land," where the ancient Jewish state had been located, as described in the Bible. Over the centuries Zionism focused on spiritual, religious, cultural, social, and historical links between Jews and the holy land. Political Zionism, with the establishment of a Jewish state as its goal, and Jewish immigration to Palestine, both developed in nineteenth century Europe, partly as responses to anti-Semitism. The defeat of the Ottoman Empire during World War I and its dismemberment during the subsequent peace conferences led to British control of Palestine and set the stage for the eventual independence of Israel.

Israel has achieved rapid development and impressive accomplishments in the social and scientific arenas. It has been the region's most politically and socially innovative state and has achieved prosperity for its people. Israel has built a democratic system unlike that of any other in the Middle East and has melded immigrants from more than seventy countries into a uniquely Israeli population. In a country almost devoid of natural resources, its people have achieved a high standard of living.

Israel's development has occurred despite the fact that it has been in a state of war since independence and continually must be ready to defend its existence. Peace and security have eluded the state that has fought six major wars with the

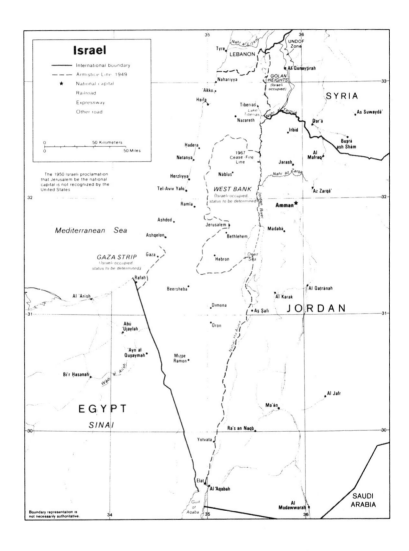

Arabs and, except for Egypt, has failed to achieve peace with its neighbors. The continuing Arab-Israeli conflict remains a central test of Israel's foreign and defense policies.

Government and Politics

Israel is a parliamentary democracy but has no formal written constitution. A number of Basic Laws have been passed that guide Israel's actions and which are intended in time to form portions of a consolidated constitutional document.

The President is the head of state and is elected by the Knesset (parliament) for a five-year term and may be reelected. His powers and functions are primarily ceremonial and his actual political power is very limited. The Prime Minister is head of government and as the chief executive officer wields considerable power. He or she is designated by the President but must secure and maintain the support of the parliament to retain office. The Prime Minister forms the cabinet (or government) whose members head the ministries. The Prime Minister determines the agenda of cabinet meetings and has the final word in policy decisions, although such decisions are often arrived at by bargaining and compromise among the coalition of parties that since independence have constituted Israel's governments. Decisions by the government determine the direction and policy of the state.

Legislative power resides in the Knesset, a unicameral body of 120 members that is the supreme authority in the state. The Knesset's main functions are similar to those of other modern parliaments and include votes of confidence or no confidence in the government, legislation, participation in the formulation of national policy, approval of budgets and taxation, election of the President, and general supervision of the activities of the administration. All members of the Knesset are elected at-large.

The judiciary consists of secular and religious court systems. The Supreme Court is the highest court and hears appeals from lower courts in civil and criminal cases and acts to protect the rights of Israeli citizens. It does not have the power of judicial review, but it may invalidate administrative actions and ordinances it regards as contrary to the law. Each major community has its own religious courts which have jurisdiction over matters of personal status such as marriage and divorce, alimony, probate, and inheritance.

Israel has a large number of political parties, many of which have their origins in Europe in the period before independence, which represent a wide spectrum of views and positions. There are also religious and special-issue parties that focus on a particular subject or theme.

Society

At independence Israel had some 806,000 citizens (650,000 Jews and 156,000 non-Jews). Israel's population by September 1991 was estimated at about 5.0 million people, some 82% of which were Jews and the remainder non-Jews, often referred to as Arabs. The non-Jewish population has quadrupled since 1948, mostly as a result of high birthrates. The Jewish population has increased more than fivefold since independence with more than 1.8 million Jewish immigrants, many of whom came to Israel from the Arab countries of the Middle East and North Africa. In the late 1980s and early 1990s large numbers of Soviet immigrants add substantially to Israel's population while smaller but more dramatic immigrations came from Ethiopia. Under the Law of Return, any Jew, with some minor exceptions, may immigrate to Israel. Immigrants are provided with housing and training to integrate them rapidly into the mainstream of Israeli society.

The land of Israel was the ancient birthplace of the Jewish people and it is there that the religious and national identity of the people was formed and developed. The earliest connections between the Jewish people and the land of Israel are recorded in the Bible when Abraham, the first of the patriarchs of Judaism, migrated to the promised land around the second millennium BC. The Bible records God's promise of the land to Abraham and his descendents.

Israel's Jews are of a single religious faith and share a spiritual heritage and elements of historical experience. Ethnically and culturally they are heterogeneous. The Jewish population is composed of immigrants from numerous countries and reflects a variety of ethnic and linguistic groups, degrees of religious observance, and cultural, historical, and political backgrounds. No single ethnic group constitutes even 20% of the total Jewish population although the largest is of Moroccan origin.

The two main groups in Israel's Jewish population are the Ashkenazim (Jews of central and east European origin) and the Sephardim or Orientals (who came to Israel from the countries of the Middle East and the Mediterranean area). Although the overwhelming majority of the Jewish population was of Ashkenazi origin at independence, the majority today are of non-Ashkenazi origin and are referred to as Edot Hamizrach (eastern, or Oriental communities), Sephardim or Orientals. Native Israelis are referred to as Sabras (the fruit of the cactus).

Geographically and demographically Israel is an Oriental country, but its culture, society, and political system are primarily Western in nature and orientation. The early Zionists laid the foundations for an essentially European culture in Palestine and subsequent immigration accelerated the trend. The Western immigrants created and developed the structure of land settlement, institutions, trade unions, political parties, and educational systems in preparation for a Western-oriented Jewish national state. Future immigrants had to adapt to a society that had formed these institutions.

After the Holocaust and the creation of Israel, whole Jewish communities were transported to Israel from the countries of the Middle East and North Africa. Massive

Oriental immigration created a situation in which a large portion of the population had societal and cultural traditions different from those of their Western coreligionists who constituted the majority and dominant element in Israel. The religious traditions of Judaism provide a common core of values and ideals, but there are major differences in outlook, frames of reference, levels of aspiration, and other social and cultural components. Israel's communal problem is one of ethnic-cultural cleavages and a socio-economic gap and consequent inequalities within the Jewish community.

Israel's non-Jewish citizenry consists primarily of the Arabs who remained in what became Israel after the 1948–1949 Arab-Israeli War and their descendents. The Arab population is composed primarily of Muslims (about 77%) and is predominantly Sunni, although some 13% are Christian (mostly Greek Catholic and Greek Orthodox) and some 10% are Druze.

Although their legal status is essentially the same as Israel's Jewish population, Israel's Arab citizens are confronted by problems qualitatively different. However, between 1948 and the mid-1960s activities of the Arab community were regarded primarily as concerns of Israel's security system, and most of the areas inhabited by the Arabs were placed under military control. The restrictions were gradually modified, and in 1966, military government was abolished. Although Israeli Arabs vote, sit in the Knesset, serve in government offices, have their own schools and courts, and prosper materially, they face difficulties in adjusting to Israel's modern, Jewish and Western-oriented society. The Arabs tend to live in separate villages and in separate sections of the major cities. They speak Arabic, attend a separate school system, and generally do not serve in the army. The Arab and Jewish communities in Israel have few points of contact, and those that exist are not intimate; they are separate societies that generally continue to hold stereotypical images of each other that often are reinforced by the tensions and problems created by the larger Arab-Israeli conflict. There is mutual suspicion and antagonism, and there is still a Jewish fear of the Arabs—a result of wars and terrorism.

Israel is a Jewish state; nevertheless, it guarantees its citizens freedom of religion and conscience and considerable autonomy under the millet system derived from the Ottoman Empire. Israel is a country of many faiths and numerous sects within them. Jews include the ultra-Orthodox and those who are atheist. Arabs are both Muslim and Christian. The Druze and the Bahai are also significant. Religious freedom is guaranteed by law and each faith is free to follow its own rituals and subscribe to its own beliefs. At the same time there have been tensions and often open clashes between the religious and secular segments of the Jewish community. The contentious religious issues are centered within the Jewish community and focus on the authority and power of the Orthodox religious authorities and their desire to mold the system in their preferred image. Debate has focused on the appropriate relationship between religion and the state and between the religious and secular authorities.

"Who is a Jew" has been at the center of a religion-state controversy in Israel and has had philosophical, theological, political, and ideological overtones with specific practical dimensions. Secular and religious authorities and ordinary citizens have faced the question in connection with immigration, marriage, divorce, inheritance, and conversion as well as in registration for identity cards and in the official collection of data and information. The question relates to the application of legislation such as the Law of Return, the Nationality Law, and others passed by the parliament.

Geography

Israel is a small country whose land borders (except with Egypt and the sea) are not permanent and recognized and whose size has not been determined precisely. Within its current frontiers (established by the 1949 armistice agreements) it is less than 8,000 square miles (some 20,700 square kilometers) and is bounded on the north by Lebanon, on the northeast by Syria, on the east by the West Bank, Jordan and the Dead Sea, on the south by the Gulf of Eilat (Aqaba), on the southwest by the Sinai Peninsula of Egypt and the Gaza Strip, and on the west by the Mediterranean Sea. The country is 265 miles long and, at its widest, some 70 miles.

Israel may be divided into four main natural land regions: The coastal plain, the highlands of Judea and the Galilee, the Rift Valley, and the Negev. The coastal plain lies along the Mediterranean and is composed of a generally narrow and sandy shoreline bordered by fertile farmland varying up to 25 miles in width from the northern border to the Israel-Egypt border in the southwest. Most Israelis live in the coastal plain and most of the industry and agriculture are located there. A series of mountain ranges run north-south from the Galilee to the Negev. The mountains of Galilee stretch southward to the Jezreel Valley, south of which are the mountains and hills of Samaria, Judea, and the Negev. Upper Galilee is the highest part of the country. Lower Galilee's hills are more broken. The highlands of Galilee are where most of Israel's Arabs live and include the city of Nazareth. Mt. Meron, Israel's highest mountain, is here. The Judean hills include Jerusalem. There is also the Carmel mountain range near Haifa.

The Rift Valley is part of the Great Syrian-African Rift—the deepest valley on earth. In Israel it includes the Jordan Valley which is located between the mountains of Judea and Samaria in the west and the mountains of Jordan to the east; the Hula Valley between the mountains of Galilee and the Golan Heights; the Jezreel Valley between the mountains of Galilee and Samaria; and the Arava, a long and arid valley running from the Dead Sea to the Red Sea. The Dead Sea, a saltwater body, is part of the Rift Valley area and is the lowest land area on earth, about 1286 feet below sea level. The Negev is an arid area of flatlands and limestone mountains that stretches southward from the Judean Desert, which lies between Jerusalem and the Dead Sea.

The Jordan River, the longest of Israel's rivers, flows from north to south through the Sea of Galilee (Lake Kinneret) and empties into the Dead Sea. Most of the other rivers are small and generally seasonal in nature, except for the Kishon (which is about 8 miles long and flows east to west and empties into the Mediterranean north of Haifa) and the Yarkon (which is about 16 miles long and flows east to west and empties into the Mediterranean at Tel Aviv).

Israel's climate generally is Mediterranean in nature— marked by hot and dry summers and cool but relatively mild winters. There is sunshine from May through mid-October and no rain falls during this season. Periods of hot and dry weather brought by easterly winds occur at the beginning and end of the summer, usually in May and September. The hot, dry, sandy, easterly desert wind of Biblical fame is commonly known as "khamsin," from the Arabic for "fifty." The rainy season begins about mid-October, but it is only in December that rainy days become frequent. Winter weather alternates between short but heavy rainy spells and sunshine. March and April are cool, with occasional rains of short duration. Nevertheless, there is a variation of climate by region, partly as a consequence of differences in altitude. North of Beersheba Israel has a Mediterranean climate, but the Negev is generally arid and cultivation there is impossible without irrigation. The Jordan Valley is hotter and drier than the coastal plain. Tiberias and the Jordan Valley enjoy warm temperatures and little rainfall. In the hilly regions (Jerusalem and Upper Galilee), temperatures drop towards the freezing point, and brief snowfalls are not unusual.

Economy

Israel's economy has made impressive progress and the economic well-being of its people has improved significantly since independence when Israel was a poor country with weak agricultural and industrial sectors and imported consumer goods, raw materials, and food. Economic growth was stimulated by a massive influx of immigrants and large governmental and private capital flows from abroad. Although virtually bereft of natural resources and faced with substantial burdens of immigrant absorption and of defense imposed by Arab hostility, Israel achieved relatively prosperous economic levels by the 1980s with a standard of living comparable to that in some Western European countries. Life expectancy is among the highest in the world; it has maintained a substantial level of social services for its population; and its GNP has made dramatic progress. Nevertheless, Israel's economy remains dependent on foreign assistance.

Israel's economy grew rapidly after independence. Between 1950 and 1972 Israel maintained a real output rate of nearly 10% per year and its output per worker nearly tripled. This was accompanied by significant increases in the standard of living. Inflation became a problem as the economy reached double-digit inflation in the early 1970s and triple-digit (more than 400 percent) by the 1984 election. It was subsequently brought down to some 15% by 1987 through the efforts of the National Unity Government. Balance of payments problems also marked the economy in the 1980s.

Israel lacks substantial natural resources—it has limited amounts of various chemicals, such as potash and phosphates, and water supplies—but this has been offset by the unusually valuable asset Israel has in its human resources. Massive immigration created problems in Israel's early years, but it also endowed Israel with skilled workers and professionals. Israel has developed its own highly regarded educational and scientific establishment. Illiteracy is virtually nonexistent, and its population is one of the most highly educated in the world. It is in the forefront of scientific accomplishment in fields such as energy technology and medical-scientific research.

Israel's only significant domestic energy source is solar power; it has no coal or hydroelectric power potential and possesses very little oil and natural gas. Energy requirements are met largely by crude oil and coal imports, and nuclear power is under study.

Israel has lacked the capital necessary for its economy to function efficiently and since 1948 it has relied on foreign capital inflows to finance the economy and for current expenditures. External sources have included loans, grants, contributions, outside investments, United States government aid, the sale of Israel bonds, German reparations and restitution payments, and Jewish donations. These sources have permitted Israel to pursue a policy of rapid economic and demographic expansion.

The country's economy today is a mixture of state and private enterprise. About 60% of the labor force is employed in service industries. The service sector remains large because of government and quasi-governmental activity, such as the machinery to integrate large immigrant populations, and the trade and transport functions connected with a high level of imports.

Agriculture traditionally has occupied a position of importance in Israel and Zionist ideology greater than its economic contribution has warranted. Its central place in Zionist ideology, dominant role in the settlement of the country, important position in absorbing new immigrants, and its security aspects have assured its priority in Israel's economic policies. The government has been involved in developing, subsidizing, and controlling agricultural activity, including fishing and forestry, since independence. The agricultural sector uses modern scientific methods and has significantly expanded the area under cultivation through irrigation drawn basically from the Jordan River. Agricultural research is extensive, and farmers are quick to adopt improved techniques and respond to changes in market conditions. Israel has become self-sufficient in food production and an exporter of various foods, including citrus and other fruits, vegetables, and poultry products. In spite of its rapid growth, agriculture's prominent position has gradually eroded to the point where it contributes about 6% of GNP and is a diminishing source of employment primarily because of improved techniques and mechanization. Farm organization is predominantly cooperative with the moshav being the most popular, while private farming is primarily the domain of non-Jewish farmers, mostly Arabs and some Druze.

Industry became an important, diverse, and fast-growing sector of the economy that contributed about one-third of the GNP by the late 1970s, and also became a major source of employment and of commodity exports. The manufacturing-sector output is similar in range, sophistication, and quality of products to that of the smaller industrialized countries. Textile manufacturers produce a range of goods including knitwear and high-fashion clothes and there are also plastics, electronics, high technology scientific and optical equipment, food processing, textiles, and clothing. Diamonds remain a major industry—Israel exports cut and polished diamonds. Israel's defense industries are dominated by government-owned plants, of which Israel Aircraft Industries is the largest. The mineral and chemical industry depends heavily on the Dead Sea which is the country's leading mineral source and includes magnesium chloride, potassium chloride (potash), table salt, and calcium and magnesium bromide. Israel produces potash, table salt, bromine, and chlorine.

Government policy supported industrial development with an export orientation to ease the country's continual balance of payments problems. Emphasis was given to science-based industries with a large value added by domestic manufacturing, particularly since the 1960s. This was the kind of export (e.g., chemicals, metal products, machinery, and electronic equipment) that, along with polished gem diamonds, grew most rapidly in the 1970s. Diamonds are the only product in which Israel has more than a peripheral share in any foreign market.

The foreign markets for Israeli products, and even the pattern of industrial growth, were shaped by the Arab boycott that precluded the possibility of Israel developing close links to the economies of its Arab neighbors. Instead the country had to seek more distant markets.

Israel's exports reached about $6 billion by 1987 and included such products as diamonds, military equipment, citrus and other fruit, textiles and clothing, processed food, fertilizer and chemical products, and electronics. Tourism is also an important earner of foreign exchange. Israeli imports include a wide range of items from diverse sources. Important are military equipment, rough diamonds, oil, chemicals, machinery, iron and steel, vehicles, ships, and aircraft. Israel's major trading partners include the United States, the Federal Republic of Germany, France, Belgium, and Luxembourg. An economic agreement with the European Common Market in the 1970s and the establishment of a free trade area with the United States in the mid-1980s were important for Israel's export market.

History

The new state of Israel came into being on May 14, 1948 with the termination of the British Mandate of Palestine, but its creation was preceded by more than fifty years of efforts by Zionist leaders to establish an independent Jewish state.

The modern history of Israel may be dated from the Jewish immigration to Palestine in the 19th century from Europe, especially Russia and Poland. The practical and modern effort to establish a state began with the founding of the Zionist movement and the creation of the World Zionist Organization by Theodor Herzl at the end of the 19th century. It was given impetus with the issuance of the Balfour Declaration (1917) in which the British Government expressed support for the establishment of a Jewish national home in Palestine. Jewish immigration to Palestine grew throughout this period, but with the advent of the Nazi regime in Germany and the Holocaust, the numbers escalated rapidly in the 1930s. With the end of World War II there was pressure for the remnants of European Jewry to be permitted to immigrate to Palestine despite British restrictions. The Arab reaction to the effort to create a Jewish state was negative and, at times, violent.

On November 29, 1947, the United Nations adopted the Partition Plan which called for the division of Palestine into a Jewish state and an Arab state and for an international administration for Jerusalem. The Plan was accepted with reluctance by the Zionists but denounced by the Arab world which prepared for war to ensure that all of Palestine would be an Arab state. With the British withdrawal from Palestine in May 1948, the new Jewish state proclaimed its independence as Israel. David Ben-Gurion became the Prime Minister and Chaim Weizmann was elected President. The new government was soon recognized by the United States and the Soviet Union, as well as by other states. The Arab League declared war on the new state and the armies of the neighboring Arab states announced that their armies would enter the area to restore order. A long and bitter war ensued between Israel and armies from Egypt, Jordan, Syria, Lebanon, and Iraq with assistance from other Arab League members.

In the spring of 1949 armistice agreements were signed between Israel and each of the bordering states (Egypt, Syria, Jordan, and Lebanon) which established a frontier (armistice line) between Israel and each of the neighboring states and portions of those areas were demilitarized. Peace negotiations to resolve the Arab-Israeli conflict were to follow, but did not. As a consequence of the war Israel encompassed more territory than had been allocated to it by the Partition Plan. At the same time portions of the territory allocated to the Palestinian Arab state came under Egyptian (the Gaza Strip) and Jordanian (the West Bank) control. Jerusalem was divided between Israel and Jordan.

Israel has fought six major wars (in 1948–49, 1956–57, 1967, 1969–70, 1973, and 1982) with the Arab states to secure its position, but peace has eluded Israel with all but Egypt.

Soon after independence Israel moved to function as a regular state. Elections for a parliament (Knesset) were held January 25, 1949 and regular parliamentary and presidential elections have been held, as required by law, since then. But, Israel's progress in its domestic life was not matched by comparable developments with the Arab states; frequent border incidents and clashes characterized the early 1950s.

Tensions continued to increase and the situation was exacerbated by external arms supplies and raids across the border between Egypt and Israel. In the summer of 1956 Egyptian President Gamal Abdul Nasser nationalized the Suez Canal and tensions grew. In late October, Israel invaded the Sinai Peninsula to destroy hostile Egyptian military positions and, in a brief war, captured the Gaza Strip and the Sinai Peninsula. Following a British and French ultimatum, their forces were interposed between Israel and Egypt along the Suez Canal. Eventually Israel was forced to withdraw from Egyptian territory and from the Gaza Strip. The United Nations Emergency Force (UNEF) was stationed on the frontier between the two states and helped ensure quiet along the border for the next decade. The sea lanes through the Strait of Tiran to Israel's port of Eilat were opened to Israeli shipping. But the hope that peace talks might follow was not realized. Although the other Arab states did not join in the hostilities, they made no effort to reach a peace agreement with Israel and their territories often became bases for attacks across the border into Israel. Israel maintained its military posture and capability to deal with the Arab threat.

In 1966 and 1967 Israel again focused on the problems associated with the Arab-Israeli conflict. Border incidents became more serious and escalation to conflict began in late 1966 and early 1967 as clashes between Israel and Syria contributed to regional tensions. In May 1967, President

Nasser of Egypt called for the removal of UNEF, mobilized the Egyptian military and moved troops and equipment into the Sinai Peninsula. Nasser also announced the closing of the Strait of Tiran to Israeli shipping destined for the port of Eilat and other factors also contributed to the growing tensions. Finally, on June 5, 1967 Israel launched a preemptive military strike against Egypt. Other Arab states joined in the hostilities that spread to include Jordan, Syria, and Iraq, among other Arab participants.

The Six Day War of June 1967 substantially modified the content of the issues central to the Arab-Israeli dispute. The realities of Arab hostility, the nature of the Arab threat, and the difficulties of achieving a settlement became more obvious. The issues of the conflict changed with the extent of the Israeli victory: Israel occupied the Sinai Peninsula, the Gaza Strip, the West Bank, East Jerusalem, and the Golan Heights. Israel adopted the position that it would not withdraw from those territories until there were negotiations with the Arab states leading to peace agreements that recognized Israel's right to exist and accepted Israel's permanent position and borders. Throughout the period between the Six Day War (1967) and the Yom Kippur War (1973), the focal point was the effort to achieve a settlement of the Arab-Israeli conflict and to secure a just and lasting peace based on United Nations Security Council Resolution 242 of November 22, 1967, which called for an exchange of peace for territory between Israel and the Arab states. Although some of the efforts were promising, peace was not achieved and there was little movement in that direction. The 1969–1970 War of Attrition (launched by Egypt against Israel along the Suez Canal in April 1969) and the 1973 Yom Kippur War marked the fourth and fifth rounds of conflict between Israel and the Arabs. It was also in this period that a restructured Palestine Liberation Organization (PLO) emerged under the leadership of Yasser Arafat and posed new challenges to Israel.

On October 6, 1973, Egyptian and Syrian military forces

attacked Israeli positions along the Suez Canal and in the Golan Heights. Despite initial Egyptian and Syrian advances, Israel pushed Syria back beyond the 1967 cease-fire line and crossed the Suez Canal to take a portion of its west bank in Egypt. The war increased Israel's dependence on the United States as no other country would provide Israel with the vast quantities of modern and sophisticated arms required for war or for the political and moral support necessary to negotiate peace.

The 1973 war was followed by renewed and intensified efforts to achieve peace between Israel and the Arabs. The postwar cease-fire was stabilized and military disengagements were achieved. A major step came in 1977 with the announcement by Egyptian President Anwar Sadat that he was prepared to negotiate peace directly with the Israelis. His November 1977 visit to Israel ultimately led to the Camp David Accords in September 1978 and the Egypt-Israel Peace Treaty signed on March 26, 1979 at the White House in Washington. The Egypt-Israel Peace Treaty was a major accomplishment that represented a significant step toward a comprehensive Arab-Israeli settlement. The process of normalization of relations between Egypt and Israel moved ahead on schedule and without major disturbances. "Normal relations" between Egypt and Israel began officially on January 26, 1980 when Israel had completed its withdrawal from two-thirds of the Sinai Peninsula, as called for in the peace treaty, and land, air, and sea borders between the two states were opened. In late February embassies were opened in Cairo and Tel Aviv, and on February 26 Ambassadors Eliahu Ben-Elisar of Israel and Saad Mortada of Egypt presented their credentials.

Despite this peace treaty with Egypt and its implementation, Israel's other borders remained tense and problems often emerged. Their successes were not followed by additional achievements of consequence despite the war in Lebanon and the Israel-Lebanon agreement of May 1983, which was later abrogated by Lebanon under Syrian pressure.

The frontier with Lebanon had been relatively quiet between the 1948–49 war and the early 1970s when the PLO was forced out of Jordan and ultimately took up positions in Lebanon. Cross-border raids and Israeli retaliations escalated tensions. The continued presence in Lebanon of missiles that had been moved there by Syria in the spring of 1981 remained an Israeli concern, as were the PLO attacks against Israeli and Jewish targets worldwide, despite a U.S.-arranged cease-fire in the summer of 1981. On June 6, 1982, Israel launched a major military action against the PLO in Lebanon (called Operation Peace for Galilee). The military objective was to ensure security for northern Israel, to destroy the PLO infrastructure that had established a state within a state in Lebanon, to eliminate a center of international terrorism, and to eliminate a base of operations from which Israel could be threatened. But the political objectives were not so precise. In many respects the results were ambiguous. The PLO withdrew its forces from Lebanon in August 1982. Israel's northern border was more secure, but the Israeli troops that remained in Lebanon until the summer of 1985 became targets of terrorists and others, and numerous casualties resulted. The costs of the War in Lebanon were high.

Israel in the International Community

Since independence Israel has sought positive relations with the members of the international community. It has joined and participated in the work of international organizations and it has sought to establish and maintain friendly relations with as many states as possible. Within the framework of this broad effort, there has been a particular focus on relations with the United States and the Soviet Union.

Israel has had a variable relationship with the Soviet Union and the members of the Eastern bloc since before independence. Although the Soviet Union supported the United Nations Partition Plan of 1947 and Israel's independence in 1948, relations deteriorated rapidly and the Soviet Union shifted to a pro-Arab position, including economic assistance and arms supply by the mid-1950s. Since 1967, when the Soviet Union and the Eastern bloc states, except Romania, broke diplomatic relations with Israel, the questions of a Soviet role in the Arab-Israeli conflict and the peace process and the status of Jews in the Soviet Union have been central themes in Israel-Soviet relations. During the Gorbachev tenure in Moscow a thaw developed and relations between Israel and the Soviet camp improved in a number of spheres. Formal diplomatic relations between Israel and the Soviet Union were restored in October 1991.

The special but central and complex relationship between Israel and the United States has been more significant. The relationship revolves around a broadly conceived ideological factor. Moreover, it is based on substantial positive perception and sentiment evident in public opinion and official statements and manifest in political-diplomatic support and military and economic assistance. However, the relationship has not been enshrined in a legally binding commitment joining the two states in a formal alliance. Undergirding the relationship is a general agreement on broad policy goals. The two states maintain a remarkable degree of parallelism and congruence on such objectives as the need to prevent major war, to resolve the Arab-Israeli conflict without the creation of a Palestinian state, and Israel's economic and social well-being. Nevertheless, there has been United States-Israeli noncongruence of policy on specific issues which have derived from various differences of perspective. The United States is an indispensable ally that provides Israel with economic, technical, military, political, diplomatic, and moral support. It is seen as the ultimate protector against the Soviet Union, and it is the primary source of Israel's sophisticated military hardware.

Israel has seen Europe and the developing world (especially Africa and Latin America) as important components of its overall policy. It has sought to maintain positive relations with Europe based on the commonality of the Judeo-Christian heritage and the memories of the Holocaust. Israel's approach to the developing world has focused on its ability to provide technical assistance in the development process. Despite substantial effort in those sectors, the centrality of the Arab-Israeli conflict has enlarged the role of the superpowers.

Israel Faces the Future

Knesset elections have often provided a focal point for a series of potentially momentous decisions Israelis must make concerning the future. In November 1988 the electorate spoke on, but did not resolve the critical issues facing the political system and selected—although not unambiguously—among alternative policy orientations and leaderships which were to help shape the future of the state. Israel's 1988 electorate was different in size and composition from that which voted in Israel's first parliamentary election nearly forty years earlier (in 1949), but its choices were perhaps even more crucial for the state and its future. As in previous elections, there were important economic issues, including an economic downturn connected to the intifada (the Arab uprising) with its disruption of normal patterns of economic activity in tourism and other service sectors which utilize large amounts of Arab labor and in manufacturing and construction. Nevertheless, while everyday economic concerns, such as employment and inflation, are not ignored, they tend to recede in significance and the focus of interest and public debate is on the "hot" issues of security, defense, and the peace process that relate to the Arab-Israeli conflict, and, more narrowly, to the intifada and Israel's reaction.

At the heart of Israel's agenda for the future is the continuing Arab-Israeli conflict, with its dimensions of potential conflict and of peace, but placed within the context of the ongoing intifada. The prospects for future conflict remain and peace seems unlikely, at least in the near term. Israel's need and desire for peace is not a subject for debate in Israel, although the means to that end are. The problem of terminating the Arab-Israeli conflict remains a dominant theme in the politics and foreign policy of Israel, and Israelis tend to divide on the procedural and substantive levels. Shimon Peres and the Labor camp tend to be committed to territorial compromise concerning the West Bank and Gaza Strip. Yitzhak Shamir and his supporters seem inclined toward the concept of Israeli retention of all of Eretz Israel (Greater Israel) and think in terms of Jewish settlements and settlers in the West Bank and Gaza. They also disagree on the mechanisms and procedures for peace negotiations. Nevertheless, the quest for peace remains a central theme of Israeli national life and Israelis are preoccupied with survival and security.

Israel has fought six major wars and countless skirmishes with the Arabs, has built an impressive and highly sophisticated but costly military capability, and holds a strategic edge over its neighbors. Despite, or perhaps because of, its battlefield successes and the specter of future combat, Israelis continuously recalculate the increasingly sophisticated military balance between themselves and the Arab world and concerns about Arab weapons acquisition, force structure, and capability, as well as willingness of Arab nations to engage in battle with Israel, are never far from the center of attention. Factors in the assessments include the sale of nuclear-capable ballistic missiles by the People's Republic of China to Saudi Arabia and rumors of sales of other missile systems to Libya and Syria. And, there is the possible utilization of chemical weapons by Syria and Iraq—especially when the latter has shown little hesitation in employing such weapons in the war with Iran. The possibility of war with potentially high levels of casualties and other unbearable costs remains a matter of public concern.

The absence of war does not foreshadow peace, and Israelis, whatever their perspective of the nature and content of the peace process, conclude that peace is not at hand. Thus, the continuing Arab-Israeli conflict remains a central test of Israeli diplomacy with peace and security as the elusive but sought-after prizes. Peace exists only with Egypt and, given the state's experiences, Israelis have developed deeply held views of the process and substance of peace and appear about equally divided as to the preferred alternative. Prime Minister Yitzhak Shamir of Likud represents those who argue that only direct, independent, open-ended, face-to-face negotiations can provide the unpressured atmosphere that is vital for reaching an agreement. He believes that Israel should not negotiate with the PLO; that Judea and Samaria (i.e., the West Bank) and Gaza are part of the Land of Israel; and that an independent sovereign state between Jordan and Israel makes no sense politically, cannot be viable economically, and can only serve as a terrorist, irredentist base from which Israel (and Jordan) will be threatened. Labor leader Shimon Peres reflects a different view and, while he sees the need for peace through direct negotiations, he believes that an international conference may be of utility and that it could not impose a solution unacceptable to Israel. Unlike Shamir, he supports territorial compromise in the West Bank (a trade of land for peace) within limits required for security.

The territories over which Israelis are divided have been a core issue in the peace process since Israel occupied them in the 1967 Six Day War, but their status took on new immediacy in the wake of the intifada. The intifada looms over politics in Israel, forcing attention to the immediate and urgent problem of tranquility and public safety and to the longer term issue of the disposition of the territories and their inhabitants. Israelis appear more supportive of a policy to quell the disturbances and restore order than they are of permanent retention of the places and peoples of the West Bank and Gaza. The ultimate status of the territories raises a more fundamental question—can Israel control indefinitely territories with a large Arab population without jeopardizing the nature and character of the Jewish state? The intifada has been a catalyst of increased attention to the issue of the territories, but it has not yet resulted in new policy directions despite extensive debate. For most Israelis, there is not yet a viable Palestinian option in the peace process and the prospects for a future in which Israel will live in peace with its neighbors in the Middle East seem to lie at a point beyond the immediate future. This perception was not significantly altered by the Madrid Peace Conference of October–November 1991 and the subsequent talks in Washington and Moscow, despite the fact that they provided an opportunity for direct, face-to-face negotiations between Israel and all of its neighbors on the complex issues of the Arab-Israeli conflict.

THE DICTIONARY

ABRAHAM. The first of the patriarchs of Judaism. He migrated from Ur of the Chaldeans to Haran and then to the Promised Land around the second millennium BC. He was the father of both Isaac and Ishmael and, as such, is considered the common ancestor of both Arabs and Jews.

ABU GHOSH. An Arab village west of Jerusalem (q.v.) on the road to Tel Aviv (q.v.) whose inhabitants were known for their friendly relations with the Jews. During Israel's War of Independence (q.v.) they did not participate in the fighting.

ABUHATZEIRA, AHARON. Born in Morocco in 1938, he immigrated to Israel in 1949 and studied History and Hebrew Literature at Bar Ilan University (q.v.). A teacher by profession, he served as Mayor of Ramla from 1971 to 1977. He was first elected to the Knesset (q.v.) on the National Religious Party (q.v.) list in December 1973, and was reelected to the Ninth Knesset on the same ticket in 1977. From June 1977 to August 1981 he served as Minister of Religious Affairs. Following a split with the National Religious Party, Abuhatzeira was elected to the Tenth Knesset in 1981 as the head of the Tami Party (q.v.) list and on August 5, 1981 he was sworn in as Minister of Labor and Social Welfare and of Immigrant Absorption. In 1984 he was again elected to the Knesset as the leader of the Tami party. In 1988 he was elected to the Knesset on the Likud (q.v.) list.

1

ACRE (AKKO). A coastal city in western Galilee (q.v.), located along the Mediterranean Sea at the northern end of Haifa Bay. The city has a long history but became well known during the British Mandate (q.v.) period because the British authorities used the medieval fortress as the country's central prison for political prisoners as well as criminals.

ADMINISTERED AREAS see OCCUPIED TERRITORIES

AGAF MODIIN (AMAN) see DIRECTOR OF MILITARY INTELLIGENCE (DMI)

AGNON, SHMUEL YOSEF (FORMERLY CZACKES). One of the central figures of modern Hebrew (q.v.) literature. Born in Buchach, Galicia, Austria in July 1888, he began writing Hebrew and Yiddish poetry at the age of nine. He settled in Palestine (q.v.) in 1907 and became secretary of the Hoveve Zion (q.v.) committee in Jaffa (q.v.). He published his first story in Palestine in *Ha'Omer* and it was about this time that he adopted the pen name Agnon. In 1913 Agnon left for Berlin but returned to Palestine in 1924 and settled in Jerusalem (q.v.). His work drew on Midrashic, Rabbinic, and Hasidic (q.v.) sources and depicted the small towns of central and eastern Europe prior to the Holocaust (q.v.). He also concentrated on the Second Aliya (q.v.) and on the characters that could be found in Jerusalem. Among his best-known books are *The Bridal Canopy, In the Heart of the Seas, Days of Awe, Betrothed,* and *A Guest in the Night.* He won the Nobel Prize for Literature 1966. He also won the Bialik Prize and the Israel Prize (q.v.) for literature. He died in 1970.

AGRANAT, SHIMON. Born in Louisville, Kentucky in 1906 and migrated to Palestine (q.v.) in 1930 where he settled in Haifa (q.v.). He was appointed a justice of the Supreme Court (q.v.) in 1950 and became Chief Justice in 1965. He served as head of the Agranat Commission of Inquiry (q.v.), established by the government in 1973.

AGRANAT COMMISSION OF INQUIRY. In November 1973 the government of Israel appointed a five-man Commission of Inquiry to investigate the events leading up to the Yom Kippur War (q.v.), including information concerning the enemy's moves and intentions, the assessments and decisions of military and civilian bodies regarding this information, and the Israel Defense Forces' (q.v.) deployments, preparedness for battle, and actions in the first phase of the fighting. The Commission was composed of Supreme Court (q.v.) Chief Justice Shimon Agranat (q.v.); Justice Moshe Landau of the Supreme Court; State Comptroller Yitzhak Nebenzahl; and two former chiefs of staff of the Israel Defense Forces, Yigael Yadin (q.v.) and Chaim Laskov (q.v.). The Commission issued an interim report in April 1974 which focused primarily on events prior to the outbreak of hostilities and the conduct of the war during its early stages. Among its findings were that Prime Minister Golda Meir (q.v.) and Defense Minister Moshe Dayan (q.v.) were not responsible for Israel's lack of preparation for the Yom Kippur War and that faulty intelligence analysis was the primary failure. Lieut. General David Elazar (q.v.) resigned as Chief of Staff of the Israel Defense Forces and Major General Yitzhak Hofi was named as his temporary replacement. The Commission's report also called for a new director of military intelligence to replace Maj. General Eliahu Zeira and the reassignment of three other intelligence officers.

AGRICULTURE. Agriculture and settlement on the land had been stressed by the immigrants to Palestine (q.v.)

and Israel since the beginning of modern political Zionism (q.v.) and the establishment of the Zionist movement. Development of the agricultural sector and the cooperative and communal agricultural settlements (the moshav (q.v.), and the kibbutz (q.v.)) has been a major feature of the Jewish communities in Palestine and Israel. In the early years of Israel's development agriculture was an important factor in assuring self-sufficiency in food and later it became an important source of foreign exchange earnings. Although declining in terms of revenues earned and people employed (due to increased mechanization and other efficiencies) agri-culture remains an important sector of the Israeli economy.

AGUDA see AGUDAT ISRAEL

AGUDAT ISRAEL (ASSOCIATION OF ISRAEL). Agudat Israel (the Aguda) is a movement which views the Torah (q.v.) as the only legitimate code of laws binding upon the Jews. It is a religiously oriented political party representing the interests of a section of Orthodox Jewry living both in and outside the Jewish state. The Aguda was established and its policies and programs delineated in Kattowitz (Katowice), Poland, in 1912 during a conference of the major East European and German-Austro-Hungarian Orthodox rabbis. It was formed, to a significant extent, in reaction to the growth of political Zionism (q.v.) with its secular majority. The original concept was to unite Orthodox groups in Eastern and Western Europe into a united front in opposition to Zionism and its efforts to alter Jewish life. But there were different perspectives on a number of issues. The Aguda was to be a Torah movement directed by a Council of Torah Sages (q.v.), which was to be the supreme authority in all matters.

Originally, Agudat Israel was ambivalent concerning

resettlement of Palestine (q.v.). Jewish law and tradition supported settling in Palestine and the Holocaust (q.v.) made it a necessity, but there was a problem because many of the new settlers did not observe Jewish law. Agudat Israel has held aloof from Zionism and has dissociated itself from the World Zionist Organization (q.v.) and the Jewish Agency (q.v.) because of its conviction that by cooperating closely with such irreligious elements, it would fail in the supreme aim of imposing the absolute rule of Jewish religion upon Jewish life. It opposed the concept of a Jewish National Home and of a Jewish State not founded on Jewish law and tradition. Agudat Israel opposed the Zionist view that Jews had to leave the Diaspora (q.v.), settle in Palestine, and build a new society there in order to live a proper Jewish life. The Orthodox groups held that the concept of "the ingathering of the exiles" (q.v.) and the return to Zion could not be separated from the Messianic redemption, for which the time had not yet come.

In Palestine Agudat Israel acquired land, founded the settlement of Mahane Yisrael, and established schools. Agudat Israel carried on an active anti-Zionist political campaign in British circles and in the world press in the 1920s. In England, it denied the Jewish Agency's right to act as the representative of the Jewish people and demanded recognition, but was turned down. In Palestine Agudat Israel was against the organization of the Jewish community along the lines of Zionist ideology, that is, within the Knesset Yisrael (q.v.). Aguda opted out of the officially recognized Jewish community (Knesset Yisrael) and it also did not recognize the Chief Rabbinate (q.v.) established by the British and set up its own rabbinical court. However, in the late 1920s, with the arrival of significant numbers of new Agudat Israel members from Europe who wanted to participate in the economic and social development of the Yishuv (q.v.) and who could not accept the idea of complete isolation from the World Zionist Organization and the Zionist movement, the Agudat Israel leadership in Palestine was reorganized. The end result was that some of the older and more conservative elements broke away from the movement and later formed the Neturei Karta (q.v.).

The genocide of European Jewry helped to convince Agudat Israel of the value of Zionism and the Aguda granted de facto recognition to Zionist work in Palestine and increased its cooperation with the agencies of the Zionist movement. At the same time it retained its reservations concerning the establishment of an independent Jewish state. Prior to Israel's independence, an arrangement was concluded with David Ben-Gurion (q.v.), then chairman of the Jewish Agency, in which Agudat Israel agreed to support the state on condition that the status quo in matters of religion be maintained. Agudat Israel then joined the Provisional Council of State and participated in Israel's first government. Since independence it has contested the various Knesset (q.v.) elections and has been represented in it. Although it boycotted the institutions of the Jewish community in Palestine, it eventually became a political party in 1948. It now accepts the state, but without ascribing any religious significance to it. It has been represented in parliament since 1948 and has supported most of the coalition governments, but, since 1952 it has refused to accept a cabinet portfolio.

The movement's voting strength lies in Jerusalem (q.v.) and Bnai Brak and consists mostly of Ashkenazim (q.v.). All crucial decisions on policy are made not by the party's Knesset members or its membership, but by the twelve-member Council of Torah Sages. Beside the Council, the party's central institutions are: the Great Assembly, composed of representatives of the local branches; the Central World Council; and the World Executive Committee. It has a youth movement (Tzeirei

Agudat Yisrael), a women's movement (Neshei Agudat Yisrael), and its own school network in which religious instruction is a major part of the curriculum. The government supplies most of the funds for the school system. Agudat Yisrael is primarily concerned with enhancing the role of religion in the state and is opposed to all forms of secularism. Its support for the coalition governments led by Menachem Begin (q.v.) was secured only after the construction of a lengthy coalition agreement containing numerous concessions to the group's religious perspectives, e.g., strict Sabbath laws and revision of legislation to accommodate Orthodox Jewish principles.

During the 1988 Knesset election campaign, Agudat Israel was strengthened by the strong support of the Lubavitcher Rebbe, Rabbi Menachem Mendel Schneerson. He was joined by the Vishnitzer Rebbe and the Gerer Rebbe in providing spiritual leadership for Agudat Israel in the final weeks of the campaign. Some observers attributed the winning of three Knesset seats to this support.

AGUDAT YISRAEL see AGUDAT ISRAEL.

AHAD HAAM ("ONE OF THE PEOPLE"). The pseudonym used by Asher Zvi Ginzberg who was born in Skvira, near Kiev, in Russia in 1856. He began to learn Hebrew (q.v.) as a youngster and developed a substantial background in Jewish literature and lore. He later settled in Odessa and engaged in commerce but came to the conclusion that the plight of Russian Jewry could only be alleviated by settlement in Palestine (q.v.). He joined the Central Committee of the Hoveve Zion (q.v.) movement, but criticized its ideas and methods. In 1895 he turned to writing as a profession and soon began editing *Hashiloah,* a Hebrew monthly. Ahad Haam became an opponent of the World Zionist Organization (q.v.) established in 1897 and he rejected the Jewish state as an immediate object of national policy. He sought instead a truly Jewish state that could be achieved only after a substantial period of national education and after the establishment of a cultural center in Palestine. This focus on cultural Zionism was in strong contrast to the political and practical Zionism of the mainstream of the Zionist movement. In 1908 he moved to London where he engaged primarily in business activities. In 1922 he settled in Tel Aviv (q.v.) and died there in 1927.

AHDUT (UNITY). A political party, led by Victor Tayar, created to contest the 1988 Knesset (q.v.) election. It did not secure the minimum number of votes to gain a seat in parliament.

AHDUT HAAVODA (UNITY OF LABOR). A Zionist, socialist association of Jewish workers in Palestine (q.v.). The association was established in 1919 by a majority of the members of the Poalei Zion (Workers of Zion) Party (q.v.), along with some members of Hapoel Hatzair (q.v.). Its ambition was to unite all Jewish workers in Eretz Israel (q.v.) and all federations and parties in the Jewish labor movement and the Zionist movement abroad. Ahdut Haavoda joined the World Alliance of Poalei Zion. It was active in aliya (q.v.), immigration, absorption, and public works.

AHDUT HAAVODA-POALEI ZION. A political party established in 1946 following an earlier split in Mapai (q.v.) by the merger of Poalei Zion (q.v.) (Workers of Zion) and smaller socialist Zionist groups. In 1948 it united with Mifleget Poalim-Hashomer Hatzair (q.v.) to form Mapam (q.v.) and, as such, contested the 1949 and 1951 Knesset (q.v.) elections. In the early 1950s it split with Mapam and reestablished itself as an independent party and, as such, won ten seats in the 1955 elections, seven in 1959, and eight in 1961. It formed the Alignment (q.v.) with Mapai and contested the 1965 and subsequent Knesset elections in that political unit.

ALIGNMENT (MAARACH). A political bloc formed in 1965 between Mapai (q.v.) and Ahdut Haavoda (q.v.). In 1968 it joined with Rafi (q.v.) to form the Israel Labor Party (q.v.). An Alignment subsequently was formed with Mapam (q.v.) to contest the elections of the Seventh Knesset (q.v.), although both Mapam and the Israel Labor Party retained their own organizations and memberships. The Alignment led Israel's government coalitions between 1965 and 1977 when it lost the elections and became the opposition in parliament. In September 1984 it joined in the National Unity Government (q.v.) with Likud (q.v.). As a consequence, Mapam and Yossi Sarid (q.v.) of the Labor Party withdrew from the Alignment while Yahad (q.v.) joined the Alignment.

ALIYA (DERIVED FROM THE HEBREW WORD FOR "ASCENT" OR "GOING UP"). The immigration of Jews from the diaspora (q.v.) to the Holy Land (Palestine (q.v.), and later, Israel). Jewish immigration to and settlement in the Land of Israel is a central concept in Zionist (q.v.) ideology, and the ingathering of the exiles (q.v.) was the primary objective of the Zionist movement. However, even before the founding of the Zionist movement, there was immigration to Eretz Israel (q.v.), the Holy Land. Throughout Jewish history prior to the modern political Zionist movement, small numbers of Jews had always migrated to the Holy Land in keeping with the Jewish religion's concept that to live and die in the Holy Land was an important precept. Immigrating to the Holy Land was an important activity and over the centuries Jews migrated to

Eretz Israel and lived in the four holy cities: Jerusalem (q.v.), Safed (q.v.), Tiberias (q.v.), and Hebron (q.v.). With the practical and political Zionism of the 19th century, beginning in the 1880s, the numbers of Jewish immigrants to Palestine grew dramatically but they also varied in number depending on practical conditions both in their countries of origin and in Palestine (and later Israel).

Immigration to Palestine traditionally has been divided into five major phases or aliyot (waves of immigration) between the 1880s and World War II. During the First Aliya (1882–1903) some 20,000 to 30,000 individuals immigrated to Palestine, primarily in groups organized by the Hoveve Zion (q.v.) and Bilu (q.v.) movements in Russia and Romania. Some arrived on their own, mostly from Galicia. The Second Aliya (q.v.) (1904–1914) involved some 35,000 to 40,000 young pioneers, mostly from Russia. In the Third Aliya (1919–1923) some 35,000 young pioneers immigrated to Palestine from Russia, Poland, and Romania. The Fourth Aliya (1924–1931) involved mainly middle-class immigrants from Poland, numbering some 88,000. The Fifth Aliya (1932–1938) consisted of some 215,000 immigrants, mainly from Central Europe. During World War II (1939–1945), immigration to Palestine continued both legally and illegally and totalled some 82,000. After World War II (1945) until the independence of Israel in May 1948, there were severe British Mandatory (q.v.) restrictions on Jewish immigration to Palestine, but some 57,000 Jews arrived. After Israeli independence the flow of immigrants to Palestine grew dramatically as Israel allowed free immigration and whole communities opted to move to the Holy Land.

ALIYA BET. A term for the illegal immigration of Jews into Palestine (q.v.) under the British Mandate (q.v.) in defiance of official British restrictions.

ALLON, YIGAL (FORMERLY PAICOVITCH). Born at Kfar Tabor (Mesha) in lower Galilee (q.v.) on October 10, 1918, he was educated at local schools, graduating in 1937 from the Kadourie Agricultural School. He later studied at Hebrew University (q.v.) and St. Antony's College, Oxford. In 1937, he helped to found and became a member of Kibbutz Ginnosar. During the Arab riots of 1936–39 in Palestine (q.v.), he served in the underground defense forces commanded by Yitzhak Sadeh (q.v.). In 1941, he helped found Palmah (q.v.), a commando unit which assisted in Allied operations in Syria and Lebanon. In 1942 he headed an underground intelligence and sabotage network in Syria and Lebanon. The following year he became the deputy commander of Palmah, and in 1945, became its commander, a post he retained until 1948. In this capacity he directed sabotage against civil and military installations of the British Mandatory (q.v.) government, and supported Aliyah Bet (q.v.), the illegal immigration of Jews into Palestine. He was commander of the southern front during the end of Israel's War of Independence (q.v.) and drove the Arab armies out of the Negev (q.v.). After Prime Minister David Ben-Gurion (q.v.) dissolved the Palmah, Allon entered politics. In 1954, he was elected to the Knesset (q.v.) and served as Minister of Labor from 1961 to 1967. In June 1967 he participated in the inner war cabinet which helped to plan the strategy of the Six Day War (q.v.). He was also the author of the "Allon plan" (q.v.). In July 1968, he became Deputy Prime Minister and Minister for Immigrant Absorption. From 1969 to 1974, he served as Deputy Prime Minister and Minister of Education and Culture, and from 1974 to 1977 was Deputy Prime Minister and Minister of Foreign Affairs. He died in 1980.

ALLON PLAN. A proposal developed by Yigal Allon (q.v.) to establish peace and secure borders for Israel after the

Six Day War (q.v.). Essentially the plan called for the return of the densely populated areas in the West Bank (q.v.) and Gaza Strip (q.v.) to Arab control as well as a return of most of the Sinai Peninsula (q.v.) to Egypt. Israel would retain control of the Jordan River valley and mountain ridges where it could establish settlements and early warning systems (of radar and other devices) to provide warnings against attacks from the east. There would be changes along the armistice lines and Israel would retain Jerusalem (q.v.) and the Etzion Bloc (q.v.), i.e., the Gush Etzion area. Other specifics were included in the detailed plan. The plan was never adopted as the official policy of Israel, but the Labor party-led (q.v.) governments of Israel until 1977 pursued its settlement policy using the Allon plan as its guideline.

ALONI, SHULAMIT. Born in Tel Aviv (q.v.), she is a writer, lawyer, and prominent figure in Israel's women's liberation movement who served as Minister Without Portfolio in the government led by Yitzhak Rabin (q.v.) in 1974. She has fought the rigid control exercised by the Orthodox rabbinate over such issues as marriage, divorce, and other areas of personal status. She was elected to parliament on the Labor Party (q.v.) list in 1965 but was dropped from the list for the 1969 and 1973 elections. She ran independently and led the Civil Rights Movement (q.v.) in the 1973 elections where it secured three seats. It subsequently joined the coalition government led by Prime Minister Yitzhak Rabin (q.v.) in 1974 but withdrew from the coalition in October of that year to protest the entry into the coalition of the National Religious Party (q.v.). Her resignation from the coalition was based on the fact that her party was pledged to a program of separation of state and religion and that the inclusion of the NRP in the government would lead to a strengthening of religious control over matters of personal status.

ALTALENA. In June 1948 a ship arrived on the coast of Israel from France with immigrants and arms and ammunition for delivery to the Irgun (q.v.). The government under Prime Minister David Ben-Gurion (q.v.) ordered that the ship and its cargo be placed at its disposal, but the Irgun refused. In the subsequent battle between the army and the Irgun, the government prevailed, and the ship was sunk. Soon afterward the Irgun was disbanded and its members were incorporated into the Israel Defense Forces (q.v.). The incident made it clear that the government would not tolerate challenges to its authority or the existence of armed forces competing with the IDF. The incident contributed to the personal animosity between Menachem Begin (q.v.) and Ben-Gurion that characterized Israeli politics in subsequent years.

AMIT, MEIR (FORMERLY SLUTZKY). Born in 1921 in Tiberias (q.v.), he joined the Hagana (q.v.) in 1936 and was a member of Kibbutz Alonim between 1939 and 1952. He served in Israel's War of Independence (q.v.), was appointed Commander of the Golani Brigade in 1950, and the head of Southern Command in 1955. He later served as Commander of the Northern Command and studied business administration in the United States. He was head of the Mossad (q.v.) from 1963 to 1968 and was Managing Director of Koor industries (q.v.) until 1977. He was one of the founding members of the Democratic Movement for Change (q.v.) in 1976 and served in the Knesset (q.v.). He served as Minister of Transport in the 1977 government led by Menachem Begin (q.v.), but in 1978 left the government and joined Shinui (q.v.). In 1980 he joined the Labor Party (q.v.). He has worked as a manager of corporations since the late 1970s.

ANGLO-AMERICAN COMMITTEE OF INQUIRY. A committee of British and American representatives appointed in November 1945 to study the question of Jewish immigration to Palestine (q.v.) and the future of the Mandate (q.v.). After numerous meetings and hearings in the region and elsewhere it issued a report on April 20, 1946. The recommendations included among others the immediate issuing of 100,000 immigration certificates for Palestine to Jewish victims of Nazi and Fascist persecution. Although United States President Harry Truman accepted much of the report, especially the recommendation concerning Jewish immigration, the British government did not accept the report. The Palestine problem was turned over to the United Nations.

AQABA, GULF OF see GULF OF AQABA

ARAB BOYCOTT OF ISRAEL. An Arab economic boycott was imposed on the Yishuv (q.v.) soon after the founding of the League of Arab States in 1945. The Arab states have maintained an economic boycott of Israel since the establishment of the state. These measures were part of the Arab anti-Israel efforts designed to weaken and ultimately to destroy the state. Until 1950 the boycott barred Arab businesses from dealing with Israel. After April 1950 foreign shippers carrying goods or immigrants to Israel were warned that they were subject to blacklisting in Arab states and would be denied access to Arab port facilities. Later, firms represented in Israel were added to the boycott list. Implementation of the boycott regulations by the Arab states against the targets have varied substantially from country to country and from time to time. Egypt (q.v.), since 1979, openly deals with Israel and some trade takes place unofficially and informally between Israel and other Arab partners.

ARAB COOPERATION AND BROTHERHOOD. An Arab political party that won seats in the Knesset (q.v.) in the elections of 1959, 1961, and 1965.

ARAB DEMOCRATIC LIST. An Arab political party that contested and won seats in the Knesset (q.v.) elections of 1949, 1951, and 1955.

ARAB DEMOCRATIC PARTY. A political party formed in 1988 by former Labor Alignment (q.v.) member of the Knesset (q.v.), Abd El-Wahab Darousha (q.v.), that contested the 1988 Knesset elections. Its platform called for appropriate and active representation for Palestinian Arabs in Israel in all state institutions. In foreign policy it called for the recognition of the right of the Palestinian Arab people to self-determination. It advocated convening an international peace conference with the participation on an equal basis of all the parties involved, including the Palestine Liberation Organization (q.v.) as the sole legitimate representative of the Palestinian people. The party called for the withdrawal of Israel from all the territories occupied in the Six Day War (q.v.) and the establishment of a Palestinian state in Judea (q.v.), Samaria (q.v.), and Gaza (q.v.), including East Jerusalem (q.v.). It won one seat.

ARAB FARMERS AND DEVELOPMENT PARTY. An Arab political party that contested the Knesset (q.v.) elections of 1951, 1955, and 1959 and won a single seat in each instance.

ARAB-ISRAELI CONFLICT. The Arab-Israeli conflict has been and continues to be the central concern and focus of Israel and affects all aspects of national life. In the period prior to Israel's independence the Arabs of Palestine (q.v.) actively opposed the Zionist efforts to create the Jewish state through attacks on Jewish settlers and settlements, through riots and demonstrations, and by opposition to Jewish immigration and land purchase in the period prior to Israel's independence. Arab opposition to the United Nations Partition Plan (q.v.) of

November 1947 which led to Israel's independence was followed by a de facto war in Palestine until the termination of the British Mandate (q.v.). With the formal end of Britain's role and the establishment of an independent Israel in May 1948 the first of six major Arab-Israeli wars began.

Israel and the Arabs have fought in Israel's War of Independence (1948–1949) (q.v.); the Sinai War (1956) (q.v.); the Six Day War (1967) (q.v.); the War of Attrition (1969-1970) (q.v.); the Yom Kippur War (1973) (q.v.); and the War in Lebanon (1982) (q.v.). In addition, there have been countless border and terrorist incidents and strikes against Israeli and Jewish targets abroad. Substantial efforts to end the conflict and achieve peace, often involving outside, especially United States (q.v.), efforts have yielded armistice agreements (1949) (q.v.); cease-fires at the end of the several conflicts; disengagement of forces agreements (q.v.) in 1974 and 1975; the Camp David Accords of 1978 (q.v.); and the Egypt-Israel Peace Treaty of 1979 (q.v.). While Israel is formally at peace with Egypt and has a de facto working arrangement with some other Arab states, resolution of the conflict has eluded Israel. *See* the individual entries for the various elements and components of the conflict and the peace efforts.

ARAB-ISRAELI WARS, ISRAEL'S WAR OF INDE-PENDENCE (1948–1949) see WAR OF INDEPEN-DENCE

ARAB-ISRAELI WARS, SINAI WAR (1956) see SINAI WAR

ARAB-ISRAELI WARS, SIX DAY WAR (1967) see SIX DAY WAR

ARAB-ISRAELI WARS, WAR IN LEBANON (1982) see WAR IN LEBANON

ARAB-ISRAELI WARS, WAR OF ATTRITION (1969–1970) see WAR OF ATTRITION

ARAB-ISRAELI WARS, YOM KIPPUR WAR (1973) see YOM KIPPUR WAR

ARAB POLITICAL PARTIES. Arab political parties have been a part of the Israeli political scene since independence, and the Arabs of Israel (q.v.) have been represented on a regular basis in the Knesset (q.v.). In the elections for the Knesset between 1949 and 1969, the majority of Israeli Arabs supported the dominant Jewish party or the Arab political party lists affiliated with it. In 1973 and 1977, this support declined; the Communist Party (q.v.) secured nearly 50% of the Arab votes in 1977. To a great extent, this reflected growing Arab nationalism and support for the Palestinians, causes espoused by the Communists. Overall Arab participation in the political process also declined during the same period. In 1981, the Alignment (q.v.) tripled its vote among the Arabs of Israel compared to 1977; this was seen as a vote for the best of the bad alternatives. Much of the turn to Labor was seen as anti-Begin (q.v.) and anti-Likud (q.v.) and grew out of disappointment with Menachem Begin's ignoring the Arab problem in Israel. There was an unexpectedly low turnout of voters and a sharp decline in support for Rakah (q.v.). In the 1988 election Rakah won four seats. See also INDIVIDUAL POLITICAL PARTIES BY NAME.

ARAB PROGRESS AND WORK. An Arab political party that contested the 1951, 1955, 1959, 1961, and 1965 Knesset (q.v.) elections and won seats in parliament.

ARABS IN ISRAEL. Israel's non-Jewish citizenry is composed mainly of the Arabs who remained in what became Israel after the 1949 Armistice Agreements (q.v.) and their descendents. By 1990 that group had grown to some 800,000, primarily as a result of a high birthrate. The Muslim population, which constitutes about three-fourths of the non-Jewish population, is predominantly Sunni. The Christians constitute about 14% of the non-Jewish population. Greek Catholics and Greek Orthodox constitute more than 70% of that number, but there are also Roman Catholics, Maronites, Armenians, Protestants, and Anglicans.

The non-Jewish communities have special positions, similar to those enjoyed under the Ottoman millet system. After Israel's War of Independence (q.v.) and the 1949 Armistice Agreements, the activities of the Arab community were regarded primarily as concerns of Israel's security system, and most of the areas inhabited by the Arabs were placed under military control. Military government was established in those districts, and special defense and security zones were created. Israel's Arabs were granted citizenship with full legal equality, but were forbidden to travel into or out of security areas without permission of the military. Military courts were established in which trials could be held in closed session. With the consent of the Minister of Defense, the military commanders could limit individual movements, impose restrictions on employment and business, issue deportation orders, search and seize, and detain a person if that were deemed necessary for security purposes. Those who argued in support of the military administration saw it as a means of controlling the Arab population and of preventing infiltration from neighboring hostile Arab states, sabotage, and espionage. It was argued that the very existence of the military administration was an important deterrent measure. However, as it became clear that Israel's

Arabs were not disloyal and as Israel's security situation improved, pressure for relaxation and then for total abolition of military restrictions on Israel's Arabs grew in the Knesset (q.v.) and in public debate. The restrictions were gradually modified, and on December 1, 1966, military government was abolished. Functions that had been exercised by the military government were transferred to relevant civilian authorities.

The non-Jewish community has undergone other substantial changes since 1948. Education has become virtually universal. Local authority has grown, and through the various local authorities the Arabs have become involved in local decision making and provision of services. The traditional life of the Arab has been altered by new agricultural methods and increased employment in other sectors of the economy—especially industry, construction, and services. Social and economic improvement have included more urbanization, modernization of villages, better infrastructure, improved health care, and expansion of educational opportunities. See also DRUZE.

ARAD. A town in the eastern Negev (q.v.), located between Beersheva (q.v.) and the Dead Sea (q.v.), founded in 1961. Its name is derived from the Bible.

ARAVA. A part of the Negev (q.v.), it is a narrow and arid plain about 100 miles long and some 10 miles wide stretching north-south from the Dead Sea (q.v.) to Eilat (q.v.). The frontier between Israel and Jordan runs through the Arava from north to south.

ARBELI-ALMOZLINO, SHOSHANA. Born in Iraq. A Labor Alignment (q.v.) Member of the Knesset (q.v.) since 1965, where she served as Deputy Speaker from 1977 to 1981.

ARCHAEOLOGY. Archaeology is a primary avocation of most Israelis and logically derives from living in a country with a long and complex past. Discovery of important archaeological sites and finds, such as Massada (q.v.) and the Dead Sea scrolls (q.v.), are considered major achievements that tend to provide a greater link between the contemporary state and the traditional states and institutions of the past. It links the modern Jewish state to the Bible and to the ancient history of the Jewish people.

ARENS, MOSHE. Born in 1925 in Kovno, Lithuania. In 1939 his family immigrated to the United States and he served in the United States Army during World War II. He secured a BS degree from the Massachusetts Institute of Technology but went to Israel at the outbreak of the War of Independence (q.v.), and served in the Irgun (q.v.) led by Menachem Begin (q.v.). After the war he settled in Mevo Betar but returned to the United States in 1951 and secured an MA degree from the California Institute of Technology in aeronautical engineering in 1953. He then worked for a number of years on jet engine development in the United States. In 1957 he took a position as an Associate Professor of Aeronautical Engineering at the Technion (q.v.). He joined Israel Aircraft Industries (q.v.) in 1962, where he was Vice President for Engineering, while continuing his relationship with the Technion. He won the Israel Defense Prize in 1971. He was active in Herut Party (q.v.) politics from the outset. He was elected to the Knesset (q.v.) in 1974 and after the Likud (q.v.) victory of 1977, he became chairman of the Knesset Foreign Affairs and Defense Committee. He voted against the Camp David Accords (q.v.), but subsequently supported the Egypt-Israel Peace Treaty (q.v.) as an established fact. He was appointed Ambassador to Washington in February 1982. He became Defense Minister in 1983 after Ariel

Sharon (q.v.) resigned the post. Arens was a well regarded technocrat and gained substantial kudos for his activities as Ambassador to Washington. His record as Defense Minister gained him similar positive reactions. He served as Minister Without Portfolio in the National Unity Government (q.v.) established in 1984 until he resigned when the government decided to halt production of the Lavi jet. Arens served again as Minister Without Portfolio from April to December 1988 when he became Foreign Minister in the Likud-led National Unity Government. In June 1990 he became Minister of Defense in a Likud-led government.

ARIDOR, YORAM. Born in Tel Aviv (q.v.) in 1933. He holds a BA in Economics and Political Science and an MJur from the Hebrew University of Jerusalem (q.v.). He was first elected to the Knesset (q.v.) on behalf of the Herut Party (q.v.) faction of Gahal (q.v.) in October 1969, and reelected to all subsequent Knessets as a member of the Likud (q.v.) bloc. He has served on the Knesset Constitution and Law Committee and as Chairman of the Knesset Interior and Environment Committee. He also served as the Chairman of the Herut faction in the Histadrut (q.v.) from 1972 to 1977, has been a member of the Herut Central Committee since 1961, and has served as Chairman of the Herut Secretariat since October 1979. From July 1977 to January 1981 he served as Deputy Minister in the Prime Minister's office. For varying lengths of time during this period he was also responsible for the activities of the Ministries of Justice; Labor and Social Welfare; Transport, Communications and Industry; and Commerce and Tourism. In January 1981 he was appointed Minister of Communications. He later became Minister of Finance in the government of Menachem Begin (q.v.) and also served as the original Finance Minister of the new government of Yitzhak Shamir (q.v.) (1983). He resigned after substantial furor developed in response to his proposal that Israel link its economy directly to the United States dollar. The proposal was part of a plan to rescue the deteriorating Israeli economy, but the so-called "dollarization" proposal had no precedent in Israel. If the plan had been adopted, it would give the Israeli shekel a fixed value in U.S. dollars and would have forced the Israeli economy to adapt by reducing inflation and cutting its huge international deficit. At the cost of a huge reduction in purchasing power there would be an end to inflation and the indexing system could be abandoned. The budget would be forced into balance. The plan also called for a further substantial devaluation of the shekel in terms of the dollar. After Aridor resigned on October 13, 1983, Prime Minister Shamir sought to calm public concerns and distanced himself from Aridor and his proposals. He subsequently served as Israel's Ambassador to the United Nations.

ARMED FORCES see HAGANA (ISRAEL DEFENSE FORCES)

ARMISTICE AGREEMENTS (1949). Treaties concluded between Israel and the neighboring Arab states after the War of Independence (q.v.). In the spring of 1949 Israel and each of the neighboring states signed an armistice agreement terminating the hostilities of Israel's War of Independence. Iraq, although a participant in the conflict, refused to do so. The agreements were to end the hostilities and pave the way for negotiations for peace. The latter did not occur. The armistice negotiations were held under the auspices of the United Nations Acting Mediator for Palestine, Ralph Bunche. Egypt (q.v.) signed the armistice agreement with Israel on February 24, 1949; Lebanon on March 23, 1949; Jordan on April 3, 1949; and Syria on July 20, 1949.

ARTS. The arts in Israel are reflected in a wide variety of cultural forms including music (q.v.), literature (q.v.), theater (q.v.), dance (q.v.), fine arts (q.v.), and cinema (q.v.). Israelis tend to be enthusiastic about the arts and are appreciative in nature. They attend concerts, theater and dance performances, movies and art exhibitions throughout the country. Music and the arts tend to be widely participated in by the population. Government support for cultural activities is substantial and is provided by the Ministry of Education and Culture through the Council for Arts and Culture. See also MUSEUMS.

ASEFAT HANIVCHARIM see ASSEMBLY OF THE ELECTED

ASHDOD. A modern city on the southern portion of the coastal plain founded in 1955, which takes its name from an ancient Philistine town that was located nearby. Its important deepwater port on the Mediterranean Sea was opened in 1966.

ASHKELON. A city located on the southern portion of the coastal plain near the site of the ancient Philistine city of Ashkelon. It was formed in 1955 by combining Migdal Gad and Afridar.

ASHKENAZI JEWS (ASHKENAZIM, plural). Jews of Eastern and Central European extraction. Ashkenazi Jews were the main components of the first waves of Zionist immigration to Palestine (q.v.), where they encountered a small Jewish community that was primarily Sephardi (q.v.) in nature. The Ashkenazi Jews had fled from the Jewish ghettos of Europe (including Russia) and sought to build a new society, primarily secular and socialist in nature. The more religious brought with them their East European customs, fashions, and language (Yiddish (q.v.)).

ASSEMBLY OF THE ELECTED (ASEFAT HA-NIVCHARIM). During the British Mandate (q.v.) period, the Yishuv (q.v.) established and developed institutions for self-government and procedures for implementing political decisions, thereby laying the foundations for the future state of Israel. All significant Jewish groups belonged to the organized Jewish community (with the exception of the ultra-Orthodox Agudat Israel (q.v.), then anti-Zionist, which refused to participate) and by secret ballot chose the Assembly of the Elected as its representative body. It was first elected in 1920. It met at least once a year, and between sessions its powers were exercised by the National Council (Vaad Leumi, q.v.) which it elected. The Assembly was formally abolished in February 1949, and its functions and authority were transferred to the Knesset (q.v.).

ASSOCIATION OF ISRAEL see AGUDAT ISRAEL

ATOMIC RESEARCH AND DEVELOPMENT. During his tenure as Prime Minister, David Ben-Gurion (q.v.) suggested that Israel's scientists begin to develop atomic energy as a source of power for a country essentially devoid of natural resources and as a component of broader scientific research. This included training scientists and engineers. In 1956 it was decided to establish a research reactor at Nahal Sorek which went critical on June 16, 1960. It became a major facility for research and teaching. It was decided to build a second experimental reactor near Dimona (q.v.) in the Negev (q.v.) which became operational in 1964. Israeli scientists established an international reputation for their work in the peaceful uses of atomic energy, but there has been more focus on whether or not Israel has developed a nuclear weapon for potential use by its defense forces. It is generally believed that Israel possesses the scientific and technological know-how, the necessary components and nuclear material, as well as the capability to develop and to deliver a nuclear weapon, but Israel has never confirmed (nor specifically denied) its existence.

ATTORNEY-GENERAL. The Attorney-General is the chief legal officer of the state. He is appointed by the Government (q.v.) nomination of the Minister of Justice and performs the functions of legal advisor to the Government, legal draftsman of all bills proposed by the Government to the Knesset (q.v.), and the representative of the State before all courts. He is administratively, but not professionally, subordinated to the Minister of Justice who is a politician representing his party in the Government. The office of Attorney-General was created in order to ensure that the Government receives independent nonpolitical advice and representation.

- B -

BAHAI. A religion founded in Persia in 1862 by Mirza Hussein Ali "Baha'ullah (Glory of God)" who was exiled from Persia in 1853 and subsequently imprisoned by the Ottoman government in Akko (Acre) (q.v.). After his death in Acre in 1892 the leadership of the movement passed to his son, Abdul-Baha. It grew out of Babism, one of the sectarian deviations of Shiite Islam. Bahai's main holy places are in Haifa (q.v.) (Tomb of the Bab) and in Bahji, near Acre (site of the Tomb of Baha'ullah). The principles of Bahaism stress the "unity of all religions, world peace, and universal education." It claims to be an all-embracing world religion.

BALFOUR DECLARATION. The Balfour Declaration was issued by the British government on November 2, 1917. Substantial effort by the Zionist organization, with a special role played by Chaim Weizmann (q.v.), preceded the government's decision, made after lengthy discussion and some divisiveness. The Declaration took the form of a letter from Arthur James Balfour, the Foreign Secretary, to Lord Rothschild, a prominent British Zionist leader. It stated: "His majesty's government view with favour the establishment in Palestine of a national home for the Jewish people, and will use their best endeavors to facilitate the achievement of this object, it being clearly understood that nothing shall be done which may prejudice the civil and religious rights of existing non-Jewish communities in Palestine, or the rights and political status enjoyed by Jews in any other country."

The Declaration was vague and sought to assuage the fears of prominent Jews in England as well as those of the non-Jewish inhabitants of Palestine (q.v.). Nevertheless, it engendered much controversy, then and since. Among the problems was the Balfour Declaration's apparent conflict with arrangements made during World War I by the British with the French and the Arabs concerning the future of the Middle East after the termination of hostilities. Foremost among those was the Hussein-McMahon Correspondence, which the Arabs saw as a promise that an independent Arab kingdom would include all of Palestine, although the British later argued that they had excluded the territory west of the Jordan River from that pledge. The Balfour Declaration provided a basis for Zionist claims to Palestine.

BANK OF ISRAEL. The central bank of the State of Israel established in accordance with the Bank of Israel Law in 1954. Its primary functions are in the area of monetary policy, where it administers, regulates, and directs the currency system and also supervises and directs the funds made available as loans to the public. It also regulates and supervises the work of commercial and other banks, including their foreign activities, in order to ensure sound practices and to protect the public interest.

BAR ILAN UNIVERSITY. An independent coeducational university founded in 1955 and located in Ramat Gan (q.v.), a suburb of Tel-Aviv (q.v.). The university, named for Rabbi Meir Bar-Ilan, was established under the auspices of the Religious Zionists of America. The university's purpose is to train students in both Jewish and secular studies.

BAR KOCHBA, SIMON. A Jewish revolutionary leader who died in 135 AD. He is credited with organizing a nearly total popular revolt against the Roman Emperor Hadrian which lasted for some three years. The rebuilding of Jerusalem (q.v.) as a Roman colony and the prohibition of circumcision were contributory factors, but it had been developing for a considerable period. The Roman counterattack, with an army of 35,000, began in 133. In 134–5, the Romans invaded Betar, Bar Kochba's last stronghold, and gradually reduced the remaining hill and cave strongholds. Bar Kochba was killed when Betar fell; records speak of the destruction of 50 fortresses and 985 villages, and of 580,000 Jewish casualties besides those who died of hunger and disease. As a result of the revolt, Judea fell into desolation, its population was annihilated, and Jerusalem was barred to Jews.

BAR KOCHBA WAR. In 63 BC the Roman leader Pompey conquered Judea (q.v.) and Jerusalem (q.v.), inaugurating a period of relative calm that ended with a revolt in 66 AD. The revolt was put down, and Titus, commander of the Roman forces, conquered Jerusalem and destroyed the Temple in 70 AD. After the revolt of Simon Bar Kochba (132–135) (q.v.), Jerusalem was destroyed, large numbers of Jews were killed or enslaved, and Jewish sovereignty over the area was terminated. Many Jews were dispersed throughout the world (a scattering known as the Diaspora) (q.v.), and the idea of an ultimate return to the Promised Land went with them.

BAR LEV, HAIM. Born on November 16, 1924 in Vienna, Austria he emigrated to Palestine (q.v.) in 1939 from Zagreb, Yugoslavia. He graduated from the Mikveh Yisrael agricultural school. While still in school he joined the Hagana (q.v.). He later joined and served in the Palmah (q.v.) (from 1942 to 1948), and during the War of Independence (q.v.) he commanded a battalion of the Negev Brigade which repulsed the Egyptian attack. In the 1956 Sinai War (q.v.), he was a colonel in command of the Armored Corps and his unit was among the first to reach the Suez Canal. From 1957 to 1961, Bar Lev was Commander of the Armored Corps. He spent time studying for his MBA at Columbia University in New York. He became commanding officer of the Northern Command in 1962. From 1964 until May 1966, when he went to Paris for advanced military courses, he served as Chief of the General Staff Branch Operations of the Israel Defense Forces (q.v.). He returned to Israel in May 1967 and was appointed Deputy Chief of Staff. Between January 1, 1968 and 1972, he served as Israel's eighth Chief of Staff. He became Chief of Staff during a period in which the Israel Defense Forces had to convert from an attack-oriented army into a defensive one without forfeiting any of its offensive qualities and capabilities. In response to continuing attacks and the escalation by President Gamal Abdul Nasser of Egypt (q.v.) in the War of Attrition (q.v.), he reversed the war of attrition and created what came to be known as the Bar Lev Line (q.v.)—the fortification system along the Suez Canal. During the 1973 Yom Kippur War (q.v.), he served as Commander of the Egyptian Front. Since his election in 1973, Bar Lev has served as a member of Knesset (q.v.) for the Alignment-Labor Party (q.v.). He served as Minister of Commerce, Industry and Development between 1972–77. In 1978 he was elected Secretary-General of the Labor Party. From 1984–88 he served as Minister of Police in the National Unity Government and he was reappointed to that post in the government established in December 1988.

BAR LEV LINE. A defensive system on the east bank of the Suez Canal constructed by the Israel Defense Forces (q.v.) during the tenure of Haim Bar Lev (q.v.) as Chief of Staff. The Bar Lev line was essentially a series of fortifications and strong points constructed along the Suez Canal to withstand artillery shelling and other weapons and tended to reduce Israeli manpower requirements and potential casualties along the Suez Canal. It was overrun by the Egyptian army in the early hours of the Yom Kippur War (q.v.).

BARAK, EHUD. Born in 1942 in Kibbutz Mishmar Hasharon. He enlisted in the Israel Defense Forces (q.v.) in 1959 and was schooled in various military educational courses and held a number of significant military assignments. His education included undergraduate studies in Physics and Mathematics at Hebrew University (q.v.) and a Master's degree from Stanford University in California in Systems Analysis. He served as Director of Military Intelligence (q.v.) and later as Deputy Chief of Staff of the Israel Defense Forces. He became Chief of Staff in April 1991.

BARAM, UZI. Born in Jerusalem (q.v.) and educated in political science and sociology at Hebrew University (q.v.). Member of the Knesset (q.v.) on the Labor Alignment (q.v.) party list. Served as Secretary General of the Labor Party from 1984 until he resigned in

January 1989, ostensibly because of his concern that Labor would lose its "identity" by joining in a national unity government led by Yitzhak Shamir (q.v.) and that this would be a political disaster for the Labor Party in future elections.

BAR-ON, MORDECHAI. He served in various capacities in the Israel Defense Forces (q.v.), including the post of Chief Education Officer. He was among the founders of the Peace Now movement (q.v.). He served his first term as a Member in the Eleventh Knesset (q.v.) elected on the Ratz (Citizens' Rights Movement) (q.v.) list.

BASIC LAW. As early as 1947, the Executive of the Vaad Leumi (q.v.) appointed a committee headed by Zerah Warhaftig to study the question of a constitution for the new state. In December 1947, the Jewish Agency (q.v.) Executive entrusted Dr. Leo Kohn, Professor of International Relations at the Hebrew University (q.v.), with the task of preparing a draft constitution. On July 8, 1949 the Provisional Council of State appointed a Constitutional Committee. The First Knesset (q.v.) devoted much time to a profound discussion of the issue of a constitution for the state of Israel. The major debate was between those who favored a written document and those who believed that the time was not appropriate for imposing rigid constitutional limitations. The latter group argued that a written constitution could not be framed because of constantly changing social conditions, primarily the result of mass immigration and a lack of experience with independent governmental institutions. There was also concern about the relationship between state and religion and the method of incorporating the precepts and ideals of Judaism into the proposed document. The discussion of these issues continued for over a year, and on June 13, 1950 the Knesset adopted a compromise that has postponed the real issue indefinitely. It was decided in principle that a written constitution would be adopted ultimately, but that for the time being there would be no formal and comprehensive document. Instead, a number of fundamental, or basic, laws would be passed dealing with specific subjects, which might in time form chapters in a consolidated constitution. A number of Basic Laws dealing with various subjects have been adopted: The Knesset (1958); The Lands of Israel (1960); The President (1964); The Government (1968); The State Economy (1975); The Army (1976); Jerusalem, The Capital of Israel (1980); and The Judiciary (1984). The Basic Laws thereby provide a definitive perspective of the formal requirements of the system in specific areas of activity, a "written" framework, in a sense, for governmental activity.

BASLE PROGRAM. On August 23, 1897, in Basle (or Basel), Switzerland, Theodor Herzl (q.v.) convened the first World Zionist Congress (q.v.) representing Jewish communities and organizations throughout the world. The Congress established the World Zionist Organization (q.v.) (WZO) and founded an effective, modern, political, Jewish national movement with the goal, enunciated in the Basle Program, the original official program of the WZO, "Zionism seeks to establish a home for the Jewish people in Palestine secured under public law." Zionism (q.v.) rejected other solutions to the "Jewish Question" and was the response to centuries of discrimination, persecution, and oppression. It sought redemption through self-determination. Herzl argued in Der Judenstaat (q.v.): "Let the sovereignty be granted us over a portion of the globe large enough to satisfy the rightful requirements of a nation; the rest we shall manage for ourselves." For the attainment of the aims of the Basle Program, the Congress envisaged the promotion of the settlement of Palestine (q.v.) by

Jewish agriculturalists, artisans, and trades people; the organization and unification of the whole of Jewry by means of appropriate local and general institutions in accordance with the laws of each country; the strengthening of Jewish national sentiment and national consciousness; and preparatory steps toward securing the consent of governments, which is necessary to attain the aim of Zionism.

BEERSHEVA (BEERSHEBA). The capital of the Negev (q.v.), it lies on its northern edge. Its name is of biblical derivation, meaning either "Well of Seven" or "Well of Oath." It is the place where Abraham (q.v.) settled. It is a new city built on an ancient site dating back to the age of the Patriarchs some 4,000 years ago. Since 1948, the city has experienced rapid industrial and residential development and has evolved from a small backward town with a population of about 4,000 to a bustling city with approximately 115,000 people by the late 1980s. It is the center of the mining and agricultural projects in that sector and the location of Ben-Gurion University (q.v.).

BEGIN, MENACHEM. Menachem Begin was born the son of Zeev-Dov and Hassia Begin in Brest-Litovsk, White Russia (later Poland), on August 16, 1913. He was educated in Brest-Litovsk at the Mizrachi Hebrew School and later studied and graduated in law at the University of Warsaw. After a short association with Hashomer Hatzair (q.v.), he became a devoted follower of Vladimir Zeev Jabotinsky (q.v.), the founder of the Revisionist Zionist Movement. At the age of 16 he joined Betar (q.v.), the youth movement affiliated with the Revisionists (q.v.), and in 1932 became the head of the Organization Department of Betar in Poland. Later, after a period of service as head of Betar in Czechoslovakia, he returned to Poland in 1937 and in 1939 became head of the movement there. Upon the outbreak of World War II, he was arrested by the Russian authorities and confined in concentration camps in Siberia and elsewhere until his release in 1941. He then joined the Polish army and was dispatched to the Middle East. After demobilization in 1943, he remained in Palestine (q.v.) and assumed command of the Irgun Tzvai Leumi (q.v.). For his activities against the British authorities as head of that organization, he was placed on their "most wanted" list, but managed to evade capture by living underground in Tel Aviv (q.v.).

With the independence of Israel in 1948 and the dissolution of the Irgun, Begin founded the Herut (Freedom) Party (q.v.) and represented it in the Knesset since its first meetings in 1949. He became Herut's leader, retaining that position until he resigned from office as Prime Minister and retired from public and political life in 1983. Herut was known for its right-wing, strongly nationalistic views, and Begin led the party's protest campaign against the reparations agreement with West Germany in 1952. He was instrumental in establishing the Gahal (q.v.) faction (a merger of Herut and the Liberal Party (q.v.)) in the Knesset in 1965. He developed a reputation as a gifted orator, writer, and political leader. He remained in opposition in parliament until the eve of the Six Day War (q.v.) of June 1967, when he joined the government of national unity as Minister Without Portfolio. He and his Gahal colleagues resigned from the government in August 1970 over opposition to its acceptance of the peace initiative of United States Secretary of State William Rogers, which implied the evacuation by Israel of territories occupied in the course of the Six Day War. Later, Gahal joined in forming the Likud bloc in opposition to the governing Labor Alignment, and Begin became its leader.

In June 1977, Begin became Israel's first non-socialist Prime Minister when the Likud bloc secured the mandate to form the government after the May Knesset election. He also became the first Israeli Prime Minister to meet officially and publically with an Arab head of state when he welcomed Egyptian President Anwar Sadat to Jerusalem in November 1977. He led Israel's delegations to the ensuing peace negotiations and signed, with Sadat and United States President Jimmy Carter, the Camp David Accords (q.v.) in September 1978. In March 1979, he and Egyptian President Sadat signed the Egypt-Israel Peace Treaty, with Carter witnessing the event, on the White House lawn. Begin and Sadat shared the 1978 Nobel Peace Prize for their efforts. For Begin and Israel, it was a momentous but difficult accomplishment. It brought peace with Israel's most populous adversary and significantly reduced the military danger to the existence of Israel by neutralizing the largest Arab army with whom Israel had fought five wars. But, it was also traumatic given the extensive tangible concessions required of Israel, especially the uprooting of Jewish settlements in Sinai.

The Knesset election of June 30, 1981 returned a Likud-led coalition government to power in Israel, contrary to early predictions which projected a significant Labor Alignment victory. Menachem Begin again became Prime Minister and his reestablished government coalition contained many of the same personalities as the outgoing group and reflected similar perspectives of Israel's situation and appropriate government policies. He also served as Minister of Foreign Affairs in 1979–80 and as Minister of Defense from May 1980 to August 1981.

The War in Lebanon (q.v.) occasioned debate and demonstration within Israel, resulted in substantial casualties, and led, at least initially, to Israel's increased international isolation and major clashes with the

United States. Many of the outcomes were muted over time, but the war left a legacy that continued to be debated long after Begin retired from public life. It was also a factor in Begin's decision to step down from the Prime Minister's office, but it was a decision he chose and was not forced to make. Within Israel, Begin's tenure was marked by prosperity for the average citizen, although there were indicators (such as rising debt and inflation levels) that this might prove costly in the long term. The standard of living rose, as did the level of expectations. The religious parties enhanced their political power and secured important concessions to their demands from a coalition which recognized their increased role in maintaining the political balance and from a Prime Minister who was, on the whole, sympathetic to their positions.

The relationship with the United States underwent significant change during Begin's tenure. The ties were often tempestuous as the two states disagreed on various aspects of the regional situation and the issues associated with resolution of the Arab-Israeli conflict. Nevertheless, United States economic and military assistance and political and diplomatic support rose to all-time high levels.

Begin's political skills were considerable and apparent. Despite his European origins and courtly manner, he was able, through his powerful oratorical skills, charismatic personality, and political and economic policies, to secure and maintain a substantial margin of popularity over other major political figures, particularly the opposition leaders. At the time of his resignation he was the most popular and highly regarded of Israeli politicians, as the public opinion polls regularly indicated.

Menachem Begin's decision to resign as Prime Minister of Israel on September 16, 1983 brought to an end a major era in Israeli politics. It was a surprise and a shock to Israelis, notwithstanding Begin's earlier statements that he would retire from politics at age 70. Although no formal reason for his resignation was forthcoming, Begin apparently believed that he could no longer perform his tasks as he felt he should and he seemed to be severely affected by the death of his wife the previous year and by the continuing casualties suffered by Israeli forces in Lebanon.

His publications include *White Nights* (describing his war-time experiences in Europe), *The Revolt* (describing the struggle against the British), and numerous articles. He died in March 1992.

BEGIN, ZE'EV BINYAMIN. Born in Jerusalem in 1943, he is the son of former Prime Minister Menachem Begin (q.v.). He earned a PhD in geology from the University of Colorado and in 1965 began working for the Israel Geological Survey prior to entering politics. A member of the Knesset (q.v.) representing Likud (q.v.) who indicated in 1991 that he would contend for the premiership when Prime Minister Yitzhak Shamir (q.v.) retires. This was seen as a direct challenge to Ariel Sharon (q.v.) who had already expressed similar intentions.

BEN YEHUDA, ELIEZER (FORMERLY PERLMAN). The pioneer of the restoration of Hebrew (q.v.) as a living, spoken language. He is generally considered "the father of the Hebrew language." He was born in Lushky, Lithuania in 1857 and died in Jerusalem (q.v.) in 1922. Ben Yehuda became interested in the restoration of the Jews to their ancient homeland and in the revival of the Jewish language. In 1881 he settled in Palestine (q.v.) with his wife and began editing and publishing dailies, weeklies, and periodicals in Hebrew. In 1889, together with several others, he established the Vaad Halashon Haivrit, the Hebrew Language Council whose main task was the coining of new Hebrew words.

Ben Yehuda developed a comprehensive dictionary of the Hebrew language containing words ranging from those found in the Bible to those in modern Hebrew literature.

BEN ZVI, YITZHAK (FORMERLY SHIMSHELEV-ITZ). Born in Poltava, Ukraine, Russia, on December 6, 1884, he was educated at a heder and then at a Russian gymnasium. He early joined Zionist groups and in 1904 made his first visit to Palestine (q.v.) and helped to found the Poalei Zion Party (q.v.). He entered Kiev University in 1905, but then strikes closed down the university for that year. During the pogroms of November 1905 he participated in Jewish self-defense groups in Poltava. In 1906, he was among the participants at the first meeting of Poalei Zion—Zionist Social Democrats of Russia. In June 1906, while his family was imprisoned by Russian police for illegal possession of weapons, he escaped to Vilna, where he attempted to coordinate Poalei Zion activites in different countries. He settled in Palestine in 1907 and that same year was the Poalei Zion delegate to the Eighth Zionist Congress at the Hague. He helped found the Hebrew socialist periodical *Ahdut* (Unity) in 1910. After his deportation from Palestine, he traveled to New York and, in 1915, founded the Hehalutz movement in America.

During World War I, Ben Zvi and David Ben-Gurion (q.v.) organized a volunteer movement for Jewish battalions in the United States. Ben Zvi then served as a soldier in the Jewish Legion (q.v.) of the British Royal Fusiliers. After returning to Palestine in 1918, he was appointed to the Palestine Advisory Council in 1920, but resigned the following year after the Jaffa riots. He was one of the founders of the Histadrut (q.v.) in 1920. He joined the Vaad Leumi (q.v.) and remained a member until Israel was established as a state. He was a member of the Knesset (q.v.) from 1948 to 1952 and also served on the Jerusalem (q.v.) Municipal Council. A signer of Israel's Declaration of Independence (q.v.), Ben Zvi was elected to the First Knesset in 1949 and to the Second Knesset in 1951. After Chaim Weizmann's (q.v.) death, he was elected President in 1952 and reelected in 1957. In 1962 he was elected for a third term, but died in office in April 1963. As President, he encouraged intellectual gatherings at his residence to discuss literary, academic, and artistic concerns.

BEN-ELISAR, ELIAHU (FORMERLY GOTTLIEB). Born in Radom, Poland on February 2, 1932 and immigrated to Palestine (q.v.) in 1942. His original family name was Gottlieb but when he changed it to Hebrew (q.v.), he did so by combining the first half of his father's two names (Eliezer Yisrael) to create Ben-Elisar. He was educated at the University of Paris in political science and international law and during his time in Paris he was enlisted by the Mossad (q.v.) where he worked until 1965. In 1965 he left the Mossad to pursue his doctorate at the University of Geneva where he wrote on the Jewish factor in the foreign policy of the Third Reich. It was published as a book in 1969. He returned to Israel and worked as a correspondent for several European newspapers. He also became involved in Herut Party (q.v.) political activities and in 1971 began to serve as head of the Information Department of the Herut Movement. He served as Director General of Prime Minister Menachem Begin's (q.v.) office and as Israel's first Ambassador to Egypt. A member of the Knesset (q.v.) on the Likud list (q.v.) he served as Chairman of the Foreign Affairs and Security Committee of the Tenth Knesset.

BEN-GURION, DAVID (FORMERLY GRUEN). Born in Plonsk, Poland on October 16, 1886. Under the influence of his father and grandfather, he became a committed Zionist in childhood. He arrived in Jaffa (q.v.) in September 1906. He was elected to the central committee of the Poalei Zion (Workers of Zion) (q.v.) and began organizing workers into unions. In 1910 he joined the editorial staff of a new Poalei Zion paper, *Ahdut* (Unity) in Jerusalem (q.v.) and began publishing articles under the name Ben-Gurion. He joined a group of young socialist Zionists who went to study at Turkish universities and moved in 1912 to the University of Constantinople, where he earned a law degree with highest honors. In 1914, he returned to Palestine (q.v.) and resumed his work as a union organizer, but in 1915 was exiled by Ottoman authorities. In May 1918 he enlisted in a Jewish Battalion of the British Royal Fusiliers and sailed to Egypt to join the expeditionary force. From 1921 to 1935, Ben-Gurion was the Secretary General of the Histadrut (q.v.) and was instrumental in the founding of the United Labor Party which eventually became Mapai (q.v.).

In the 1920s and 1930s, Chaim Weizmann (q.v.), the head of the World Zionist Organization (q.v.) and chief diplomat of the Zionist movement, ran overall Zionist affairs while Ben-Gurion headed Zionist activities in Palestine where his major rival was Vladimir Jabotinsky (q.v.). Convinced that Revisionist Zionists (q.v.) under Jabotinsky were endangering the drive toward eventual statehood, Ben-Gurion sought to undermine and discredit Revisionism. When Menachem Begin (q.v.) became the leader of Revisionism in the 1940s and increased militant actions against the British, Ben-Gurion intensified his efforts to discredit Revisionism and its leader. In 1935 he defeated the forces of Chaim Weizmann and was elected Chairman of the Jewish Agency (q.v.) Executive, a post in which he served from 1935 to 1948. Recognized as the founder of Israel, he served as Prime Minister from 1948 to 1963, except for two years from December 1953 to 1955 when he voluntarily retired to Sde Boker (q.v.) in the

Negev (q.v.) to seek respite from the rigors of his long political career and to dramatize the significance of pioneering and reclaiming the desert. In 1955, when Pinhas Lavon (q.v.) was forced to resign as Minister of Defense, Ben-Gurion left Sde Boker to become Minister of Defense in the government headed by Moshe Sharett (q.v.). After the election of 1955, Ben-Gurion undertook to form a new government. However, the eruption of the Lavon Affair (q.v.) in 1960 brought disarray to Mapai (q.v.) and Ben-Gurion's political strength eroded. It was also the period of the Eichmann (q.v.) trial. He resigned as Prime Minister in June 1963. In 1965 he founded a new political party, Rafi (q.v.), and remained in the Knesset until he resigned in 1970. He died on December 1, 1973.

BEN-GURION UNIVERSITY. Located in Beersheva (q.v.), the capital of the Negev (q.v.), it was founded in 1969 with a mandate to spearhead social, agricultural, and industrial growth in Israel's arid southern region.

BERMAN, YITZHAK. Born in Russia in 1913 and immigrated to Palestine (q.v.) in 1921. After completing his schooling in Jerusalem (q.v.), he studied law in London. He served in the British army from 1942 to 1945. He joined the Irgun (q.v.) and served in the Israel Defense Forces (q.v.). He then entered the world of business, in which he was active until 1954, when he opened a private law practice. In 1968 he became active in the Liberal Party (q.v.). He was first elected to the Ninth Knesset (q.v.) on behalf of the Liberal Party faction of the Likud (q.v.) bloc in May 1977, and he served as Chairman of the House Committee until his election to the position of Speaker of the Knesset on March 12, 1980. After being reelected to the Tenth Knesset, he was sworn in as Minister of Energy and Infrastructure on August 5, 1981 and served until 1982 when he resigned.

BERNADOTTE PLAN. The Bernadotte Plan, submitted by Count Folke Bernadotte of Sweden to the United Nations in 1948, called on Israel to relinquish control over the Southern Negev (q.v.), in return for retention of western and central Galilee (q.v.). The Plan also called for the repatriation of all Arab refugees who had fled from Palestine (q.v.) during the War of Independence (q.v.), the merger of the Arab part of Palestine with Jordan, and that Haifa (q.v.) be made an international port. The proposal raised opposition from both Jews and Arabs, and was rejected by the Political Committee of the United Nations General Assembly in early December 1948. Bernadotte was assassinated in Jerusalem on September 17, 1948.

BET SHEAN. A town in the Bet Shean Valley south of the Sea of Galilee (q.v.), it was captured by Israeli forces in May 1948. Archaeological digs indicate that there were Canaanite (q.v.) towns here in the Bronze age and the town has had a long and eventful history.

BETAR. Hebrew acronym for Brit Yosef Trumpeldor (Joseph Trumpeldor (q.v.) pact). A revisionist Zionist youth movement founded in 1923 in Riga, named after Joseph Trumpeldor, and affiliated with the Revisionist Movement (q.v.). The movement's ideological mentor was Vladimir Zeev Jabotinsky (q.v.). Betar's ideological tenets were: Jewish statehood; territorial integrity of the homeland; ingathering of the exiles (q.v.); the centrality of the Zionist idea; cultivation of the Hebrew language; social justice; military preparedness for defense; national service; and *hadar*—a code of honor and strict personal behavior. Following Israel's War of Independence (q.v.), Betar founded agricultural and rural settlements. It also supports a sports society by the same name.

BETHLEHEM. A town in the West Bank (q.v.), it lies about five miles (eight kilometers) south of Jerusalem (q.v.) and is the birthplace of Jesus Christ. Bethlehem is chiefly a religious shrine with many churches and other religious institutions. Bethlehem was a walled city during the time of King David (q.v.) who was born there. Christian crusaders captured it in the first Crusade, but later lost it to Turkish Muslims. The Ottoman Turks gained control of the area in the 1500s. In 1917, during World War I, British forces led by General Allenby took the town. It was part of the West Bank area annexed by Jordan in 1949. Israel took control of the city during the Six Day War (q.v.) of 1967.

BIALIK, HAIM NAHMAN. One of the most influential Hebrew poets and writers of modern times. He was born in Radi, Russia in 1873 and died in Vienna in 1934. In many of his poems he stressed the vital role of the Bet Hamidrash (House of Study) and extolled the tradition of learning in Jewish life, but his main preoccupation was with the rebirth of the Jewish people and their return to Zion (q.v.). In 1924 he settled in Palestine (q.v.) and played an important and active role in numerous cultural institutions and was also a President of the Vaad Halashon Haivrit, the Hebrew Language (q.v.) Council.

BILTMORE PROGRAM. After World War I, when the British mandate (q.v.) replaced Ottoman rule in Palestine (q.v.), the focus of Zionist political and diplomatic endeavor was Britain. However, during and after World War II, political necessity and reality resulted in a shift in focus to the United States. The Biltmore Program was adopted by the Extraordinary Zionist Conference in New York on May ll, 1942 in response to Britain's policy toward the Jewish national home particularly the restrictions on land sales and immigration to Jews. The

Program became the basis for Zionist effort until Israel's independence and was a harbinger of change. It rejected efforts to restrict Jewish immigration and settlement in Palestine and called for the fulfillment of the Balfour Declaration (q.v.) and the mandate, urging that "Palestine be established as a Jewish Commonwealth." The Biltmore Program reflected the urgency of the situation in which the Jewish leadership found itself as a consequence of the Holocaust (q.v.) and the need to provide for the displaced Jews of Europe.

BILU MOVEMENT. A Zionist society and movement of Palestinian pioneers from the nonreligious, Jewish-Russian intellectual leadership, founded in Kharkov in 1882, who spearheaded the First Aliya (q.v.). It derived its name from the Hebrew acronym of the Biblical verse: "Bet Yaakov Lkhu Vnelha" ("House of Jacob, come ye and let us go," Isaiah 2:5), which served as its slogan. Its aim was the national renaissance of the Jewish people, the development of its productiveness, and its return to agriculture. The society was founded after the pogroms of 1882, and the first group of Bilu settlers in Palestine arrived in July 1882. Although their concrete achievements of establishing settlements were limited, the moral and historical effect of the movement was substantial because the ideals it represented continued to inspire successive generations.

BITON, CHARLEY. Born in Casablanca, Morocco in 1947 and emigrated to Israel in 1949. One of the founders of the Black Panthers (q.v.) movement. Elected to the Eleventh and Twelfth Knessets (q.v.) on the Democratic Front for Peace and Equality (q.v.) list.

BLACK PANTHERS. Although there had been riots in the Oriental (q.v.) neighborhood of Wadi Salib (q.v.) in 1959, no significant movement developed in the Oriental community until the 1970s. Then a militant protest group formed by some young Orientals of North African background, who chose to call themselves Black Panthers, took to the streets to oppose what they regarded as discrimination against the Oriental Jewish community. They helped to generate awareness and a plethora of public investigation and study commissions. Demands for more educational and social services were part of the effort to achieve improvement in the Oriental community's socioeconomic status. These efforts achieved some amelioration of the situation, but did not effect substantial change. See also "ORIENTAL REVOLT."

BNAI ISRAEL OF INDIA. A Jewish community indigenous to western India near Bombay whose origins are a mystery. In 1947 there were some 24,000 members of the community living in India, but most subsequently immigrated to Israel. In 1961 a controversy erupted in Israel as to whether the Bnai Israel were Jews according to Jewish law. The controversy ended in 1964, when Prime Minister Levi Eshkol (q.v.) declared adherents of the Bnai Israel as Jews in every respect.

BRIT SHALOM. A Jewish organization based in Palestine (q.v.) and devoted to the promotion of a working arrangement between Zionism (q.v.) and Arab nationalism. The main goal was to promote a bi-national state in Palestine rather than a Jewish state. It was a small and loosely shaped organization composed primarily of intellectuals and other well-known figures and reached its peak in the 1920s and 1930s. In many respects it was more of a debating society and study group than an active political organziation. Martin Buber (q.v.) and Judah Magnes (q.v.) were among its prominent members.

BRITISH MANDATE FOR PALESTINE. At the end of World War I the great powers dismantled the Ottoman Empire. Great Britain was granted control over Palestine (q.v.) under the League of Nations Mandate System and retained control of the territory from 1922 to 1948. It was during the Mandatory period that most of the political, economic, and social institutions of Israel were formed, its political parties launched, and the careers of its political elite begun. In the spring of 1947, the British turned the problem of the future of the Mandate over to the United Nations which established a Special Committee on Palestine (UNSCOP) (q.v.) to review the situation and to offer suggestions for disposition of the territory. UNSCOP's majority report, which called for the partition of Palestine, was adopted by the United Nations General Assembly on November 29, 1947. The British terminated the Mandate and its presence in Palestine on May 15, 1948.

BUBER, MARTIN. A Jewish religious philosopher born in Vienna in 1878 and died in Jerusalem (q.v.) in 1965. Buber was the author of many books on Jewish philosophy, general philosophy, Hasidism (q.v.), theology, Zionist theory, and the Bible. His fame, which was greater in the non-Jewish world than in Israel itself, was based primarily on his philosophy of a dialogue between God and man, as expressed in his books *Between Man and Man* (1947) and *I and Thou* (1958). He joined Judah Magnes (q.v.) and the Ihud (q.v.) movement and advocated Arab-Jewish rapprochement as well as an Arab-Jewish bi-national state in Palestine (q.v.).

BURG, YOSEF. Born in Dresden, Germany in 1909. From 1928 to 1931 he completed his rabbinical studies at the seminary in Berlin and studied in the Faculty of Humanities at Berlin University. In 1933 he received a PhD from the University of Leipzig. In 1938 he emigrated to Palestine (q.v.) and, from 1939 to 1951, he served as a member of the World Zionist Council. Between 1946 and 1949 he carried out a number of rescue missions in Europe. Initially elected on behalf of the National Religious Party (q.v.) to the First Knesset (q.v.) in January 1949, Dr. Burg was reelected to subsequent Knessets. He served as Deputy Speaker in the First Knesset; as Minister of Health from 1951 to 1952; Minister of Posts from 1952 to 1958; Minister of Social Welfare from 1959 to 1970; and as Minister of the Interior from 1970 to 1984. On August 5, 1981, in addition to his post as Minister of the Interior and as Chairman of the Ministerial Committee on Negotiations for Autonomy for the Arab Residents of Judea (q.v.), Samaria (q.v.), and the Gaza District (q.v.), Dr. Burg assumed the post of Minister of Religious Affairs. In the Government of National Unity (q.v.), he served as Minister of Religion from 1984 until his resignation from the post in 1986.

- C -

CABINET. The cabinet or government is the central policy-making body of the Israeli governmental system. After Knesset (q.v.) elections are held, the member of parliament entrusted by the President (q.v.) with the task of forming the government establishes a cabinet, with himself or herself as Prime Minister and a number of ministers who are usually, but not necessarily, members of the Knesset. The Prime Minister may appoint any number of ministers, and there is no formal requirement regarding the size of the cabinet or the distribution of ministerial portfolios.

The government is constituted upon obtaining a vote of confidence from the parliament, which must approve the composition of the government, the distribution of functions among the ministers, and the basic lines of its policy. The cabinet is collectively responsible to the Knesset, reports to it, and remains in office as long as it enjoys the confidence of that body. Until March 1990 there had never been a successful motion of no confidence by the Knesset causing the ouster of a government. A government's tenure may also be terminated by ending the Knesset's tenure and scheduling new elections; by the resignation of the government on its own initiative; or by the resignation or death of the Prime Minister. After obtaining the confidence of the parliament, the cabinet decides Israel's policies in all spheres, subject to Knesset approval, and generally initiates the largest portion of legislation. Increasingly much of the cabinet's work has been conducted by a small and select group of ministers meeting informally in kitchen cabinets (q.v.), for example, as occurred when Golda Meir (q.v.) was the Prime Minister, or in ministerial committees on issues such as security and defense. Ministries are divided among the parties forming the coalition in accordance with the agreement reached by the parties and generally reflect their size and influence. The Prime Minister may select a replacement, subject to Knesset confirmation, for a minister who resigns or dies in office. The most important positions in the cabinet are Prime Minister, Defense Minister, Foreign Minister, and Finance Minister. (See the tables on pages xxxi–xxxiii for a listing of the individuals who have held these key posts since Israel became independent.)

The government is headed by the Prime Minister. The number of ministers, most of whom hold specific portfolios, is not fixed and may change from government to government. Although the Prime Minister must be a Knesset member, the ministers need not be, but usually are. The government, whose policy-making powers are very wide, is collectively responsible to the Knesset and subject to its confidence. Following each election, the president calls on a Knesset member, usually the leader of the party with the largest Knesset representation, to form a government and to head it. That person has 21 days to complete the task, and, should he or she fail, may receive an extension or the President may turn to another Knesset member. This procedure may be repeated as many times as necessary, until a government can be formed. Since the government requires the Knesset's confidence to function, it must enjoy the support of at least 61 of its 120 members. To date, no party has received enough Knesset seats to be able to form a government by itself; thus, all Israeli governments have been based on coalitions between two or more parties, with those remaining outside the government making up the opposition. The coalition is based on agreement among the parties that make up the government, defining common policy goals and the principles which are to guide its activities. The coalition agreement is not a legally binding document. The government usually serves for four years.

CAMP DAVID ACCORDS. Egyptian President Anwar Sadat's (q.v.) historic visit to Jerusalem (q.v.) in November 1977 was followed by negotiations in which the United States—and President Jimmy Carter (q.v.) personally—played an active and often crucial role. In September 1978, President Carter, President Anwar Sadat of Egypt, Prime Minister Menachem Begin (q.v.) of Israel, and their senior aides held an extraordinary series of meetings for thirteen days at Camp David, Maryland, during which they discussed the Arab-Israeli conflict. On September 17, 1978, at the White House they announced the conclusion of two accords that provided the basis for continuing negotiations for peace: a "Framework for Peace in the Middle East" and a "Framework for the Conclusion of a Peace Treaty Between Egypt and Israel." The Middle East framework set forth general principles and some specifics to govern a comprehensive peace settlement, focusing on the future of the West Bank (q.v.) and the Gaza Strip (q.v.). It called for a transitional period of no more than five years during which Israel's military government would be withdrawn (although Israeli forces could remain in specified areas to ensure Israel's security) and a self-governing authority would be elected by the inhabitants of these areas. It also provided that "Egypt, Israel, Jordan and the representatives of the Palestinian people" should participate in negotiations to resolve the final status of the West Bank and Gaza, Israel's relations with Jordan based on United Nations Security Council Resolution 242 (q.v.), and Israel's right to live within secure and recognized borders. The Egypt-Israel framework called for Israel's withdrawal from the Sinai Peninsula (q.v.) and the establishment of normal, peaceful relations between the two states. In addition to the two frameworks, there was a series of accompanying letters clarifying the parties' positions on certain issues. The Egyptian cabinet approved the accords on September 19 and on September 28 the Israeli Knesset (q.v.) voted 84–19 (with 17 abstentions) to endorse them. The Camp David Accords led to negotiations and the Egypt-Israel Peace Treaty (q.v.).

CANAAN, LAND OF. The biblical name for the area known as Palestine (q.v.), and later Israel. Prior to its conquest by the Hebrews under Joshua, the Judges, King Saul (q.v.), and King David (q.v.), the area of Palestine was known as the Land of Canaan, the name being inherited from the Canaanites, who inhabited parts of the area.

CARTER, JIMMY. President of the United States from 1977 to 1981 who played an active role in negotiations between Israel and Egypt that led to the Camp David Accords (q.v.) and the Egypt-Israel Peace Treaty (q.v.).

CENTER LIBERAL PARTY see LIBERAL CENTER PARTY

CENTER-SHINUI MOVEMENT. A politial bloc made up of three parties: Shinui (q.v.), the Independent Liberals (q.v.), and the Liberal Center (q.v.) which contested the Twelfth Knesset (q.v.) elections in 1988 and won two seats in parliament. It campaigned on a platform that claimed it was the only political body combining an aspiration for peace based on compromise, a socio-economic concept encouraging a free and enterprising economy, the protection of individual rights, and opposition to religious coercion. It also claimed that it would not join a coalition government formed by the Likud (q.v.) and the religious parties (q.v.). It also differed from the Labor Alignment (q.v.) in its approach to the economy and focused on a free economy encouraging growth and creativity rather than the failed bureaucratic approaches of the Labor Alignment. In the political realm the movement favored a peace agreement with the Arabs, arguing that this would free Israel from the cycle of war and bloodshed and prevent it from becoming a bi-national state which would rule over another people. Such a peace agreement would be based on the principle of land for peace. Israel's security would be guaranteed by secure border adjustments, security arrangements, and the demilitarization of evacuated areas. The party further believes that the solution to the Palestinian problem and the intifada (q.v.) lies in the establishment of a Jordanian-Palestinian confederation. If the Palestine Liberation Organization (q.v.) unequivocally recognized Israel and renounced terrorism the party would be prepared to conduct negotiations with it.

CHEN (WOMEN'S ARMY CORPS). Since its inception, women have served in the Israel Defense Forces (IDF) (q.v.). During the War of Independence (q.v.) women soldiers participated occasionally in combat, but since 1949, no women have been allowed to do so. Women generally serve in the army for two years. However, women over 24, married women, and women with religious objections are exempt from military service. The Women's Corps is responsible for the placement, conditions of service, and well-being of women in the service. Women serve as clerks, drivers, radar operators, nurses, medical doctors, social workers, teachers, instructors at the various service branch schools, in various intelligence duties, in the legal service of the IDF, and in administrative capacities.

CHIEF RABBINATE. Established in 1921 under the auspices of the British Mandatory (q.v.) government as the supreme religious authority of the Jewish community in Palestine (q.v.). The powers of the Chief Rabbinate were redefined in the 1928 regulations of Knesset Yisrael (q.v.), which divided its authority between an Ashkenazi (q.v.) Chief Rabbi and a Sephardi (q.v.) Chief Rabbi. Membership in the Chief Rabbinate Council was also equally divided between the Ashkenazi and Sephardi communities. The Rabbinate deals with all matters of personal status, matrimony, and burial among the Jews of Israel, and regulates the public observance of Kashrut (dietary laws) and the Sabbath. The Conservative and Reform Jewish movements are not represented in the Chief Rabbinate, and their rabbis are not recognized for purposes of performing various rituals governed by laws such as marriage and conversions.

CINEMA. Israelis began directing and producing their own feature films in 1960. Feature films aimed at the local market are produced, but a growing number of Israeli filmmakers are dealing with the country's culture and society in films that have universal appeal, and some have received international acclaim and popularity. Cinema exports continue to grow as more Israeli-made films become successful abroad and more dollar-earning foreign and co-productions are filmed on location in the country. A large variety of documentary and educational films are also made in Israel.

CITIZENS' RIGHTS AND PEACE MOVEMENT (CRM—HATNUA LEZHUIOT HAEZRAH ULE-SHALOM—RATZ). The Citizens' Rights Movement is a social-liberal political party established by Shulamit Aloni (q.v.), a former Labor Party (q.v.) member and civil rights activist, in August 1973, although it began to develop following the Yom Kippur War (q.v.) when there was substantial discontent with the Labor Party. It calls for electoral reform; the introduction of a Basic Law (q.v.) protecting human rights; recognition of a Palestinian entity and the Palestinian right to self-determination; the separation of religion and state; and equal rights for women. In the elections to the Eighth Knesset (q.v.) which took place on December 31, 1973, the CRM won three seats and joined the government coalition for a brief period in 1974. It gained only one seat in the elections to both the Ninth Knesset (1977) and the Tenth Knesset (1981), but following the 1981 elections Aloni joined the Alignment (q.v.) so that it would have the same number of seats (48) as the Likud (q.v.) bloc and thus it would be blocked in its efforts to form the new government. The tactic failed.

The party changed character in the 1980s, becoming a party whose membership is drawn from a variety of older groups. Yossi Sarid (q.v.), a former Labor Party member, assumed a significant role in shaping the party's dovish foreign policy. The CRM broke away from the Alignment just before the elections to the Eleventh Knesset and ran on a platform which called for complete equality for all citizens, irrespective of religion, nationality, race, or sex; freedom of religion, conscience, language, education, and culture; opposition to religious coercion; recognition of the right of the Palestinian people to self-determination; negotiations with any representative of the Palestinians on the basis of mutual recognition; rejection of wars of choice and the use of the IDF for political purposes outside the state. The CRM gained three seats in the 1984 election, and refused, on principle, to join the Government of National Unity (q.v.). The party is now composed of the historical CRM, including liberals and secularists; the academic of the "group of 100" (including former Peace Now (q.v.) and Labor Party doves); and former Shelli (q.v.) members. Its constituency is primarily the "middle class" Ashkenazi (q.v.) population, and its platform emphasizes civil rights for all Israelis. Its original focus was on human and civil rights and it opposes discrimination based on religion, sex, or ethnic identification. It advocates a peace settlement with the Arabs and the Palestinians. In the 1988 Knesset election it supported a platform which recognized the right of the Palestinian people to self-determination and called on the Palestine Liberation Organization (q.v.) to recognize Israel's right to a sovereign and secure existence, so that the PLO would be able to participate in peace negotiations as the representative of the Palestinian people. It believes that the Palestinian people should ultimately decide on what form their self-determination should take. On domestic issues, it stood for the separation of religion and state.

CITRUS. Citrus products make up a large share of Israel's agricultural exports which, in turn, represent a significant portion of Israel's total exports. Citrus fruits are major crops and their export in substantial numbers—primarily to Western Europe—have helped to earn important foreign exchange for Israel.

CIVIL RIGHTS MOVEMENT see CITIZENS' RIGHTS AND PEACE MOVEMENT

COHEN, GEULA. Born in Tel Aviv (q.v.) in 1925 to parents of Yemenite and Moroccan background. In her youth she was a member of Betar (q.v.) and the Irgun (q.v.) and in 1943 she joined Lehi (q.v.). Later she was arrested and sentenced to prison by the British authorities in Palestine. She graduated from Hebrew University (q.v.) and worked as a journalist. After the Six Day War (q.v.) she became involved in the question of Soviet Jewry and in 1970 joined Herut (q.v.). She was elected to the Eighth Knesset (q.v.). She left Herut (q.v.) in June 1979 in opposition to the Camp David Accords (q.v.) and the Arab-Israeli peace process. She was elected to the Tenth and subsequent Knessets on the Tehiya (q.v.) ticket, a party she helped to found and has since helped to lead. She has been a strong supporter of nationalist positions and has been active in promoting Jewish settlement in Judea (q.v.) and Samaria (q.v.).

COHEN-ORGAD, YIGAL. Born in Tel Aviv (q.v.), Yigal Cohen-Orgad is an economist who was trained at Hebrew University (q.v.) and is a member of the Knesset (q.v.) who has been elected on the Likud (q.v.) list. He served as Finance Minister from the Fall of 1983 until the Government of National Unity (q.v.) acceded to power in the Fall of 1984. As Finance Minister, he introduced austerity measures and sought to strengthen the balance of payments through export-led growth and a cut in imports. In order to promote this growth, public and private consumption had to be restricted, and he sought to promote those sectors focusing on production and export. He initiated a variety of budgetary cuts, including the slashing subsidies, in order to reduce government expenditures. He also initiated new revenue-raising measures, including: education fees; taxes on early pensions; higher income tax in the higher brackets; and a cut in fringe benefits for civil servants and public-sector workers. He is regarded as a hardliner on foreign policy, having opposed the Camp David Accords (q.v.) and the Egypt-Israel Peace Treaty (q.v.). He supports continued Jewish settlement in the West Bank (q.v.) and Gaza Strip (q.v.).

COMMUNIST PARTY. The Communist movement began in Palestine in 1919 during the British Mandate (q.v.) and has existed continuously since that time, although it has been plagued by internal divisions and splits. Although isolated from the mainstream of political life and prevented from joining the government, Communist parties have been legal in Israel since independence and have been represented in the Knesset (q.v.) continuously. On average, the Communists secure four or five seats in the Knesset.

The Israel Communist Party (Miflaga Kommunistit Yisraelit; Maki) was founded in 1948 and split in 1965. The splinter group, the New Communist List (q.v.) (Reshima Komunistit Hadasha; Rakah) was pro-Moscow, strongly anti-Zionist, and primarily drew its membership from Israel's Arab population. In the 1981 elections, the Rakah-led Democratic Front for Peace and Equality (DFPE) (q.v.) won four seats in the Knesset. Its platform called for the total withdrawal of Israel from the occupied territories; equal rights for the Arab community; the establishment of a democratic, socialist, secular state in Palestine (q.v.); peace with the Arab states; and a nonaligned foreign policy.

Meir Wilner (q.v.) is the party's General Secretary; and Tawfiq Toubi (q.v.) is Deputy Secretary General. Membership in the Communist parties and voting support are overwhelmingly Arab, generally as a form of dissent, but its leadership usually is divided between Jews and Arabs. Since 1977, only the Democratic Front for Peace and Equality has won seats in the Knesset.

CONSTITUTION see BASIC LAW

CORFU, HAIM. Haim Corfu was born in Jerusalem (q.v.) in 1921 and studied law at the Hebrew University (q.v.). He served on the Jerusalem City Council. In the Seventh and Eighth Knessets (q.v.) he was a member of the Finance Committee, and in the Ninth Knesset he was a member of both the Defense and Foreign Affairs Committees and the House Committee, as well as being the Coalition Chairman. He is a member of the Herut (q.v.) Executive. On August 5, 1981 he was sworn in as Minister of Transport and served in that position in the Government of National Unity (q.v.).

COUNCIL OF STATE (MOETZET HAMEDINA HAZ-MANIT). Israel's Declaration of Independence (q.v.) provided for the transformation of the thirty-seven member People's Council into the Provisional State Council, which was to serve as the country's provisional legislature for the first nine months of independence. The executive arm of the People's Council, the People's Administration, consisting of thirteen members, became the Provisional Government by the same instrument. In keeping with its provisional functions, the Council sought to confine its legislative activity to a minimum. Its first enactment was for the continuance in force of virtually the whole body of mandatory law as well as of the regulations and orders that had been issued by the Jewish Agency (q.v.) for Palestine. Nevertheless, in meeting emergent demands of the new state, the Council, during its short life of forty weekly sittings, passed ninety-eight ordinances, including important organic laws, fiscal measures, and amendments to mandatory ordinances. The Council met for the last time on February 10, 1949 and ceased to exist with the convocation of the Constituent Assembly on February 14, 1949.

COUNCIL OF TORAH SAGES (MOETZET GEDOLEI HATORAH). The supreme authority in all matters relating to Agudat Israel (q.v.), a religious-oriented political party. The Council, instituted in the 1920s, is a group of revered scholars and rabbis, heads of Yeshivas (religious schools), and members of Hasidic (q.v.) dynasties who represent the various factions of the Aguda movement. Council members are chosen for their scholarly merit and prestige in the realm of Orthodox Jewry. The Council of Torah Sages continues to be the supreme decision-making body for Aguda adherents, and its decisions are sovereign in all questions affecting the membership, including religious and political matters, such as joining or remaining in a government coalition. This authority derives from the personal standing and reputation of its members, who have achieved recognition as qualified interpreters of the halacha (q.v.) and are viewed with high esteem by members of Aguda. The Council traditionally has not permitted its representatives in the Knesset (q.v.) to accept ministerial appointments, but they have held important committee chairmanships.

CRM see CITIZENS' RIGHTS AND PEACE MOVEMENT

CUNNINGHAM, ALAN GORDON. Born in Dublin in 1887, he was a soldier who served as the last British High Commissioner for Palestine (q.v.). He had a distinguished military career and achieved the rank of General in 1945 and in that year was appointed High Commissioner for Palestine. He left Palestine on May 14, 1948 when the State of Israel declared its independence.

- D -

DALIYAT AL-CARMEL. A Druze (q.v.) village on Mount Carmel.

DANCE. In the early years, dance was mainly folk dance. Based on ethnic and traditional motifs, it became over the decades increasingly Israeli in style, tempo, and spirit. While folk dancing is still a popular form of community enjoyment, some of these dances have been transformed into stage art and are performed in Israel and abroad by two major companies: the Inbal Dance Theatre and the Jerusalem Dance Company. Growing in prominence and popularity is art-dance performed by such companies as Batsheva, Bat-Dor, and the Kibbutz Dance Company. There is also a classical company, the Israel Ballet, and Kol U'Demama (Sound and Silence), a company of deaf dancers.

DAROUSHA, ABD EL-WAHAB. A member of the Knesset (q.v.) who resigned from the Labor Alignment (q.v.) in 1988 and was recognized as a one-man parliamentary faction. His Arab Democratic Party (q.v.) contested the 1988 Knesset election, and he won a seat in parliament.

DAVAR (THE WORD). A daily newspaper published in Tel Aviv (q.v.). It was founded in 1925 by the Histadrut (q.v.) and was the third Hebrew (q.v.) daily newspaper to appear in Palestine (q.v.) under the British Mandate (q.v.). As a result of the dominance of the labor movement in the leadership of the World Zionist Organization (q.v.) and the Jewish Agency (q.v.) under the Mandate and in the government of Israel after independence, *Davar* became, for all practical purposes, the unofficial organ of the leadership and government of Israel.

DAVID. King of Israel c. 1004–965 BC. Second King of Israel, he unified the Jewish tribes, pacified the area, and made Israel into a major regional force. He fought the Philistines and conquered Jerusalem (q.v.). By expanding his territory, making Jerusalem his capital, and awakening a national consciousness, he laid the foundation of a Jewish state. He had a son, Solomon (q.v.), and established a dynasty which lasted some four hundred years. Jewish tradition teaches that the Messiah will be a descendent of the House of David.

DAYAN, MOSHE. Moshe Dayan was born in Kibbutz Degania (q.v.) on May 20, 1915, but grew up in Nahalal (q.v.). Dayan was one of the first to join the Palmah (q.v.) when it was established, on May 18, 1941, and served under Orde Wingate in his night squads. From 1939 to 1941 Dayan was detained by the British in Acre, but was released in order to take part in an allied venture against the Vichy French in Syria in 1941. On June 7, 1941 Dayan headed a squad of Hagana (q.v.) members who joined the British in an operation which was intended to destroy bridges in Syria. During an assault on a police station he lost his left eye. In July 1948, he was made the commanding officer of Jerusalem, while it was under siege. In that capacity he took part in informal negotiations with King Abdullah of Jordan and later served as a member of the Israeli delegation to the armistice negotiations in Rhodes. Between 1950 and 1953 Dayan served as Commander of the Southern and Northern commands of the Israel Defense Forces (q.v.) and later head of the General Branch of Operations in the General Staff. In December 1953 he was appointed Chief of Staff. He was nominated after a stormy cabinet defense committee meeting, and with David Ben-Gurion's (q.v.) support.

Dayan led the IDF during the Sinai War of 1956 (q.v.) and was discharged from the IDF in January 1958. In November 1959 he was elected as a member of the Knesset (q.v.) on the Mapai (q.v.) list and became Minister of Agriculture in Prime Minister David Ben-Gurion's government. In 1963 Ben-Gurion left his party over the Lavon Affair (q.v.) and established Rafi (q.v.).

After much hesitation Dayan joined Ben-Gurion and Shimon Peres (q.v.) (who served during this period as Deputy Defense Minister). Nevertheless, he continued to serve as Minister of Agriculture under Prime Minister Levi Eshkol (q.v.). Dayan brought to Israeli agriculture methods of long-range planning and national allocation of resources such as water. He resigned from the cabinet on November 4, 1964 when Eshkol tried to prevent him from participating in the formation of defense policy. In 1965 he was elected to the Sixth Knesset on the Rafi ticket. Dayan went briefly to Vietnam to observe and write about the war.

Just prior to the Six Day War (q.v.), by popular demand, Prime Minister Levi Eshkol was forced, against his expressed will, to appoint Dayan to the post of Minister of Defense. Although Dayan did not have time to change the IDF's operational plans his position as Minister of Defense inspired the country with confidence and helped Eshkol to decide on a preemptive strike. After the war Dayan supported the research and development functions of the Ministry of Defense as a means of replenishing the equipment and ammunition of the IDF, in light of the French arms embargo. He also initiated the open bridges (q.v.) policy providing an infrastructure for coexistence between Israel and the Arabs. When Eshkol died suddenly in February 1969 and was succeeded by Golda Meir (q.v.), Dayan remained as Minister of Defense. He was among those blamed by the public for the delay in the mobilization of Israel's reserve forces at the time of the Yom Kippur War (q.v.). Nevertheless, Dayan continued to serve under Golda Meir's leadership after the elections of December 31, 1973.

When Golda Meir resigned in April 1974, however, Prime Minister Yitzhak Rabin (q.v.) did not include Dayan in the cabinet. Between 1974 and 1977, Dayan served as a member of the Knesset and was active in archaeological excavations. When Menachem Begin (q.v.) became Prime Minister after the May 1977 elections Dayan joined the government as Foreign Minister and in that capacity played a crucial role in the negotiations that led to the Camp David Accords (q.v.) and the Egypt-Israel Peace Treaty (q.v.). Dayan resigned in 1979 over the differences of viewpoint and policy between himself and the Prime Minister in regard to autonomy negotiations. On April 4, 1981 Dayan established a new political party, Telem (q.v.), which had as one of its primary goals to support Dayan's proposals concerning the occupied territories (q.v.). The party secured two mandates in the 1981 Knesset elections. Dayan died on October 16, 1981.

DEAD SEA. The lowest point on earth. Located about 30 miles east of Jerusalem (q.v.) and shared by Jordan and Israel, it is 49 miles long and 11 miles wide, has a 1,309 foot maximum depth, and is 1,299 feet below sea level. Its salty water has a high content of minerals and other chemical elements including: magnesium chloride (52%); sodium chloride (cooking salt, 30%); calcium chloride (12%); potassium chloride (4.36%); and magnesium bromide (1.46%). One of Israel's major industries is the extraction of these minerals from the Dead Sea. The Dead Sea has also become a major tourist attraction for both Israeli and international visitors who seek to benefit from the medicinal value of its mineral waters.

DEAD SEA SCROLLS. The Dead Sea scrolls are the oldest discovered manuscripts of the Old Testament. The scrolls, dating from 167 BC to 237 AD, were discovered by two shepherd boys in 1947 in a cave in the hills of Qumran, south of Jericho (q.v.). Written in Hebrew (q.v.), the scrolls contain biblical texts, biblical commentaries, and fragments of Apocrypha. In addition, some texts describe in detail the way of life of the Jewish sect whose members wrote the scrolls.

DECLARATION OF INDEPENDENCE. The United Nations partition plan (q.v.) of November 1947 provided for the establishment of a Jewish state in Palestine (q.v.). The date of the termination of the British Mandate (q.v.) was set for May 15, 1948, and with that date nearing, the Zionist General Council decided that the Jewish people would establish an independent regime in their homeland. This decision, put forth in a resolution, paved the way for the Declaration of Independence. A five-man committee was established to prepare the Declaration, and a four-man committee, including David Ben-Gurion (q.v.), worked out the final draft. The Declaration of Independence was read on May 14, 1948, and went into effect the following day. The Declaration provides for a Jewish state in the Land of Israel and it recalls the religious and spiritual connection of the Jewish people to the land of Israel, but it does not mention boundaries. Nevertheless it notes that "it will guarantee freedom of religion and conscience, of language, education, and culture." The document does not address the meaning of a Jewish state or the roles that would be played by religious forces and movements (especially by their political parties) in such an entity.

DEGANIA. The first kibbutz (q.v.). In 1909 a group of Russian immigrants built a cooperative worker's settlement located at the exit of the Jordan River (q.v.) from Lake Kinneret (q.v.) on a site which commanded the approach to Galilee (q.v.) and Haifa (q.v.), on land purchased by the Jewish National Fund (q.v.). Degania was established as a completely integrated communal settlement where its members lived and worked together. Part of the original land was given to another group of settlers who founded Degania Bet in 1919. Subsequently the original settlement became known as Degania Aleph. Degania served as a prototype for all subsequent communal settlements.

DEGEL HATORAH. A religious political party which secured two seats in the 1988 Knesset (q.v.) election. The party was founded by Rabbi Eliezer Shach, the head of the Ponevesher Yeshiva and a former member of the presidium of the Moetzet Gedolei Hatorah (Council of Torah Sages) (q.v.) who decided that Agudat Israel (q.v.) was not loyal to its original ideals and objectives. Among its faults was its connection to the Chabad Hasidim (q.v.) and its leader, Rabbi Menachem Mendel Schneerson, the Lubavitcher Rebbe, which Rabbi Shach considered heretical. Rabbi Avraham Ravitz served as its political leader. He has expressed dovish views on foreign policy. The party supported the Likud-led (q.v.) government established in June 1990.

DEMOCRATIC FRONT FOR PEACE AND EQUALITY (HADASH). In 1977, Rakah (q.v.) and some members of the Israeli Black Panthers (q.v.) joined to form the Hadash (acronym for Hazit Demokratit Leshalom Uleshivyon) political party. Hadash, the Democratic Front for Peace and Equality, contested Knesset (q.v.) elections beginning in 1977. Its program has called for: Israeli withdrawal from all the territories occupied in the Six Day War (q.v.); the establishment of an independent Palestinian state; recognition of the Palestine Liberation Organization (q.v.) as the representative of the Palestinians; and a number of measures to improve the situation of the disadvantaged classes in Israel.

DEMOCRATIC MOVEMENT. One of the remaining units of the Democratic Movement for Change (q.v.) after it disintegrated in 1978. The Movement remained in the government coalition, but the party ceased to exist in 1981.

DEMOCRATIC MOVEMENT FOR CHANGE (HAT-NUA HADEMOCRATIT LESHINUI) (DMC). The DMC was a political party formed in 1976 in order to contest the 1977 Knesset (q.v.) election. In May 1976 Professor Yigael Yadin (q.v.) appeared on Israeli television and announced that he would form a new political party to contest the next election with a program that concentrated on domestic political reform. He suggested that the party would play a key role in any future government coalition. He had decided to enter politics and create the party because the country urgently needed certain reforms to enable it to combat social and economic ills. Yadin believed that electoral reform must be the Nation's first priority because the electoral system, which was based on proportional representation, had created a leadership crisis. He called for reductions in the number of government ministries and drastic cuts in the government budget.

The nucleus of the party was soon formed around academic and governmental personalities. The Shinui (Change) (q.v.) Movement headed by Amnon Rubinstein (q.v.) joined and the party took the name of Democratic Movement for Change. The DMC contested the 1977 election and won fifteen seats. The unexpected Likud (q.v.) victory provided the base for DMC's efforts to influence the nature and direction of Israeli politics. The main goal of the DMC was still to become a partner in the coalition with a significant political role. During the '77 election campaign it had stressed a number of crucial points: it wanted a significant reduction in the number of government ministries; an economic program designed to reduce inflation; programs for disadvantaged areas; electoral reform; and support for DMC views on foreign policy. The DMC soon entered into negotiations to enter the Likud-led government coalition, but there were problems resulting from divergent foreign policy views and positions. Ultimately the DMC would join the coalition. Unlike other political parties, however, its membership cut across the spectrum of political ideologies and party affiliations. After joining the coalition government, the party split into several smaller groups and disintegrated by the time of the 1981 Knesset elections.

DER JUDENSTAAT. Theodor Herzl (q.v.) was the driving force for the creation of the political ideology and worldwide movement of modern political Zionism (q.v.). Herzl wrote *Der Judenstaat (The Jewish State)*, published in Vienna on February 14, 1896, in which he assessed the situation and problems of the Jews and proposed a practical plan for resolution of the Jewish question. It contains an examination of the status of the Jewish people and a detailed plan for creating a state in which Jews would reconstitute their national life in a territory of their own. Herzl sets forth his concept of a Jewish homeland, believing this was the only solution to the Jewish problem. Herzl's pamphlet was the catalyst for a campaign to influence European leaders on behalf of the Zionist cause. As a result of this initiative, the first World Zionist Congress (q.v.) was convened in Basle (q.v.) in 1897, at which the World Zionist Organization (q.v.) was established. Subsequently, Herzl traveled widely to publicize and gain support for his ideas.

DERECH ERETZ (MANNERS). A political party, led by Tal Urbach, created to contest the 1968 Knesset (q.v.) election. It failed to secure the votes necessary to gain a seat in parliament.

DERI, RABBI ARYE. Born in Morocco in 1959, Deri was brought to Israel by his family in 1968. He was educated at Yeshivat Hebron in Jerusalem (q.v.). He became Secretary General of the Shas (q.v.) Party in 1985, and has remained in that position since. He became Minister of Interior in the government established in December 1988 although he was not a member of the Knesset (q.v.), and retained that position in the government established in June 1990.

DEVELOPMENT TOWNS. Towns built in Israel since independence, primarily in regions remote from the old population centers. They were begun in the 1950s and had several goals. These included the dispersal of population and industry for both economic and security reasons and the development of administrative and economic centers for the more rural areas of the country. The idea was to create new urban centers, as opposed to additional farming villages which had been the pattern in the pre-state period. This would also provide facilities for the immigration and integration of the large numbers of new immigrants to the country. Among the development towns are Kiryat Shmona, Maalot, Karmiel, Migdal Haemek, Bet Shemesh, Ashdod (q.v.), Netivot, Arad (q.v.), Dimona (q.v.), and Mitzpe Ramon.

DIAMONDS. The diamond industry in Israel dates back to 1939. Its pioneers were industrialists who had come to Palestine (q.v.) from Belgium and Holland before World War II and members of the Jewish community in Palestine. The industry expanded dramatically during World War II when the European countries were cut off from their from source of raw diamonds and from their traditional markets. The industry diminished immediately after the war, but began to grow in the 1950s. Israel has since become a major force in the production of finished and polished diamonds and a major factor in the world trade of diamonds although these precious stones are not found naturally in the country. In 1988 exports of cut diamonds reached a record of $2.548 billion.

DIASPORA. A Greek word meaning "scattering," that has been used since the Babylonian exile of 586 BC to refer to the dispersion of the Jews and the Jewish communities outside of Israel. It is interchangeable with the Hebrew (q.v.) term Galut.

DIMONA. A development town in the central Negev (q.v.). Founded in 1955, its name is derived from the book of Joshua in the Bible. It has become a center for textile and other manufacturing activities. Israel, with French technical assistance, established a uranium/heavy water nuclear reactor in Dimona in 1964.

DINITZ, SIMHA. Born in Tel Aviv (q.v.) in June 1929. He was educated in the United States (University of Cincinnati and Georgetown University) where he received Bachelors and Masters degrees. He served as political advisor to Prime Minister Golda Meir (q.v.), Director General of Prime Minister Meir's office (1969–1973) and as Ambassador to the United States (1973–1978). Later he served as Vice President of Hebrew University (q.v.) and then as a Labor Alignment (q.v.) member of the Knesset (q.v.). He later became Chairman of the World Zionist Organization (q.v.) and Jewish Agency (q.v.).

DIRECTOR OF MILITARY INTELLIGENCE (DMI). The Director of Military Intelligence heads the Intelligence Branch (AMAN, acronym for Agaf Modiin) of the Israel Defense Forces (q.v.) General Staff. Its function is to provide intelligence for the planning of Israel's defense policy and for war and to provide intelligence to the IDF and other government bodies, especially the cabinet. The first head of AMAN was Isar

Beeri (1948–1949). He was followed by Haim Herzog (q.v.) (1949–1950 and 1959–1962). Benjamin Gibli served from 1950 to 1955. Yehoshafat Harkabi held the post from 1955 to 1959. Subsequent holders of the position included: Meir Amit, 1962 to 1964; Aharon Yariv, 1964 to 1972; Eliahu Zeira, 1972 to 1974; Shlomo Gazit, 1974 to 1978; Yehoshua Saguy, 1978 to 1983; Ehud Barak (q.v.), 1983 to 1985; Amnon Reshef beginning in 1985; Amnon Shahak, 1986–1991; and Uri Saguy, 1991–.

DISENGAGEMENT OF FORCES see ISRAEL-EGYPT DISENGAGEMENT OF FORCES AGREEMENT (1974); ISRAEL-SYRIA DISENGAGEMENT OF FORCES AGREEMENT (1974)

DMC see DEMOCRATIC MOVEMENT FOR CHANGE

DORI, YAACOV. Born in Odessa, Russia in 1899 he was brought to Palestine (q.v.) as a child and joined the Jewish Legion (q.v.). He later studied engineering in Belgium. After returning to Palestine he joined the Technical Department of the Zionist executive and became active in the Hagana (q.v.). He became Chief of Staff of the Hagana in 1938 and in 1948 and 1949 he was Chief of Staff of the Israel Defense Forces (q.v.). In this capacity he commanded the Israeli army in the War of Independence (q.v.). From 1951 to 1965 he served as president of the Technion (q.v.).

DREYFUS, ALFRED. A French Jew, and artillery Captain attached to the general staff of the French Army. In 1894, he was accused of selling military secrets to Germany, and placed on trial for espionage and treason. He was tried by a military court, and sentenced to life in prison. His sentence was contested by a minority group consisting mainly of intellectuals, called Dreyfusards, who claimed the evidence was based on forged documents. Among other developments, it led Emile Zola to write his famous *"J'accuse"* in 1898. Public opinion became so aroused that the military was forced to reopen the case. Dreyfus was again found guilty, but the sentence was reduced to ten years in prison. Dissatisfaction with the verdict persisted, and in 1906 Dreyfus was exonerated. The sharp controversy which the case triggered caused a wave of anti-Semitic demonstrations and riots throughout France. The Dreyfus trial was considered an important indicator of growing anti-Jewish sentiment in Europe and helped to awaken a Jewish nationalistic feeling. Theodor Herzl (q.v.) covered the first Dreyfus trial as a newspaper correspondent and later said that this convinced him that assimilation was not the solution to the problem of anti-Semitism.

DRUCKMAN, HAIM. Born in Poland he was one of the founders of the Bnai Akiva youth movement. He split from the National Religious Party (q.v.) and helped to establish the Morasha (Heritage) Party (q.v.). He was elected to Eleventh Knesset (q.v.) on the Morasha list.

DRUZE (sometimes DRUSE). The Druze are a self-governing religious community that broke from Islam in the eleventh century, whose members live primarily in Syria and Lebanon. They number some 70,000 (about 9% of Israel's non-Jewish population). Their religious practices are highly secretive and complex and the community is very tightly knit. The Druze are considered a separate community by the state of Israel, and they are the only Arabs conscripted into the Israel Defense Forces (q.v.). Druze soldiers have fought in all the Arab-Israeli wars for Israel.

DULZIN, ARYE LEON. Born in Minsk, Russia on March 31, 1913, he emigrated to Mexico in 1928 where he became active in Zionist matters. He served as Secretary General of the Zionist Federation of Mexico and as its President (from 1938 to 1942). He settled in Israel in 1956 and became a member of the Executive of the Jewish Agency (q.v.). He served on a number of other boards and in various executive positions and was involved in the activities of the Liberal Party (q.v.). In 1969 he became Minister Without Portfolio in the government. He served as Treasurer of the Jewish Agency from 1968 to 1978 and was elected Chairman of the World Zionist Organization (q.v.) and Jewish Agency in 1978. He retired in 1987. In 1986 he broke with the Liberal party and helped to form the Liberal Center Party (q.v.). He died in Tel Aviv in September 1989.

- E -

EARTHQUAKE. The Yom Kippur War (q.v.) resulted in an Israeli military victory, but unleashed tensions in the economic, political, and psychological arenas in Israel. Protest groups focusing on various aspects of the resulting situation were formed. Israelis were concerned with war losses, the failure of military intelligence, initial battlefield reverses, questions about war-associated political decisions, and deteriorating economic and social conditions at home accompanied by diplomatic reverses abroad. This malaise affected the body politic during much of the tenure of Yitzhak Rabin (q.v.) as Prime Minister (1974 to 1977), but seemed to reach a crucial level in conjunction with the 1977 Knesset (q.v.) election when many of the forces set in motion by the Yom Kippur War and its aftermath seemed to coalesce, causing a major fissure or "Earthquake" in the political landscape in Israel. The body politic gave the largest number of votes to the Likud (q.v.) led by Menachem Begin (q.v.) and Labor (q.v.) lost a substantial number of seats compared to the 1973 election. The results ended Labor's dominance of Israeli political life that had begun in the Yishuv (q.v.) period. Menachem Begin subsequently formed a Likud-led coalition government. This sudden shift in political direction, together with the aftershocks it caused, have been likened to an "Earthquake," the descriptive term often attached to this period in Israeli political development.

EAST FOR PEACE (HAMIZRACH LESHALOM). An Oriental-based peace group organized by a group of intellectuals after the War in Lebanon (q.v.) in part to counter the hardline image of Oriental Jews (q.v.). This group believes that peace is essential for Israel and that Oriental Jews should play a role in the effort to achieve it.

EAST JERUSALEM see JERUSALEM

EBAN, ABBA (FORMERLY AUBREY). Born in Cape Town, South Africa in 1915 to Lithuanian-Jewish parents, he grew up in England. While a student of Oriental languages and classics at Cambridge University, he founded the University Labour Society, was president of the Students' Union, and was active in debating and Zionist (q.v.) circles. During World War II, he served as a major to the British minister of state in Cairo and then as an intelligence officer in Jerusalem (q.v.). In 1946 he became the political information officer in London for the Jewish Agency (q.v.), and the following year, the liaison officer for the Jewish Agency with the United Nations Special Committee on Palestine (q.v.). In May 1948, he became Israel's permanent delegate to the United Nations. From 1950 to 1959, he served as both Israel's Ambassador to the United States and to the United Nations. In 1959, he was elected to the Knesset (q.v.) on the Mapai (q.v.) list. He served as Minister of Education and Culture from 1960 to 1963, and was Deputy Prime Minister in 1964 to 1965. He also served as President of the Weizmann Institute of Science (q.v.) at Rehovot from 1959 to 1966. In 1966, he became Minister of Foreign Affairs. In this position, which he held until 1974, he sought to strengthen Israel's relations with the United States and with the European Economic Community. During the Six Day War (q.v.), Eban presented Israel's position at the United Nations. He served as chairman of the Knesset Committee for Security and Foreign Affairs from 1984 to 1988. In 1988 the Labor Party (q.v.) dropped him from its list of candidates for the Knesset election.

EDOT HAMIZRACH see ORIENTAL JEWS

EDRI, RAPHAEL. Born in Morocco in 1937, he served as Director General of Shikun Ovdim housing company. He served as a Labor Party (q.v.) member of the Knesset (q.v.) beginning in 1981. He became Minister Without Portfolio in the Government established in December 1988.

EDUCATION. Education has been a priority for Israel since independence although there was already a substantial growth of Jewish education under the British Mandate (q.v.). During its initial years the educational system was characterized by tremendous expansion which resulted from large-scale immigration (primarily from the Middle East and North Africa with large numbers of children) and the Compulsory Education Law of 1949. The educational system required facilities (schoolrooms) and teachers to deal with these needs and initially there were shortages of both. The system faced additional challenges created by the substantial immigration from numerous countries with different linguistic and educational backgrounds. The integration of Jews coming from all parts of the world continues as a basic challenge given differences among the various Jewish communities in education, lifestyle, history, tradition, and culture. The challenge to revive Hebrew (q.v.) as a living language and the centerpiece of the system was compounded by the need to blend the cultures of the numerous immigrants from the various countries of the world.

Education is a basic element of Jewish tradition and is given a high priority in Israeli society. In 1949 the Knesset passed the Compulsory Education Law which made regular school attendance obligatory for all children from age 5 to 14 and tuition fees were abolished in government schools for these nine years. Since 1978 school attendance has been mandatory to age 16 and free to age 18.

Because of the special characteristics of Israel's major communities—Jewish, Arab (q.v.) and Druze (q.v.)—which differ in language, history, and culture, two basic school systems are maintained: the Jewish system, with instruction in Hebrew; and the Arab/Druze system, with instruction in Arabic. Both systems are financed by and accountable to the Ministry of Education and Culture, but enjoy a large measure of internal independence. The Arab/Druze education system, with separate schools for Arab and Druze pupils, provides the standard academic and vocational curricula, adapted to emphasize Arab or Druze culture and history. Religious instruction in Islam or Christianity is provided by Arab schools if the community elders so determine. Due to the Compulsory Education Law and changes in traditional Arab/Druze attitudes towards formal education, there has been a substantial increase in general school attendance, particularly at the high school level, as well as in the number of female pupils.

Higher education was begun during the British Mandate with the establishment of the Hebrew University (q.v.) in Jerusalem (q.v.) in 1925; the Technion (q.v.), known also as the Israel Institute of Technology in Haifa (q.v.) in 1924; and the Weizmann Institute of Science (q.v.) in Rehovot in 1934. Since independence additional institutions have been created including Bar-Ilan University (q.v.) (1955), Tel Aviv University (q.v.) (1956), Haifa University (1963), and Ben Gurion University (q.v.) (1969).

EGYPT. Israel's neighbor to the west and the southwest with which it fought in the War of Independence (q.v.), the Sinai War (q.v.), the Six Day War (q.v.), the War of Attrition (q.v.), and the Yom Kippur War (q.v.).

During the War of Independence Egyptian forces succeeded in retaining a portion of the territory that was to have been a part of the Arab state in Palestine (q.v.) and known since as the Gaza Strip (q.v.). Egypt retained the territory under military control until 1967, except for a brief period in 1956–1957 when Israel held the territory during and immediately after the Sinai War. Following the Egyptian revolution and the accession of Gamal Abdul Nasser to power in the 1950s the stage was set for a second round. Cross border raids from Gaza into Israel and a substantial increase in the armaments of the Egyptian army, as well as the increased activism of the Nasser regime, helped to provide the context for the Sinai War. The conclusion of that conflict was followed by a decade of relative calm along the Egypt-Israel frontier which was broken by the Six Day War in which Israel took the Gaza Strip and the Sinai Peninsula (q.v.). A War of Attrition initiated by Nasser in the spring of 1969 was terminated by a cease-fire in the summer of 1970. The Egyptian- and Syrian-initiated Yom Kippur War of October 1973 was followed by movement in the direction of a settlement. United States Secretary of

State Henry Kissinger helped to arrange a disengagement agreement (q.v.) which was signed in January 1974 and the Sinai II (q.v.) agreement of September 1975. Following the 1977 initiative of President Anwar Sadat (q.v.), Israel and Egypt began negotiations for peace, which led to the Camp David Accords (q.v.) in September 1978 and the Egypt-Israel Peace Treaty (q.v.) of March 1979. Peace and the normalization of relations followed—ambassadors were exchanged, trade and tourism developed, and continued contacts were sustained between the two states. Nevertheless, the relationship between the two countries could best be characterized by the concept of a "cold peace" in which formal ties exist and some intercourse occurs but their links could not be characterized as friendly or warm in nature.

EGYPT-ISRAEL DISENGAGEMENT OF FORCES AGREEMENT (1974) see ISRAEL-EGYPT DISENGAGEMENT FORCES AGREEMENT

EGYPT-ISRAEL PEACE TREATY (1979). A peace treaty signed in Washington, DC, in March 1979, between the Arab Republic of Egypt and the State of Israel, under the auspices of the United States which ended the state of war between the two countries. See also JIMMY CARTER, MENACHEM BEGIN, ANWAR SADAT, CAMP DAVID ACCORDS.

EHRLICH, SIMHA. Born in Lublin, Poland, in 1915, Simha Ehrlich received a traditional Jewish education and at an early age he became an active member of the General Zionist Youth Movement, emigrating to Palestine (q.v.) at the age of nineteen. During his first years in the country he worked as a agricultural laborer and studied commerce and economics. He began his public and political career in the Union of General Zionists and rose through its ranks.

He was elected to the Tel Aviv (q.v.) Municipal Council in 1955 and continued to serve on it until his election to the Seventh Knesset (q.v.) in 1969. In 1962 he became Deputy Mayor of Tel Aviv. He also became President of the National Secretariat of the Liberal Party (q.v.) and later, Chairman of its National Secretariat and member of the Gahal (q.v.) Executive Committee. During the Seventh and Eighth Knessets, Ehrlich served on the Knesset Finance Committee and was Chairman of its Sub-Committee for the Defense Budget. In the Ninth Knesset, he served as Minister of Finance from June 1977 until November 1979 when he was appointed Deputy Prime Minister. While serving as Finance Minister he declared a new economic plan designed to eliminate the government from the economy and apply free market principles. The plan sought to modify the existing socialist system, check inflation, cut the foreign trade deficit, increase the growth rate, and promote foreign investment. On August 5, 1981, following his reelection to the Tenth Knesset, he was sworn in as Deputy Prime Minister and Minister of Agriculture. He died in 1983.

EICHMANN, ADOLF. Adolf Eichmann was a German SS officer who presided over the execution of Adolf Hitler's "final solution," the extermination of European Jews. Captured by Americans at the end of the war, Eichmann escaped to Argentina where he was recaptured by Israeli agents in 1960. Eichmann was tried in public on charges of crimes against the Jewish people and war crimes against humanity. The trial began in Jerusalem on April 11, 1961 and on December 11, 1961 the court found him guilty and sentenced him to death. After appeals he was executed on May 31, 1962. The trial focused world attention on the tragedy of European Jewry and the systematic efforts of Nazi Germany to exterminate the Jewish communities of Europe in the Holocaust (q.v.).

EILAT (ELAT, ELATH). Israel's southernmost city, it is a deepwater port on the Gulf of Aqaba (q.v.) connecting Israel with the Red Sea and the Indian Ocean. It is named for the ancient city of Eilat which is mentioned in the Bible as a city through which the Israelites passed during their desert wanderings. It later served as a port city for numerous empires and conquerers of the area. Prior to the opening of the Suez Canal to Israeli shipping, Eilat was Israel's major gateway for goods from the Far East, the Indian Ocean, Asia, and East Africa. Eilat's natural beauty and seaside location make it a year-round resort. Modern Eilat was founded in 1948. Its importance increased after 1950 when Egypt banned Israeli ships from the Suez Canal. Without the canal, the Gulf of Aqaba became Israel's only outlet to the Red Sea. But Egypt also blocked the entrance to the Gulf at the Straits of Tiran (q.v.). The Gulf was opened as a result of the Sinai War of 1956 (q.v.). Eilat then grew rapidly in both size and importance. Egypt's blockade of the Gulf in 1967 was a major cause of the Six Day War (q.v.). Eilat also serves as an important center for oil; a pipeline carries oil from the city to Israel's Mediterranean coast and from there it is either exported or sent to a refinery in Haifa.

EITAN, RAPHAEL (FORMERLY KAMINSKY; NICK-NAMED "RAFUL"). Born in 1929 in Tel Adashim, he pursued a military career. He was educated at Tel Aviv (q.v.) and Haifa universities. He joined the Palmah (q.v.) at the age of 17. He served as Chief of Staff of the Israel Defense Forces (q.v.) from 1978 to 1983. He first joined the Knesset (q.v.) in 1984 on the Tehiya (q.v.)-Tsomet (q.v.) list. In June 1990 he joined the government as Minister of Agriculture.

EL AL. El Al was a Syrian village in the Golan Heights (q.v.), which surrendered to Israel during the Six Day

War (q.v.). It became a settlement developed by Israel in an effort to expand the Jewish population of the Heights.

EL AL (UPWARD). Israel's national airline. One of the first decisions of the new state of Israel after independence was to establish a national airline to ensure that the state, surrounded by hostile neighbors, would have an air link to the outside world. Among its first activities was flying whole communities of immigrants to Israel. It has grown to become a significant international air carrier.

ELAZAR, DAVID (NICKNAMED "DADO"). Born in Zaghreb, Yugoslavia in 1925, he was brought to Palestine (q.v.) as part of the Youth Aliya in 1940. In 1946 he joined the Palmah (q.v.). In the War of Independence (q.v.) he participated in the fighting for Jerusalem (q.v.) and later in the Sinai Peninsula (q.v.). After a period as a training officer and as an operations officer in the Central Command he took a leave of absence in 1953 to study Economics and Middle Eastern Studies at Hebrew University (q.v.). In the Sinai War of 1956 (q.v.) he fought in the Gaza Strip (q.v.). In 1961 he was promoted to the rank of Major General. In November 1964 he was appointed Commander of the Northern Command which, during the 1967 war, captured the Golan Heights (q.v.). He was appointed head of the Staff Branch in 1969 and he served as the Chief of Staff of the Israel Defense Forces (q.v.) from January 1972 until April 1974. He resigned in April 1974 after the release of the findings of the Agranat Commission of Inquiry (q.v.) which blamed him for the initial setbacks at the beginning of the Yom Kippur War (q.v.), for excessive confidence in the ability of the army to contain the Egyptian and Syrian attacks without calling up the reserves, for incorrect assessments and a lack of preparedness of the IDF at the outbreak of the war. The commission recommended the termination of his role as Chief of Staff. He later joined the Zim shipping company as Managing Director and died in April 1976.

ELIAV, ARIE (NICKNAMED "LOVA"). Born in Moscow in 1921 he immigrated to Palestine (q.v.) with his parents in 1924. Eliav was educated at Herzliya High School (q.v.) in Tel Aviv (q.v.). He served in the Hagana (q.v.) from 1936 to 1940 and from 1940 to 1945 with the British army. He served in the IDF (q.v.) during the War of Independence (q.v.). From 1958 to 1960 Arie Eliav served as the First Secretary in the Israeli Embassy in Moscow. He served as the Secretary General of the Labor Party (q.v.) from 1969 until 1971. Following the Six Day War (q.v.), Eliav became increasingly critical of the Labor Party (q.v.), particularly its policies toward the Arab (q.v.) population. He eventually split from the Labor party, and formed a leftist group the Independent Socialists. In 1977 this party joined other leftist groups and formed the Shelli (Peace for Israel) Party (q.v.). The party advocated the establishment of an Arab Palestinian state alongside Israel, Israel's withdrawal to pre-1967 borders, and negotiations with the Palestine Liberation Organization (q.v.). After serving in the Knesset (q.v.) for thirteen years, Eliav resigned in 1977. He joined the Israel Labor Party (q.v.) in 1986 and was elected to the Knesset in 1988 on the Maarach (q.v.) list. He received the Israel Prize (q.v.) in 1988.

ENGLAND. Israel's relationship with England (the United Kingdom, Great Britain) antedates Israel's independence. It can be traced to the period of World War I when, among other arrangements concerning Palestine (q.v.), the British government issued the Balfour Declaration (q.v.) which endorsed the concept of a national home for the Jewish people in Palestine. The Declaration was seen as support for the Zionist claim to a Jewish state in Palestine. The British were granted the Mandate (q.v.) over Palestine after the end of the war and retained their control until the establishment of Israel's independence in May 1948. Britain did not support the establishment of the Jewish state and supplied arms to the Arab states during the War of Independence (q.v.) in addition to supporting the Arab position in the United Nations. Britain recognized Israel in 1949.

In May 1950 Britain joined with France (q.v.) and the United States (q.v.) in a Tripartite Declaration to limit arms sales to the region in an effort to ensure regional stability. The ensuing years were marked by a coolness in relations while Britain retained close links with many of Israel's Arab neighbors. Nevertheless, in the fall of 1956 England joined with France and Israel in a tripartite plan to deal with the policies and activities of President Gamal Abdul Nasser of Egypt. Nasser sought to accelerate the British withdrawal from Egypt and the Suez Canal zone and to undermine British influence elsewhere in the Arab world. In July 1956 he nationalized the Suez Canal which the British regarded as having economic value and strategic significance. Israel invaded Egypt at the end of October 1956 in the Sinai War (q.v.) and England and France soon joined in after giving both Egypt and Israel an ultimatum. The convergence of interests and the marriage of convenience that resulted soon came apart under the pressure of the international community, especially the United States.

In the 1960s there was a small growth and improvement in relations between Israel and England which included the sale of some military equipment to Israel. At the same time, England was in the process of reordering its relationship with the Arab states of the Middle East, especially its former colonial territories. Sympathy for Israel was widespread in England at the outbreak of the Six Day War (q.v.). It was Britain's United Nations representative who was instrumental in the drafting of United Nations Security Council Resolution 242 (q.v.), but Britain did not play a major role in trying to achieve peace in the years immediately following the 1967 war.

The succeeding years saw a variation in the relationship with links alternately improving and declining, based on changes in personality in decision-making positions in both Britain and Israel. Britain's role in the European community and its advocacy of the Venice Declaration of 1980 which sought a resolution of the Arab-Israeli conflict on terms deemed problematic by Israel remained an irritant in the relationship. Nevertheless other factors, such as a common opposition to Middle East originated terrorism, proved to be positive factors in the relationship.

ENTEBBE AIRPORT RAID see ENTEBBE OPERATION

ENTEBBE OPERATION. On July 4, 1976, an Israeli commando operation, codenamed "Thunderbolt," freed 103 hostages taken from a hijacked jetliner and held at Entebbe airport, Uganda. The jetliner, Air France flight 139 originating in Tel Aviv (q.v.), was hijacked on June 27, 1976 by Arab and German terrorists on a flight between Athens and Paris. The plane was flown to Uganda, then under the control of Idi Amin. Israel refused to give in to the hijacker's demands for the release of numerous terrorists held in Israel. After a week of negotiations, Israeli commandos, under the command of Brigadier General Dan Shomron (q.v.), staged a dramatic and successful raid that later was renamed "Operation Jonathan" in memory of Jonathan (Yoni) Netanyahu, an Israeli officer who was killed during the rescue.

ERETZ ISRAEL (OR ERETZ YISRAEL). Eretz Israel or Eretz Yisrael is a Hebrew term meaning "Land of Israel," used to refer to Palestine (q.v.). The term is found in the Bible, Talmud (q.v.) and later literature, and refers to the land of ancient Israel: all of Palestine, including Judea (q.v.) and Samaria (q.v.).

ESHKOL, LEVI (FORMERLY SHKOLNIK). Levi Eshkol was born in Oratovo in the Kiev district of the Ukraine, on October 25, 1895. In January 1914 he set out as part of a contingent representing the youth organization, Hapoel Hatzair (The Young Worker) (q.v.), to the port of Trieste where he sailed for Jaffa (q.v.). At first he served as a common farm laborer and watchman, but soon became involved in the building of a pumping station and was elected to the Workers' Agricultural Council of Petah Tikva (q.v.). He entered military service in the Jewish Legion (q.v.) and upon demobilization in 1920 he helped to create Degania Bet (q.v.). When the Histadrut (q.v.) was created in 1920 Eshkol joined the executive board and when Mapai (q.v.) was founded in 1929 he was elected to its Central Council. David Ben-Gurion (q.v.) became a powerful figure in the party and with him Eshkol was drawn into the party leadership. Eshkol increasingly was seen as a political appendage to Ben-Gurion because of the parallels in their careers and their friendship.

After Israel's independence Eshkol was appointed as Director-General of the Ministry of Defense. He was appointed head of the Land Settlement Department of the Jewish Agency (q.v.) in 1949. In 1951 he became Minister of Agriculture and Development and the following year Minister of Finance. Eshkol replaced Ben-Gurion as Prime Minister in June 1963 and served in that position until his death on February 6, 1969. He and Ben-Gurion split over the Lavon Affair (q.v.) which led to the defection of Ben-Gurion from Mapai and the creation of ·Rafi (q.v.). Eshkol was known for his contributions to Israel's economic development in a crucial period and for his skills as a compromiser. He led Israel through the Six Day War (q.v.) and the crisis that preceded it. He was considered one of the more dovish of Israel's leaders, and did not wish to formally annex areas inhabited by large numbers of Arabs. Nevertheless, on June 27, 1967 he issued an administrative order to apply Israeli law and administration to East Jerusalem (q.v.).

ETHIOPIAN JEWS see OPERATION MOSES

ETZEL see IRGUN

ETZION BLOC (GUSH ETZION). Jewish settlements in the hills of Judea (q.v.) between Jerusalem (q.v.) and Hebron (q.v.) taken by Jordan during the War of Independence (q.v.). After numerous attacks by the Jordanian Arab Legion and other Arabs the Etzion Bloc of settlements fell on May 14, 1948. It included Kfar Etzion, Massuot Yitzhak, Ein Tzurim, and Rvadim. The group derives its name from Kfar Etzion, the oldest (founded 1943) of the settlements. The area was recaptured by Israel during the Six Day War (q.v.) of 1967. Subsequently settlements were reestablished in the area.

EXODUS 1947. A ship bringing illegal immigrants to Palestine under the auspices of the Hagana (q.v.) in 1947. The ship, originally named the President Warfield, was purchased by the Hagana to transport immigrants to Palestine (q.v.). It departed from France in July 1947 with a shipload of immigrants, but the British escorted the ship to Haifa (q.v.) and boarded it. The refugees were refused permission to enter Palestine and were forced to return in British ships to Europe, mostly to Germany. See also BRITISH MANDATE.

- F -

FALASHAS (JEWS OF ETHIOPIA) see OPERATION MOSES

FIGHTERS LIST. A political party based largely on members and sympathizers of Lehi (the Stern Gang) (q.v.). It contested and won a seat in the first Knesset (q.v.), but did not contest the second Knesset election and ceased to be a political force.

FINE ARTS. Boris Schatz established the Bezalel School of Arts and Crafts in Jerusalem (q.v.) at the beginning of the twentieth century and marked the inauguration of formal art activity in Palestine (q.v.). The period since has been characterized by intense vitality and development. Art in Israel has been stimulated by great historical events, the rich body of literature created in the country, international trends, as well as by the influence of major local artists. Israel's artistic life is concentrated in three cities: Jerusalem, Haifa (q.v.), and Tel Aviv (q.v.). Tel Aviv tends to be the focus of the richness and excitement of Israeli art, but an important creative factor is the kibbutz (q.v.) movement, which encourages talented artists among its members. Artists also live and pursue their work in artists' villages and in the artists' quarters of Safed (q.v.) and Jaffa (q.v.).

FIRST ALIYA see ALIYA

FLATTO-SHARON, SHMUEL. Born in Lodz, Poland in 1930 and immigrated as a child to France. He became a successful businessman. He ran for election in the 1977 Knesset (q.v.) election and again in 1981. When he first ran for parliament he neither spoke nor understood Hebrew (q.v.) and was a new immigrant. France had requested his extradition to stand trial on charges of illegal financial transactions, embezzlement, and fraud. Nevertheless, he won more than enough votes to secure a seat in the parliament and as a member of the Knesset he gained immunity from extradition. He was later convicted in Israel of bribing voters in the 1977 election.

FRANCE. The relationship between France and Israel has evolved through a series of stages over the years as had France's relationship with the Zionist movement in the earlier decades of the twentieth century. Although France voted for the Palestine Partition Plan (q.v.) in November 1947 and recognized Israel after independence in 1949, relations between the two states remained cool. In 1950 France joined with the United States and England in a Tripartite Declaration that sought to stabilize the situation in the Middle East by limiting arms supply to the region. In subsequent years the relationship between the two states improved and by 1954–1955 France and Israel had signed a number of agreements relating to arms supply and nuclear energy. A political-military marriage of convenience between Israel and France developed as the revolt against France in Algeria gained support from President Gamal Abdul Nasser in Egypt and Nasser clashed with France over the nationalization of the Suez Canal. France and Britain reached agreement with Israel, which led to the Sinai War (q.v.) in October 1956. France became Israel's primary supplier of military equipment (including tanks and aircraft) until the Six Day War (q.v.) and close links were established in other sectors as well. France also assisted Israel in the construction of a nuclear reactor at Dimona (q.v.) in the Negev (q.v.).

However, after Charles de Gaulle came to power in France in 1958 and suggested a need to resolve the Algerian issue, relations between Israel and France began to cool—a trend that accelerated after the accord in 1962 that led to Algerian independence. The Six Day War of 1967 became a more significant watershed as

France announced in early June an embargo on arms shipments to the Middle East, a decision that severely and negatively affected Israel since France was Israel's primary arms supplier. De Gaulle's antipathy to Israel and its policies grew after the 1967 war and the trend accelerated even further when Georges Pompidou became President. After Israel's raid on Beirut airport in December 1968 (following a terrorist attack on an El Al (q.v.) aircraft in Athens, Greece), France imposed a total embargo on arms deliveries to Israel. In December 1969 Israel smuggled five gunboats (that had been built for Israel and paid for) out of Cherbourg harbor. This led to an intensification of the embargo and a deterioration in relations that was further compounded by growing French dependence on Arab oil and a desire to sell military equipment to the Arab states. Among the factors in the relationship were French efforts to secure the Venice Declaration of the European Community in 1980 which was condemned by Israel.

Relations improved when François Mitterrand became President and paid a state visit to Israel in early 1982. Relations in other sectors also improved in subsequent years despite some interruption in the trend as a result of the War in Lebanon (q.v.) of 1982.

FREE CENTER PARTY (HAMERKAZ HAHOFSHI). Founded by Shmuel Tamir (q.v.) in 1967, when he and two other Knesset (q.v.) members split from the Herut (q.v.) party because of ideological differences. In 1973 the Free Center rejoined Herut. Subsequently, the larger portion of the Free Center, excluding Tamir, joined the La'am (q.v.) faction (organized in 1977) within Likud. Tamir joined Yigael Yadin's (q.v.) Democratic Movement (q.v.).

FREE TRADE AREA. The United States Congress, in October 1984, authorized the President to negotiate a free trade area with Israel. The idea was broached during a meeting between President Ronald Reagan and Prime Minister Yitzhak Shamir (q.v.) in November 1983 and subsequently the President sought the requisite Congressional approval to negotiate such an agreement. Under the arrangement, Israel became the first country in the world to enjoy a bilateral free trade arrangement with the United States. It allows Israel access to its largest single trading partner on substantially improved terms, thereby aiding its export capability. Israel eventually will gain virtually complete and permanent duty-free access to the world's largest market.

FUNDAMENTAL LAWS see BASIC LAWS

- G -

GABRIEL MISSILE. A missile, developed by Israel, which was the first operational sea-to-sea missile in the Western world. The Gabriel has earned hundreds of millions of dollars for Israel. It has been purchased by South Africa and Argentina, among others.

GADNA (THE ISRAELI YOUTH CORPS). Gadna began operating some ten years before the establishment of the state. Over the years it has had a variety of names and tasks, but its primary purpose has remained to (a) educate the youth on good citizenship, loyalty, and preparation for national service, (b) make the youth aware of national security problems, and (c) develop the physical fitness of youth. During the riots in Palestine (q.v.) in the period 1936–1939 the leaders of the Yishuv (q.v.) reached the conclusion that all able-bodied individuals were essential and the mobilization of young boys was begun. A number of groups were established. In the summer of 1948 the Chief of Staff of the Israel

Defense Forces (q.v.) signed the order for the establishment of Gadna. The intent was not to send these youngsters into combat, but occasionally this was done during the War of Independence (q.v.). The basic purpose is to train and prepare Israeli youth between the ages of 14 and 18 for national duty.

GAHAL. In 1965 Herut (q.v.) was joined by the former General Zionists (q.v.) in the Liberal Party (q.v.) to form the parliamentary bloc Gahal (acronym for Gush Herut Liberalim—bloc of Herut and the Liberals), under the leadership of Menachem Begin (q.v.). The Gahal Agreement was signed on April 25, 1965. Among other elements, the agreement fixes the ratio of Herut and Liberal members of parliament and the locations of candidates from the two parties on the Gahal election list. Each of the parties gets eleven of the first twenty-two slots on the list, one going to each party, with Herut getting the first, the Liberals the second, and so on. From that point to the fortieth position, Herut gets eleven seats and the Liberals get seven. From that point on the agreement again provides for one each. Gahal joined the national unity government formed on the eve of the Six Day War (q.v.) and was represented in the cabinet by Menachem Begin (q.v.) and Joseph Saphir. Likud (q.v.) (Unity) was formed in 1973 as a parliamentary bloc by the combination of Gahal and La'am (q.v.) (Toward the People), and Menachem Begin retained his dominant role.

GALILEE. The northernmost section of Israel. Divided into an Upper Galilee (mostly mountainous) and a Lower Galilee (more hilly in nature).

GALILI, ISRAEL (FORMERLY BERCZENKO). Born in Brailov, Ukraine, Russia in 1910 Israel Galili was taken to Palestine (q.v.) at the age of four. There he became active in various Zionist and labor activities at a young age and remained active throughout his life. He helped found Kibbutz Naan where he remained a member. He joined the Hagana (q.v.) and rose through the ranks to become Deputy Commander in Chief. In the provisional government of Israel established in 1948, he served as Deputy Minister of Defense. He was a member of Ahdut Haavoda (q.v.) and served in the Knesset (q.v.) from its inception. In 1966 he became a member of the Cabinet without portfolio. He played an especially important role in foreign policy and security decisions when Golda Meir (q.v.) was Prime Minister and was a significant member of her kitchen cabinet (q.v.). He died in 1986.

GALUT see DIASPORA

GAZA DISTRICT see GAZA STRIP

GAZA STRIP. The southernmost section of the coastal plain of Mandatory Palestine (q.v.). It is some 25 miles long and between 4 and 8 miles in width. Its major city is Gaza and there is substantial citrus agriculture. Although it lies between Israel and Egypt (q.v.), it belongs to neither and its disposition remains a matter of dispute. The territory, heavily populated by Palestinians, was to have been part of a Palestinian Arab state under the terms of the 1947 United Nations Partition Plan (q.v.) for Palestine. However, it was taken by the Egyptian army during the 1948–1949 war with Israel and placed under Egyptian military administration. Held briefly by Israel in 1956–1957, the Gaza Strip was then returned to Egyptian control, where it remained until 1967 when Israel again occupied the area during the Six Day War (q.v.). Egypt did not claim sovereignty over the Gaza Strip as a part of the Egypt-Israel Peace Treaty (q.v.), and negotiations concerning its status have made little progress. Violence and protests directed at Israel and the Israeli administration in the area have increased considerably since late 1987, and both Jews and Arabs have been killed during the course of the intifada (q.v.).

GENERAL FEDERATION OF LABOR see HISTADRUT

GENERAL ZIONIST PARTY (HATZIONIM HAKLALIYIM). In June 1946, the General Zionists A and B, previously separate parties, joined to form the General Zionist Party. The General Zionists, Group A, in the main represented middle-class interests as well as members of the liberal professions. Group B was more outspokenly right wing. The social outlook of the party was largely determined by the fact that it relied for support mainly upon the industrialists, merchants, citrus growers, and landlords, and the various professional associations formed by them. When the General Zionist Party was created, its constituent elements survived within it as organized groupings and real cohesion was never achieved. After Israeli independence the rift between the two groups became greater. The crisis culminated in August 1948 with a split of the Party when the former General Zionists A broke away to take part in the formation of the new Progressive Party (q.v.). The party represented a large section of the secular non-socialist element among the Jewish population of Israel and sought to portray itself as a center party in the early 1950s. It was represented in the Knesset (q.v.) from 1949 to 1961.

GERMANY, FEDERAL REPUBLIC OF. The relationship between Israel and the Federal Republic of Germany (West Germany or Germany) has been described by observers as "special." The complex relationship grows out of developments related to the Holocaust (q.v.) and the crimes committed by the Germans against the Jews and the subsequent efforts on the part of Germany to normalize its relationship with Israel and to integrate itself into the international system.

Germany's approach to Israel had its origins in the views and policies of Germany's first postwar Chancellor, Konrad Adenauer, who believed that there should be reconciliation between Germany and the Jewish people. Adenauer admitted the crimes committed by Germany against the Jewish people and argued that the rehabilitation of the Jews through moral and material reparations by Germany was essential. Israel was to receive material restitution from Germany. After negotiations which began in the early 1950s, a restitution agreement was signed by Israel, Germany, and the Conference of Jewish Material Claims Against Germany in September 1952, despite strong Arab opposition. The agreement was of great importance to Israel as it provided substantial economic support at a crucial time for the young state. Germany subsequently became a supplier of military equipment to the Jewish state. Nevertheless and despite the significance of this agreement for Israel, there was strong opposition in Israel to any arrangement with Germany and diplomatic relations between the two states were not a realistic option. For Germany the agreement was crucial in helping to reestablish its international position and to help prepare the way for its reintegration into the Western European alliance structure.

Despite various high level and other meetings and continued economic assistance and military sales, a number of issues precluded substantial movement toward a diplomatic relationship between Israel and Germany for some time. These included the trial of Adolf Eichmann (q.v.), which rekindled old memories, and the activities of German scientists in assisting in the development of Arab military capabilities. Diplomatic relations were not established until 1965. Although many Israelis remained concerned about dealing with the successor state to Nazi Germany, contacts between Israel and Germany flourished in all sectors and at all levels. Germany has become a major trading partner and its aid to Israel has been indispensable to the economic growth of the state. Although Germany has become increasingly critical of some of Israel's policies concerning the Palestinians and the Arab-Israeli conflict the Holocaust factor continues to play a special role in Germany's approach to Israel.

GIMLAIM (PENSIONERS) PARTY. A political party, led by Abba Gefen, that contested the 1988 Knesset (q.v.) election but failed to gain sufficient votes for a mandate in parliament.

GINZBERG, ASHER ZVI see AHAD HAAM

GOLAN HEIGHTS. A zone east of the Huleh Valley (q.v.) and the Sea of Galilee (q.v.) that abuts Mount Hermon (q.v.). It is a sparse territory some 41 miles long and 15 miles wide. The border between Israel and Syria has been in dispute since the establishment of the Jewish state in 1948. In 1949 the armistice agreement (q.v.) designated small areas on the western side of the border as demilitarized zones. Many of the clashes between Syria and Israel between 1949 and 1967 developed from Israel's efforts to assert control over these parcels of land.

In the Six Day War (q.v.), Israel occupied the Syrian territory known as the Golan Heights and began to establish settlements there. It was placed under military administration. During the Yom Kippur War (q.v.), Syria briefly recaptured a portion of the Golan Heights, but Israel quickly took additional Syrian territory. The Israel-Syria Disengagement of Forces Agreement (q.v.)

of 1974 resulted in Syria's regaining some territory lost in 1967. No major incidents and only a few minor ones have occurred since 1974. Since the late 1970s the focus of Israeli-Syrian tension has been in Lebanon (q.v.) because of the use by the Palestine Liberation Organization (q.v.) of Syrian-controlled Lebanese territory for strikes against Israel.

On December 14, 1981, the Government of Israel presented a bill to the Knesset (q.v.) which applied the law, jurisdiction, and administration of the state to the Golan Heights. The bill passed all three readings required in the Knesset and was adopted by a vote of 63 in favor and 21 against. Explaining this action, Prime Minister Menachem Begin (q.v.) declared, "in this matter of the Golan Heights there is a universal, or nearly universal, national consensus in Israel." Begin also stated that the law did not alter Israel's readiness to negotiate all outstanding issues with Syria, including the issue of final borders. The government cited several reasons for proposing the bill to the Knesset. After fourteen years of administration, the Syrians had rejected all efforts to bring them into a peace process. The Syrians had refused to accept the Camp David peace process, had installed missiles in Lebanon which were a direct threat to Israel, and in their occupation of Lebanon directly aided the PLO in its border attacks against Israel.

The action by the Knesset changed the status of the Golan Heights from military to civil jurisdiction. The Druze farmers who live there had the option of receiving Israeli citizenship. The population of the Golan numbers 6,700 Jews in 27 farms and villages, 12,000 Druze in four villages, and one village of 600 Alawite Muslims.

Following the Knesset vote on the Golan bill, the United States condemned the act, stating that the swift nature of the Israeli action surprised the United States, was harmful to the peace process, and violated the

Camp David accords (q.v.). In a prepared statement, the State Department spokesman said, ". . . We have stated that we do not recognize Israel's action, which we consider to be without legal effect. In our view, their action is inconsistent with both the letter and the spirit of UN Security Council Resolution 242 and 338. We continue to believe that the final status of the Golan Heights can only be determined through negotiations between Syria and Israel based upon Resolutions 242 and 338." On December 17, 1981 the United Nations Security Council adopted unanimously a resolution holding ". . . that the Israeli decision to impose its laws, jurisdiction and administration in the occupied Syrian Golan Heights is null and void and without international legal effect; [and that] Demands that Israel, the occupying power, should rescind forthwith its decision." The United States voted in favor of a Syrian-sponsored United Nations Security Council resolution condemning the Israeli action and demanding that Israel rescind the legislation. The United States also announced that it was suspending the U.S.-Israel Memorandum of Understanding on Strategic Cooperation (q.v.). Additionally, the U.S. administration canceled several bilateral economic agreements that would have provided Israel with opportunities to sell Israeli-made arms to nations friendly to the United States, using U.S. credit dollars. The administration also canceled several planned purchases of Israeli-made arms.

GONEN, SHMUEL (FORMERLY GORODISH). He came to Palestine (q.v.) with his parents from Lithuania when he was three years old and attended a yeshiva. He joined the Hagana (q.v.) in 1944 and rose through the ranks to become a general officer. He gained fame in the June War of 1967 (q.v.) when his tank brigade broke through Egyptian defenses in northern Sinai. After the Yom Kippur War (q.v.) he was among those criticized by the Agranat Commission (q.v.) and was suspended. The suspension was later reversed on condition that he not be appointed as a corps commander. He retired from the army in 1976 and went into private business. He died in September 1991.

GORDON, AHARON DAVID. A Hebrew (q.v.) writer and spiritual mentor of labor Zionists who believed in settlement of the land. Gordon was born in Troyanov, Russia in 1856. He was given a position in the financial management of Baron Guenzburg's estate and remained in this position for 23 years. In 1903, because he had to find other employment, he decided to move to Palestine (q.v.) which he did the following year. Five years later he brought his family. He became involved in manual agricultural work but also, beginning in 1909, started writing articles concerning his outlook on labor, Zionism (q.v.) and Jewish destiny, which became known as "the religion of labor." He died in Degania (q.v.) in 1922.

GOREN, RABBI SHLOMO. Born in Poland in 1917 and immigrated to Palestine (q.v.) in 1925, Shlomo Goren was educated at Hebrew University (q.v.) and served as Chief Rabbi of Tel Aviv-Jaffa (q.v.). He has also served as Chief Chaplain of the Israel Defense Forces (q.v.) and as Ashkenazi Chief Rabbi (q.v.) of Israel. See also RABBINATE OF ISRAEL.

GOVERNMENT see CABINET

GOVERNMENT OF NATIONAL UNITY. A coalition government of Labor (q.v.) and Likud (q.v.) formed following the 1984 Knesset (q.v.) election which lasted until the 1988 Knesset election. A variant was formed following the 1988 election. See also ROTATION and WALL-TO-WALL COALITION.

GREAT BRITAIN see ENGLAND

GULF OF AQABA. Israel also refers to it as the Gulf of Eilat, derived from the port city of Eilat (q.v.) at its head. The Gulf of Aqaba is about 100 miles long with a coastline shared by Israel, Egypt, Jordan, and Saudi Arabia. At its northern end are the Israeli port of Eilat and the Jordanian port of Aqaba. At the southern end, where the Gulf meets the Red Sea, there are two islands: Tiran and Sanafir. The navigable channel is between Tiran and the coast of the Sinai Peninsula (q.v.) and is three nautical miles wide. The point on the Sinai coast directly facing Tiran is Ras Nasrani, near Sharm el-Sheikh (q.v.). Egypt set up gun emplacements there to prevent shipping through the Strait of Tiran (q.v.). Israel destroyed the guns on November 3, 1956.

Israel's use of the Strait of Tiran and the Gulf of Aqaba has been a factor in the relations between Egypt and Israel and in the Sinai (q.v.) and Six Day (q.v.) Wars. Since the Israeli occupation of the Sinai Peninsula in 1956 and later withdrawal in 1957, Israeli ships have used the Strait and the Gulf, except for a brief interruption in 1967. Nasser's announced blockade of the Strait in 1967 was considered by Israel as a war provocation and by the United States as a major act leading to the conflict. To avoid a repetition of the blockade, the United Nations adopted Security Council Resolution 242 (q.v.) of November 1967, the basic document in the quest for an Arab-Israeli peace settlement. Resolution 242 called for freedom of navigation in international waterways, including the Strait of Tiran and Gulf of Aqaba.

The narrowness of the Gulf of Aqaba and the disparate claims by the coastal states have the potential to cause problems of maritime boundary delimitations. Both Egypt and Saudi Arabia have claimed 12-mile territorial seas and additional six-mile contiguous zones.

Israel has claimed six-mile territorial seas, and Jordan has claimed three miles without any contiguous zones.

Since the Gulf of Aqaba is very deep and because no natural resources have been discovered in it, no disputes over exploitation rights have arisen, but disputes over navigation, mostly concerning shipping to and from Eilat, have occurred. After the Israeli occupation of the western shore of the Strait of Tiran in 1967, ships of all states again enjoyed the right of passage through the Strait and the Gulf. To ensure freedom of navigation the 1979 Egypt-Israel Peace Treaty (q.v.) provided that after Israel withdrew from the shores and entrances of the Gulf of Aqaba in 1982, the area would be controlled by a multinational force established by the concerned parties and stationed in the area of Sharm el-Sheikh.

GULF OF EILAT see GULF OF AQABA

GUR, MORDECHAI (NICKNAMED "MOTTA"). Mordechai Gur was born in Jerusalem (q.v.) on May 5, 1930. At the age of seventeen, he joined the youth battalion of the Hagana (q.v.) during the Mandate (q.v.) period and later served in the Palmah (q.v.). After the War of Independence (q.v.) he attended Hebrew University (q.v.) and studied politics and Oriental studies while still in the military. He became a paratrooper and helped to develop the Israeli style of commando raids on Arab targets across the lines before the Sinai War (q.v.). He commanded the Golani Brigade from 1961 to 1963. During the Six Day War (q.v.) he commanded the paratroop brigade that captured East Jerusalem and the walled city. In August 1967 he became Commander of the Gaza Strip (q.v.) and Northern Sinai. He is a graduate of Ecole de Guerre, Paris. He served as military attaché in Washington from August 1972 until December 1973. He served as Chief of Staff of the Israel Defense Forces (q.v.) from 1974 to 1978, taking over after David Elazar (q.v.) resigned from that post. After leaving the IDF in 1978, he became Director General of a division of Koor industries (q.v.). In 1981 he ran for the Knesset (q.v.) on the Labor Party (q.v.) list.and won a seat. He served as Minister of Health in the Government of National Unity (q.v.) established in 1984 and became Minister Without Portfolio in the Government established in December 1988. Gur is also well known in Israel for his children's books about a paratrooper unit and their fighting mascot, a dog named Azit.

GUSH EMUNIM (BLOC OF THE FAITHFUL). A movement which promotes the establishment of Jewish settlements in Judea (q.v.), Samaria (q.v.), and Gaza (q.v.) as a means of promoting retention of these areas, especially the West Bank (q.v.). It is an aggressive (sometimes even illegal) settlement movement that combines religious fundamentalism and secular Zionism (q.v.) to create a new political force. Its leaders assert a biblically based Jewish claim to Judea and Samaria, but profess a belief that peaceful and productive coexistence with the Arabs is both possible and desirable. Gush Emunim became active after the Six Day War (q.v.) in establishing Jewish settlements in the occupied territories. But it was not until after the Yom Kippur War (q.v.) that it organized politically in order to oppose further territorial concessions and to promote the extension of Israeli sovereignty over the occupied territories. The founding meeting of Gush Emunim took place in 1974 at Kfar Etzion, a West Bank kibbutz that had been seized by the Arabs in Israel's War of Independence (q.v.) and which was recovered by Israel in the Six Day War. Among those playing leading roles in the movement's founding were: Rabbi Moshe Levinger (q.v.), the leader of the Kiryat Arba (q.v.) settlers; Hanan Porat, one of the revivers of Jewish settlement in Gush Etzion (q.v.); Rabbi Haim Druckman (q.v.), educator, who was one of the leaders of the Bnai

Akiva religious youth movement and subsequently became a member of the Knesset (q.v.); Rabbi Eliezer Waldman; and Rabbi Yohanan Fried.

Gush Emunim began as a faction within the National Religious Party (q.v.), but because of distrust of the NRP's position concerning the future of Judea and Samaria, the Gush left the party and declared its independence. The Gush Emunim people—mostly yeshiva graduates, rabbis, and teachers—launched an information campaign to explain their position. Gush Emunim has since refused to identify with any political party and has gained a unique political status. During the tenure of the government of Yitzhak Rabin (q.v.) from 1974 to 1977 Gush Emunim protested the disengagement agreements with Egypt (q.v.) and Syria (q.v.), staged demonstrations in Judea and Samaria to emphasize the Jewish attachment to those parts of the Land of Israel, and engaged in settlement operations in the occupied territories. Among its activities, Gush Emunim has held a mass rally in Tel Aviv's Malkhei Yisrael Square to urge recognition of Judea and Samaria as inseparable parts of the country. Gush Emunim's primary commitment is to settlement beyond the 1949 Armistice Agreement (q.v.) demarcation lines, which had served as the de facto borders between Israel and the Jordanian-annexed West Bank and between Israel and the Egyptian-administered Gaza Strip and Sinai from the 1949 to 1967. Gush Emunim has continued to push for settlements in all parts of Eretz Israel (q.v.).

Gush Emunim's spiritual authorities and political leaders were educated in Yeshivat Merkaz Harav, whose founder was Avraham Yitzhak Hacohen Kook (q.v.), the first Ashkenazi (q.v.) Chief Rabbi of Eretz Yisrael. Kook believed that the era of redemption for the Jewish people had already begun with the rise of modern Zionism and the growing Zionist enterprise in Palestine (q.v.). Israel's victory in the Six Day War transformed the status of Kook's theology. It seemed clear to his students that they were living in the messianic age and believed that redemption might be at hand. Kook's views were expounded by his son, Rabbi Zvi Yehuda Kook (q.v.), who succeeded him as the head of Yeshivat Merkaz Harav. Gush Emunim has become a highly complex social and institutional system comprised of a settlement organization, regional and municipal councils, and independent economic corporations. In addition, its spiritual leadership is composed of distinguished rabbis and scholars.

GUSH ETZION see ETZION BLOC

- H -

HAARETZ (THE LAND). A daily newspaper not affiliated with any political party. It was founded as *Hadashot Haaretz,* and first appeared in Jerusalem (q.v.) on June 18, 1919. It was later transferred to Tel Aviv (q.v.). It was the first Hebrew language (q.v.) daily to be published in Palestine (q.v.) after World War I.

HABAD. Acronym for Hokhmah, Binah, Daat (wisdom, comprehension, knowledge). A central stream of Hasidut (whose adherents are called Hasidim (q.v.)), its founder was Rabbi Shneur Zalman of Lyady. It began in Belorussia, in a town called Lubavitch (therefore these Hasidim are called Lubavitchers, and their rabbi is the Rabbi of Lubavitch—the Lubavitcher Rebbe).

HABIMAH (THE STAGE). A theater company founded in Moscow in 1914 that took the name Habimah in 1917 as the world's first professional Hebrew theater. It first performed in 1918 and settled in Palestine (q.v.) in 1931. It later became Israel's National Theater.

HADASH see DEMOCRATIC FRONT FOR PEACE AND EQUALITY

HADASSAH. The organization of Zionist women in America, founded in 1912 at the instigation of Henrietta Szold. (The name Hadasah is the Hebrew name for Esther, a Jewish Queen who dedicated herself to the saving of her people. It is also the equivalent of myrtle, a plant indigenous to Israel). Its activities in Palestine (q.v.) and Israel were limited at first to health and medical care, and then extended to include social and educational projects. At the Second Zionist Congress, Theodor Herzl (q.v.) asked Mrs. Richard Gottheil to direct her energies to enlisting the interest of her American colleagues in the principles of Zionism (q.v.). Mrs. Gottheil joined a group of the Daughters of Zion which met in New York and introduced the name "Hadassah Circle." In 1907 Henrietta Szold joined this group and, in 1909, she and her mother visited Palestine. On her return Szold described the distressing social and health situation in Palestine and the group developed a program of action. On February 24, 1912, the national organization of "Daughters of Zion" was established and the New York chapter retained the name "Hadassah." At the suggestion of Professor Israel Friedlander the Daughters of Zion adopted the motto "The healing of the daughter of my people." Hadassah began its involvement in health and medical services in Palestine and Israel in 1913 and has continued in those areas since.

HAGANA (DEFENSE). The security force of the Yishuv (q.v.) was established in Palestine (q.v.) in 1920 as a clandestine defense organization for the purpose of protecting Jewish life and property against Arab attacks. In 1941 it created a commando or "striking" force, the Palmah (q.v.) (a full-time military force of volunteers, something of a professional and elite unit) which later provided a large proportion of the senior officers in the early years of the Israel Defense Forces (q.v.). Officially Hagana ceased to exist on May 31, 1948 when the Israel Defense Forces were constituted.

HAGANA BET see IRGUN

HAIFA. A major deepwater port city on the Bay of Haifa on the eastern end of the Mediterranean Sea, it lies on and around Mount Carmel. It is the administrative center of the north of Israel and is an important manufacturing and cultural center. The city is composed of three sections: (1) the lower section, which spreads around the bottom of Mount Carmel, includes port facilities, warehouses, and apartment buildings; (2) the main business district covers most of the mountain slopes, and (3) the upper part of Haifa consists mostly of large houses, apartments buildings, and gardens and parks on top of the mountain.

Many religious landmarks are located in Haifa, including the Bahai (q.v.) Temple, the Monastery of Our Lady of Mount Carmel, and Elijah's Cave. Haifa has two universities. The city's industries include oil refining and the manufacture of cement, chemicals, electronic equipment, glass, steel, and textiles. Haifa is also a shipping and railroad center. People lived in what is now the Haifa area about 3,000 years ago. Haifa was a small town until the mid-1850s, when it was first used as a port.

HAKIBBUTZ HAARTZI. Hakibbutz Haartzi came into being as settlement federation in 1927. Its ideological foundations are Zionism (q.v.) and socialism. This federation advocates the combination of settlement with the class struggle, and for many years demanded of its members total identification with the kibbutz (q.v.)

federation's political philosophy, a concept which was termed "collective ideology." However, in the course of time the intensity of this collective ideology diminished, and today some members of Hakibbutz Haartzi publicly identify with other political parties (noticeably on the left). It was from this kibbutz movement that Hashomer Hatzair (q.v.) developed, and this party founded with Sia Bet in 1949 the United Workers Party—Mapam (q.v.).

HAKIBBUTZ HAMEUHAD (UNITED KIBBUTZ). Hakibbutz Hameuhad was founded in 1927 by the association of Kibbutz En Harod and other kibbutz settlements. Its program was finally crystallized in 1936: establishing large collective settlements that could grow even larger and which could engage in all spheres of industry. Each kibbutz (q.v.) was an autonomous unit. This kibbutz federation regards itself as fulfilling the historic mission of the Ahdut Haavoda (q.v.) Party (founded in 1919) within the Mapai (q.v.) Party and its heir—the Israel Labor Party (q.v.). Because of differences of opinion on ideological and political party matters, Hakibbutz Hameuhad split into two factions in 1951 and Ihud Hakvutzot Vehakibbutzim (q.v.) was formed. Both are reunited in the United Kibbutz Movement (q.v.). Between 1944 and 1968 Hakibbutz Hameuhad provided the political base for the Sia Bet faction that split from Mapai in 1944 to form the Ahdut Haavoda Party. It united with Mapai and Rafi (q.v.) to found the Israel Labor Party in 1968.

HAKOAH HASHAKET (THE QUIET FORCE). A political party created to contest the 1988 Knesset (q.v.) election. Led by Yaacov Gross, it failed to secure a seat in parliament.

HALACHA. Jewish religious law.

HALUTZ (PIONEER). A term used in the Zionist (q.v.) movement and in Israel to designate an individual who devoted himself or herself to the ideals of upbuilding Jewish Palestine (q.v.) with physical labor, especially in agriculture.

HAMIZRACH LESHALOM see EAST FOR PEACE

HAMMER, ZEVULUN. Born in Haifa (q.v.) in 1936. He received a BA in Education and Jewish Studies from Bar Ilan University (q.v.) in 1964 and is a graduate of the National Defense College. First elected on behalf of the National Religious Party (q.v.) to the Seventh Knesset (q.v.) in October 1969, and reelected to subsequent Knessets, Hammer has served as Deputy Minister of Education and Culture and has been a member of the Defense and Foreign Affairs and Education and Culture Committees of the Knesset. Hammer served as Minister of Welfare from 1975 to 1976, and became Minister of Education and Culture in June 1977. He served as Minister of Education and Culture from 1977 to 1984 and as Minister of Religious Affairs from October 1986 to December 1988. He again became Minister of Religious Affairs in the government established in December 1988. In June 1990 he assumed the portfolio of Minister of Education and Culture.

HAOLAM HAZEH. A political party founded in 1965, which focused on peace as the supreme aim and called for negotiations for a peace settlement between Israel and the Palestinian Arab state that should arise in the Land of Israel. It also called for free state welfare services for all. It won one seat in the Knesset (q.v.) elected in 1965 and two seats in the Knesset elected in 1969.

HAPOEL HAMIZRAHI (WORKERS OF THE SPIRITUAL CENTER) see MIZRAHI

HAPOEL HATZAIR (THE YOUNG WORKER). A Zionist socialist political party established in 1905 by East European pioneers in Palestine (q.v.). In general it sought to distinguish itself from the other socialist groups, especially Poalei Zion (q.v.). It established Degania (q.v.)—the first kibbutz (q.v.). In 1930 it joined with Ahdut Haavoda (q.v.) to found Mapai (q.v.).

HAREL (FORMERLY HALPERIN), ISSER. One of the founders of the Israeli intelligence service. He was born in Russia in 1912 and immigrated to Palestine (q.v.) in 1931. He was one of the original founders of Kibbutz Shfaim. He was active in the Hagana (q.v.). During the War of Independence (q.v.), he headed the Hagana's Information Service (SHAI) and was member of the National Command. In 1952, he was appointed head of the Mossad Lemodiin Vetafkidim Meyuhadim (q.v.), the central intelligence and security service of Israel. During his service in this post, he commanded the special operation to capture the Nazi war criminal Adolf Eichmann (q.v.). In 1963, he resigned his post over a disagreement with Prime Minister David Ben-Gurion (q.v.) on the question of German scientists in Egypt. In 1965, he was appointed an intelligence consultant to Prime Minister Levi Eshkol (q.v.), but he resigned this post after a short tenure. He is author of several books, among them: *Jihad, The House on Garibaldi Street,* and *An Anthology of Betrayal.*

HASHOMER HATZAIR. Literally "the young guard." The oldest of the Jewish youth movements in Israel and abroad. The movement strives to instill in its members national values, Zionist (q.v.) awareness, and socialist ideals, as well as to prepare them for kibbutz (q.v.) life. Hakibbutz Haartzi (q.v.) is its affiliate.

HASIDIM (HEBREW PLURAL, THE PIOUS). A religious movement founded by Israel Baal Shem Tov around 1735. He was not a Rabbi but journeyed widely as an itinerant preacher and proclaimed a philosophy of faith, love, and joy. His preaching was widely acclaimed and condemned. The Vilner Gaon excommunicated him. His philosophy spread throughout Eastern Europe where most Jews were concentrated at that time and had a revolutionary effect on Jewish life. It also generated strong opponents (the Mitnagdim). Hasidim are still a vital aspect of contemporary Judaism and numerous Hasidic dynasties of prominent Rabbis continue to have large groups of followers in Israel and abroad.

HATIKVA (THE HOPE). Anthem of the Zionist (q.v.) movement and the national anthem of the State of Israel which expresses the hope and yearning of the Jew for the return to Zion. It was written by Naftali Herz Imber and first published in Jerusalem (q.v.) in 1886.

HATNUA HAKIBBUTZIT HAMEUHEDET see UNITED KIBBUTZ MOVEMENT

HAUSNER, GIDEON M. An Israeli jurist who was born in Lvov, Galicia, on September 26, 1915. He was brought to Palestine (q.v.) in 1927. He graduated from the Hebrew University of Jerusalem (q.v.) in 1940 and from the Jerusalem Law School in 1941. He was in private law practice from 1946 to 1960. From 1960 to 1963 he served as Attorney General (q.v.) of the State of Israel. In that position he was the chief prosecutor at the Eichmann (q.v.) trial. He was elected to the Knesset (q.v.) on the Independent Liberal Party (q.v.) ticket in 1965 and served until 1977.

HAZIT DEMOKRATIT LESHALOM ULESHIYYON (HADASH) see DEMOCRATIC FRONT FOR PEACE AND EQUALITY

HEALTH. Palestine (q.v.), at the beginning of the twentieth century, was a backward area with substantial diseases, including malaria and numerous other ailments, as well as high infant mortality rates and other indicators of poor medical circumstances. Israel's situation is quite different. When the state was established in 1948, the government created a Ministry of Health to serve as an administrative organ to supervise the functioning of the existing health organizations and to deal with the needs of the new state. Numerous health care-related organizations have been created. These include voluntary organizations such as the Kupat Holim (q.v.), the Hadassah Medical Organization, the Magen David Adom (q.v.), and various other groups.

The basis of Israel's health care system was developed during the British Mandate (q.v.) by the British authorities as well as by Jewish organizations in Palestine and in the Diaspora (q.v.). The tradition of health care provision antedates the founding of the state and in some instances even the Zionist movement. Jewish clinics established in Jerusalem (q.v.) in the nineteenth century provided services to all citizens of the city and some have evolved into modern hospitals such as Bikur Holim and Shaare Zedek. In 1913 Hadassah (q.v.) sent two trained nurses to work in Jerusalem—from this small beginning there eventually evolved the massive Hadassah-Hebrew University Medical Center with its attendant hospitals, clinics, and schools of medicine. Kupat Holim, Israel's first health insurance arrangement and the largest today, was established by the Histadrut (q.v.) soon after the latter's founding in 1920 to provide health care for its members. More than 80% of Israel's population is insured through Kupat Holim today. Kupat Holim operates a vast network of facilities with thousands of staff throughout Israel. Thus, by the time Israel became independent there was a substantial health-services infrastructure.

However, the post-independence wave of new immigrants that included Holocaust (q.v.) survivors from Europe as well as substantial immigration from developing countries brought with them health problems which challenged the existing system to meet the needs and to expand to provide services that were new and different from those provided to that time. From that starting point, Israel has created a modern health care system that rivals many of those in the most developed states, and Israel's achievements in the health field are among the most impressive in the world. Health insurance is voluntary, but virtually all of the population is insured under one or another health scheme.

HEBREW LANGUAGE. The official language of the State of Israel, Hebrew, is a Semitic language in which most of the Bible, the Mishna and parts of the Talmud (q.v.) and much of Rabbinic and secular Jewish literature are written. It is written from right to left. Until the Babylonian Exile (in 586 BC) Hebrew was the sole language of the Jews. After the exile Aramaic came into widespread use although some Hebrew was still utilized. Both the Babylonian and Jerusalem Talmuds are written in Aramaic rather than Hebrew. In countries of the Diaspora (q.v.) the Jewish communities adopted local languages and substantially limited their use of Hebrew as a language of communication although it remained a language of Jewish literature and prayer. As the language of the Bible and prayer it was considered the sacred tongue. When the first pioneers came to Palestine (q.v.) in the 1880s it seemed natural to use Hebrew as the vernacular language. The revival of the Hebrew language was closely associated with Eliezer Ben Yehuda (q.v.) who arrived in Palestine in 1881 and sought to promote the use of Hebrew as a spoken language. There was opposition from skeptics who felt that the language was not rich enough to deal with contemporary matters and from the ultra-religious who objected to the use of the sacred tongue for practical everyday concerns. There was a vocabulary gap as a consequence of centuries of limited use. Ben Yehuda founded the Vaad Halashon Haivrit (Hebrew Language Council) in 1890 for the purpose of coining and creating new Hebrew words for modern usage. After the independence of Israel this body became the Akademiya Lalashon Haivrit (the Hebrew Language Academy). Hebrew made great strides among the pioneers who arrived in Palestine prior to 1948 and was well entrenched by the time of Israel's independence and the immigration to Israel of hundreds of thousands of new immigrants in the late 1940s and early 1950s who would have to learn Hebrew to become integrated into the society of the new state.

HEBREW UNIVERSITY. A prominent institution of higher learning located in Jerusalem (q.v.). Hebrew University was formally opened on April 1, 1925 on Mount Scopus (q.v.) and remained there until the War of Independence (q.v.) when in 1948 it became an enclave in Jordanian-held territory. The main focus of University life then was transferred to a new campus at Givat Ram. After Israel recaptured the surrounding areas and restored the Mount Scopus campus to the University during the Six Day War (q.v.), the University embarked on an ambitious scheme to dramatically increase its activities on the Mount Scopus campus. Judah Magnus (q.v.) was instrumental in the creation of the University, serving as its first president.

HEBRON (HEVRON). Sometimes referred to as Kiryat Arba (q.v.). A town southwest of Jerusalem (q.v.) in the hills of Judea (q.v.). It is one of the oldest cities in the world and played an important part in the ancient history of the Jewish people. It was the residence of the

Jewish patriarchs and served as King David's (q.v.) capital before he conquered Jerusalem. According to Jewish tradition Abraham (q.v.), Isaac, and Jacob and their wives (Sarah, Rebecca, and Leah) are buried in the cave of Machpela in Hebron. The traditional site of the cave, over which a mosque was erected, is one of the most sacred of Jewish shrines. Between Israel's War of Independence (q.v.) and the Six Day War, when Israel captured the city, Israelis had no access to the city or the cave. The Arabs call it Al Halil. The meaning of the name Al Halil is "the friend" or "lover," the nickname given to Abraham, considered a holy man in Islam, who lived and was buried in Hebron. His full nickname, Al Halil Al Rachman, means "the lover the God." In Isaiah's prophesy, God calls Abraham "my friend" (Isaiah, 41:8), and in the Book of Second Chronicles, he is called "Abraham, God's friend" (2 Chronicles, 20:7). In the Koran, it is written: ". . . saintly Abraham, whom Allah himself chose to be his friend [in Arabic: Ibrahim Hallilian]" (Koran, 4, Women, 125). The Jewish legend finds in the name Hebron a combination of the two words Haver-Naeh, meaning a nice company or friend, which alludes to Abraham, since it was said, "a nice friend—that is Abraham" (Genesis, 4:13).

HERUT PARTY (TENAUT HAHERUT—FREEDOM MOVEMENT). A political party founded by the Irgun (q.v.) in 1948 after the independence of Israel and the dissolution of the Irgun. Herut is descended from the Revisionist movement (q.v.) of Vladimir Zeev Jabotinsky (q.v.). The party was based largely on the members and supporters of the Irgun which grew out of the Revisionist (New Zionist) Organization (q.v.). The Revisionists advocated militant ultra-nationalistic action as the means to achieve Jewish statehood. Revisionism called for the creation of a Jewish state in "Greater Israel" (all Palestine (q.v.) and Jordan); rapid mass immigration of Jews into Palestine; formation of a free-enterprise economy; rapid industrialization—as opposed to agricultural settlements—to increase employment opportunities; a ban on strikes; and a strong army. In order to effect these policies, and because they were outnumbered by leftist and moderate elements in the World Zionist Organization (q.v.), the Revisionists formed the New Zionist Organization in 1935. Their rejection of the socialist and liberal Zionist leadership and its conciliatory policy toward the mandatory power led Revisionists to form two paramilitary groups: Irgun Tzvai Leumi (Etzel) (q.v.), founded in 1937, and the even more radical Lehi (Stern Gang) (q.v.), founded in 1939–40. The Irgun was commanded by Menachem Begin (q.v.) after 1943. Betar (q.v.), the Revisionist youth movement, was founded by Jabotinsky in 1920 and continues as the Herut youth wing. Begin founded Herut in June 1948 to advocate the Revisionist program within the new political context of the State of Israel. Herut's political orientation has changed little over the years. It advocates the "inalienable" right of Jews to settle anywhere in Israel, in its historic entirety, including Judea (q.v.) and Samaria (q.v.) (the West Bank). Herut advocates the unification of Eretz Israel (q.v.) within its historic boundaries and favors a national economy based on private initiative and free competition. Other policies include a minimum of economic controls, a restructured free enterprise system to attract capital investment, and the right to strike. Within Herut and Likud (q.v.), Menachem Begin was the primary force from Israel's independence until his retirement in 1983. He was regarded by many as a heroic figure because of his role as a leader of the underground in the Israeli struggle for independence. He was also a skillful politician and a charismatic figure. Upon Begin's retirement, Yitzhak Shamir (q.v.) became Prime Minister and party leader, although he was challenged within

Herut, especially by David Levy (q.v.) and Ariel Sharon (q.v.). In 1965 Herut combined with the Liberal Party (q.v.) to form Gahal (q.v.). In 1973 Gahal and several small parties combined to form Likud (q.v.).

HERZL, THEODOR. The founder of modern political Zionism (q.v.), he was the driving force in the creation of the political ideology and the worldwide movement that led to the establishment of Israel. He was born in Pest, Hungary on May 2, 1860. He was an assimilated Jew who later moved from Hungary to Vienna. He studied law but became involved in literature and wrote short stories and plays. He worked as the Paris correspondent of the Viennese daily newspaper *Neue Freie Presse* from 1891 to 1895. Growing anti-Semitism in France contributed to Herzl's interest in the Jewish problem. As a journalist, he observed the trial of Alfred Dreyfus (q.v.) and was affected by the false accusations leveled against the French Jewish army officer and by the episodes of anti-Semitism that accompanied the trial and the disgrace of Dreyfus. Herzl wrote *Der Judenstaat* (q.v.) (*The Jewish State*), published in Vienna in 1896, in which he assessed the situation and problems of the Jews and proposed a practical plan—the establishment of a Jewish state—for resolution of the Jewish question. Herzl argued: "Let the sovereignty be granted us over a portion of the globe large enough to satisfy the rightful requirements of a nation; the rest we shall manage for ourselves." Subsequently, Herzl traveled widely to publicize and gain support for his ideas. He found backing among the masses of East European Jewry and opposition among the leadership and wealthier segments of the Western Jewish communities.

On August 23, 1897, in Basle, Switzerland, Herzl convened the first World Zionist Congress representing Jewish communities and organizations throughout the world. The congress established the World Zionist

Organization (WZO) (q.v.) and founded an effective, modern, political, Jewish national movement with the goal, enunciated in the Basle Program (q.v.), the original official program of the WZO: "Zionism seeks to establish a home for the Jewish people in Palestine secured under public law." Zionism rejected other solutions to the "Jewish Question" and was the response to centuries of discrimination, persecution, and oppression. It sought redemption through self-determination. Herzl died in Austria on July 3, 1904, and he was buried in Vienna. In August 1949 his remains were reinterred on Mount Herzl (q.v.) in Jerusalem (q.v.).

HERZLIYA HIGH SCHOOL (GYMNASIA HERZL-IYA). First Hebrew (q.v.) High School in Palestine (q.v.). It was founded in Jaffa (q.v.) in 1905 for the purpose of providing a Jewish and secular education using Hebrew as the language of instruction. It was originally called the Gymnasia Ivrit of Jaffa and later renamed for Theodor Herzl (q.v.). It helped to educate generations of Jewish youth.

HERZOG, CHAIM. Born in Ireland in 1918, the son of Rabbi Isaac Halevi Herzog (q.v.), who later became the first Chief Rabbi of the State of Israel. He received an education in Ireland, at the University of London, at Cambridge, and at Hebron Yeshiva in Jerusalem (q.v.). He immigrated to Palestine (q.v.) in 1935. During World War II, he served in the British Army and became head of intelligence in the northern zone of Germany. During Israel's War of Independence (q.v.) in 1948, he served as an officer in the battle for Latrun (q.v.). He was Director of Military Intelligence (q.v.) from 1948 to 1950 and from 1959 to 1962. He served as military attaché in Washington from 1950–1954 and then became the commanding chief of the Jerusalem district from 1954–1957. He was Chief of Staff of the southern command from 1957–1959. After retiring from the army in 1962, he directed an industrial investment company. Beginning in 1967 with the Six Day War (q.v.), he was the leading military commentator for Israel Broadcasting Services. He was the first military commander of the West Bank (q.v.) after the Six Day War (q.v.). He served as Israel's representative at the United Nations from 1975 to 1978, and was elected to the Tenth Knesset (q.v.) in 1981. In 1983, he was elected President (q.v.) of Israel and was reelected in 1988.

HERZOG, ISAAC HALEVI. Chief Rabbi of Israel. He was born in Lomza, Russian Poland, in 1888 and died in Jerusalem (q.v.) in 1959. He was educated in England where he was ordained and attained a doctorate from the University of London. He served as a Rabbi in Belfast and became Chief Rabbi of the Irish Free State in 1925. He was chosen Chief Rabbi of Palestine (q.v.) in 1936. His son, Chaim Herzog (q.v.), became a significant figure in the Israel Defense Forces (q.v.), and became President (q.v.) of Israel, while his younger son, Jacob David Herzog, became an important figure in Israel's foreign policy and political establishment. See also CHIEF RABBINATE.

HEVRAT OVDIM. The cooperative association of all members of the Histadrut (q.v.) organized in 1923. It serves as the ultimate authority—legislative, supervisory, and managerial—for all of the Histadrut's economic enterprises, as well as their official legal framework. These enterprises are independent, with Hevrat Ovdim supervising management, authorizing plans, and overseeing operations.

HIBBAT ZION MOVEMENT see HOVEVE ZION

HILLEL, SHLOMO. Shlomo Hillel was born on April 23, 1923, the youngest of eleven children of a merchant in

Baghdad, Iraq. In 1933 he went to Palestine (q.v.) and studied at the Herzliya High School (q.v.) in Tel Aviv (q.v.). He was one of the founders of Kibbutz Maagen Michael. In 1946 he returned to Iraq to help organize the emigration of Iraqi Jews, and was active in the "illegal immigration" from Arab countries to pre-independence Israel. Following Israel's independence he was involved in the arrangements for the emigration in the early 1950s of virtually all of Iraq's Jewish community. He became a Mapai (q.v.) member of the Knesset (q.v.), but resigned in 1959. He joined the Israeli diplomatic corps and served as Israel's Ambassador to a number of French-speaking African countries and in 1963 became head of the African division of the Foreign Ministry. He became Minister of Police in December 1969 and served as Minister of Interior and Police from 1973 to 1977. In 1984 he was elected Speaker of the Eleventh Knesset. He was reelected to parliament in 1988.

HISTADRUT (GENERAL FEDERATION OF LABOR). The General Federation of Labor in Israel was founded in Haifa, Palestine (q.v.) in December 1920 as a federation of Jewish labor. It later admitted Arabs to full membership. The purpose was to unite and organize all workers, to raise their standard of living, and to defend their economic interests, as well as to represent their interests in other areas. It is the country's biggest employer, controlling some 60% of the country's industry. It controls the Hapoel sports organization, the Naamat women's organizations, and the biggest health insurance fund—Kupat Holim (q.v.). The Histadrut provides a wide range of services to its members. It cooperates with the government in numerous areas related to foreign and domestic policy and carries out many functions which are normally government activities in other modern states. Many of its leaders have served in major government posts (including that of

Prime Minister) before and after working in Histadrut. Its decision-making bodies are organized along partisan political lines, and the organization as a whole has long been closely aligned with the leaders and policies of the Israel Labor Party (q.v.).

The Histadrut's constitution stated: "The General Federation unites all workers in the land, as long as they live by their own toil without exploitation of another's labor, for the arrangement of all settlement and economic matters as well as cultural affairs of workers in the land, for the upbuilding of a Jewish workers' commonwealth in Eretz Israel." The convention also established a workers bank (now known as Bank Hapoalim), Israel's biggest. The Histadrut evolved into a major institution in the Yishuv and in the State of Israel.

The Histadrut has a number of elements. The General Convention is the supreme authority of the Histadrut and is its legislature. Its decisions bind all members and all units of the organization. It is elected once every four years in general, direct, secret, and proportional elections. The convention chooses the Council (Moetzet Hahistadrut) whose composition is based on and reflects the political makeup of the Convention. The Histadrut Council is the supreme institution of the Histadrut between conventions. The Histadrut Executive is the governing executive body. It is chosen by the Council in keeping with the party makeup of the Histadrut Convention. It chooses the Central Committee and the Secretary General. The Histadrut Central Committee is its Cabinet. It is chosen by the Executive and formally serves as its secretariat, conducting the day-to-day operations of the Labor Federation. It is composed only of members of the ruling coalition. The Histadrut Secretary General is chair of the Executive and of the Council and is extremely powerful. Among the more prominent early Secretaries General of the Histadrut were: David Ben-Gurion (q.v.) (1921–1935); David

Remez (1935–1945); Yosef Sprinzak (1945–1949); Pinhas Lavon (q.v.) (1945–1950, 1955–1961); Mordechai Namir (1951–1955); Aharon Becker (1961–1969); Yitzhak Ben-Aharon (1969–1973); Yeruham Meshel (1973–1984); and Israel Kessar (1984-) (q.v.).

HOLOCAUST (THE SHOAH). Its origins were in Germany in January 1933 when the Nazis took power. It ended with the surrender of Nazi Germany at the end of World War II in May 1945. The period of Nazi control of Germany saw increasingly negative actions against Jews in the territories under Nazi Germany's control—an ever-increasing area as Adolf Hitler's military successes conquered more and more countries, and their populations. Under Nazi Germany millions of European Jews lived in agony and fear and millions were tortured and killed. Israel remembers the Holocaust each year on the 27th day of Nisan of the Jewish calendar—known as Yom Hashoah. The Holocaust continues to have a major effect on Israel's collective psychology and on virtually every aspect of Israeli politics and foreign and security policy.

HOROWITZ, DAVID. Born on February 15, 1899 at Drogobych near Lvov in the Ukraine and educated at Lvov and Vienna, David Horowitz emigrated to Palestine (q.v.) in 1920. He became a member of the Executive Committee of the Histadrut (q.v.) in 1923, but also worked with a number of enterprises, served on government committees, and became director of the Economic Department of the Jewish Agency (q.v.). After Israel's independence Horowitz became director general of the Ministry of Finance. In 1954 he became Governor of the Bank of Israel (q.v.), a position in which he was responsible for the stability of Israel's currency at home and abroad and for the management of the public debt, among other functions.

HOVEVE ZION (LOVERS OF ZION). A movement that was established in 1882, as a direct reaction to the widespread pogroms in Russia (especially Odessa) in 1881, for the purpose of encouraging Jewish settlement in Palestine (q.v.) and achieving a Jewish national revival there. The founders concluded that the way to save the Jewish people was to return to Zion (q.v.) and rebuild the land. They generally favored practical Zionism (q.v.)—settlement in Israel. The members of the Hibbat Zion movement joined farm villages or established new ones (such as Rishon Le-Zion (q.v.), Zichron Yaakov, and Rosh Pina) in conformity with their view that immigration and settlement in Palestine would alleviate the problems of the communities in Europe.

HULEH VALLEY. A region in the upper and eastern portion of the Galilee (q.v.), bounding the Golan Heights (q.v.). Swamps were formed around Lake Huleh and were the cause of malarial conditions leading to high mortality rates and low living standards. Although earlier plans existed, Israel launched a major effort to drain the swamps beginning in 1951. By 1958 the project was concluded and successful; fertile land in the valley was reclaimed, water was made available for irrigation, and the threat of malaria was eliminated.

HURVITZ, YIGAEL. Born in Nahalat Yehuda in 1918, Yigael Hurvitz originally worked in agriculture, but became an industrialist. He was first elected to the Seventh Knesset (q.v.) in October 1969 on the State List (q.v.) and was reelected subsequently. He later served as chairman of the La'am Party (q.v.) faction of the Likud (q.v.). He became Minister of Industry, Commerce and Tourism in 1977, but resigned in September 1978. He replaced Simha Ehrlich (q.v.) as Minister of Finance in November 1979. He advocated hard-line economic policies, promoted austerity, and sought sharp cuts in subsidies, a reduction in civil service employment, some wage freezes, and other measures to reduce government expenditure. The Israeli pound was replaced by the shekel (the term drawn from the Bible), worth ten Israeli pounds. Hurvitz later resigned his position and left Likud, and was elected to the Knesset in 1981 on Moshe Dayan's (q.v.) Telem Party (q.v.) list. In 1984 he entered the Knesset as the leader of the Ometz (Courage) (q.v.) list. He served as Minister Without Portfolio in the Government of National Unity (q.v.) established in 1984. Hurvitz was elected to the Knesset on the Likud list in 1988.

- I -

IAI see ISRAEL AIRCRAFT INDUSTRIES

IDF see ISRAEL DEFENSE FORCES

IHUD. A Jewish group in Palestine (q.v.) during the British Mandate (q.v.) that advocated an Arab-Jewish bi-national state in Palestine. Judah Magnes (q.v.) believed that a determined effort should be made to avert a direct clash between Arabs and Jews. Along with others such as Martin Buber (q.v.), he helped to form, in 1942, a group called Ihud (Unity). It advocated a bi-national solution to the problem of Palestine and argued for that view before the United Nations Special Committee on Palestine (q.v.). After the establishment of Israel, Ihud (and Magnes) argued for the establishment of a confederation in the Middle East that would include Israel and Arab states.

IHUD HAKVUTZOT VEHAKIBBUTZIM. Founded in 1951 by the merger of Hever Hakvutzot with a group of kibbutzim (q.v.) that broke away from Hakibbutz Hameuhad (q.v.). It provides economic, organizational, and social services to the kibbutzim of the Oved Hatzioni and Poalei Agudat Israel (q.v.). Its members generally identify with the basic principles of the Israel Labor Party (q.v.).

IMMIGRATION see ALIYA

INDEPENDENCE, DECLARATION OF see DECLARATION OF INDEPENDENCE

INDEPENDENT LIBERAL PARTY (HALIBERALIM HAATZMAIM). A political party formed in 1965 by members of the Progressive (q.v.) faction in the Liberal Party (q.v.). The Liberal Party split when the majority decided to join with Herut (q.v.) to form Gahal (q.v.). Those who were concerned with the apparent rightward shift formed the new party. It contested the Knesset (q.v.) elections beginning in 1965, and joined in the governments led by Labor (q.v.) until 1977, when they lost their last Knesset seat. They later joined the Labor Alignment.

INGATHERING OF THE EXILES (KIBBUTZ GALUYOT). The concept that the exiled Jewish communites in the Diaspora (q.v.) would be gathered in Israel was derived from the Bible. The ingathering of the exiles became an important element in Zionism (q.v.) during the pre-State period and was enshrined in the Law of Return (q.v.) passed by the Knesset (q.v.) after independence. See ALIYA.

INTIFADA. Arab uprising in the West Bank (q.v.) and Gaza Strip (q.v.), which began in December 1987 in strong and violent opposition to continued Israeli occupation of those territories. The Palestinian uprising became a test of wills and policy between Palestinians in the territories occupied by Israel in the Six Day War (q.v.) and Israel. Israel sought to end the uprising and restore law and order in the West Bank and Gaza Strip. The Palestinians saw the uprising as a means to end Israeli occupation and to promote an independent Palestinian state. Palestinians sought to accelerate the political process and, in particular, to gain a representative role for the Palestine Liberation Organization (q.v.) in negotiations with Israel and the United States.

Confrontation and violence marked the evolution of the intifada with a growing toll of casualties on both sides. For the Palestinians the intifada seemed to provide a catharsis, but also a high cost in casualties, imprisonment, loss of education and employment, and growing divisions within the Palestinian population. For Israel the intifada posed a major challenge on a number of counts, including damage to its international image, divisions within the body politic on how to respond, the monetary costs of increased military reserve duty, and the costs of other disruptions of the economy.

The intifada began with a series of incidents (the stabbing to death of an Israeli by a Palestinian in Gaza City, a traffic accident in which four Palestinians were killed, and subsequent riots in the Jabaliya refugee camp) in early December 1987. Over the ensuing period the violence seemed to grow and to gain increasing international attention for the status of the Palestinians in the West Bank and Gaza Strip. Eventually Defense Minister Yitzhak Rabin (q.v.) argued that this was not classical terrorism, but civilian violence carried out by a considerable portion of the Palestinian population by means available to every individual, such as stones, Molotov cocktails, barricades, and burning tires. The difficulty was to devise a means to defuse the violence. For both sides the intifada became a test of political wills portending continuing confrontations over time.

IRAN. Iran, like Israel, is a non-Arab state located in the predominantly Arab Middle East. Iran opposed the creation of the Jewish state in the United Nations General Assembly vote in November 1947 on the Palestine Partition Plan (q.v.) but, subsequently, established diplomatic relations with Israel. During the reign of the Shah mutually beneficial relations developed between Israel and Iran that involved, among other activities, the sale of oil to Israel and Israeli assistance with various developmental projects in Iran. Positive, if low profile, political linkages were established. Following the Iranian Revolution, diplomatic relations between the two states were broken as the Islamic Republic of Iran established close formal links with the Palestine Liberation Organization (q.v.). Under the Ayatollah Khomeini, Iran called for the termination of the Jewish state and the liberation of Jerusalem (q.v.) from Israeli control. Hostility and vituperative rhetoric have been the hallmarks of Iran's approach to Israel since the accession of the Islamic Republican regime in Teheran.

IRAQ. An Arab state in the Middle East situated in the northeastern portion of the Arabian Peninsula on the Persian Gulf. Although Iraq does not border Israel, it has been an active participant in the Arab-Israeli conflict for much of the period since 1947, and has fought against Israel in Israel's War of Independence (q.v.), the Six Day War (q.v.), and the Yom Kippur War (q.v.). It remains in a state of war with Israel and has been associated with the Arab confrontation states. Iraq was among those Arab states that took the lead against Egyptian President Anwar Sadat's overtures to Israel in 1977 and 1978, it opposed the Egypt-Israel Peace Treaty of 1979 (q.v.), and it harbored and supported anti-Israel Palestinian terrorist groups. In 1981 Israel destroyed Iraq's Osirak nuclear reactor arguing it was developing nuclear weapons. At the same time, during the course of the Iran-Iraq War (from 1980 to the cease-fire of 1988), it was preoccupied with developments in the Gulf area and the cause against Israel became of much lesser consequence. With the end of Gulf hostilities, Israel became increasingly concerned about Iraqi intentions, particularly with the large size, capability and battle experience of Iraq's military, its ability and willingness to use missiles and chemical-biological warfare in its war with Iran, and its support of the Palestinian cause against Israel. The Iraqi attack against and occupation of Kuwait in August 1990 and the crisis which followed confirmed many Israeli fears. During the war between Iraq and the international coalition Iraq launched 39 Scud missiles against Israel that killed and wounded Israelis and caused substantial property damage. This unprovoked attack occasioned substantial concern and debate in Israel about an appropriate response. The government decided that it would accede to requests by the United States that it not respond militarily to the aggressive acts by Iraq.

IRGUN (IRGUN TZVAI LEUMI—ETZEL). Also called Hagana Bet. A Jewish military organization in Palestine (q.v.) formed in 1931 and headed by Abraham Tehomi (formerly Silber), organized on a military basis and stressed military training and discipline. In its early years, civilian backing was provided by a broadly based board consisting of representatives of all non-socialist parties in the Yishuv (q.v.). The rank and file of the organization consisted overwhelmingly of members of Betar (q.v.) and young Revisionists, but the Revisionist movement had at that stage no decisive influence over the body. In 1937 Tehomi reached an agreement with the Hagana (q.v.) for the merger of the two defense bodies. This led to a split in Etzel in April 1937. Etzel asserted that only active retaliation would deter the

Arabs. Its ideology, based on the teachings of Vladimir Zeev Jabotinsky (q.v.), was built on the principle that armed Jewish force was the prerequisite for the Jewish State and that every Jew had a natural right to enter Palestine. Irgun's first commander was Robert Bitker, who was succeeded by Moshe Rosenberg and then by David Raziel. Its symbol was a hand holding a rifle over the map of Palestine, including Transjordan, with the motto "rak kach" ("only thus"). The Jewish Agency (q.v.) strongly denounced Irgun's "dissident activities," which the British administration countered by suppression and mass arrests. Until May 1939, Irgun's activities were limited to retaliation against Arab attacks. After the publication of the British White Paper of 1939, the British Mandatory (q.v.) authorities became Irgun's main target. Another major field of activity was the organization of Aliya Bet (q.v.) (illegal immigration) and helping "illegal" immigrants land safely.

With the outbreak of World War II, Irgun announced the cessation of anti-British action and offered its cooperation in the common struggle against Nazi Germany. Its Commander in Chief, David Raziel, was killed in Iraq in May 1941 while leading Irgun volunteers on a special mission for the British. Raziel's successor was Yaakov Meridor (q.v.), who in turn was replaced by Menachem Begin (q.v.) in December 1943, who remained in command until 1948.

In January 1944, Irgun declared that the truce was over and that a renewed state of war existed with the British. Irgun demanded the liberation of Palestine from British occupation. Its attacks were directed against government institutions such as immigration, land registry, and income tax offices and police and radio stations. Limited cooperation was established in the late fall of 1945 between Irgun, Lehi (q.v.), and Hagana with the formation of the Hebrew Resistance movement. Cooperation between the three forces lasted, with occasional setbacks, until August 1946. On July 22, Etzel blew up the British Army headquarters and the Secretariat of the Palestine government in the King David Hotel in Jerusalem (q.v.).

When, after the United Nations adopted the Palestine Partition Plan (q.v.) on November 29, 1947, organized Arab bands launched murderous anti-Jewish attacks, Irgun vigorously counterattacked. Among these was the capture, on April 10, 1948 of the village of Deir Yassin by Irgun-Lehi forces, which resulted in 240 Arab civilian casualties.

When the State of Israel was proclaimed on May 14, Irgun announced that it would disband and transfer its men to the Israel Defense Forces (q.v.). For several weeks, however, until full integration was completed, Irgun formations continued to function as separate units.

On June 20, 1948, a cargo ship, the "Altalena" (q.v.), purchased and equipped in Europe by Irgun and its sympathizers, and carrying 800 volunteers and large quantities of arms and ammunition, reached Israel's shores. Irgun demanded that 20% of the arms be allocated to its still independent units in Jerusalem, but the Israeli government ordered the surrender of all arms and of the ship. When the order was not complied with, government troops opened fire on the ship, which consequently went up in flames off Tel Aviv. On September 1, 1948, the remaining units disbanded and joined the Israel Defense Forces.

IRGUN TZVAI LEUMI (NATIONAL MILITARY ORGANIZATION, ETZEL) see IRGUN

ISRAEL AIRCRAFT INDUSTRIES (IAI). Israel Aircraft Industries is the centerpiece of Israel's armaments industry. It has grown rapidly, from a company of less than a hundred employees when founded to more than twenty thousand by the 1980s. IAI produces a wide range of items, some under license, including aircraft (such as the Fouga-Magister), ammunition, armor, radar/sonar, and gyroscopes.

The idea to form an aircraft industry combining the special security needs of Israel with the development of industry originated in the Ministry of Defense during the 1950s. The reasons were that Israel's strategic situation depended on a capability to manufacture arms, the high costs of foreign-made arms, and the fear of an arms embargo. Maintenance was a problem for both the air force and El Al (q.v.), which was dependent upon maintenance facilities abroad. The need to establish an aeronautical and technological center in Israel was acute.

Al Shwimmer, an American aeronautical engineer who served in the Israeli air force, established a small factory in California called Intercontinental Airways, which dealt mainly with repairing old airplanes. In 1951, he met with Shimon Peres (q.v.), then the head of an Israeli arms acquisition delegation, and proposed that his company look for scrap metal for Mustang planes (which were then very popular in the Israeli air force), renovate the planes, and send them to Israel. The idea was broached to David Ben-Gurion (q.v.) who accepted it. Ben-Gurion proposed that Shwimmer relocate the factory to Israel. This was the beginning of Israel Aircraft Industries. Shwimmer submitted his proposal for the establishment of an aircraft industry to the Prime Minister. The proposal included two projects calling for: (1) the establishment of a base in Israel that would be able to repair and overhaul all types of aircraft, both military and civilian, including engines; and (2) the independent production of planes in Israel. The second project was not accepted by the government since it seemed unrealistic. The first, however, was to be fulfilled by creating Bedek, a company established in

1951 according to a special agreement between Shwimmer and the government. The factory grew quickly. In the early 1960s Bedek's management decided to proceed with the original proposal to attempt to produce new aircraft in Israel. Among the problems they encountered was the lack of a crystallized and experienced engineering body. This problem was reflected in the manufacturing of the Fuga and the "Stratocruiser." However, this problem was solved by the mid-1960s.

On March 31, 1968, Bedek was transformed from a subdivision of the Ministry of Defense to an independent company. It then was divided into three units: the Bedek-Metosim unit, which primarily dealt with the repair and rebuilding of airplanes; the aircraft manufacturing unit, which was focusing on the manufacture of new aircraft; and the engineering unit, which dealt with research and development. That same year, the company took upon itself, for the first time, the design and manufacture of a whole plane, the Arava, which was a light plane carrying up to 20 people that could land and take off on short runways. The Arava was produced in both a civilian and military version. In the early 1970s Bedek revised its goals and decided to produce a fighter plane. The first such plane was the Kfir.

Other than production and repair of aircraft, Israel Aircraft Industries also deals with the production of other sophisticated weapons systems, such as the Mazlat (the Hebrew acronym for pilotless aircraft). Among these weapons systems was the "Gabriel" (q.v.), a sea-to-sea missile. The Gabriel later became one of IAI's primary export items. In addition, IAI produces several ships, such as the Dabour class corvettes, armored vehicles, electrical and communication systems, helicopters, etc. Many of these products are produced by one of the company's numerous subsidiaries, including Alta, Tama, Mabat, Shahal, Pamal, and others.

ISRAEL BONDS see STATE OF ISRAEL BONDS

ISRAEL COMMUNISTS see COMMUNIST PARTY

ISRAEL DEFENSE FORCES (ZAHAL) (IDF). Israel's military is under a unified command of land, air, and sea forces. It is subject to the authority of the Government (q.v.) and carries out its policy. The Minister of Defense is in charge of the IDF. The Minister is a civilian, although he or she may have had a previous career in the professional military (e.g., Moshe Dayan (q.v.), Ezer Weizman (q.v.), and Yitzhak Rabin (q.v.)). A special ministerial committee generally headed by the Prime Minister deals with security matters on behalf of the government. Military service in the armed forces is compulsory and eligible men and women are drafted at 18. Men serve for three years, women for two. Men remain liable for reserve duty until 45 while women remain liable until they reach 24. Israel's Arab (q.v.) citizens are not required to serve but they can, and some do, volunteer. Druze (q.v.) men have been drafted into the IDF since 1957 at the request of their communities. The IDF is composed of a small standing force consisting of career officers, noncommissioned officers and draftees, as well as reserve officers. The reserve forces are regularly called to active status for training and service and they constitute the bulk of the military personnel. The IDF is responsible for the security of the country and its primary task is to defend the state from the enemy. Nevertheless, it performs other tasks which serve the public good. It helps in the absorption of new immigrants, the enhancement of education for recruits, and the provision of teachers to some developing areas.

ISRAEL-EGYPT DISENGAGEMENT OF FORCES AGREEMENT (1974). In late October 1973 the United Nations Security Council adopted Resolution 338 (q.v.),

which called for an immediate cease-fire in the Yom
Kippur War, the implementation of United Nations
Security Council Resolution 242 (q.v.), and explicitly
required negotiations "between the parties." Subsequently, United States Secretary of State Henry Kissinger negotiated the Israel-Egypt Disengagement of
Forces Agreement of 1974. It brought about the reaffirmation of the cease-fire achieved at the end of the
Yom Kippur War (q.v.), the disengagement and separation of Israeli and Egyptian military forces, and the
creation of disengagement zones between the opposing
forces.

ISRAEL LABOR PARTY (MIFLEGET HAAVODA HA-
ISRAELIT). On January 21, 1968 Mapai (q.v.) merged
with two other labor parties, Ahdut Haavoda (q.v.) and
Rafi (q.v.), to form the Israel Labor Party. The merger
of the labor parties did not eliminate the differences
between the coalition's components, but instead shifted
the quarrels to the intraparty sphere. It was within the
confines of the Labor Party that the problems of political
leadership and succession for the government of Israel
were resolved. Beginning with the 1969 Knesset (q.v.)
election, the Labor Party was joined in an election
alliance (the Alignment (q.v.)) with Mapam (q.v.),
although both parties retained their own organizational
structures and ideological positions. The new party
retained Labor's dominant position until 1977, when
lackluster leadership, corruption scandals, and the
founding of the Democratic Movement for Change
(q.v.) made way for the Likud (q.v.) victory. Likud was
also successful in 1981. In 1984, Shimon Peres (q.v.) was
given the mandate to form the new government. He
formed a Government of National Unity (q.v.) with
himself as Prime Minister for an initial period of two
years.

Labor's policies are Zionist (q.v.) and socialist. They

include: support for the immigration of Jews to Israel; establishment of a social welfare state; and a state-planned and publicly regulated economy with room for the participation of private capital, full employment, minimum wages, and the right to strike. Labor stands for the separation of religion and the state, although it has historically made major concessions to the religious parties in this area. It supports equality for minorities, including the Arabs of Israel (q.v.), and believes in a negotiated settlement with the Arab states without prior conditions, i.e., it has not rejected the possibility of returning some of the occupied territories (q.v.) to Arab sovereignty. It has pursued the "Jordan option" (q.v.) as the preferred means of achieving peace. Shimon Peres is the party's head. Peres, once an ally of Moshe Dayan (q.v.) and David Ben-Gurion (q.v.) in Rafi, served as Defense Minister in Rabin's government (1974–77). In 1984, he became Prime Minister in the National Unity Government. Yitzhak Rabin remains Peres's chief rival for the leadership of the Labor Party and the Alignment. A former Prime Minister, Chief of Staff during the Six Day War (q.v.), and former ambassador to the United States, Rabin served as Minister of Defense in the Government of National Unity formed in 1984 and continued in that position in the government formed in December 1988. Peres became Minister of Finance in December 1988 when Labor again joined with Likud to form the government. Disagreements between Labor and Likud over various issues of domestic and foreign policy marked the tenure of the government and reached a climax in the spring of 1990. In a dispute over the appropriate response to the United States' efforts to develop further movement toward an Arab-Israeli settlement, Shamir dismissed Shimon Peres from the government and the other Labor ministers resigned. A subsequent vote of no confidence terminated the government and Shimon Peres, on behalf of Labor, was given the opportunity to form a government but ultimately failed and the mandate was given to Shamir. Rabin challenged Peres's leadership of the party in the summer of 1990 but failed to oust him.

ISRAEL-LEBANON AGREEMENT OF MAY 17, 1983. In the wake of the War in Lebanon (q.v.) in 1982, Israel engaged in negotiations with Lebanon under the auspices of the United States, concerning the withdrawal of foreign forces from Lebanon and related arrangements. After months of discussion, an agreement was reached. The May 17, 1983 agreement provided for the withdrawal of Israeli forces from Lebanon and noted that "they consider the existing international boundary between Israel and Lebanon inviolable." Israel committed itself to withdraw from southern Lebanon in return for specific security arrangements in the south and some elements of normalization approaching, but not quite becoming, a peace treaty. It was an important milestone in Israel's relations with the Arab states. Although signed and ratified by both states, Lebanon abrogated the agreement in March 1984 under heavy pressure from Syria.

ISRAEL PHILHARMONIC ORCHESTRA. Originally the Palestine Orchestra, it opened its first season in 1936 with Arturo Toscanini conducting. It has grown in stature since and is based at the Heichal Hatarbut in Tel Aviv (q.v.).

ISRAEL PRIZE. An award given by the Israel Ministry of Education and Culture on Independence Day annually for outstanding achievement in various fields, including Jewish studies, Torah, humanities, sciences, and the arts.

ISRAEL-SYRIA DISENGAGEMENT OF FORCES AGREEMENT (1974). An agreement between Syria and Israel achieved in May 1974 through the shuttle diplomacy of United States Secretary of State Henry Kissinger. It brought about the reaffirmation of the cease-fire achieved at the end of the Yom Kippur War (q.v.), the disengagement and separation of Israeli and Syrian military forces on the Golan Heights (q.v.), and the creation of disengagement zones between the opposing armies.

ISRAELI ARABS see ARABS IN ISRAEL; DRUZE

- J -

JABOTINSKY, VLADIMIR ZEEV. Born in Odessa, Russia in 1880, Vladimir Jabotinsky was the founder of the World Union of Zionist Revisionists in 1925, which later branched off into the New Zionist Organization (q.v.). The union advocated the establishment of a Jewish state, increased Jewish immigration, and militant opposition to the British Mandatory (q.v.) authorities in Palestine (q.v.). His philosophy provided the ideological basis for the Herut Party (q.v.). He studied law in Bern and Rome, but became interested in the Zionist cause with the growth of pogroms in Russia. After the beginning of World War I Jabotinsky promoted the idea of a Jewish Legion (q.v.) as a component of the British army and he later joined it. In March 1921 he joined the Zionist Executive but resigned in January 1923 because of dissatisfaction with British policy and with lack of resistance to the British anti-Zionist policy. In 1923 Jabotinsky founded Brit Trumpeldor (Betar) (q.v.) and in 1925 the World Union of Zionists-Revisionists was formed in Paris and he became President. Jabotinsky later seceded from the World Zionist Organization (q.v.) and founded (in Vienna in 1935) the New Zionist Organization, of which he became President. He campaigned against the British plans for the partition of

Palestine and advocated and promoted illegal Jewish immigration to Palestine. He died in New York in 1940. Jabotinsky's remains were transferred to Israel and reburied on Mount Herzl (q.v.) in Jerusalem (q.v.) in July 1964. His influence on Israel's history and politics is substantial as indicated by his role as the ideological forebear of the Herut (q.v.) and Likud (q.v.) political parties and especially in the influence of his ideas on the thinking and policies of Menachem Begin (q.v.) and Yitzhak Shamir (q.v.).

JAFFA (YAFO). An ancient city adjoining Tel Aviv and with which it merged in 1950 to form the city of Tel Aviv-Yafo (q.v.), Jaffa is one of the oldest seaport cities in the world. Ancient Egyptian records confirm its existence and it has been an important seaport since Biblical times, when it was called Joppa by the Greeks. Most of the Arab population of the city fled during Israel's War of Independence (q.v.).

JARRING, GUNNAR. Then Swedish Ambassador to the USSR who was appointed by United Nations Secretary General U Thant in November 1967 as a Special Representative to assist in Arab-Israeli peace efforts based on the principles in United Nations Security Council Resolution 242 (q.v.) of November 22, 1967.

JERICHO. Located northwest of the northern end of the Dead Sea (q.v.). Ancient Jericho is considered by some to be the oldest city in the world—dating back to 7,000 BC. It is mentioned in the Bible and was conquered by the Israelites led by Joshua when they entered the Land of Canaan (q.v.). The city has been built and rebuilt throughout the centuries.

JERUSALEM. Jerusalem is Israel's largest city and its declared capital. It is a Holy City of Jews, Christians, and Muslims. In 1947 when the United Nations voted to partition Palestine (q.v.) into a Jewish state and an Arab state, Jerusalem was to be internationalized. However, the city was divided between Jordan (East Jerusalem, including the walled city) and Israel (West Jerusalem, the new city) during Israel's War of Independence (q.v.). Israel made its portion of Jerusalem its capital. Nevertheless, most countries did not accept that decision and many retained their embassies in Tel Aviv. In the Six Day War (q.v.) Israel gained control of East Jerusalem and merged it with the western portion of the city.

On July 30, 1980 the Knesset (q.v.) passed the Basic Law (q.v.): Jerusalem, Capital of Israel, 5740–1980. It declared: "Jerusalem united in its entirety is the capital of Israel. Jerusalem is the seat of the President of the State, the Knesset, the Government and the Supreme Court. The Holy Places shall be protected from desecration and any other violation and from anything likely to violate the freedom of access of the members of the different religions to the places sacred to them or their feelings with regard to those places." It also provided that the government would work for the development and prosperity of the city and the welfare of its inhabitants and would give special priority to this activity.

West Jerusalem is the modern part of the city. East Jerusalem includes the walled old city, the site of many ancient Holy Places. Jews consider Jerusalem a Holy City because it was their political and religious center in Biblical times. About 1000 BC King David (q.v.) made Jerusalem the capital of the united Israelite tribes. David's son, King Solomon (q.v.), built the first Temple of the Jews in the city. Christians consider Jerusalem holy because Jesus was crucified there and many events in his life took place in the city. Muslims believe that Muhammed, the founder of Islam, ascended to heaven from Jerusalem, and the city is the third holiest in Islam after Mecca and Medina in Saudi Arabia. The city is the site of numerous Holy Places. Among the more prominent are the Wailing Wall (q.v.) and the Church of the Holy Sepulcher (which is believed to stand on the hill of Calvary, or Golgotha, where Jesus was crucified and buried). The Church is shared by several Christian sects, and the Dome of the Rock (which stands near the Wailing Wall) was built over the rock from which, according to Muslim belief, Muhammed rose to heaven. In Jewish tradition it was on this rock that Abraham (q.v.) prepared to sacrifice his son Isaac as God commanded.

JERUSALEM POST. English-language daily newspaper founded in 1932 in Jerusalem (q.v.) as the *Palestine Post.* Its founding editor was Gershon Agron. It has no formal political party affiliation. It was renamed the *Jerusalem Post* on April 23, 1950.

JEWISH AGENCY (JEWISH AGENCY FOR PALESTINE, JEWISH AGENCY FOR ISRAEL). Established in the 1920s under the terms of the Palestine Mandate (q.v.) to advise and cooperate with the British authorities in the task of establishing the Jewish National Home in Palestine (q.v.). Article 4 of the Mandate for Palestine provided for the recognition of an appropriate "Jewish Agency" as a "public body for the purpose of advising and cooperating with the Administration of Palestine in such economic, social and other matters as may affect the establishment of the Jewish National Home and the interests of the Jewish population in Palestine, and subject always to the control of the Administration, to assist and take part in the development of the country." Article 6 of the Mandate stipulated that the British administration of Palestine should, "in cooperation with the Jewish Agency," encourage settlement by Jews on the land. Article 11 provided that the administration might arrange with the Jewish Agency "to construct or operate, upon fair and equitable terms, any public works, services and utilities, and to develop any of the natural resources of the country, insofar as these matters are not directly undertaken by the Administration." The Mandate itself recognized the World Zionist Organization (WZO) (q.v.) as such Jewish Agency (article 4) and directed the WZO to "take steps in consultation with His Britannic Majesty's Government to secure the cooperation of all Jews who are willing to assist in the establishment of the Jewish National Home." The WZO, on its part, undertook to take steps to secure such cooperation.

The Zionist Organization performed its functions until a Jewish Agency for Palestine (which included non-Zionist and Zionist Jews) was formally constituted in 1929. It provided the apparatus for worldwide Jewish participation in the building of the Jewish home in Palestine. The Jewish Agency worked with the government of the Yishuv (q.v.) and, particularly, with the Vaad Leumi (q.v.). Generally, the Agency promoted immigration, settlement, economic development, and mobilized support for Jewish efforts in Palestine. Its political department acted as the "foreign ministry" of the quasi-government in Palestine. It negotiated with the Palestine Government and Great Britain, and it represented the cause of the Jewish national home before appropriate organs of the League of Nations and the United Nations. The Jewish Agency's officials, along with those of the Vaad Leumi and other organs of the Yishuv, provided Israel's ministries with a trained core of civil servants and political leaders. David Ben-Gurion (q.v.), who served as Israel's first Prime Minister and Minister of Defense, was Chairman of the Executive of the Jewish Agency and Moshe Shertok (later Sharett) (q.v.), was a director of the Agency's political department. One of the main tasks of the Jewish Agency during the period of the British administration of Palestine was to represent the Zionist movement and world Jewry at large before the Mandatory government, the League of Nations, and the British government in London. It also served as part of the governing structure of the Yishuv. It promoted Zionism, encouraged and facilitated immigration, raised funds, engaged in social-welfare activities, promoted Jewish culture, developed economic enterprises, and formulated domestic and external policies for the Jewish community.

It was realized long before May 15, 1948 that the future independent and sovereign Jewish state would be fully responsible for the conduct of its domestic and foreign affairs and that some functions hitherto exercised by the Jewish Agency would have to be transferred to the state. On the other hand, it was obvious that the state would not and could not deal with all matters that had been in the purview of the Jewish Agency (in particular, immigration, absorption of immigrants, and settlement), not only for financial reasons but also because they were global Jewish responsibility and not an internal affair of Israel. It was felt that the Jewish Agency would be needed to express the partnership of the Jewish people all over the world with Israel in the historic enterprise of building the State and to channel and utilize properly the aid that was expected and forthcoming from Diaspora (q.v.) Jewry.

The Jewish Agency/World Zionist Organization, even though nongovernmental, performs functions instrumental to Zionism and important to the government's activities; its personnel often move to and from positions of responsibility within the government. Upon independence the government of Israel began to assume many of the functions previously performed by this institution and formalized its relationship with it through legislation and administrative decisions. The Jewish Agency today is responsible for the organization of Jewish immigration to Israel; the reception, assistance, and settlement of immigrants; care of children; and aid to cultural projects and institutions of higher learning. It fosters Hebrew education and culture in the Diaspora, guides and assists Zionist youth movements, and organizes the work of the Jewish people in support of Israel.

The mutual relations of the state and the Jewish Agency were put on a firm legal basis by the Law on the Status of the World Zionist Organization—Jewish Agency of 5713 (1952), Article 4 of which declares: "The State of Israel recognized the WZO as the authorized agency that will continue to operate in the State of Israel for the development and settlement of the country, the absorption of immigrants from the diaspora and the coordination of the activities in Israel of Jewish institutions and organizations active in those fields." After the Six Day War (q.v.) of 1967 it was suggested that while the WZO-Jewish Agency should remain in charge of immigration, the absorption and integration of immigrants should become largely a responsibility of the government. A new Ministry for the Absorption of Immigrants was established.

JEWISH BRIGADE. Established formally by a decision of the British government in September 1944 to join in the Allied fight against the Axis in World War II. Its origins go back to 1939 when some 130,000 Palestinian Jews registered as volunteers for military service against the Axis. During the war the members of the unit served in various capacities in the fight against Nazi Germany and its allies.

JEWISH LEGION. Military units formed by Jewish volunteers in World War I to fight alongside British troops for the liberation of Palestine (q.v.) from the Turks.

JEWISH NATIONAL FUND (KEREN KAYEMET LE ISRAEL). Various organizations and units were created to carry on the work of the World Zionist Organization (q.v.), including the Jewish National Fund (JNF), founded in 1901 at the Fifth Zionist Congress and charged with land purchase and development in Palestine (q.v.). It now focuses on afforestation and reclamation of land in Israel. In 1960 the Knesset passed the Israel Land Administration Act which transferred ownership of the land owned by the Keren Kayemet to the State of Israel.

THE JEWISH STATE see *DER JUDENSTAAT*

JEZREEL VALLEY. Known also as the Plain of Esdraelon. It separates the Galilee (q.v.) from Samaria (q.v.) and is Israel's most extensive valley. It is Israel's major granary and has been settled since ancient times.

JOINT EMERGENCY COMMITTEE. A Joint Emergency Committee, composed of members of the Executive of the Jewish Agency (q.v.) and the Vaad Leumi (National Council) (q.v.) of the Jewish community in Palestine (q.v.), was formed in the autumn of 1947, at which time the United Nations was considering the future of the Palestine Mandate (q.v.) and it had become obvious that the British were intent on withdrawal. The Committee was formed to make appropriate arrangements for the transfer of power from the Mandatory administration to the government of the proposed Jewish State and it sought to fill the void created by the disintegration of the British role. It drafted a legal code and a proposed constitution; it developed a roster of experienced civil servants willing to serve the future government; and it instituted vigorous recruitment for the Hagana (q.v.) to preserve the security of the Jewish community of Palestine. It disbanded in March 1948 and was succeeded by the Peoples Council, which became the *de facto* government of Israel upon independence.

JORDAN (FORMERLY TRANSJORDAN). The Hashemite Kingdom of Jordan is Israel's neighbor to the east with which it has fought in several wars and with which it is often seen as being in a *de facto* state of peace. Following the War of Independence (q.v.), Jordan and Israel signed an Armistice Agreement (q.v.) which established the frontiers between the two states during the period from 1949 to 1967. During the war Jordan occupied a portion of the territory of the Palestine Mandate (q.v.) that had been allocated to the Arab state of Palestine and retained control of that area which became known as the West Bank (q.v.). It later annexed that territory. The frontier between the two states varied from peaceful to one across which raids and reprisals took place. Jordan joined in the Arab fighting against Israel in the Six Day War (q.v.) during which time Israel took control of the West Bank and East Jerusalem (q.v.) from Jordan, but abstained during both the Sinai War (q.v.) and the War of Attrition (q.v.). During the Yom Kippur War (q.v.) King Hussein committed only token forces to the battle against Israel and these fought alongside Syrian troops in the Golan Heights (q.v.).

Negotiations between senior Israeli officials and King Abdullah took place prior to the creation of Israel and substantial high level contacts between the two states have continued over the years since. The open bridges policy (q.v.) of Moshe Dayan (q.v.) increased the flow of people and goods across the Jordan River between Jordan and Israel. Numerous other contacts of various kinds at various levels and on numerous themes have taken place. The concept of a Jordanian option (q.v.) has assumed that Jordan could represent the Palestinians as a means of resolving the Arab-Isareli conflict (q.v.).

JORDAN OPTION. An approach to a peaceful resolution of the Arab-Israeli conflict which suggested that Israel and Jordan would negotiate to determine the future of the West Bank (Judea and Samaria, q.v.) and Gaza (q.v.) since Jordan had been the power controlling the West Bank and appeared amenable to possible participation in a peace process. It has been a major element of Labor Party (q.v.) policy.

JORDAN RIVER. The Jordan, some 205 miles long, flows north to south through the Sea of Galilee (q.v.) and ends in the Dead Sea (q.v.) and forms the boundary between Palestine (q.v.) and Transjordan. The Jordan originates in the snows and rains of Mount Hermon (q.v.) and its sources are the Hasbani River (in Lebanon), the Banias River in Syria, and the Dan in Israel.

JORDANIAN OPTION see JORDAN OPTION

JUDAH see JUDEA

JUDEA. The Kingdom of Judah (Judea) maintained its capital at Jerusalem until 586 BC, when the Babylonians destroyed the Temple, ended the kingdom, and took the leadership and much of the Jewish population in exile to Babylon. Under Cyrus of Persia the Jews were allowed to return to Jerusalem, and the rebuilding of the Temple began.

JUDEA AND SAMARIA. Terms used in Israel to refer to the West Bank.

JUNE WAR (1967) see SIX DAY WAR

- K -

KACH (THUS). A political party on the extreme right of Israel's political spectrum founded and led by Rabbi Meir Kahane (q.v.) until his death. It is essentially a secular nationalist movement that focuses on the Arab challenges to Israel and its Jewish character. In the 1984 election, after failure in previous attempts, Kach succeeded in gaining nearly twenty-six thousand votes and a seat in the Knesset (q.v.). Kahane had campaigned on a theme of "making Israel Jewish again" by seeking the expulsion of the Arabs from Israel, as well as from the West Bank (q.v.) and Gaza (q.v.). Initially, the party was banned from participation in the election by the Central Elections Committee, but the ruling was reversed by the Supreme Court (q.v.)—a move that gained the party additional publicity and probably facilitated its efforts to secure a Knesset seat. Despite Kahane's success in the '84 elections he was considered an extremist, even by many on the right, and his political ideology and programs remain marginal in Israel and are considered by the majority of Israelis in that vein. He was ruled out as a political ally and coalition partner by all the major factions in the Knesset, including Tehiya (q.v.). Kach was banned from participation in the 1988 Knesset election by the Central Elections Committee on the grounds that it was racist. After the murder of Rabbi Kahane, Rabbi Avraham Toledano was chosen as his successor in March 1991.

KAHAN COMMISSION OF INQUIRY. Toward the end of the War in Lebanon (q.v.) Christian Phalangist forces massacred Palestinians at the Sabra and Shatila (q.v.) refugee camps in the Beirut area. Some alleged that the Israeli Army should have known and could have prevented the massacres since the camps were within the Army's supposed range of control. The resultant anguish within Israel led to the decision to create a Commission of Inquiry. At a meeting of the Cabinet on September 28, 1982 the Government of Israel decided to establish a Commission of Inquiry. "The matter which will be subjected to inquiry is: all the facts and factors connected with the atrocity carried out by a unit of the Lebanese Forces against the civilian population in the Shatila and Sabra camps.'' The Commission of Inquiry consisted of Yitzhak Kahan, President of the Supreme Court (q.v.) who served as Commission Chairman; Aharon Barak, Justice of the Supreme Court; and Yona Efrat, a reserve Major General in the Israel Defense Forces (q.v.). Its final report was issued in February 1983. Among other recommendations it was suggested that Major General Yehoshua Saguy not continue as Director of Military Intelligence (q.v.) and that Division Commander Brigadier General Amos Yaron not serve in the capacity of a field commander in the Israel Defense Forces. Among other results of the report and recommendations was the resignation of Ariel Sharon (q.v.) as Minister of Defense.

KAHANE, RABBI MEIR. He was born in Brooklyn, New York, in 1932, the son of an Orthodox Rabbi, and became an ordained Rabbi in the 1950s. In 1946 he joined Betar (q.v.). He studied at the Mirrer Yeshiva in Brooklyn and later attended Brooklyn College and then studied law at New York University. He founded the Jewish Defense League in 1968 as a response to vicious outbreaks of anti-Semitism in New York and a perceived need to change the Jewish image. The Jewish Defense League became known for its violent methods, especially those designed to call attention to the plight of Soviet Jewry. He moved to Israel in 1971. In Israel he was arrested numerous times and served some months in prison in 1981 under preventive detention for threatening violence against Palestinian protesters in the West Bank (q.v.). He headed the Kach party (q.v.) which he founded. He was elected to the Knesset (q.v.) in 1984. A prolific author, Kahane advocated the necessity of retaining Israel's Jewish character as its first priority. Thus, he proposed that the Arabs should leave Israel and go to other locations in the Arab world because of the violence they have perpetrated against the Jews, and because their growing numbers would threaten the Jewish nature of the Israeli state. Kahane was assassinated while on a speaking engagement in New York City in the fall of 1990.

KAPLAN, ELIEZER. Born in Minsk, Russia in 1891. He was educated in Russia and became active in Zionist affairs. He visited Palestine (q.v.) briefly in 1920 and settled there in 1923. In 1933 he became a member of the Executive of the Jewish Agency (q.v.), becoming the head of its Finance and Administrative Department. He was a central figure in the planning and organizing of economic and development projects in Palestine. After the independence of Israel he became the first Minister of Finance and later Deputy Prime Minister. He died in Genoa, Italy while on a trip in 1952.

KATZAV, MOSHE. Born in 1945 in Iran, he graduated from the Hebrew University of Jerusalem (q.v.) and served as mayor of Kiryat Malachi. He was first elected to the Knesset (q.v.) in 1977. He was Minister of Labor and Social Affairs in the National Unity Government (q.v.) established in 1984 and became Minister of Transport in the government established in December 1988. He retained the latter position in the Shamir-led (q.v.) government established in June 1990.

KATZIR (FORMERLY KATCHALSKI), EPHRAIM. Born in Kiev, Russia on May 16, 1916. He was brought to Palestine (q.v.) by his parents in 1922 and was educated at Hebrew University of Jerusalem (q.v.), where he received his master's degree in 1937 and his doctorate in 1941. From 1941 to 1948 he held posts at Hebrew University and as a research fellow at Brooklyn Polytechnic Institute and at Columbia University. During Israel's War of Independence (q.v.) he headed the science corps of the Hagana (q.v.). In 1949 he joined the Department of Biophysics at the Weizmann Institute of Science (q.v.) in Rehovot and became department head. He did research on proteins and polyamino acids and is a member of numerous scientific organizations. He became President (q.v.) of Israel in April 1973 and remained in that post until 1978. In keeping with government policy that government officials adopt Hebrew names, he changed his name from Katchalski to Katzir. In 1978 he became the head of the Center for Biotechnology at Tel Aviv University (q.v.) and a professor at the Weizmann Institute.

KATZ-OZ, AVRAHAM. Born in Tel Aviv (q.v.) in 1934 and a member of Kibbutz Nahal Oz. He was educated at the Hebrew University (q.v.) where he received an MSc in agriculture. He has been a Labor Alignment (q.v.) member of the Knesset (q.v.) since 1981. He became Minister of Agriculture in the government established in December 1988.

KEREN HAYESOD (PALESTINE FOUNDATION FUND). The major fund-raising and financial institution of the World Zionist Organization (q.v.) that financed its activities in Palestine (q.v.). The 1920 Zionist conference created the fund to finance immigration to Palestine and rural settlement there and in March 1921 it was registered as a British company. In the subsequent years it was the agency that funded the building of the Jewish State in Palestine and Israel. Its funds came from contributions and financed activities in the areas of immigration, absorption, settlement, water resource development, and economic investment. Keren Hayesod was incorporated as an Israeli company by a special act of the Knesset (q.v.), the Keren Hayesod Law of January 18, 1956.

KEREN KAYEMET LE ISRAEL see JEWISH NATIONAL FUND

KESSAR, ISRAEL. Born in 1931 in Sana, Yemen. He immigrated to Palestine (q.v.) in 1933 and was educated in Jerusalem (q.v.). He received a BA in economics and sociology and an MA in labor studies from Tel Aviv University (q.v.). Beginning in 1984 he served as a Member of the Knesset (q.v.) on the Maarach (q.v.) list and as Secretary General of the Histadrut (q.v.).

KHARTOUM ARAB SUMMIT. At the Khartoum Arab Summit at the end of the summer of 1967, the Arab states agreed to unite their efforts "to eliminate the effects of the [Israeli] aggression" in the Six Day War (q.v.) and to secure Israeli withdrawal from the occupied territories within the framework of "the main principles" to which they adhere: "no peace with Israel, no recognition of Israel, no negotiation with it, and adherence to the rights of the Palestinian people in their country."

KIBBUTZ. The kibbutz (a word meaning collective settlement that comes from the Hebrew (q.v.) for group) is a socialist experiment—a voluntary grouping of individuals who hold property in common and have their needs satisfied by the commune. Every kibbutz member participates in the work. All the needs of the members, including education, recreation, medical care, and vacations, are provided by the kibbutz. The earliest kibbutzim (plural of kibbutz) were founded by pioneer immigrants from Eastern Europe who sought to join socialism and Zionism (q.v.) and thus build a new kind of society. They have been maintained by a second and third generation as well as by new members. Initially, the kibbutzim focused on the ideal of working the land and became known for their crops, poultry, orchards, and dairy farming. As modern techniques, especially automation, were introduced and as land and water became less available, many of the kibbutzim shifted their activities or branched out into new areas, such as industry and tourism, to supplement the agricultural pursuits. Kibbutz factories now manufacture electronic products, furniture, plastics, household appliances, farm machinery, and irrigation-system components. See also HAKIBBUTZ HAARTZI, HAKIBBUTZ HAMEUHAD, IHUD HAKVUTZOT VEHAKIBBUTZIM, and UNITED KIBBUTZ MOVEMENT.

KING-CRANE COMMISSION. At the time of World War I, perhaps the most significant American concern and its first political involvement in the Middle East was the formation of an investigating commission that was sent to the region and offered suggestions concerning its future. At a meeting of the Big Four in March 1919, Wilson proposed that a commission visit Syria to elucidate the state of opinion in the region and report on its findings to the peace conference. The United States sent two Americans, Henry C. King, President of Oberlin College, and Charles R. Crane, a manufacturer, to the area but neither the British nor the French joined the commission. The King-Crane Commission was the first significant American involvement in the political affairs of the area although, in the final analysis, the inquiry had no real impact. Neither the Allies nor the United States gave it serious consideration. King and Crane arrived in Palestine (q.v.) in June 1919, conducted interviews and studied reports and documents. In August the Commission submitted its report to the American delegation for use at the peace conference. Generally, it argued against the Zionist objectives and sought to include Palestine within a larger Syrian mandate that would include Lebanon and Palestine.

KING DAVID see DAVID

KING SAUL see SAUL

KING SOLOMON see SOLOMON

KIRYAT ARBA. A Jewish settlement established at Hebron after the Six Day War (q.v.). The name Kiryat Arba or Kiryat Haarbah, is mentioned in the Bible: "Kiryat Arba, that is Hebron" (Joshua, 15:54), "Hebron, formally called Kiryat Arba" (Judges, 1:10), "Kiryat Arba, that is Hebron" (Genesis, 35:27), and "some of the men of Judah lived in Kiryat Arba and its villages" (Nehemiah, 11:25). In the Cave of Machpela in Hebron are the tombs of Abraham (q.v.), Isaac and Jacob and their wives (Sarah, Rebecca and Leah, respectively). An old Jewish tradition has it that this cave is also the burial place of Adam and Eve who lived in Hebron after their banishment from the Garden of Eden. The name Kiryat Arba (Town of the Four) was chosen to allude to the four pairs who are buried there.

KITCHEN CABINET. Although the Cabinet has been the primary policy-making body of Israel and it decides Israel's policies in all areas of activity subject to the approval of the Knesset (q.v.), at times much of the Cabinet's work has been conducted by a small and select group of ministers meeting informally. When Golda Meir (q.v.) was Prime Minister these informal meetings generally were referred to as the kitchen cabinet.

KNESSET (PARLIAMENT). The Knesset is the supreme authority in the state, and its laws are theoretically the source of all power and authority, although in reality decisions are made by the Prime Minister and the Government (or Cabinet) (q.v.) and ratified. The Knesset's name is derived from the Knesset Hagedola (q.v.) (Great Assembly), the supreme legislative body of the Jewish people after the Biblical period and prior to the Maccabean Revolt. The modern body is based, to a large extent, on the British model, adapted to Israel's needs and special requirements. It is a unicameral body of 120 members elected for four-year terms by general, national, direct, equal, secret, and proportional suffrage in accordance with the Knesset Elections Law. Citizens may be elected to the Knesset if they are at least 21 years of age. The entire country elects all members; there are no separate constituencies. This system derives from that used by the World Zionist Organization (WZO) (q.v.) and the Histadrut (q.v.) and other elements in the Yishuv (q.v.) prior to Israel's independence. All Israeli citizens age 18 and over may vote in Knesset elections without regard to sex, religion, or other factors, unless deprived of that right by a court of law. Voters cast their ballots for individual parties, each with rival lists of candidates, rather than for individual candidates. Each party may present the voter with a list of up to 120 names—its choices for Knesset seats. An important part of the Knesset's work is done within the framework of its major committees: House Committee, Finance Committee, Economics Committee, Foreign Affairs and Defense Committee, Internal Affairs and Environment Committee, Constitution, Law and Justice Committee, Immigration and Absorption Committee, Education and Culture Committee, Labor and Welfare Committee, and State Control Committee.

KNESSET ELECTIONS. The Knesset (q.v.) is elected every four years, but may dissolve itself and call for new elections before the end of its term. Elections to the Knesset are general, nationwide, direct, equal, secret, and proportional. The entire country is a single constituency. According to the Basic Law: The Knesset (1958/5718) (q.v.), every citizen is eligible to vote from age 18, provided the courts have not deprived the individual of this right by law, and to be elected from age 21. Prior to elections, each party presents its list of candidates and its platform. There is no rule regarding the way candidates are to be chosen and the order in which they are to be presented in each list, since this is the sole prerogative of the parties or the groups submitting the list. Some parties make use of an organizing committee, while others select candidates in the party centers or in the branches. In some instances the person at the head of the list decides who should follow him on the list and in what order, while in others secret elections are held beforehand, with the participation of all the members of the group or party in question. In recent years lists comprising several parties generally reserve certain places on the lists for each of the parties they contain, each such party filling those places in its own way or according to its own regulations.

Parties represented in the outgoing Knesset are automatically eligible to stand for reelection. Additional parties may stand for election, provided they obtain the requisite number of signatures of eligible voters and deposit a bond, which is refunded if they succeed in receiving at least 1% of the national vote. A Treasury allocation for each Knesset member is granted to each party represented in the outgoing Knesset, in order to wage their election campaign. New parties receive a similar allocation retroactively for each Knesset member they actually elect. The State Comptroller (q.v.) reviews the disbursement of all campaign expenditures. The President (q.v.), the State Comptroller, judges and other senior public officials, as well as the Chief of Staff of the Israel Defense Forces (q.v.) and other high-ranking army officers, are disqualified from presenting their candidacy for the Knesset, unless they have resigned their positions by a specified date (one hundred days) prior to the elections.

A central elections committee, headed by a justice of the Supreme Court (q.v.) and including representatives of the parties holding seats in the Knesset, is responsible for conducting the elections. The Eleventh Knesset barred the submission of lists whose platform negated the existence of the Jewish State or its democratic character. On election day, each voter casts a ballot for one party—its list of candidates and its platform as a whole, having been presented prior to the election. Knesset seats are assigned in proportion to each party's percentage of the total national vote. Knesset seats are allocated according to the sequence in which the candidates appear on their respective party lists. Ever since the establishment of Israel, a large number of small parties have received representation in the Knesset, thus ensuring the representation of a wide spectrum of political views.

KNESSET HAGEDOLA (GREAT ASSEMBLY). Literally "The Great Assembly." The supreme Jewish council during the early period following the return from the Babylonian exile (from c. 538 BCE).

KNESSET YISRAEL. The term used to refer to the organizational structure of the Yishuv (q.v.) during the British Mandate (q.v.).

KOLLEK, THEODORE (TEDDY). Born in Vienna in 1911 he early became involved in Zionism (q.v.). He settled in Palestine (q.v.) in 1934 and was one of the founders of Kibbutz Ein Gev. From 1940 to 1947 he served on the staff of the Political Department of the Jewish Agency (q.v.). After Israel's independence he became the number two official in Israel's embassy in Washington. He served as Director General of the Prime Minister's Office from 1952 to 1964. Affiliated with Mapai (q.v.) he followed David Ben-Gurion (q.v.)

when he left the party and founded Rafi (q.v.). At the head of the Rafi ticket he was elected Mayor of Jerusalem (q.v.) in 1965 and has been reelected continuously since. When Jerusalem was reunited as a consequence of the 1967 war it posed a particular challenge to the Mayor who had to extend the services of the city to East Jerusalem and was now mayor of the entire city. He heads the One Jerusalem party, a loose coalition of Labor party members and personal supporters of Kollek, that established control of Jerusalem's city council in 1978.

KOOK, RABBI AVRAHAM YITZHAK HACOHEN. Chief Rabbi of Palestine (q.v.). He was born in Griva, Latvia in 1865 and died in Jerusalem (q.v.) in 1935. He studied in various Eastern European Yeshivot and served as Rabbi for a number of communities. In 1904 he settled in Palestine where he served as Rabbi of the Jewish community of Jaffa (q.v.). Stranded in Europe during World War I, he returned to Palestine in 1919 and became the Rabbi of the Ashkenazi (q.v.) community of Jerusalem. When the Chief Rabbinate (q.v.) of Palestine was established in 1921 he was chosen Ashkenazi Chief Rabbi of Palestine and held that position until his death. He developed a nationalist-religious philosophy and pursued the Zionist ideal. He established his own yeshiva in Jerusalem (Merkaz Harav) where he focused on the ideal of a religious-national renaissance for the Jewish people. He was outspoken in his criticism of the administration of the British Mandate (q.v.) in Palestine.

KOOK, RABBI ZVI YEHUDA. Born in Lithuania in 1891 he was educated at Jewish religious schools as well as at the university in Germany. He immigrated with his parents to Palestine (q.v.) in 1904 where his father, Rabbi Avraham Yitzhak Hacohen Kook (q.v.), later became Chief Rabbi. He became head of the Merkaz Harav Yeshiva and published numerous religious and other commentaries. He was an ardent Zionist. He participated in Gush Emunim (q.v.) activities and became the movement's spiritual mentor. He died in 1982.

KOOR INDUSTRIES. An umbrella organization for industrial and craft concerns. It was established in 1944 as part of Solel Boneh, a construction concern whose aim was to develop heavy industry factories. The establishment of Koor was part of the Histadrut's (q.v.) general plan to ensure basic industry for the Yishuv (q.v.) which would maximize the use of existing raw materials, would enable a planned distribution of the factories such that they would provide employment in development towns and areas, and would help the balance of payments both by creating local products to replace imports, and in supporting the export industry. Such an industry was also to be the basis for an independent security industry, a source of training for Jewish workers, and it was hoped that it would ensure the Labor movement's special place in defining the direction and development of the economy in the future. In 1958, Solel Boneh was reorganized and divided into three companies: (1) construction and public works throughout the country; (2) construction and pavement abroad; and (3) different types of industrial production. This made Koor an independent company, which rapidly became the largest concern in Israel. Despite its status as Israel's largest conglomerate, Koor experienced severe economic difficulties in the late 1980s. It sold off various subsidiaries, closed unprofitable units and defaulted on some bank loans. In the fall of 1991 United States and Israeli banks, the government of Israel, and Hevrat Ovdim (q.v.) signed a financial restructuring agreement designed to rescue Koor.

KUPAT HOLIM (SICK FUND). A comprehensive health insurance scheme of the Histadrut (q.v.) founded in 1911. When the Histadrut was formed in 1920 two health insurance schemes merged into a joint sick fund which maintained its own medical staff. It provided medical services for its members and new immigrants who were given Kupat Holim coverage on arrival. It has clinics throughout Israel as well as numerous other facilities including hospitals.

- L -

LA'AM PARTY (TOWARD THE PEOPLE). One of the components that formed Likud (q.v.) in 1973. It was composed of parts of the Free Center Party (q.v.), the State List (q.v.), and the Land of Israel Movement (q.v.).

LABOR ALIGNMENT see ALIGNMENT

LABOR PARTY see ISRAEL LABOR PARTY

LADINO. A Judeo-Spanish language, generally spoken by Iberian Jews, and originally written in medieval Hebrew (q.v.) letters and later in Latin letters, much as the Ashkenazi Jews (q.v.) spoke Yiddish (q.v.).

LAKE KINNERET see SEA OF GALILEE

LAKE TIBERIAS see SEA OF GALILEE

LAND DAY. An annual commemoration by Israel's Arab population (q.v.) of the killing on March 30, 1976 of demonstrators who had been protesting the confiscation of Arab land in the Galilee (q.v.).

LAND OF ISRAEL MOVEMENT. A political movement that began its efforts shortly after the Six Day War (q.v.) and argued that Israel should retain the territories occupied (West Bank (q.v.) and Gaza Strip (q.v.)) in the war and establish settlements there. Much of its program and its supporters were later incorporated into Gush Emunim (q.v.) and Tehiya (q.v.).

LANDAU, HAIM. Born in Cracow, Poland, in 1916. In 1935 he immigrated to Palestine (q.v.) and enrolled at the Technion (q.v.) in Haifa (q.v.), where he received a degree in construction engineering in 1944. Shortly after his arrival in Palestine, he joined the Irgun Tzvai Leumi (q.v.). In 1944 he served as Deputy Commander of the Irgun and was subsequently appointed chief of its general command, a post which he held until 1948. One of the founding members of the Herut Party (q.v.), he was elected to the First Knesset (q.v.) in January 1949, and reelected to all subsequent Knessets until the Ninth. In December 1969 he joined the Government of National Unity (q.v.) as Minister of Development, a position he held until the resignation of Gahal (q.v.) from that government in August 1970. He was appointed Minister Without Portfolio in January 1978. In January 1979 he was appointed Minister of Transport. He died in 1981.

LASKOV, CHAIM. Born in Russia and immigrated to Palestine (q.v.) with his parents in 1925. His father was murdered by Arabs in 1930 in Haifa (q.v.), where he studied in the "Reali" high school. He joined the Hagana (q.v.) at a young age and entered Orde Wingate's Special Night Squadrons. Following the outbreak of World War II, he joined the British army and served in North Africa and Europe. He was released from the army with the rank of Major. After World War II, he organized the purchasing of weapons in Europe to be smuggled into Israel. When he returned to Israel, he became the chief training and education officer of the Hagana. He commanded the first armored battalion of the Israel Defense Forces (q.v.) in the War of Independence (q.v.), and later the Seventh Brigade during the battles to free the Galilee (q.v.). After the war, he received the rank of Major General, and became the head of the training and education branch of the IDF. He was appointed head of the air force in 1953, the armored corps in 1956, the Commander of a division in the Sinai War (q.v.), and later the Commander of the southern command. He served as Chief of Staff of the IDF between 1958-1961, and from November 1972 on, he became the Commissioner of Soldiers' Complaints in the Defense Ministry. He was a member of the Agranat Commission of Inquiry (q.v.) that was established after the Yom Kippur War (q.v.). He died in 1982.

LATRUN. A locality with a monastery at the foot of the Judean hills on the road from Tel Aviv (q.v.) to Jerusalem (q.v.). The monastery was founded in the nineteenth century by French Trappist Monks. It is located at a strategic crossroads linking the Mediterranean coast to Jerusalem where the coastal plain meets the Judean hills. The Ayalon Valley where Joshua completed the conquest of Canaan (q.v.) is here. During the British Mandate (q.v.) a police fortress was built at the strategic location as was a detention camp where many Jewish political prisoners were held. A major effort was made by the Jews during Israel's War of Independence (q.v.) to take this area in order to open the road from Tel Aviv to Jerusalem, but it failed and an alternative "Burma Road" had to be built. The area was captured by Israel during the Six Day War (q.v.).

LAVON, PINHAS (FORMERLY LUBIANIKER). He was the key figure in the "affair" that clouded Israel's political life for almost a decade from the mid-1950s to the mid-1960s. The affair resulted in the downfall of a government and split the country's ruling party. He was born in Poland and attended Lvov University. He immigrated to Palestine (q.v.) at 25. He became active in the Mapai Party (q.v.) and served as its Secretary from 1935 to 1937. After Israel's independence he was elected to the First Knesset (q.v.). He served as Minister of Agriculture and then of Supply and Rationing before becoming Minister of Defense in 1953. He died on January 24, 1976. See LAVON AFFAIR.

LAVON AFFAIR. Pinhas Lavon (q.v.) was Israel's Defense Minister in 1954 when Israeli agents were arrested in Egypt, apparently for trying to bomb United States facilities in Cairo and Alexandria and other targets in an effort to turn the United Kingdom and the United States against Egypt. The government of Prime Minister Moshe Sharett (q.v.) had not been consulted and Lavon claimed that he had not been aware of the plan. However, Colonel Binyamin Gibli, head of military intelligence, insisted that Lavon had personally in-structed him to proceed. An inquiry was ordered but no conclusion was reached. Lavon resigned from the government and was elected Secretary General of the Histadrut (q.v.). As a consequence of later revelations the Cabinet was convinced that the evidence against Lavon had been fabricated and the Government issued a statement that the 1954 operation had been ordered without Lavon's knowledge. Prime Minister David Ben-Gurion (q.v.), who had been outvoted in the Cabinet, called the resolution a miscarriage of justice. In protest against the intrusion of the executive into the sphere of the judiciary, Ben-Gurion resigned and brought down the government. He told his party that he would not accept a mandate to form a new government as long as Lavon represented the party as Secretary

General of the Histadrut. The party's central committee ousted Lavon in 1961.

LAW OF RETURN (1950). The law was adopted by the Knesset (q.v.) on July 5, 1950. It assures virtually unlimited and unfettered Jewish immigration to Israel by providing that every Jew has the right to immigrate to Israel to settle there unless the applicant is engaged in an activity "directed against the Jewish people" or one that may "endanger public health or the security of the state." An amendment in 1954 also restricted those likely to endanger public welfare. The 1950 law has provided the formal basis for the substantial immigration (aliya) (q.v.) that has taken place since independence. The concept of unlimited immigration, which has been reinforced by the programs and actions of successive governments and has had overwhelming support in parliament and from Israel's Jewish population, has brought hundreds of thousands of Jewish immigrants to Israel from more than seventy countries.

LEBANON. Israel's neighbor to the north. During the War of Independence (q.v.) Lebanon joined in the fighting against Israel despite that country's Christian majority and the control of the body politic by that segment of the Lebanese population. Lebanon essentially abstained from participation in the Sinai (q.v.) and Six Day Wars (q.v.) and the War of Attrition (q.v.). After the Palestine Liberation Organization (q.v.) was ousted from Jordan in September 1970 it moved into Lebanon via Syria (q.v.) and established a base of operations. Attacks against targets in Israel by the PLO from Lebanon led to Isareli retaliatory strikes as well as two major military operations: Operation Litani (q.v.) and Operation Peace for Galilee (q.v.). While the PLO was building its base of operations and striking against Israel, these developments were contributing to the disintegration of Lebanon which had already begun because of disagreements among the various Lebanese factions over the distribution of socioeconomic and political power. A civil war broke out in Lebanon in 1975 and has continued since. Meanwhile, with the absence of effective control from Beirut, the PLO was able to use Lebanese territory for attacks into Israel. After a number of these strikes into Israel, Israel launched Operation Litani in March 1978. Despite the subsequent establishment of the United Nations Interim Force in Lebanon (UNIFIL) periodic attacks into Israel continued. In June 1982 Israel launched Operation Peace for Galilee, the War in Lebanon (q.v.), to rectify the situation. Subsequently the United States (q.v.) brokered an agreement between Israel and Lebanon— the May 17, 1983 agreement (q.v.)—which called for the withdrawal of Israeli forces from Lebanon. The agreement was subsequently abrogated by the Lebanese government. Israel completed its withdrawal from Lebanon in 1985 while a security zone was established in Lebanon along Israel's northern border.

LEBANON WAR (1982) see WAR IN LEBANON

LEHI (LOHAMEI HERUT YISRAEL—FIGHTERS FOR THE FREEDOM OF ISRAEL, STERN GROUP) see STERN (GANG) GROUP

LEVINGER, RABBI MOSHE. Rabbi Levinger was born in Jerusalem (q.v.) in 1935. He planned and initiated the Jewish return to Hebron (q.v.) at Passover in 1968 and continues to live there. He was involved in the creation of Gush Emunim (q.v.) and has been among its leaders and activists. In May 1990 he entered Eyal prison to begin serving a five-month jail sentence for causing the death of a shopkeeper in Hebron in September 1988.

LEVY, DAVID. David Levy was born in Rabat, Morocco in 1938, and has lived in the development town (q.v.) of Bet Shean (q.v.) since immigrating to Israel in 1957. A former construction worker, he began his political career in the Histadrut (q.v.) and served as chairman of its Likud (q.v.) faction. He was the Likud candidate for the position of Secretary General of the Histadrut in the 1977 and 1981 elections. He was first elected on behalf of the Herut Party (q.v.) faction of Gahal (q.v.) to the Seventh Knesset (q.v.) in October 1969, and has been reelected to all subsequent Knessets on behalf of the same faction in the Likud bloc. Levy was appointed Minister of Immigrant Absorption in June 1977, and Minister of Construction and Housing in January 1978. In August 1981 he became Deputy Prime Minister and Minister of Construction and Housing and retained those posts in the National Unity Government (q.v.) established in 1984. He has been a vocal advocate of the need for Israel to be strong, secure, and self-sufficient and that this would lead to peace. He has been an equally strong opponent of the creation of a Palestinian state. An interesting sidelight is that as his career has grown and he has matured as a politician, David Levy jokes became rather widespread. They tended to impugn his intelligence, his knowledge (or lack of it) of English, and other factors. Soon after his rise to the top of the political leadership the jokes began to disappear. In the government established in December 1988 he became Deputy Prime Minister and Minister of Construction and Housing. He served as Deputy Prime Minister and Minister of Foreign Affairs in the Shamir-led (q.v.) government established in June 1990.

LEVY, MOSHE. Born in 1936 in Tel Aviv (q.v.) he studied economics and the history of Islamic countries at the Hebrew University (q.v.). He joined the Israel Defense Forces (q.v.) in 1954 and served in the Golani Brigade and in the paratroopers and held a series of commands. He was in command of the Central Command from 1977 to 1982 and from 1982 to 1983 served as Deputy Chief of Staff of the Israel Defense Forces. He served as Chief of Staff of the IDF from 1983 to 1987.

LIBERAL CENTER PARTY. This party was formed in 1985 by Liberal Party (q.v.) members who left the Likud (q.v.). Its leaders include Tel Aviv (q.v.) Mayor Shlomo Lahat and then Jewish Agency (q.v.) Chairman Arye Leon Dulzin (q.v.), as well as former minister and Knesset Speaker Yitzhak Berman (q.v.). Its political platform opposed the annexation of the occupied territories (q.v.) as well as the "bi-national state" which would result from such annexation. It argued that Israel must be a Jewish and Zionist state and should be prepared to give up territories for peace. Jerusalem (q.v.) was not a matter for negotiation, and the party rejected the creation of an independent Palestinian state between Israel and Jordan. The party's platform also stressed the equality of all Israeli citizens regardless of religion, race, or sex. It became part of the Center-Shinui (q.v.) political bloc.

LIBERAL PARTY (HAMIFLAGA HALIBERALIT). The Liberal Party was established during the Fifth Knesset (q.v.) by a merger of the General Zionist Party (Hatzionim Haklaliyim) (q.v.) and the Progressive Party (Hamiflaga Haprogressivit) (q.v.). The party's beginnings can be traced to middle-of-the-road Zionists (q.v.) who wanted to unify all Zionists without regard to socialist, Revisionist (q.v.), or religious feelings. They stressed industrial development and private enterprise. This group split into two wings in 1935: General Zionists A, the larger of the two groups which was led by Chaim Weizmann (q.v.), on the left; and General Zionists B, on the right. Both were comprised of industrialists, merchants, landlords, white-collar professionals, and intellectuals. The two factions merged in 1946 to form the General Zionist Party; then split again in 1948, when the one group formed the Progressive Party; and then merged once again in 1961 as the Liberal Party. The party won 17 seats in the 1961 Knesset election, the same as Herut (q.v.). In 1965, Herut and the Liberals set up an electoral alliance called Gahal (q.v.). Seven Liberals in the Knesset refused to join Gahal and formed the Independent Liberal Party (q.v.). From 1965 to 1977, the Independent Liberals averaged about 3.5% of the vote and retained four or five Knesset seats. In 1971, they won only one seat, and in 1981, with only 0.6% of the vote, they disappeared from the Knesset. In the meantime, in 1973, retired General Ariel Sharon (q.v.), then a member of the Liberal Party within Gahal, advocated a wider union of parties which could present itself as a genuine alternative to the Labor Alignment (q.v.). Sharon and Ezer Weizman (q.v.) successfully brought the Free Center Party (q.v.), the State List (q.v.), and the Land of Israel Movement (q.v.) (a nonparty group advocating immediate Israeli settlement and development of the occupied territories) into the Herut-Liberal alliance to form Likud. The Liberals are presently led by Yitzhak Moda'i (q.v.), who has favored a formal merger of the Liberal Party with Herut.

LIKUD (UNION). Likud was established in 1973 and the alliance crystalized at the time of the 1977 elections. It consisted of: the Gahal (q.v.) alliance (Herut (q.v.) and the Liberals (q.v.)); the La'am (q.v.) alliance (the State List (q.v.) and the Free Center (q.v.)); Ahdut (a one-man faction in the Knesset); and Shlomzion (q.v.), Ariel Sharon's (q.v.) former party.

Likud came to power in Israel in 1977, ousting the Labor Party-led (q.v.) government for the first time since Israel became independent. Although it retained its government position after the 1981 elections, its majority in the Knesset (q.v.) seldom exceeded two or three votes. In 1984, it lost its plurality and joined with the Labor Alignment to form a Government of National Unity (q.v.) in which it shared power and ministerial positions. In the 1988 Knesset election it again emerged as the dominant party but without a majority. A Likud-dominated government with Yitzhak Shamir (q.v.) as Prime Minister and with Labor as the junior partner was formed in December 1988. Likud is right of center, strongly nationalist, and assertive in foreign policy. It has focused on retaining the territories west of the Jordan River occupied by Israel in the Six Day War (q.v.) and has strongly opposed negotiations with the Palestine Liberation Organization (q.v.), regarding the PLO as a terrorist organization committed to the destruction of Israel. It has emphasized the need for economic and social betterment of Israel's disadvantaged, primarily in the Oriental (q.v.) Jewish community. Its economic programs regard free enterprise as the preferred mechanism and it has campaigned on themes of dismantling the socialist mechanisms established during the Labor Party's control of the Israeli polity and economy. Since the retirement of Menachem Begin (q.v.) from political life, Yitzhak Shamir has been the party leader. Among the other major party figures are Moshe Arens (q.v.), Ariel Sharon, David Levy (q.v.), and Yitzhak Moda'i (q.v.).

LITANI OPERATION see OPERATION LITANI

LITERATURE. Hebrew (q.v.) literature accompanied the return of the Jewish people to Palestine (q.v.) and the Zionist movement since its inception at the end of the 19th century. Authors wrote in Hebrew to describe daily life, their concerns and dreams, the encounter with the

Arabs, and cultural and social tensions. Some writers depicted the Zionist settler in a romantic way and viewed the Arab with ambivalence, while others were more pessimistic in outlook regarding the future of relations between Jews and Arabs. Initially the group of Hebrew authors included some native-born writers, but mainly they were immigrants from Eastern Europe. Prominent among the latter were Haim Nahman Bialik (q.v.), Shaul Tchernichovsky (q.v.), and Shmuel Yosef Agnon (q.v.), corecipient of the 1966 Nobel Prize for Literature. The roots of the poetry and prose of most of these writers were in the world and traditions of European Jewry as well as in themes derived from the achievements in Palestine to which they had come as pioneers. The new Hebrew literature since the 1960s has included the works of Amos Oz (q.v.) and A.B. Yehoshua (q.v.). This literature experiments with various styles or prose writing, but also with speculation and some skepticism regarding the political and social activities of Israeli society.

Israeli prose and poetry draw images and expressions from the Bible, various Jewish sources such as the Talmud (q.v.), Mishna, and Kabbala, and the traditions of the Diaspora (q.v.). The trend of mixing the sacred with the everyday is especially evident in modern Hebrew poetry. Although the poetry of writers such as Avraham Shlonsky and Nathan Alterman tended toward classical structure and ordered rhyming and reflected the events and voices of the country, a change in the character of poetry appeared with Natan Zach. The poetry of the younger generation experiments with form and language and is typified by its critical attitude toward realism and the attempt of many poets to replace reality with personal experience.

Israelis are the "people of the book" and per capita publishing rates are among the highest in the world. All forms of literature—serious and popular—are produced and read in substantial quantities.

LOHAMEI HERUT YISRAEL see STERN (GANG) GROUP

- M -

MAABAROT (TRANSIT CAMPS). Temporary accommodations provided by Israel for mass immigration between 1950 and 1954, to facilitate absorption of the new immigrants into the Israeli system. The conditions in the camps were problematic and demonstrations and other difficulties resulted. More permanent housing was soon constructed and a new system for immigrant absorption was devised and put into effect in 1954. See ALIYA.

MAAPILIM. The illegal immigrants who entered Palestine (q.v.) despite the strict immigration quotas imposed by the British Mandatory (q.v.) authorities. The beginning of such immigration, called haapalah, dates to 1934. It peaked in the post-World War II period, with the aim of providing refuge for Holocaust (q.v.) survivors.

MAARACH see ALIGNMENT

MAARIV. An afternoon daily Hebrew language (q.v.), politically independent newspaper which first appeared on February 15, 1948.

MACMICHAEL, SIR HAROLD (ALFRED). A British public servant who joined the Sudan Political Service in 1905 and served successively as Inspector in the Provinces of Kordofan, Blue Nile, and Khartoum and as a political and intelligence officer with the Expeditionary Force that reoccupied Darfur in 1916. Subsequently he became Sub-Governor of Darfur Province and later Assistant Civil Secretary. From 1926 to 1933 he was Civil Secretary and periodically Acting Governor General. From 1933 to 1937 he served as High Commissioner and Commander in Chief of Tanganyika Territory. He served as High Commissioner and Commander in Chief for Palestine (q.v.) (and also as High Commissioner for Transjordan) from 1938 to 1944. His appointment was partially designed to reassure the Arab world that the problem of Palestine would be handled sympathetically since he had a reputation as a renowned Arabic scholar and had prepared several publications on the Sudan. His tenure in Palestine was characterized by increasing Arab-Jewish tension and the intensification of efforts by both communities to secure their goals for the future of Palestine. It was a period during which the plight of European Jewry became critical and there was an accelerated deterioration of relations between the Jewish community and the British Government over the issue of Jewish immigration. By the time he left Palestine at the end of August 1944 there was virtually no contact between the High Commissioner and the Jewish quasi-government in Palestine.

MADRID PEACE CONFERENCE. An Arab-Israeli peace conference convened in Madrid, Spain beginning October 30, 1991, at the invitation of the United States and the USSR. In an opening plenary session, Israeli and Syrian, Egyptian, Lebanese, and Jordanian-Palestinian delegations met and delivered speeches and responses. These were followed by bilateral negotiations between Israel and each of the Arab delegations. The conference was an important step on the road to peace in that it involved direct, bilateral, public and official peace negotiations between Israel and its Arab neighbors.

MAFDAL see NATIONAL RELIGIOUS PARTY

MAGEN DAVID (SHIELD OF DAVID). A Jewish symbol. It appears on the flag of the state of Israel as it did on the flag of the Zionist movement. It consists of two superimposed triangles which form a six-pointed star. Although an ancient symbol it apparently became widely used in Europe for the Jewish communities in the 16th and 17th centuries. In 1897 the First Zionist Congress chose it as the symbol of the movement and of the World Zionist Organization (q.v.). It was employed by the Nazis during the Holocaust (q.v.) as a means of identifying Jews. The Flag and Emblem Law of Israel of May 24, 1949 incorporated the Magen David into the flag of Israel.

MAGEN DAVID ADOM (RED SHIELD OF DAVID). Israel's equivalent of the Red Cross which provides emergency medical services. The first group was founded in Tel Aviv (q.v.) in 1930 and in 1935 a national organization was formed. After Israel's independence it sought to affiliate with the International Red Cross, but this was rejected as the Red Cross refused to recognize the Magen David Adom symbol, a red six-pointed star. This remains the case although there are some relations between the two organizations.

MAGIC CARPET see OPERATION MAGIC CARPET

MAGNES, JUDAH LEON. Born in San Francisco in 1877, he died in New York in 1948. He was ordained as a Rabbi at Hebrew Union College in 1900. An ardent Zionist, he was active in many of the Zionist organizations prior to his settling in Palestine (q.v.) in 1922. He helped found the American Jewish Committee, which sought to speak for the Jewish Community in the United States and to act in its defense against anti-Semitism, and served on its Executive Committee from 1906 to 1918. He helped found Hebrew University (q.v.) and became its Chancellor in 1925. After reorganization he became the President of the University in 1935, a post in which he remained until he died. He became an advocate of a bi-national state in Palestine as a means of preventing bloodshed which he believed would be associated with efforts to establish a Jewish State and in 1929 helped found Brit Shalom (q.v.). In 1942 he founded the Ihud (q.v.) (Unity) organization for better understanding between Arabs and Jews. He continued to advocate a bi-national state until after the establishment of Israel.

MAHAL. Acronym for Mitnadvei Hutz Laeretz (foreign volunteers). A group of some 3,000 Jewish and non-Jewish soldiers who came to Palestine (q.v.) to fight in Israel's War of Independence (q.v.).

MAKI see COMMUNIST PARTY

MAKLEFF, MORDECHAI. Born in Palestine (q.v.) in 1920, he volunteered in the 1930s to serve in the Hagana (q.v.). During World War II, he served in the British army in Orde Wingate's "Special Night Squadrons." Following the war, he left the British army with the rank of major. In the War of Independence (q.v.), he took part in combat as a brigade commander along the northern front. He became commander of military intelligence and served as the Deputy Chief of Staff in 1951–1952. He served as Chief of Staff of the Israel Defense Forces (q.v.) in 1952–1953. Following his retirement from the military, he became General Manager of Israel's electric company, the Israel Chemicals company, and held other public posts. He died in 1978.

MANDATE see BRITISH MANDATE

MAPAI (MIFLEGET POALEI ERETZ YISRAEL—ISRAEL WORKERS PARTY). Mapai originated with the union of two smaller political parties, Ahdut

Haavoda (q.v.) and Hapoel Hatzair (q.v.), in 1930, but the roots of the movement can be traced to the turn of the century in Europe, especially Russia. Its program focused on the development of the Jewish people in Israel as a free working people rooted in an agricultural and industrial economy and developing its own Hebrew (q.v.) culture. It supported membership in the world movement of the working class and cooperation in the struggle to eliminate class subjugation and social injustice in any form. It endorsed the building of a Jewish commonwealth focusing on labor, equality, and freedom. Its program was a combination of Zionist and socialist ideologies. Mapai soon became the dominant party in the Yishuv (q.v.). The two parties which formed it had established the Histadrut (q.v.) in 1920, and under their leadership it became the embodiment of the Jewish community in Palestine (q.v.). Mapai controlled the Histadrut as well as the National Council (q.v.) and the Jewish Agency (q.v.). Many of the noted figures in the creation of Israel came from Mapai, including David Ben-Gurion (q.v.), Moshe Sharett (formerly Shertok) (q.v.), Golda Meir (formerly Meyerson) (q.v.), Moshe Dayan (q.v.), and others. In the elections for the Knesset (q.v.) from Israel's independence until 1965, when it ran in the framework of the Alignment (q.v.), it won the largest number of seats and its leader was given the mandate to form the government. All of Israel's Prime Ministers and Histadrut Secretaries General as well as many other senior members of the Israeli administrations and political elite were Mapai members in the period from its founding until its merger into the Israel Labor Party (q.v.). It was the leading member of all government coalitions and generally held the key portfolios of Defense, Foreign Affairs, and Finance as well as the post of Prime Minister. The party permeated the government, the bureaucracy, the economy, and most of the other institutions of Israel. Political advancement in Israel and party membership were generally coincident. In 1965 Mapai joined with Ahdut Haavoda to form the Alignment to contest the Knesset election. In 1968 the Alignment joined with Rafi (q.v.) to form the Israel Labor Party.

MAPAM (MIFLEGET POALIM HAMEUHEDET— UNITED WORKERS PARTY). Mapam was organized in 1948 when Hashomer Hatzair (q.v.) merged with radical elements from Ahdut Haavoda (q.v.). It is a left-wing socialist-Zionist Jewish-Arab party. From its beginnings, the party was more Marxist than Mapai (q.v.) The former Ahdut Haavoda members left in 1954 because of Mapam's pro-Soviet orientation and acceptance of Arabs (q.v.) as party members. Although the party's domestic policy was essentially indistinguishable from Mapai's, Mapam's share of the vote in national elections declined steadily before it joined the Alignment (q.v.) for the 1969 elections. Mapam ended its alliance with Labor (q.v.) in September 1984 over the issue of the formation of a Government of National Unity (q.v.) with Likud (q.v.). The veteran leader, Victor Shemtov (q.v.), retired as party head. It has supported the principle of compromise concerning the trade of territories for peace in the Arab-Israeli conflict (q.v.). It supports the return of most of the territories, except for minor border changes required for security, in exchange for peace. It has expressed its readiness to negotiate with any authorized Palestinian (q.v.) element that will declare its willingness to recognize Israel and to cease terrorism.

MASSADA. A natural rock fortress in the Judean desert on the shore of the Dead Sea (q.v.), located south of Ein Gedi, where a group of Jewish Zealots held out against a Roman siege for seven months in 73 AD. When the Romans finally entered the fortress they found that the defenders had committed suicide rather than be taken alive. This heroic stand has led to the pledge of Israeli youngsters that "Massada shall not fall again." Excavations of the site by archaeologist Yigael Yadin (q.v.) have documented much of the historical writings of Josephus concerning Massada.

MEA SHEARIM. A neighborhood of Jerusalem (q.v.) located near the former Jordanian border and the Mandelbaum Gate. It was one of the first neighborhoods built outside the walls of the old city of Jerusalem, around 1874. The first residents were Orthodox Jews who sought to escape the crowded conditions in the old Jerusalem community. The name is derived from the book of Genesis in the Bible. It has become the symbol of religious extremism because the neighborhood is under the influence of the Neturei Karta (q.v.), though not all who live there are members of that group. The inhabitants of the area tend to be traditional and religious in their outlook.

MECHDAL. A Hebrew (q.v.) word meaning omission. A term widely used in Israel in the aftermath of the Yom Kippur War (q.v.) to refer to the failures of the government and of the military to be fully prepared for the outbreak of the Yom Kippur War and to respond to the inital attacks. See also AGRANAT COMMISSION OF INQUIRY.

MEIMAD (DIMENSION). Tenua Mercazit Datit. The Movement of the Religious Center. Founded in 1988 as a reaction to the move to the right of the National Religious Party (q.v.), it is a dovish religious party drawing much of its membership from those formerly affiliated with the National Religious Party. It has been described as a balanced religious Zionist party that is not locked into any particular conception. Meimad seeks to promote dialogue and lessen polarization within Israeli society. On matters of peace and security it follows the principle that "the good of the people and State of Israel takes precedence over political control over the entire Land of Israel." Its leaders include Rabbi Yehuda Amital, the prominent head of the Har Etzion yeshiva in Alon Shvut, and Rabbi Dr. Daniel Tropper, the head of the Gesher movement which works for understanding between the Orthodox Jews and others. It did not win any seats in the November 1988 parliamentary election.

MEIR, GOLDA (FORMERLY MEYERSON). Born Golda Mabovitch on May 3, 1898 in Kiev, Russia. In 1903 the family moved to Pinsk and, three years later, settled in Milwaukee. She graduated from high school in Milwaukee and attended the Milwaukee Normal School for Teachers. At age 17 she joined the Poalei Zion (Workers of Zion) Party (q.v.). She married Morris Meyerson in December 1917 and in 1921 they moved to Palestine (q.v.). They settled in Kibbutz Merhaviah, but later moved to Tel Aviv (q.v.) and then to Jerusalem (q.v.). In 1928 she became Secretary of the Women's Labor Council of the Histadrut (q.v.) in Tel Aviv. When Mapai (q.v.) was formed in 1930 by the merger of Ahdut Haavoda (q.v.) and Hapoel Hatzair (q.v.) (The Young Worker), she quickly became a major figure in the new party.

In 1934 she was invited to join the Executive Committee of the Histadrut and became head of its Political Department. In 1946, when the British Mandatory (q.v.) authorities arrested virtually all the members of the Jewish Agency (q.v.) Executive and the Vaad Leumi (q.v.) that they could find in Palestine, she became acting head of the Political Department of the Jewish Agency replacing Moshe Shertok (later Sharett) (q.v.), who was imprisoned in Latrun (q.v.). In the months immediately preceding Israel's Declaration of Independence (q.v.) she met secretly with King Abdullah of Transjordan to dissuade him from joining the Arab League in attacking Jewish Palestine, but her efforts failed. In early June 1948, she was appointed Israel's first Minister to Moscow, but returned to Israel in April 1949. She was elected to the First Knesset (q.v.) in 1949 on the Mapai ticket and became Minister of Labor in the government, a post she held until 1956, when she became Foreign Minister for a decade under Prime Minister David Ben-Gurion (q.v.) and Levi Eshkol (q.v.). As Minister of Labor her principal function was the absorption of hundreds of thousands of immigrants who arrived in Israel in the first years after independence. She initiated large-scale housing and road-building programs and strongly supported unlimited immigration, and she helped to provide employment and medical care for the immigrants.

When she succeeded Moshe Sharett as Foreign Minister in 1956, she Hebraicized her name and became known as Golda Meir. As Foreign Minister she concentrated on Israel's aid to African and other developing nations as a means of strengthening Israel's international position. She resigned as Foreign Minister in January 1966 and was succeeded by Abba Eban (q.v.). Because of her enormous popularity in Mapai, she was prevailed on to accept appointment as General Secretary of Mapai, and, in that position, was Prime Minister Levi Eshkol's closest advisor. In January 1968 she was instrumental in facilitating the union of Mapai, Rafi (q.v.), and Ahdut Haavoda as the Israel Labor Party (q.v.). After serving for two years as Secretary General, she retired from public life.

Following Eshkol's death in February 1969, party leaders prevailed upon her to succeed Eshkol and she became Israel's fourth Prime Minister in March 1969. She retained the national unity government that Eshkol had constructed at the time of the Six Day War (q.v.). In the Knesset election at the end of October, the Labor Party won 56 seats, and she once again became Prime Minister. She led Israel through the trauma of the Yom Kippur War (q.v.) and its aftermath. Following the 1973 election, which was postponed until December 31, she had great difficulty in forming a government with Moshe Dayan (q.v.) continuing in his role as Minister of Defense. In April 1974 she resigned. She died on December 8, 1978.

MEMORANDUM OF UNDERSTANDING (MOU). In November 1981, Israel and the United States negotiated and signed a Memorandum of Understanding on Strategic Cooperation in which it was agreed that United States-Israel strategic cooperation "is designed against the threat to peace and security of the region caused by the Soviet Union or Soviet-controlled forces from outside the region introduced into the region." The MOU was suspended in December 1981 in the wake of the Israel's extension of its law and jurisdiction to the Golan Heights (q.v.), but additional memoranda were signed in subsequent years.

MERIDOR, DAN. Born in Jerusalem (q.v.) on April 23, 1947 and graduated from the Faculty of Law of Hebrew University (q.v.). A lawyer by profession he served as Government (q.v.) Secretary from 1982 to 1984. He was first elected to the Knesset (q.v.) on the Likud (q.v.) list in 1984. He became Minister of Justice in the government established in December 1988 and retained that position in the government of June 1990.

MERIDOR, YAAKOV. Born in Poland in 1913. In 1932 he emigrated to Palestine (q.v.), where in the following year, he joined the Irgun (q.v.), which he commanded from 1941 to 1943. He served in the First through the Sixth Knessets (q.v.). He is the founder and chairman of the Board of Directors of Maritime Fruit Carriers Ltd., and serves on the Board of Directors of the Atlantic Fisheries and Shipping Co., Ltd. On August 5, 1981, following his election to the Tenth Knesset, he was sworn in as Minister of Economic Affairs. He is the author of *Long is the Road to Freedom.*

MILITARY see HAGANA; ISRAEL DEFENSE FORCES

MILO, RONNIE. Born in Tel Aviv (q.v.) on November 26, 1949, Milo was educated at the faculty of law of Tel Aviv University (q.v.). A lawyer by profession, Milo was first elected to the Knesset (q.v.) on the Likud (q.v.) list in 1977. He became Minister of Ecology and Environmental Protection in the government established in December 1988 and assumed the position of Minister of Police in the Government established in June 1990.

MIZRAHI. Mizrahi came into being in 1902, although its central concept can be identified as early as the 1880s. The founders of the movement did not see an inherent contradiction between Judaism and Zionism (q.v.). Mizrahi and its labor offshoot, Hapoel Hamizrahi (founded in 1922), functioned as part of the World Zionist Organization (q.v.) and the Yishuv (q.v.) institutions in Palestine (q.v.). The fundamental principle on which the Mizrahi and Hapoel Hamizrahi were based is adherence to Jewish religion and tradition. Both parties sought to secure the adoption of the religious precepts of Judaism in the everyday life of the Jewish community, and to found the State of Israel constitutionally upon Jewish religious law.

The difference between the two parties was in the social composition of their membership, which gave each a distinctive social outlook. The attitude of Mizrahi on internal social issues was largely determined by the fact that its members were drawn almost entirely from the middle-class element. As distinct from the Mizrahi, Hapoel Hamizrahi was composed exclusively of Orthodox working-class elements. In addition to being a political party, Hapoel Hamizrahi served as a professional organization, fulfilling all the functions which the Histadrut performs for its members. In the 1951 Knesset (q.v.) election Mizrahi won two seats and Hapoel Hamizrahi won eight seats. In 1955 Mizrahi and Hapoel Hamizrahi formed the National Religious Party (q.v.) to contest the Knesset election as a religious party seeking to combine religious concerns and a moderate socialist orientation in economic matters within a Zionist framework.

MODA'I, YITZHAK. Born in Tel Aviv (q.v.) in 1926. He received a BSc in Chemical Industrial Engineering from the Technion (q.v.) in 1947, a graduate degree in Economics from the University of London in 1957, and a law degree from the Tel Aviv branch of Hebrew University (q.v.) in 1959. He served as Israel's Assistant Military Attaché in London in 1951–52, on the Israel-Syria and Israel-Lebanon Mixed Armistice Commissions, and as an observer, on behalf of Israel, at several sessions of the Council of Europe. After the Six Day War (q.v.) he served as Military Governor of Gaza (q.v.) and was involved in private industry. First elected on behalf of the Liberal Party (q.v.) faction of Likud (q.v.) to the Eighth Knesset (q.v.) in December 1973, and reelected to the Ninth, he has served on the Economics and State Control Committees of the Knesset. He served as President of the Israel-America Chamber of Commerce and General Manager of Revlon (Israel) Ltd. Moda'i served as Minister of Energy and Infrastructure from 1977 to 1981, and as Minister of Communications from 1979 to 1981. On August 5, 1981 he was sworn in as Minister Without

Portfolio. He became Minister of Finance in the National Unity Government (q.v.) established in 1984 and later served as Minister Without Portfolio. He became Minister of Economics and Planning in the government established in December 1988. In June 1990 he assumed the position of Minister of Finance in the new Shamir-led (q.v.) government.

MOETZET GEDOLEI HATORAH see COUNCIL OF TORAH SAGES

MOETZET HACHMEI HATORAH see SEPHARDI TORAH GUARDIANS

MOKED. A political party formed by the combination of the Israel Communist Party (q.v.) and Tchelet Adom (Blue-Red) Movement that won a seat in the Knesset (q.v.) in the 1973 election. It later merged into Shelli (q.v.).

MOLEDET (HOMELAND) PARTY. A political party created for the 1988 Knesset (q.v.) election by Israel Defense Forces (q.v.) Reserve General Rehavam ("Gandhi") Zeevi. It advocates the transfer of the Arab population of the occupied territories (q.v.) to Arab countries. It won a seat in the Knesset elected in November 1988. It joined the coalition government headed by Prime Minister Shamir (q.v.) in February 1991.

MONTEFIORE, MOSES. Born in England in 1784. He first visited Palestine (q.v.) in 1827 and made six subsequent visits. He sought to assist the Jews of Palestine first through schemes to develop agriculture and later in bringing industry to the country. He inspired the founding of some agricultural colonies. The Yemin Moshe quarter of Jerusalem was developed due to his efforts and later was named after him. He died in 1885.

MORASHA (HERITAGE). A political party created by a religious-nationalist splinter group from the National Religious Party (q.v.) (NRP) that joined with Poalei Agudat Israel (q.v.) to contest the 1984 Knesset (q.v.) election. The party advocated more Jewish settlement of the West Bank (q.v.) and claimed the support of Gush Emunim (q.v.). Hanan Porat and Rabbi Haim Druckman (q.v.), formerly of the NRP, were leaders of the party, which combined religious orthodoxy and a demand for more territory. It merged with the NRP faction in the Knesset in July 1986.

MOSHAV (MOSHAV OVDIM). A cooperative agricultural settlement. A moshav is a village composed of a number of families—the average is about sixty—each of which maintains its own household, farms its own land, and earns its income from what it produces. The moshav leases its land from the Israel Lands Authority or the Jewish National Fund (q.v.) (Keren Kayemet Le Israel) and, in turn, distributes land to each of its members. Each family belongs to the cooperative that owns the heavy machinery and deals collectively with marketing and supplies and provides services such as education and medical care. Families are duty-bound to mutual assistance in cases of need as a result of some misfortune or national service. Hired labor is forbidden except under special circumstances and then only after the village committee has given its approval. Full response is expected to the needs of the nation and the labor movement. However, over the years there have appeared some deviations from the principles of moshav living. Some now engage in industry under similar conditions. The first moshav, Nahalal (q.v.), was founded in 1921 in the Jezreel Valley (q.v.). Private homes, rather than communal living, are the rule, as are private plots of land and individual budgets. Moshavim (plural of moshav) have become more numerous than kibbutzim (q.v.). Many of the post-independence immigrants to Israel were attracted to the concept of cooperative activity based on the family unit rather than the kibbutz's socialist communal-living approach. The moshavim are organized in the countrywide Tnaut Moshavei Haovdim—the Moshav Movement. They belong to the Agricultural Workers Union and to the Histadrut (q.v.).

MOSHAV SHITUFI. It is the middle way in settlement between the kibbutz (q.v.) and the moshav ovdim (q.v.). It resembles the kibbutz in its communal production and is like the moshav in its individual family-consumer framework. The first moshav shitufi was set up in 1936 at Kfar Hittim.

MOSHAVA (LITERALLY "COLONY"). A private farming village. The first was founded in Palestine (q.v.) in 1878 and known as Petah Tikva (q.v.). Others included Rishon Le Zion (q.v.), Rosh Pina, and Nes Ziona.

MOSSAD—HAMOSSAD LEMODIIN VETAFKIDIM MEYUHADIM. The Institute for Intelligence and Special Missions. Created on September 1, 1951 it is Israel's equivalent of the United States Central Intelligence Agency. Among its missions are the collection of political, social, economic and military information in and on foreign countries, especially all aspects of Arab politics, society, and foreign policy.

MOU see MEMORANDUM OF UNDERSTANDING

MOUNT HERZL (HAR HERZL). A hill on the Western outskirts of Jerusalem (q.v.) on which is located the grave of Theodor Herzl (q.v.) whose remains were transferred there from Vienna in 1949. Other prominent Zionist and Israeli figures are also buried there.

MOUNT SCOPUS (HAR HATZOFIM). A hill in Jerusalem (q.v.). Site of the first campus of the Hebrew University (q.v.) of Jerusalem which was cut off from Jewish Jerusalem during the War of Independence (q.v.), but remained under Israel's control. The enclave was held by a small contingent of Israelis who were periodically relieved by convoys under United Nations escort. In the Six Day War (q.v.), however, Israel recaptured the surrounding territory and the Hebrew University began to rebuild and expand its facilities on Mt. Scopus.

MOUNT ZION. A hill in Jerusalem (q.v.) located outside of Zion gate of the old walled city. An old tradition places the tomb of King David (q.v.) on Mount Zion.

MOVEMENT FOR DISCHARGED SOLDIERS. A party led by Ben-Zion Koren created to contest the 1988 Knesset election (q.v.). It failed to secure sufficient votes to win a seat in parliament.

MOVEMENT FOR MOSHAVIM, DEVELOPMENT TOWNS AND NEIGHBORHOODS. A political party, led by Raanan Zaim, which contested the 1988 Knesset (q.v.) election, but failed to secure a seat.

MUSEUMS. Israel has more than 80 museums of varying sizes which draw more than nine million visits a year. They focus on archaeology (q.v.), ethnology, local history, ancient and modern art, and crafts. Among the major museums are: The Israel Museum in Jerusalem (q.v.), opened in 1965, incorporating the Bezalel Museum (est. 1906) with its large collection of Jewish folk and ceremonial art. The main areas are devoted to archaeology, Judaica, a sculpture garden, and impressionist and Israeli painting. The Shrine of the Book houses the Dead Sea Scrolls (q.v.). The Rockefeller

Museum, also in Jerusalem, has an extensive collection of regional archaeology, and the Ticho House contains a gallery in a century-old Jerusalem family home. The Tel Aviv Museum, founded in 1926, opened its new building in 1971. It houses a comprehensive collection of classical and contemporary art, including Israeli art and a sculpture garden. It houses performing arts and its Helena Rubinstein Pavilion features temporary exhibits and the Rubinstein art collection. The Ha'aretz Museum in Ramat Aviv (est. 1953), has pavilions devoted to glass, coins, ethnology, ceramics, and archaeology as well as a planetarium. The Beersheba Museum (est. 1953), focuses on prehistory and the history of the Negev (q.v.). The Art Museum at Kibbutz Ein Harod (est. 1953), houses a Judaica collection and Jewish and Israeli painting and sculpture. The Institute for Islamic Art in Jerusaelm (est. 1974) has exhibitions displaying a thousand years of Islamic art.

Beit Hatefutzot (The Museum of the Diaspora, est. 1978), located on the Tel Aviv University (q.v.) campus, traces the history of Diaspora (q.v.) Jewry through the ages and throughout the world. The Yad Vashem (q.v.) collection deals with the Holocaust (q.v.).

MUSIC. The early immigrants to Palestine (q.v.) from Eastern Europe brought their songs with them, often translating the original lyrics into Hebrew (q.v.) or writing new Hebrew words for traditional tunes. New works gave expression to the pioneering and its associated hardships, to the return to manual labor and to the soil, and to new hopes. These were set to musical styles drawn from many foreign lands or were variations of Middle Eastern themes. With the growing threat of Nazism in Germany during the 1930s and the developing Holocaust (q.v.), music teachers and students, composers, instrumentalists and singers, as well as music lovers, immigrated to Palestine. Existing music schools were expanded and new ones founded. The Palestine Orchestra (which became the Israel Philharmonic Orchestra (q.v.)) was established in 1936 through the efforts of Bronislaw Huberman and a radio orchestra was formed which became the Jerusalem Symphony Orchestra of the Israel Broadcasting Authority. Other orchestras were founded in various parts of the country and major choral groups were established and performed frequently in concert and with major orchestras throughout Israel and abroad. Israeli audiences tend to be enthusiastic and demonstrative.

- N -

NAHAL. (Derived from the Hebrew (q.v.) words—Noar Halutzi Lohaim—meaning Fighting Pioneering Youth.) It is the formation within the Israel Defense Forces (q.v.) which combines military training and operations with pioneering settlement and agricultural training. After completing basic training Nahal groups are allocated to settlements for a period of combined agriculture and military training. The Nahal program derived from the security needs of the pioneering agricultural settlements that developed from the immigration to Palestine (q.v.) starting in the latter part of the nineteenth century. The hostile environment and security situation in Palestine helped to dictate the requirement for self-defense against armed attack. The Nahal program was formalized in the summer of 1948 by Prime Minister David Ben-Gurion (q.v.) for the specific purpose of encouraging the flow of people into the agricultural settlements and maintaining the pioneering spirit. The Nahal was the natural continuation of the pioneering traditions of the waves of immigration to Israel. Since its establishment Nahal has created new settlements and assisted in the establishment of others.

It has opened up undeveloped areas and created a presence at 'sensitive border points. Originally a unit within Gadna (q.v.) it was separated from it in September 1949.

NAHALAL. An agricultural settlement in the western Jezreel Valley (q.v.). Founded in 1921, it was the first moshav ovdim (q.v.) and became the prototype of this type of settlement. It was laid out in a circle with the houses grouped around a central section of public buildings.

NAHARIYA. A city on the coast of western Galilee (q.v.), it derives its name from Gaton, the small river (nahar) on whose banks it is situated. It was founded in 1934 by immigrants from Germany as an agricultural settlement but has become a popular tourist center.

NASI see PRESIDENT

NATIONAL COUNCIL see VAAD LEUMI

NATIONAL MILITARY ORGANIZATION see IRGUN

NATIONAL RELIGIOUS PARTY (NRP) (MIFLAGA DATIT LEUMIT—MAFDAL). Political parties with a religious orientation have played a major role in Israel's political life. The National Religious Party was founded in 1956 by Mizrahi (q.v.) as a religious party seeking to combine religious concerns and a moderate socialist orientation in economic matters within a Zionist framework. It was a merger of Mizrahi, formally established as a party in Palestine (q.v.) in 1918, and Hapoel Hamizrahi (Mizrahi Worker), founded in 1922. Hapoel retained a degree of independence as the trade-union section of the party responsible for immigration and absorption, labor and vocational affairs, housing, settlement, culture, pension funds and economic affairs, etc. The central NRP organization was responsible for policy, party organization, religion and rabbinical relations, and publications.

From its beginning, this party of Orthodox religious Zionists began to have an impact, electing 19% of the delegates to the Twelfth Zionist Congress in 1921. After Israel's independence, the NRP served in every government except for a brief period from 1958 to 1959, when it left the coalition over the question of who should be considered a Jew for purposes of immigration. The party is overseen by the World Center, a council elected by the world conference of the party. The conference also elects the chairman of the World Center, the party leader. Delegates to the conference are elected from local party branches by the party members. The World Center supervises the party's women's and youth organizations. The former has over 50,000 members in Israel and is active in providing nurseries and kindergartens and cultural and vocational education for its members. The best known of the party's youth organizations is Bnai Akiva. The NRP also has a sports organization, Elitzur. In addition, the United Mizrahi Bank and the Mishav construction company are also NRP enterprises. Bar Ilan University (q.v.) and the Mosad HaRav book publishing house were established by Mizrahi and are a part of the NRP operation.

The NRP was founded to emphasize the need for legislation based on Jewish religious law (Halacha) and protective of a "Torah true" tradition. It actively supports Jewish immigration, the development of the private sector, and government support of all Halachically necessary religious activities, including a religious school system and rabbinical councils in every city. These aims have been constant since the founding of NRP's predecessors, and they have been realized to a large degree. With only some minor intraparty disagreement, the NRP view was that it was organized for religious purposes and had no particular role to play in political, economic, or foreign affairs. It was able to cooperate effectively with Mapai (q.v.) and the Israel Labor Party (q.v.) primarily because of its willingness to defer to the left on foreign and defense questions in return for support in religious matters.

With Israel's capture of the West Bank (q.v.) and the Sinai Peninsula (q.v.) in 1967, however, NRP attitudes began to change. The capture of ancient Israeli cities— Hebron (q.v.), Shechem (Nablus), and Old Jerusalem (q.v.)—was seen as a miraculous achievement in fulfillment of the covenant between God and the Jewish people. The NRP believed that the return of any of the territory of historic Israel would be a repudiation of that covenant. On that basis, NRP "hawks" sought to focus the party's efforts on the rapid settlement of the new territory with the aim of securing it for Israel in perpetuity. Although "hawks" are to be found in all of the NRP factions, they appear to be concentrated in the Youth Faction, which originally sought to reform the party organization, in part to increase the opportunities for newer and younger members in the party and government. They also wanted to increase NRP's independence in the coalition with the Labor Party. After 1967, the Youth Faction sought to appeal to nontraditional voters with the slogan "no return of any part of Eretz [historic land of] Israel." Largely because both groups are composed of the same people, the Youth Faction has strong but informal ties with Gush Emunim (q.v.), the leading movement of West Bank settlers. In some respects, the Youth Faction considers itself the political representation of the Gush Emunim.

Youth Faction leaders have come to increasing prominence in both the NRP and the government. Nevertheless, the NRP also encompasses other factions which represent more flexible (i.e. moderate) points of view on the future of the West Bank. The factionalism of the NRP reflects both personal conflicts and differing policy perspectives. Yosef Burg (q.v.) served as the party leader from its founding to the mid-1980s and has served in most Israeli cabinets. A man of great political skill, he has worked successfully to maintain and expand the religious foundation of the state. His seniority and role as head of the largest faction (Lamifneh) secured his dominant position in the party, but he did not dictate its positions or policies. His influence was, in part, the result of his shrewd use of patronage in allocating jobs in the party and the party-controlled institutions. As a government minister, he was also able to distribute many public jobs in the religious and educational establishments and a variety of posts controlled by the Ministry of the Interior.

The Youth Faction leader is Zevulun Hammer (q.v.) (who served as Minister of Education). Hammer became Party General Secretary in 1984. Between the 1984 and 1988 elections the NRP went through a significant reorganization and there was a clear move to the right on political and educational issues. In 1988 Professor Avner Shaki (q.v.) was elected to head the ticket and Zevulun Hammer was placed in the second position. The party's election platform reflected a hawkish tendency. There was an expectation that it could unite all elements of the party and some recent defectors around the candidates and the platform. However, one of the results was the creation of Meimad (q.v.). Led by Shaki in the 1988 Knesset election, NRP supported a program that there would be only one state between the Jordan River and the Mediterranean Sea—the State of Israel. No independent national Arab entity will exist within the limits of the Land of Israel. No part of Israel will be given over to a foreign government or authority and no Jewish settlement will be uprooted. The NRP, however, was prepared for direct negotiations with neighboring Arab states based on any realistic peace proposal.

NATIONAL UNITY GOVERNMENT (NUG) see GOVERNMENT OF NATIONAL UNITY

NATIONAL WATER CARRIER. The national water carrier, put into operation in 1964, brings water from Lake Tiberias (q.v.) through a series of pipes, aqueducts, open canals, reservoirs, tunnels, dams, and pumping stations to various parts of the country, including the northern Negev (q.v.).

NAVON, YITZHAK. Born in Jerusalem (q.v.) on April 19, 1921 of prominent Sephardi (q.v.) lineage. The Navon family is one of the oldest and most distinguished Jerusalem families. On his father's side he came from a wealthy Sephardi family which arrived in Palestine (q.v.) from Constantinople in the 17th century. On his maternal side he is of Moroccan background. Navon received an education at religious schools and at Hebrew University (q.v.), where he studied Hebrew Literature, Arabic, Islamic Culture, and Pedagogy. In 1951, he became political secretary to Foreign Minister Moshe Sharett (q.v.). He served as head of Prime Minister David Ben-Gurion's (q.v.) office from 1952 to 1963. In 1965, after resigning from the civil service, he was elected to the Knesset (q.v.) on the Rafi (q.v.) ticket. In 1972 he was elected Chairman of the World Zionist Council. He served from 1978 to 1983 as the fifth President (q.v.) of Israel. He became Deputy Prime Minister and Minister of Education and Culture in the 1984 National Unity Government (q.v.) and retained those posts in the government established in December 1988. He tended to combine liberal values and Labor socialist ideology with dovish views of foreign policy issues. He often expressed his views publicly during his tenure as President and was a very popular figure in that position.

NAZARETH. A town in northern Israel that was the home of Jesus Christ during his early youth. It was located in the Roman province of Galilee. The Old Testament does not mention Nazareth but Nathanael in the New Testament expressed the attitude of the times when he said, "Can something good come out of Nazareth?" Nazareth remained insignificant for many years after the time of Christ, but in about 600 AD pilgrims visited the town and a large basilica was built. The Arabs later captured the city. The Crusaders built several churches there, but the Ottoman Turks forced Christians to leave in 1517. A new town of Nazareth stands on the site of the old town. The population of Nazareth today is far larger than its population in Biblical times. The Latin Church of the Annunciation, completed in 1730, now rises where some people think the home of Mary, the mother of Jesus, stood. Since the 1700s, several religious denominations have constructed churches and monasteries in Nazareth. An ancient well, called Mary's Well, still flows and people still take water from it. It is the principal Arab city in Israel and most of its inhabitants are Christian although there is a small Muslim minority.

NEEMAN, YUVAL. Born in Tel Aviv (q.v.) in 1925. He was educated at the Technion (q.v.) and holds a PhD from London University. He is a Professor of Physics and served as President of Tel Aviv University (q.v.). He was the founder and Chairman of the Tehiya (q.v.) movement from its inception in 1979. He served as Minister of Science and Development in the government from 1982 to 1984. He previously served as Chief Scientist of the Ministry of Defense and is the recipient of numerous awards and prizes in science. He became

Minister of Science and Development in the government established in June 1990.

NEGEV. The triangular southern half of Israel. It extends from Beersheva (q.v.) south to the port of Eilat (q.v.) on the Gulf of Aqaba (q.v.). The Negev is a semidesert tableland from 1,000 to 2,000 feet (300 to 610 meters) above sea level. It has limestone mountains and flatlands and is covered by a layer of fertile loam, which must have water to grow crops. The Israelis have farmed part of the Negev by irrigation with water brought through the National Water Carrier (q.v.) from Lake Kinneret (the Sea of Galilee (q.v.)) through canals and pipelines. They have also mined phosphates and copper.

NETUREI KARTA (ARAMAIC: GUARDIANS OF THE CITY). A group of religious extremists who live primarily in the Mea Shearim (q.v.) (Hundred Gates) section of Jerusalem (q.v.) and in Bnei Brak. It derives its name from a passage in the Talmud (q.v.) which refers to those who devote themselves to the study of the Torah (q.v.) as the guardians of the city. The group adheres to strict Orthodox views and follows the lifestyles that were brought to Israel from Eastern Europe. Their dress codes are the traditional long coat and black hats of Eastern European origin. They oppose Zionism (q.v.) and have refused to accept Israel as a Jewish state. They oppose the use of the Hebrew language (q.v.) for everyday communication because it is the holy language and because to do so would imply acceptance of Israel as the Jewish state. They believe that a Jewish state can be established only by God. Neturei Karta strongly opposes Israel and has indicated a willingness to work with groups such as the Palestine Liberation Organization (q.v.) and the Arab states to oppose the Zionist enterprise.

The group has close ties with the Satmar Rebbe and those of similar views who are headquartered in Brooklyn, New York. According to their doctrine, any attempt to regain the Holy Land by force or against the will of God is considered a sin. The Zionists, in their view, have usurped the holy name "Israel" and have exploited the Jewish religion and the Holy Land to reinforce their positions. Neturei Karta spokespersons have made clear their opposition to Israel and political Zionism in numerous ways. They do not recognize Israel, do not use its currency, do not speak its language (speaking Yiddish (q.v.) instead), do not go to its schools or hospitals, do not pay taxes, and do not accept any assistance or social security from the state. They see themselves as the original Jewish settlers, the Palestinian Jews who made their way to the Holy Land with the clear intent of worshipping God in his "back yard". They claim to have no political ambitions. They do not recognize the Israeli flag and have no "right" to a flag of their own. They have raised the Palestinian flag because they have said it is a flag of a state they consider to be theirs. They have indicated that they wish to be part of a proposed Palestinian state and to be represented in a joint Palestinian-Jordanian delegation to struggle against the common Zionist enemy.

NEW COMMUNIST LIST (RAKAH). Descended from the Socialist Workers' Party of Palestine (founded in 1919), the party was renamed the Communist Party of Palestine in 1921 and the Communist Party of Israel (Maki) in 1948. A pro-Soviet anti-Zionist group formed Rakah in 1965. It had both Jewish and Arab membership and campaigned for a socialist system in Israel, a lasting peace between Israel and the Arab countries, and the Palestinian Arab people. It favored full implementation of United Nations Security Council Resolutions 242 (q.v.) and 338 (q.v.); Israel's withdrawal from all Arab territories occupied since 1967; formation of a Palestinian Arab state in the West Bank (q.v.) and Gaza Strip (q.v.); recognition of the national rights of the State of Israel and of the Palestine people; democratic rights and defense of working class interests; and demands an end of alleged discrimination against Arab minority in Israel and against Sephardic Jewish communities. It contested the 1984 Knesset (q.v.) election as Hadash (Democratic Front for Peace and Equality) (q.v.), an alliance with the Black Panther (q.v.) movement of Sephardic Jews, winning four seats in the Knesset (q.v.). Its Secretary General is Meir Wilner (q.v.).

NEW LIBERAL PARTY. A political party founded in 1987 as a merger of three groups: Shinui (q.v.), the Liberal Center Party (q.v.), and the Independent Liberal Party (q.v.). Its leaders included Amnon Rubinstein (q.v.), Yitzhak Berman (q.v.), and Moshe Kol.

NEW ZIONIST ORGANIZATION. A worldwide Zionist organization created after members of the Union of Zionists-Revisionists voted to secede from the World Zionist Organization (q.v.). Its aims, articulated at its Constituent Congress in September 1935, included the creation of a Jewish majority on both sides of the Jordan River and the establishment of a Jewish state in Palestine (q.v.).

NISSIM, MOSHE. Born in Jerusalem (q.v.) in 1935, he received a law degree from Hebrew University (q.v.) in 1957. He was first elected on behalf of the General Zionists (q.v.) to the Fourth Knesset (q.v.) in November 1959. He has been elected to all Knessets since 1969 on behalf of the Liberal Party (q.v.) faction of Gahal (q.v.) and the Likud (q.v.) bloc respectively. Moshe Nissim has also served on the Defense and Foreign Affairs, Constitution, Law and Justice, Labor and

House Committees of the Knesset. In the Eighth Knesset he was Co-Chairman of the Likud Knesset faction and, since February 1978, has served as Chairman of the Executive Committee of the Likud. He was appointed Minister Without Portfolio on January 10, 1978 and became Minister of Justice on August 13, 1980. He served as Minister of Finance from April 1986 until December 1988. He became Minister Without Portfolio in the Government established in December 1988. He became Deputy Prime Minister and Minister of Industry and Trade in the Likud-led (q.v.) government established in June 1990.

NRP see NATIONAL RELIGIOUS PARTY

- O -

OCCUPIED TERRITORIES. In the Six Day War (q.v.) Israel occupied various Arab and Arab-held territories including the Sinai Peninsula (q.v.), the Gaza Strip (q.v.), the West Bank (q.v.), East Jerusalem (q.v.) and the Golan Heights (q.v.). Although commonly referred to as occupied territories they are often referred to in Israel as the administered areas.

OCTOBER WAR (1973) see YOM KIPPUR WAR

OFEQ 2. The Ofeq (Horizon) 2 experimental space satellite, produced by Israel Aircraft Industries (q.v.), was launched into space on April 3, 1990, from a site in central Israel. It was similar to but a more advanced model of Ofeq 1, which was put into orbit in September 1988.

OLEH (JEWISH IMMIGRANT TO ISRAEL) see ALIYA

OLMERT, EHUD. Born in Binyamina on September 30, 1945. He was educated at Hebrew University (q.v.) and is a lawyer by profession. He has served as a Likud (q.v.) member of the Knesset (q.v.) since 1977 and became Minister Without Portfolio in the government established in December 1988. He became Minister of Health in the June 1990 government.

OMETZ (COURAGE TO CURE THE ECONOMY). A political party founded in 1982 by Yigael Hurvitz (q.v.), an industrialist who had served, under Likud (q.v.), as Minister of Industry, Commerce and Tourism and, later, as Minister of Finance. The party's primary position was that drastic measures were needed to deal with Israel's substantial economic problems. The party won one Knesset (q.v.) seat in the 1984 election and Hurvitz joined the Government of National Unity (q.v.) as Minister Without Portfolio in 1984.

OPEN BRIDGES POLICY. The term refers to the bridges across the Jordan River between Jordan and the West Bank (q.v.) and Israel as well as to the links between Israel and Jordan developed after the Six Day War (q.v.) of 1967. Moshe Dayan (q.v.), who was Minister of Defense, allowed the shipment of goods (mostly agricultural produce) and later the crossing of people between the two sides of the river.

OPERATION ALI BABA (OPERATION EZRA AND NEHEMIA). The airborne transfer to Israel of virtually all of Iraq's ancient Jewish community (about 123,000), which migrated to Israel in 1950.

OPERATION ENTEBBE see ENTEBBE OPERATION

OPERATION EXODUS. The name given to the effort begun in 1990 to achieve the emigration of Soviet Jews from the USSR (q.v.) and to resettle them in Israel. In 1990–1991 more than 350,000 Soviet Jews arrived in Israel for resettlement and absorption.

OPERATION EZRA AND NEHEMIA see OPERATION ALI BABA

OPERATION JONATHAN see ENTEBBE OPERATION

OPERATION LITANI. In 1978 Israel launched an invasion of southern Lebanon to drive the Palestinians from their positions close to the Israeli border from which they had been launching attacks against Israel since before the Yom Kippur War (q.v.).

OPERATION MAGIC CARPET. The airborne transfer to Israel in 1949–1950 of virtually the entire Jewish community of Yemen.

OPERATION MOSES. A massive airlift in late 1984 and early 1985 that brought thousands of Falashas (Jews of Ethiopia) to Israel from refugee camps in the Sudan.

OPERATION PEACE FOR GALILEE see WAR IN LEBANON

OPERATION SOLOMON. An airlift of some 15,000 Ethiopian Jews from Addis Ababa, Ethiopia to Israel carried out by the government of Israel on the weekend of May 24–25, 1991.

ORIENTAL JEWS. Originally, the term was used to refer to the Jews from Spain who were expelled from the Iberian Peninsula during the Inquisition, but currently the term is used when referring to Jews of non-Western European descent. They hold strong traditional beliefs of the Sephardim and often their educational and living standards are lower than the Ashkenazi Jews (q.v.). They constitute a majority of the country's population. Israel's non-Ashkenazi Jews are referred to as Edot Hamizrach (eastern, or Oriental, communities), Sephardim, or Oriental Jews. The term Sephardim (derived from the Hebrew name for Spain) is often used to refer to all Jews whose origin is in the Arab world and Muslim lands, although it properly refers to the Jews of Spain and the Iberian Peninsula and the communities they established in areas to which they migrated after their expulsion from the Iberian peninsula during the Spanish Inquisition. The Iberian Jews generally spoke Ladino (q.v.), a Judeo-Spanish language originally written in medieval Hebrew letters and later in Latin letters (much as the Ashkenazi Jews spoke Yiddish (q.v.)), whereas those of the Middle Eastern communities did not. Most of the Oriental immigration came after Israel's independence from the eastern Arab states (such as Iraq) and from Iran, where the Jews had resided for more than two thousand years and often had substantial centers of learning. The community is diverse and pluralistic, although a collective "Oriental" identity appears to be emerging.

"ORIENTAL REVOLT". The lack of substantial political organization in the Oriental Jewish (q.v.) population in the first decades after Israel's independence meant that its method of expression was by casting votes for, or withholding them from, the major established political parties. This seemed to reach a plateau in the 1981 Knesset (q.v.) elections, when the Oriental vote for Likud (q.v.) led the Israeli media to speak of an "Oriental revolt," and the Jewish ethnic issue became more public during the campaign. It seemed to suggest full-scale Oriental efforts to be heard in the electoral process and to follow the pattern foreshadowed in the 1977 election and replicated in the 1984 election, although the ethnic issue was all but eliminated from the latter campaign.

OZ, AMOS. Born in Jerusalem (q.v.) in 1939. Educated at the Hebrew University (q.v.) of Jerusalem (BA) and at Oxford University (MA). A member of Kibbutz Hulda. Widely published author of novels, short stories, essays, and articles in Israel and abroad including *My Michael; Touch the Water, Touch the Wind;* and *In the Land of Israel.*

- P -

PALESTINE. The geographical area of which part is occupied by the State of Israel. Palestine is one of the names for the territory that has also been known as the Holy Land or the Land of Israel (Eretz Israel (q.v.)). The name is derived from the fact that it was called Palestina by the Greeks and the Romans because of the Philistines who lived in part of the region. During the period of Ottoman control it was generally known by the Arabic Filastin, although it was part of the province of Syria. The League of Nations' Palestine Mandate (q.v.) awarded to the British included territory on both sides of the Jordan River but Transjordan was soon separated and only the area west of the river was referred to as the Palestine Mandate between 1922 and 1948. With the establishment of Israel and the first Arab-Israeli War (q.v.) Palestine ceased to exist as a geographical or political unit.

PALESTINE LIBERATION ORGANIZATION (PLO). An organization originally created and established by the Arab League in 1964 which claims to represent the Palestinian people wherever they may live. Its original leader was Ahmed Shukeiri, but after the Six Day War (q.v.) and the substantial Israeli victory with its occupation of the West Bank (q.v.) and Gaza Strip (q.v.), Yasser Arafat took over the leadership of Fatah and subsequently of the PLO. He has remained its Chairman since and has been the international representative and symbol of the PLO. He gives voice to its demands and guides its overall direction and policy. The status of the PLO as the "sole legitimate representative" of the Palestinians as claimed by the PLO and by the Arab states has posed a major stumbling block in negotiations for settlement of the Arab-Israeli conflict since Israel continues to see it as a terrorist organization with which it cannot and will not negotiate. See also PALESTINE NATIONAL COVENANT.

PALESTINE MANDATE see BRITISH MANDATE

PALESTINE NATIONAL COVENANT. The Covenant was adopted by the Palestine Liberation Organization (PLO) (q.v.) in 1964. Its central theme is the elimination of Israel and its replacement by a Palestinian state established in all of Palestine (q.v.). It was rewritten by the Palestine National Council in Cairo in July 1968. At the core of the Covenant is Article 20 which declares that the "Balfour Declaration, the Mandate for Palestine and everything that has been based upon them, are deemed null and void." Although various Palestinian leaders have suggested that the Covenant has been superseded in part by subsequent statements and declarations, the Covenant remains formally unchanged as the guide to Palestinian objectives.

PALESTINE PARTITION PLAN. A plan adopted by the United Nation's General Assembly on November 29, 1947 dividing the Palestine Mandate (q.v.) into an Arab state, a Jewish state, and an internationalized sector including Jerusalem (q.v.). It provided the basis for Israel's independence.

PALMAH (ACRONYM FOR PLUGOT MAHATZ— ASSAULT COMPANIES). Commando units of the Hagana (q.v.) in Palestine (q.v.) and later the shock batallions of the Israel Defense Forces (q.v.): In May 1941 the Hagana created a full-time military force of volunteers, something of a professional and elite unit. The Palmah played a key role in Israel's War of Independence (q.v.) but afterward its units became part of the Israel Defense Forces.

PARLIAMENT see KNESSET

PARTITION PLAN see PALESTINE PARTITION PLAN

PATT, GIDEON (FORMERLY GIDEON MARCUS– after his mother died and his aunt Haya Patt adopted him his name was changed). Born in Jerusalem (q.v.) in 1933, Gideon Patt studied in religious schools and at the Merkaz Harav yeshiva. After serving in the army he entered politics. He went to the United States to work for Nahum Goldmann, then Chairman of the World Zionist Organization (q.v.). He received a BSc in Economics, International Trade and Labor Relations from New York University in 1963. He worked as an adviser to Yosef Sapir, Minister of Commerce and Industry, from 1964 to 1970. He joined the Knesset (q.v.) on behalf of the Liberal Party (q.v.) faction of Gahal (q.v.) in January 1970. He has continued to serve as a Member of the Knesset representing the same faction within the Likud bloc since, focusing his parliamentary activity on economic affairs and serving on the Economics, Interior and Finance Committees of the Knesset. In January 1979 he was appointed Minister of Industry, Commerce and Tourism and on August 5, 1981, he was sworn in as Minister of Commerce and Industry. Patt served as Minister of Science and development in the National Unity Government established in 1984. In December 1988 he became Minister of Tourism and retained that portfolio in the government established by Yitzhak Shamir in June 1990.

PEACE FOR GALILEE see WAR IN LEBANON

PEACE MOVEMENT. Within Israel, between the Six Day (q.v.) and Yom Kippur Wars (q.v.), two alternatives to the official position developed that focused on the occupied territories (q.v.) and their disposition. Some argued that Israel should retain the territories occupied in 1967 and establish settlements there. The Peace Movement, which was composed of a number of small groups on the left, took time to become established, in part because the official position preempted the Movement's main arguments by making overtures to the Arab states that indicated Israel was prepared to return territory for peace and to be magnanimous in victory. When it became clear that Israel's insistence on direct negotiations for peace was unsuccessful in achieving its objective and when the government began to show an interest in establishing settlements and retaining territories, the Peace Movement became more prominent. It argued that the failure of the peace process could be attributed to the government of Israel for not taking greater initiatives. See also PEACE NOW.

PEACE NOW (SHALOM ACHSHAV). An interest group established in the spring of 1978 when reserve army officers wrote to Prime Minister Menachem Begin (q.v.) urging him to pursue peace vigorously. It has worked to keep the subject on the public agenda with rallies and demonstrations. Among its positions is the view that there should be territorial compromise and Israel should relinquish some of the occupied territories (q.v.). It was prominent in protests against the War in Lebanon (q.v.) and the Sabra and Shatila (q.v.) camp massacres.

PEEL COMMISSION. British Royal Commission appointed in May 1937 to investigate unrest in Palestine (q.v.). The Peel Royal Commission recommended partition of the Palestine Mandate into an Arab state united with Transjordan and a Jewish state, while retaining a British enclave. The recommendation was later abandoned, but in 1939, in a new White Paper, the British dramatically restricted Jewish immigration to Palestine. See also BRITISH MANDATE.

PELED, MATITYAHU. Retired from the Israel Defense Forces (q.v.) as a Brigadier General. Served in the Knesset (q.v.) representing the Progressive List for Peace (q.v.) in the 1984 parliamentary session.

PERES, SHIMON (FORMERLY PERSKY). Born on August 16, 1923 in the town of Vishneva, Poland, to Isaac and Sarah Persky. Because of British restrictions and the financial burdens associated with immigration Isaac Persky emigrated to Palestine (q.v.) in 1931, leaving his wife and two sons behind. The family was reunited in Palestine in 1934. He became involved in the largest of the movements Hashomer Hatzair (q.v.) (Young Guard), and later joined Hanoar Haoved (Working Youth). By 1941 Peres was a leader in the Kibbutz movement in Palestine and he continued his efforts within Hanoar Haoved. In 1942 he joined Kibbutz Alumot and he remained a member until 1957. Peres's military career began in the Hagana (q.v.). He rose to the rank of position commander by his late teens, and in 1947 he accepted Levi Eshkol's (q.v.) offer to serve as Director of Manpower and in that capacity was active in the procurement and manufacture of arms for the Israel Defense Forces (IDF) (q.v.). His successful efforts to develop and acquire arms both at home and abroad gained him recognition as one of the pioneers of Israel's defense industry.

After Israel's War of Independence (q.v.) in 1949, Peres asked Prime Minister David Ben-Gurion (q.v.) for a leave of absence to study abroad. Ben-Gurion granted the leave provided Peres continue his arms acquisition efforts in the United States where he chose to study at Harvard University and New York University. He returned to Israel and in February 1952 was appointed to serve as Deputy Director-General of the Defense Ministry. In October 1952 he became acting Director-General of the Defense Ministry. As Director-General of the Defense Ministry Peres continued his efforts to acquire high quality weapons for the IDF. Peres spent much of his time fostering Franco-Israeli relations and France remained Israel's primary supplier of major weapons systems until after the Six Day War (q.v.) of 1967. Peres's efforts included gaining French consent to provide Israel with an atomic reactor located at Dimona (q.v.). Peres was instrumental in the creation of Bedek, which later came to be known as the Israel Aircraft Industries (IAI) (q.v.).

Peres's Knesset (q.v.) career began in 1959 when he was elected to parliament as a member of the Mapai (q.v.) party although he continued to serve as Deputy Minister of Defense. Peres was included in Ben-Gurion's cabinet which gave him a larger role in policy debates. In 1963 David Ben-Gurion resigned and was replaced by Levi Eshkol (q.v.) as Prime Minister and Minister of Defense. Ben-Gurion's retirement from politics lasted only two years before he returned to the political arena in June 1965 as the leader of a new political party called Rafi (q.v.). Peres resigned his position in the government to join Ben-Gurion and become Secretary General of the new party. He managed the party's campaign efforts in the 1965 election in which it won ten seats. But the government did not include Rafi or any of its members. In 1968, Rafi joined with Mapai and Ahdut Haavoda (q.v.) to form the Israel

Labor Party (q.v.). Between 1969 and 1973 Peres held a variety of cabinet posts including Minister of Absorption, Minister of Transport, Minister of Information, Minister of Communications, and Minister Without Portfolio, with responsibility for economic development in the occupied territories.

Then in April 1974 Golda Meir (q.v.) submitted her resignation as Prime Minister. The two candidates who emerged were Peres, who was serving as Minister of Information, and Yitzhak Rabin (q.v.), Minister of Labor. Rabin who was the preferred choice of the party establishment, won a close vote over Peres in the Labor Party's central committee. However, Peres's performance established him as the number two man in the party. The new government was established in June 1974 with Rabin as Prime Minister and Peres as Minister of Defense. Relations between Peres and Rabin were strained during the term of the government. Disputes arose over domestic and foreign policy, the selection of personnel, and the scope of their authority.

Peres formally announced his intention to challenge Rabin for the party leadership in January 1977. The showdown took place at the Labor Party convention the following month where Rabin prevailed by a slim majority. However, a series of scandals including the disclosure that Rabin's wife maintained bank accounts in the United States in violation of Israeli currency laws, led Rabin to resign from the chairmanship of the Labor Party in April 1977, just one month prior to the Knesset elections. Peres became the party's new leader and candidate for the premiership. Despite Peres's efforts, a Likud-led government won a plurality of Knesset seats and succeeded in forming the government. In June 1977 Peres was elected Labor Party Chairman. The 1981 election was Peres's second loss to Begin. In the 1984 election Labor secured 44 seats to Likud's (q.v.) 41, and although he received the mandate to form the government Peres was unable to form a majority coalition. This led to the formation of a National Unity Government (NUG) (q.v.), which was a new experiment in Israeli politics. A rotation (q.v.) agreement was adopted which called for Peres to serve as Prime Minister for the first half of the 50-month term while Shamir served as Foreign Minister. After 25 months the two rotated positions for the balance of the term. During his tenure as Prime Minister Peres presided over Israel's withdrawal from Lebanon, and confronted the economic problems with austerity measures. He conducted an active foreign policy. Among Peres's successes was a summit meeting with King Hassan of Morocco in July 1986. Israel's special relationship with the United States improved considerably during Peres's tenure, which was a change from the tension which frequently characterized relations during Begin and Shamir's tenure in office. The 1988 Knesset election, as in 1984, did not produce a clear victory for either Labor or Likud. Shamir was given the mandate to form a coalition by President Chaim Herzog (q.v.). The central difference between the 1988 coalition agreement and the 1984 agreement was that Shamir would serve as Prime Minister for the duration of the government. Peres accepted the position of Finance Minister. Peres and the other Labor Party ministers left the government in the spring of 1990 and forced a vote of confidence in the Knesset which the Shamir-led government lost. Peres subsequently sought to form a government during the spring of 1990, but was unsuccessful. In June 1990 Shamir was able to form a government which gained the confidence of the Knesset. Peres reverted to the role of leader of the opposition in the Knesset.

PERETZ, YITZHAK HAIM. Born in 1939 in Morocco and an ordained Rabbi, Peretz served as Chief Rabbi of Raanana. Elected to the Knesset (q.v.) on the Shas (q.v.) list, he served in the Government of National Unity (q.v.) established in 1984 as a Minister Without Portfolio (until December 1984); as Minister of the Interior (from December 1984 to January 1987); and as Minister Without Portfolio (from May 1987 to December 1988). He became Minister of Immigration and Absorption in the government formed in December 1988 and retained that position in the government established in June 1990.

PETAH TIKVA. A city on the coastal plain of Israel northeast of Tel Aviv (q.v.). It was founded in 1878 as an agricultural settlement and developed into the first modern Jewish moshava (private village) in the country and became known as the "mother of moshavot". It has become a growing and thriving city.

PLO see PALESTINE LIBERATION ORGANIZATION

POALEI AGUDAT ISRAEL (WORKERS OF THE AS-SOCIATION OF ISRAEL). A religious labor movement dedicated to the building of the Land of Israel in the spirit of the Torah (q.v.). Founded in 1922 in Poland to counteract the growth of secularism, socialism, and antireligious tendencies among workers, this organization was the labor wing of Agudat Israel (q.v.). Within Agudat Israel, it fought for the development of the land and the building of a Jewish state in the spirit of the Torah and tradition. In the late 1920s the first Poalei Agudat Israel pioneers arrived in Palestine (q.v.). In 1933 they founded Kibbutz Hafetz Hayim. In 1946, it founded the World Union of Poalei Agudat Israel. Its members joined the Hagana (q.v.) to fight the Arab invasion in 1948 and it joined the trade union department of the Histadrut (q.v.) under a special arrangement. In 1960 it officially split from Agudat Israel and became independent. It joined with a splinter group from the National Religious Party (q.v.) to form Morasha (q.v.) to contest the 1984 Knesset (q.v.) election.

POALEI ZION. Literally "workers of Zion." A Zionist socialist workers' party, which began in Russia, Austria, and the United States in the late 19th and early 20th centuries. Influenced by Dov Ber Borochov, Poalei Zion's platform was based on Marxist principles developed along nationalist lines. The party's worldwide movement was continually involved in arguments on such fundamental issues as cooperative settlement activity in Eretz Israel initiated by the labor class; membership in the Zionist movement (which included members of the bourgeoisie); and the party's relationship to the Communist International.

"POLITICIDE". A term developed to describe the destruction of a state, that is, the Arab goal of destroying Israel. Between 1949 and 1967 Israel was prepared for peace with the Arab states on the basis of the 1949 armistice (q.v.) lines with minor modifications, but after the events of May and June 1967, including the Six Day War (q.v.), the stark reality of "politicide" began to enter into these considerations, and many argued for a need to change the security situation.

PORUSH, MENACHEM. An ordained Rabbi. Born in Jerusalem (q.v.) on April 2, 1916, he was educated at religious schools. He served as a correspondent for foreign newspapers from 1932 to 1938 and as an editor for *Kol Israel* from 1936 to 1949. He was first elected to the Knesset (q.v.) as a member for Agudat Israel (q.v.) in 1959. He served as Vice Mayor of Jerusalem from 1969 to 1974. He served as Deputy Minister of Labor and Social Affairs in the National Unity Government (q.v.) established in 1984. He was reelected to the Knesset in the 1988 elections.

PRESIDENT (NASI). Nasi in Hebrew means "prince" or, now, President. The title Nasi is derived from the head of the Sanhedrin, the assembly of Jewish scholars which served as both a legislature and supreme court until the fifth century. The President is elected by a simple majority of the Knesset (q.v.) for a five-year term and may be elected for no more than two consecutive terms. He is head of state and has powers that are essentially representative character. In the sphere of foreign affairs these functions include signing instruments that relate to treaties ratified by the Knesset; appointing diplomatic and consular representatives; receiving foreign diplomatic representatives; and issuing consular exequaturs (official written accreditations). In the domestic sphere, the President has the power to grant pardons and reprieves and to commute sentences.

Subsequent to nomination by the appropriate body, the head of state appoints civil judges; dayanim (judges of the Jewish religious courts); kadis (judges of Muslim religious courts); the state comptroller (q.v.), the president of the Magen David Adom Association (q.v.) (Red Shield of David, or Israel's equivalent of the Red Cross); and the Governor of the Bank of Israel (q.v.), as well as other officials as determined by law. The President signs all laws passed by the Knesset, with the exception of those relating to presidential powers, and all documents to which the state seal is affixed. Official documents signed by the President require the counter-signature of the Prime Minister or other duly authorized minister, with the exception of those where another procedure is laid down, as in the case of the judges.

The President's powers and functions relating to the formation of the government fall into a different category. After elections, or the resignation or death of the Prime Minister, the President consults with representatives of the parties in parliament and selects a member of the Knesset to form a government. Although anyone may be chosen, traditionally the member has been the leader of the largest party in the Knesset. Until 1984, this formal discretion has not been accompanied by any real choice because the political composition of the Knesset had determined the selection. Nevertheless, situations are conceivable in which different party combinations might gain the support of the Knesset, and in such instances the President would fulfill a crucial political role in determining the person chosen to form a cabinet. The President also receives the resignation of the government. Another aspect of the presidential role that could have potential political significance in the future is the office's public position and prestige potential—the President makes visits throughout the country, delivers speeches, and formally opens the first session of each Knesset. Generally, however, these activities up to now have been ceremonial in nature.

PROGRESSIVE LIST FOR PEACE (PLP). An Arab-Jewish political party led by Palestinian lawyer Muhammad Miari from Haifa (q.v.) and two prominent Jewish leftists, Matityahu Peled (q.v.) and Uri Avneri, but supported primarily by Israeli Arabs (q.v.). The party held its first convention in August 1985. It called for the government to recognize the Palestine Liberation Organization (q.v.) as the sole legitimate representative of the Palestinians with whom peace talks can be conducted. It called on Israel to withdraw totally from all territories occupied in 1967, foremost among which is Arab Jerusalem (q.v.), and restore them to the Palestinian Arab people. It called for a continuation of the struggle against racism, fascism, and Kahanism. It supports the establishment of a Palestinian state in the West Bank (q.v.) and the Gaza Strip (q.v.) alongside Israel. It also endorses an international conference for peace in the Middle East which would include the five permanent members of the United Nations Security

Council as well as Israel and the PLO and all other parties to the conflict.

PROGRESSIVE PARTY (HAMIFLAGA HAPROGRES-SIVIT). A political party established in October 1948 by combining Haoved Hazioni, the Aliya Hadasha, and the left wing of the General Zionists (q.v.). Its focus was on domestic social and related issues. Pinhas Rosen represented the party in government coalitions and served as Minister of Justice. In April 1961 the Progressive Party united with the General Zionist Party to form the Liberal Party (q.v.). In 1965 the former General Zionists decided to establish a parliamentary bloc with the Herut Party (q.v.). The former Progressives opposed this move and many split from the Liberal Party to establish the Independent Liberal Party (q.v.).

- Q -

QUMRAN see DEAD SEA SCROLLS

- R -

RABBINATE OF ISRAEL. The origins of the institution of the Chief Rabbinate of Israel date back when Palestine (q.v.) was part of the Ottoman Empire. According to Ottoman regulations, the Sultan would appoint one eminent Turkish Rabbi as Chief Rabbi of the Jews of the Ottoman Empire, which included Palestine. Residing in Constantinople and bearing the title Hakham (Haham) Bashi (literally, "Chief Sage"), he was the official spokesman of the Jewish community to the authorities, and by firman (the Sultan's command) he exercised broad authority over all the religious activities and spiritual concerns of members of the Jewish community throughout the Ottoman Empire. The Hakham Bashi of Jerusalem (q.v.) had the title Rishon Le-Zion (q.v.) (First in Zion). The Rishon Le-Zion gradually came to assume authority over all the religious affairs of the Jews of Palestine. The post of Hakham Bashi was always held by a Rabbi of the Sephardi (q.v.) community in Jerusalem, which originally constituted the majority of the Yishuv (q.v.).

Sir Herbert Samuel (q.v.), the first High Commissioner for Palestine, appointed a commission headed by Norman Bentwich, then Legal Secretary of the mandatory government, which recommended the establishment of an electoral college of 100 members to choose two Chief Rabbis and a Council of the Chief Rabbinate (q.v.). In 1921 the electoral college met in Jerusalem and it elected Rabbis Avraham Yitzhak Hacohen Kook (q.v.) and Yaakov Meir as Chief Rabbis and presidents of the Council of the Chief Rabbinate of Palestine. The mandatory government accepted the newly organized Chief Rabbinate of Palestine as exercising sole jurisdiction in matters of personal status. The office of Hakham Bashi was abolished, and the judgments of the Rabbinate were enforced by the civil courts. On January 12, 1936, new elections were held and Rabbi Isaac Halevi Herzog (q.v.) was chosen Ashkenazi Chief Rabbi and Rabbi Meir reelected Sephardi Chief Rabbi. As Rabbi Meir was ill, Rabbi Ben-Zion Meir Hay Uziel was elected his acting representative. In 1945 Chief Rabbis Herzog and Uziel were reelected.

After the independence of Israel, the first elections for the Council of the Chief Rabbinate were held in March, 1955. Chief Rabbi Herzog was reelected and Rabbi Yitzhak Rahamim Nissim was chosen to replace Rabbi Uziel, who had died in 1953. In 1964 Rabbi Nissim was reelected Sephardi Chief Rabbi, and Rabbi Issar Yehuda Unterman, the Chief Rabbi of Tel Aviv, was elected Ashkenazi Chief Rabbi to succeed Chief

Rabbi Herzog, who had died in 1959. See also CHIEF RABBINATE.

RABIN, YITZHAK. Born in Jerusalem (q.v.) on March 1, 1922, to Russian immigrants to Palestine (q.v.). He entered the prestigious Kadourie Agricultural School in the Galilee (q.v.) in 1937 and, after graduation in 1940, he moved to Kibbutz Ramat Yohanan. He joined the Hagana (q.v.) in May 1941 and subsequently served in the Palmah (q.v.). Later, he was arrested in a massive sweep by British Mandatory (q.v.) authorities and he spent a brief period in a British prison. In October 1947, he was appointed Deputy Commander of the Palmah. A month before Israel declared its independence on May 14, 1948, he was put in charge of the Palmah's Harel Brigade and was assigned the task of eliminating Arab strongholds along the Tel Aviv (q.v.)-Jerusalem (q.v.) road.

Rabin's military career included a variety of positions in the Israel Defense Forces (q.v.) during Israel's formative years, including head of the army's tactical operations division from 1950 to 1952, head of the training branch from 1954 to 1956, and Commanding Officer of the northern command from 1956 to 1959. He was then appointed Army Chief of Operations and came into conflict with then Deputy Defense Minister Shimon Peres (q.v.) over the question of who should determine the priorities in the acquisition and manufacture of arms. Rabin believed that the decision should be made by professional soldiers rather than by civilians in the defense ministry. It developed into a bitter personal feud. Rabin was appointed Chief of Staff of the IDF in January 1964 and during his tenure focused on the restructuring of the army and on acquiring more advanced weaponry. In the Six Day War (q.v.) Rabin's army won a decisive victory over its Arab adversaries in six days, radically transforming the situation in the Middle East. In February 1968 he became Israel's

Ambassador to the United States and, in March 1973, returned to Israel.

After the Knesset (q.v.) election of December 1973 Rabin was invited by Golda Meir (q.v.) to join the new cabinet as Defense Minister because of Moshe Dayan's (q.v.) refusal to serve in the new government. When Dayan suddenly announced his willingness to join, Rabin became Minister of Labor. But, Golda Meir resigned following publication of the Agranat Commission's (q.v.) interim report. On April 22, 1974, Rabin was chosen by the Labor Party (q.v.) central committee to succeed Golda Meir as Prime Minister, but Peres's strong showing in the vote earned him the post of Defense Minister, from which he tried to undermine Rabin's authority at almost every turn in the hope of replacing him. Rabin served as Prime Minister from June 1974 to May 1977 during which time he concentrated on rebuilding the IDF to which the successful raid at Entebbe (q.v.) airport contributed by restoring the army's and nation's self-confidence. He also successfully negotiated a second disengagement of forces agreement with Egypt brokered by the United States. Rabin's term as Prime Minister ended prematurely in 1977 after a cabinet dispute led to the scheduling of early elections. A month before the election, Rabin was forced to step down after admitting that he and his wife had maintained an illegal bank account in the United States. Peres was designated to head the Labor Party list in the election, but Labor was defeated at the polls. For the next four years, Rabin found himself in Peres's political shadow and the relationship between the two was highly contentious. Rabin challenged Peres for the party's leadership at its national convention in December 1980 but lost. In 1984, Rabin became Minister of Defense in the National Unity Government (q.v.) that was formed following the July 1984 election and remained in that position under both Shimon Peres and Yitzhak Shamir (q.v.). He once again became Minister of Defense in the government established in December 1988. He left the government with the other Labor ministers in the spring of 1990. Subsequently, Rabin failed in his challenge to Shimon Peres in the summer of 1990 for the leadership of the party.

RABINOWITZ, YEHOSHUA. Born in Poland on November 13, 1911. He immigrated to Palestine (q.v.) in 1934 and joined Mapai (q.v.) in the mid-1950s. He was elected to the Tel Aviv (q.v.) city council in 1956, became Deputy Mayor in 1959 and became Mayor of Tel Aviv-Jaffa in 1969. He was defeated for reelection in 1973. He became Finance Minister in the government established by Yitzhak Rabin (q.v.) in 1974 and remained in office until 1977.

RACHEL, TOMB OF. The Bible relates that Rachel, one of the matriarchs of the Jewish people, was buried on the way to Bethlehem and a site near that city has been regarded as that spot since ancient times. It has been a place of Jewish pilgrimage.

RAFI (RESHIMAT POALEI ISRAEL—ISRAEL LABOR LIST). A political party founded in July 1965 by David Ben-Gurion (q.v.) and seven other Knesset (q.v.) members. The founders seceded from Mapai (q.v.) over the issue of the Lavon Affair (q.v.). Teddy Kollek (q.v.), its candidate, was elected mayor of Jerusalem (q.v.) in 1965. In the Knesset elections it secured ten seats. It remained in opposition to the government until the eve of the Six Day War (q.v.) when it joined the Government of National Unity (q.v.) and Moshe Dayan (a member) became Minister of Defense. In January 1968 it joined Mapai and Ahdut Haavoda (q.v.) to form the Israel Labor Party (q.v.). Ben-Gurion and some of his followers opposed Rafi joining in the Israel Labor Party and established a new party—Reshima Mamlakhtit (State List) (q.v.). In the Knesset elections of 1969 it won four seats.

RAKAH (RESHIMA KOMUNISTIT HADASHA—NEW COMMUNIST LIST) see NEW COMMUNIST LIST and COMMUNIST PARTY

RAMADAN WAR see YOM KIPPUR WAR

RAMAT GAN. A city on the outskirts of Tel Aviv (q.v.) founded in 1914 and into which the first settlers moved in 1922. Since Israel's independence it has become one of the most important industrial centers of the country. Among its important activities is the Diamond Center— the focal point of Israel's important diamond (q.v.) industry. Bar Ilan University (q.v.) is located there.

RATZ see CITIZENS' RIGHTS AND PEACE MOVEMENT

RELIGIOUS AFFAIRS, MINISTRY OF. The Ministry of Religious Affairs has primary responsibility for meeting Jewish religious requirements, such as the supply of ritually killed and prepared (kosher) meat, for overseeing rabbinical courts and religious schools, as well as for looking after the autonomous religious needs of the non-Jewish communities.

RELIGIOUS PARTIES see AGUDAT ISRAEL, DEGEL HATORAH, HAPOEL HAMIZRAHI, MEIMAD, MIZRAHI, MORASHA, NATIONAL RELIGIOUS PARTY, POALEI AGUDAT ISRAEL, SHAS, TAMI, TORAH RELIGIOUS FRONT, UNITED RELIGIOUS FRONT

RESOLUTION 242 see UNITED NATIONS SECURITY COUNCIL RESOLUTION 242

RESOLUTION 338 see UNITED NATIONS SECURITY COUNCIL RESOLUTION 338

REVISIONISTS. A Zionist political party, founded in 1925 by Vladimir Zeev Jabotinsky (q.v.). It reflected the demand for a revision of the Zionist Executive's conciliatory policy toward the British Mandatory (q.v.) government and of the system and pace of Zionist activity in Palestine (q.v.). In the Revisionist conception, the Zionist aim was to provide an integral solution to the worldwide Jewish problem in all its aspects—political, economic, and spiritual. To attain this objective, the Revisionists demanded that the entire mandated territory of Palestine, on both sides of the Jordan River, be turned into a Jewish State with a Jewish majority. The contention of the Revisionists was that worldwide political pressure must be exerted to induce Britain to abide by the letter and spirit of the Palestine Mandate. They stressed the imperative necessity of bringing to Palestine the largest number of Jews within the shortest possible time. The financial instrument of the movement was the Keren Tel Hai (Tel Hai Fund). Within the World Zionist Organization (WZO) (q.v.), Revisionism met with increasingly strong resistance, particularly from the labor groups. The World Union of Zionists-Revisionists was founded in 1925 as an integral part of the WZO with Jabotinsky as President. The Revisionists strongly opposed expansion of the Jewish Agency (q.v.) through inclusion of prominent non-Zionists, which, they felt, would impair the national character, independence, and freedom of political action of the Zionist movement. From 1929, when the expanded Jewish Agency took over the political prerogatives of the WZO, Jabotinsky consistently urged increasing independence for the Revisionists. In 1935 a referendum held among Revisionists resulted in their secession from the World Zionist Organization and the establishment of an independent New Zionist Organization (NZO) (q.v.).

Eleven years later, when ideological and tactical differences between the NZO and the WZO had diminished,
the NZO decided to give up its separate existence. The
United Zionists-Revisionists (the merger of the Revisionist Union and the Jewish State party) participated in
the elections to the 22d Zionist Congress in Basle in 1946.

RISHON LE-ZION (FIRST IN ZION). Title of the Sephardi
(q.v.) Chief Rabbi of Israel. Prior to the creation of the
Chief Rabbinate the title was used for the head of the
Sephardi Rabbis of Jerusalem (q.v.). See RABBINATE
OF ISRAEL and CHIEF RABBINATE.

RISHON LE ZION (FIRST IN ZION). A city founded in
1882 by immigrants from Russia. The name is derived
from the Bible.

ROSENNE, MEIR. Born in Iasi, Romania, on February 19,
1931 and immigrated to Palestine (q.v.) at the age of 13.
He studied at the Sorbonne where he received his MA in
Political Science and his PhD with honors in International Law. He is a graduate of the Institute for
Advanced International Studies in Paris. Ambassador
Rosenne joined the Israel government service in 1953
and served in a variety of positions. Between 1971 and
1979 he was legal adviser to the Israel Foreign Ministry.
In this capacity he served as the legal adviser to the
Israel delegation to the negotiations at Kilometer 101,
the Geneva Peace Talks (1973), and the related negotiations with the Egyptian and Syrian delegations following
the Yom Kippur War (q.v.). He participated in the
negotiations leading to the Egypt-Israel Peace Treaty
(q.v.) in 1979 and, until September 1979, he was head of
the Israeli team to the autonomy negotiations with
Egypt. He became Ambassador to France in 1979 and
served in that capacity until May 1983, when he was
nominated to be Israel's Ambassador to the United

States. Subsequent to his service as Ambassador to the United States he became head of the Israel Bonds Organization (q.v.).

ROSH HANIKRA. Border point on the Israel-Lebanon frontier at the Mediterranean Sea.

ROTATION. The coalition agreement between Labor (q.v.) and Likud (q.v.) which established the Government of National Unity (q.v.) in 1984 provided for the "rotation" of the positions of Prime Minister and Foreign Minister between Yitzhak Shamir (q.v.) of Likud and Shimon Peres (q.v.) of the Alignment. During the first 25 months of the government, Peres was to serve as Prime Minister and Shamir as Foreign Minister. They would then "rotate" and Shamir would become Prime Minister and Peres Foreign Minister for the second 25 months. Despite dire predictions concerning the fate of the agreement and the government established under its terms, the rotation took place in October 1986 as scheduled and the government served its full term.

RUBINSTEIN, AMNON. Born in 1931 in Tel Aviv (q.v.), he graduated from the Law Faculty of Hebrew University (q.v.) in Jerusalem and received his PhD from the London School of Economics. A lawyer by profession, he served as Dean of the Faculty of Law of Tel Aviv University (q.v.) and as Professor of Law. Chairman of the Shinui (q.v.) faction in the Tenth Knesset (q.v.). He served as Minister of Communications in the 1984 Government of National Unity (q.v.).

- S -

SABRA. A term commonly used to refer to native born Israelis. It is derived from the name of the cactus plant (in Hebrew, Tzabar) which grows in Israel. The plant has a sweet and juicy fruit encased in a tough skin that has numerous thorns. This is supposed to characterize the Israelis who are seen as tough on the outside but gentle inside.

SABRA AND SHATILA REFUGEE CAMPS. Among the tragic aspects of the War in Lebanon (q.v.) of 1982 was the massacre by Christian Phalangist forces of Palestinians at the Sabra and Shatila refugee camps in the Beirut area. The resultant anguish within Israel over possible Israeli involvement led to the decision to create a Commission of Inquiry, headed by Supreme Court Chief Justice Yitzhak Kahan. See also KAHAN COMMISSION OF INQUIRY.

SADAT, ANWAR. Became President of Egypt (q.v.) after the death of Gamal Abdul Nasser and led Egypt in the Yom Kippur War (q.v.). He proposed direct negotiations with Israel to resolve the Arab-Israeli conflict and visited Israel in November 1977. He signed the Camp David Accords (q.v.) of 1978 and the Egypt-Israel Peace Treaty (q.v.) of 1979 and established the process of peace and normalization of relations between Egypt and Israel. Sadat was assassinated while reviewing a military parade in Cairo in October 1981.

SADEH, YITZHAK. Born in Lublin in Russian Poland in 1890. He served in the Russian Army in World War I, but settled in Palestine (q.v.) in 1920. He soon became active in the Hagana (q.v.) and in 1941 founded Palmah (q.v.) and served as its commander until 1945. At the beginning of the War of Independence (q.v.) he served in the command of the Hagana and when the Israel Defense Forces (q.v.) was established he became commander of the 8th Armored Brigade. After the war he resigned from the Israel Defense Forces and assumed a leading role in the Mapam Party (q.v.). He died in Petah Tikva (q.v.) in 1952.

SAFED (TZEFAT). A city in upper Galilee (q.v.) in which Jews have lived for centuries. Beginning in the 16th century it became an important center of Jewish learning. It has become a center for artists and tourists.

SAMARIA. Northern section of the highlands of Palestine (q.v.), north of Judea (q.v.), it is 31 miles long and 23 miles wide. The area is very densely populated. The area was part of the West Bank (Judea and Samaria, q.v.) occupied by Jordan in Israel's War of Independence (q.v.) and was taken by Israel from Jordan in the Six Day War (q.v.).

SAMUEL, HERBERT LOUIS. First Viscount. Born in Liverpool, England in 1870. He entered politics and with the outbreak of World War I developed an interest in the subject of Zionism (q.v.) and the creation of a Jewish National Home. He was appointed the first High Commissioner of Palestine (q.v.) and served from 1920 to 1925, during which time he established the foundations of the civil administration of Palestine.

SAPIR (FORMERLY KOSLOWSKY), PINHAS. Born in Suwalki, Russian Poland on October 15, 1907, he immigrated to Palestine (q.v.) in 1929, took the name Sapir, and settled in Kfar Saba where he worked in the orange groves. He held a number of local positions and worked with the Mekorot Water Company from 1937 to 1947. In February 1948 he was put in charge of the quartermaster branch of the Hagana (q.v.). During the War of Independence (q.v.) he travelled abroad to purchase arms. Later in 1948 he was appointed Director General of the Ministry of Defense and from 1953 to 1955 he served as Director General of the Ministry of

Finance. In 1955 he was appointed Minister of Commerce and Industry and in 1963 became Minister of Finance. In 1968 he became Secretary General of the Israel Labor Party (q.v.). In 1969 he again became Minister of Finance until June 1974. He died in 1975 while serving as Chairman of the Jewish Agency (q.v.) and the World Zionist Organization (q.v.).

SARID, YOSSI. Born in Rehovot and worked as a journalist. He shifted from the Labor Alignment (q.v.) to the Citizens' Rights Movement (q.v.) after the 1984 election. Member of the Knesset (q.v.). He has emerged as a leading and high-profile left-wing politician.

SAUL. The first King of Israel (c.1020–1004 BC). Most of his reign was spent in wars against the enemies of Israel.

SAVIDOR, MENACHEM. Born in Russia in 1918. After moving with his family to Poland in 1923 he became active in the Betar (q.v.) youth movement. After high school he completed studies in philology in Vilna. In 1941 he immigrated to Palestine (q.v.) and joined the British army, serving in the Jewish Brigade (q.v.). He later served in the Israel Defense Forces (q.v.) where he rose to the rank of Lieutenant Colonel. He became Director General of the Transport Ministry and director general of Israel Railways. After running unsuccessfully for Mayor of Tel Aviv (q.v.) in 1973 he was elected in 1977 to the Knesset (q.v.) and in 1981 became Speaker. He left politics in 1984 and died in November 1988.

SCOPUS, MOUNT see MOUNT SCOPUS

SDE BOKER. A kibbutz in the Negev (q.v.) founded in 1952 and chosen by David Ben-Gurion (q.v.) as his residence when not in Tel Aviv (q.v.) or Jerusalem (q.v.). His house remains and he is buried at the kibbutz.

SEA OF GALILEE. The Sea of Galilee is a small (14 miles long and 8 miles across at its broadest point) freshwater lake in northern Israel and is often mentioned in the Bible. It is called the Sea of Kinnereth (Lake Kinneret) in the Old Testament. The name Galilee is used in the New Testament. It is also called Lake Tiberias for a city on its shore. The Sea of Galilee lies on the Jordan plain in Israel 30 miles from the Mediterranean Sea. It touches the Golan Heights (q.v.) on the northeast. The Jordan River (q.v.) flows southward through it.

SECOND ALIYA. The Second Aliya (1904–1914) was the most significant in terms of Israel's future political system. Some 40,000 immigrants of Russian and Eastern European origin laid the foundations of the labor movement and established the first Jewish labor parties and kibbutzim (q.v.). They were secularists who sought to modernize and secularize Jewish life in the Diaspora (q.v.), and they brought their political ideas, especially socialist ideology, to Palestine (q.v.) and thereby provided the foundations of the future political system.

SEPHARDI, SEPHARDIM see ORIENTAL JEWS

SEPHARDI TORAH GUARDIANS (SHAS). A political party established by individuals of Sephardic background who split from Agudat Israel (q.v.) and first contested the 1984 Knesset (q.v.) election. While ideologically close to Agudat Israel positions, the founders of this party perceived discrimination and consequently wished to get the funds, political jobs, and other forms of support of which they had felt deprived. Among the founders of the party was Rabbi Nissim Zeev of Jerusalem (q.v.), while Rabbi Yitzhak Haim Peretz (q.v.) was the leader of the Knesset list. Shas formed a council of sages known as Moetzet Hachmei Hatorah and its leadership was closely linked to the former Sephardic Chief Rabbi of Israel, Ovadia Yosef (q.v.). It argued that the Torah was its platform and regarded itself as a movement of spiritual awakening. Despite a split in the party and the creation of Yahad Shivtei Yisrael (Yishai (q.v.)), it won six seats in the 1988 Knesset election to emerge as the third largest party in the parliament and the largest of the religious parties. Rabbi Ovadia Yosef resigned his position on the Supreme Rabbinical Court in order to campaign actively for Shas. In the spring of 1990 five of the six Shas members of the Knesset abstained (one vote was cast expressing confidence in the government) in the vote of confidence that led to the ouster of the government. In June 1990 Shas joined the newly established Likud-led government of Yitzhak Shamir (q.v.).

SEPHARDIM PARTY. An ethnic based political party that represented an effort to organize Sephardic (q.v.) and Oriental Jews (q.v.) and succeeded in electing four members to the First Knesset (q.v.) and two to the Second Knesset. Toward the end of the tenure of the first Knesset the party split along economic lines and it eventually disappeared when one of its most prominent leaders, Bechor Shitreet, was coopted by Mapai (q.v.) to serve as Minister of Police in a series of governments led by David Ben-Gurion (q.v.).

SHABAK see SHIN BET

SHAHAL, MOSHE. Born in Iraq on May 20, 1935. He studied at Haifa University and graduated from the Law Faculty of Tel Aviv University (q.v.). Shahal is a lawyer by profession and has been a member of the Knesset (q.v.) since 1969 on the Labor Alignment (q.v.) list. He became Minister of Energy and Infrastructure in 1984 and retained that post in the government established in December 1988.

SHAI. Acronym for Sherut Yediot (information service). The intelligence service of the Hagana (q.v.) was established in 1940.

SHAKI, AVNER. Born in Safed in 1928, he graduated from the Faculty of Law of Hebrew University (q.v.). Shaki is a leader of the National Religious Party (q.v.), a Bar-Ilan University Professor, and an expert on Jewish law. He served as a member of the Knesset (q.v.) from 1969 to 1973 and again beginning in 1984. He became a Minister Without Portfolio in the government established in December 1988. He became Minister of Religious Affairs in the Shamir-led (q.v.) government established in June 1990.

SHALOM ACHSHAV see PEACE NOW

SHAMIR, YITZHAK (FORMERLY YZERNITZKY). Born in Rozhinay in eastern Poland in 1915. He was educated at a Hebrew secondary school in Bialystok, where he became a disciple of Vladimir (Zeev) Jabotinsky (q.v.) and joined the Revisionist youth movement, Betar (q.v.). He studied law at Warsaw University until 1935 when he emigrated to Palestine (q.v.) and changed his name to Shamir. He completed his studies at Hebrew University (q.v.) in Jerusalem (q.v.).

Shamir joined the Irgun (q.v.) in 1937 and rose through the ranks of the organization into leadership positions. Menachem Begin (q.v.) became the commander of the Irgun in 1943 and remained its leader until its dissolution in 1948. In 1940 the Irgun suspended attacks against the British Mandatory (q.v.) authorities in Palestine and offered its cooperation in the war effort against Germany. This caused a split in the organization and led to the creation of a smaller and more militant group which Shamir joined. This faction, LEHI, (Lohamei Herut Yisrael—Israel Freedom Fighters) was

known as the "Stern Gang" (q.v.), named after Abraham Stern (Yair), the group's first leader, and viewed
the British as the main obstacle to the establishment of
a Jewish state in Palestine. After Stern was killed by
British police in 1942, Shamir helped to reorganize
LEHI, establishing a high command known as LEHI
Central which included Shamir, Nathan Yellin-Mor,
and Dr. Israel Scheib (Eldad). Shamir directed LEHI's
operations, which became increasingly violent. A terror
campaign was conducted against the British which
included the assassination of Lord Moyne, Britain's
senior Middle East official who was stationed in Cairo,
in 1944. Two members were captured, tried, convicted,
and executed for the crime. The Stern Gang was also
suspected in the assassination of Swedish Count Folke
Bernadotte, who sought to mediate an end to Israel's
War of Independence (q.v.) on behalf of the United
Nations. But, these charges were never substantiated
and Shamir has refused to comment on the matter. He
was arrested twice by British authorities, in 1941 and
1946, but managed to escape both times. He was sent to
a detention camp in Eritrea, but he escaped and traveled
through Ethiopia to Djibouti, ultimately arriving in
France where he was given political asylum. He remained in France until he returned to the newly
established State of Israel in May 1948.

Shamir found it difficult to enter Israel's new political
system, which was dominated by former Hagana (q.v.)
members and others who had been associated with the
Labor Zionist movement. Shamir sought election to the
Knesset (q.v.) in 1949 with a list of candidates comprised
of former LEHI members, but this effort failed. Shamir
did not pursue elective office again until he joined the
Herut Party (q.v.) of Menachem Begin in 1970. During
the period from 1948 to 1955 he remained in private life
where he was active in a number of commercial ventures
including directing an association of cinema owners.

These were not particularly successful. Isser Harel (q.v.), then head of the Mossad (q.v.), recruited Shamir into the organization in 1955 where his operational experience from the Mandate period could be put to use. He spent a decade with the Mossad and rose to a senior position. For a part of that time he was stationed in Paris. Shamir left the Mossad in 1965 and returned to private life where he pursued commercial interests but with only moderate success. He remained active in public life primarily through his efforts at increasing Soviet Jewish immigration to Israel. In 1970 Menachem Begin offered him a position in Herut, which Shamir had recently joined, and he was elected to the Executive Committee and became the Director of the Immigration Department.

Shamir successfully ran for election to the Knesset for the first time on the Herut list in 1973 and became a member of the State Comptroller Committee and the Defense and Foreign Affairs Committee. He directed the party's Organization Department, and in 1975 he was elected Chairman of Herut's Executive Committee, a post to which he was reelected unanimously two years later. The 1977 Knesset election was a watershed in Israeli politics. Likud (q.v.), into which Herut had merged, secured the largest number of votes and Menachem Begin became Israel's first non-Labor Prime Minister. Shamir was elected Speaker of the Knesset in June 1977 and continued to be a loyal supporter of Begin. Loyalty characterized Shamir's service to Begin both within the party and in the Begin-led governments in which he served. The most significant issue which separated the two was Begin's decision to negotiate and sign the Camp David Accords (q.v.) and the Egypt-Israel Peace Treaty (q.v.). Shamir opposed the treaty, as did other Likud leaders including Moshe Arens (q.v.) and Ariel Sharon (q.v.), because he believed Israel was sacrificing too much in return for what he viewed as uncertain guarantees of peace. The withdrawal from the Sinai Peninsula (q.v.) and the relinquishing of the security buffer it provided and the sophisticated air bases located there, as well as the dismantling of Jewish settlements, was seen as too high a price for Israel to pay. Shamir abstained on the final Knesset vote when the treaty was approved.

Begin appointed Shamir as his Foreign Minister in March 1980. Shamir's view of the Camp David process changed during his tenure as Foreign Minister when he was responsible for implementing the agreements reached and he became an advocate of that approach for future negotiations between Israel and the Arab states. Shamir was also active in efforts to re-establish diplomatic relations with several African states which had been severed at the time of the Yom Kippur War (q.v.). He also supported legislation declaring united Jerusalem the eternal capital of Israel, as well as the bombing of the Iraqi nuclear reactor in June 1981, and the annexation of the Golan Heights (q.v.) in December 1981. He saw these actions as contributing to Israel's security. After the 1981 Knesset election Begin succeeded in establishing a Likud-led coalition that subsequently received the endorsement of the Knesset and Shamir continued to serve as Foreign Minister. During this term in office Shamir was criticized by the Kahan Commission (q.v.) because he failed to pass on to appropriate individuals information he received from Communications Minister Mordechai Zipori (q.v.) suggesting that massacres were taking place in the Sabra and Shatila (q.v.) camps near Beirut in September 1982.

Menachem Begin resigned from office in September 1983 and thereby brought to an end a major era in Israeli history and politics. Shamir was the compromise choice to follow Begin and he formed the new government. On October 10, 1983, the Knesset endorsed the government and its programs and Yitzhak Shamir became the Prime Minister of Israel, but many viewed him as an interim leader who would last only until the next Knesset election in 1984. The 1984 Knesset election results were inconclusive and after a period of intense, lengthy and complex negotiations, Labor and Likud formed, in September 1984, a Government of National Unity (q.v.), the basis of which was a series of compromises and concessions. According to the terms of the agreement Shamir and Peres each were to serve for 25 months as Prime Minister while the other held the position of Vice Prime Minister and Foreign Minister. Peres was Prime Minister during the first period, and rotated (q.v.) positions with Shamir as agreed in October 1986. The 1988 Knesset election, as in 1984, did not demonstrate a clear preference for either Likud or Labor among the electorate. After weeks of intensive negotiations Shamir entered into a new coalition agreement with Labor which placed Labor in an equal position with Likud in the government. The distribution of cabinet portfolios among the two blocs was to be equal, but Shamir would remain the Prime Minister for the full tenure of the government. Disagreement within the cabinet reached a climax in the spring of 1990 that led a vote of no confidence in the government. Shamir headed a caretaker government and, after an abortive effort by Shimon Peres to form a new government, formed a Likud-led government composed of right of center and religious political parties that won Knesset approval in June 1990.

SHAPIRA, YOSEF. Born in Jerusalem (q.v.) in 1926, Shapira graduated from yeshiva. He served as the World Secretary of the Bnei Akiva youth movement and of the World Executive of the Mizrahi (q.v.) movement. Additionally, he served in the Government of National Unity (q.v.) established in 1984 as Minister Without Portfolio representing the Morasha (q.v.) Party.

SHAPIRO, AVRAHAM. Born in Romania, Shapiro made aliya (q.v.) in 1949. He became an ordained Rabbi and is also the owner of a large carpet and textile industry. Shapiro is an Agudat Israel (q.v.) member of the Knesset (q.v.). He entered politics at the summons of the Gerer Rebbe (the Rabbi of Gur) to aid Agudat Israel.

SHAREF, ZE'EV. Born in Izvor-Szeletin, Romania in 1906, Sharef became active in the Poalei Zion (q.v.) youth movement in Romania. He settled in Palestine (q.v.) in 1925 and subsequently held a series of official and semiofficial posts in support of the Zionist movement and the Jewish community in Palestine. From 1943 to 1947 he served as secretary of the Political Department of the Jewish Agency (q.v.). He then was charged by the Provisional Council of State with the task of preparing the administrative machinery essential for the functioning of the new state upon termination of the British Mandate (q.v.). From 1948 to 1957 he was Secretary of the Cabinet and from 1957 to 1959 he served as Director General of the Prime Minister's Office. He held a number of other civil service positions and in 1965 was elected to the Knesset (q.v.) on the Labor Alignment (q.v.) list. He was named Minister of Commerce and Industry in 1966 and assumed the portfolio of Finance as well in 1968. In December 1969 he became Minister of Housing.

SHARETT, MOSHE (FORMERLY SHERTOK). Born in Kherson, Russia in 1894 and raised in a Zionist household, Moshe Sharett immigrated with his family to Palestine (q.v.) in 1906, settling in an Arab village in the Samarian Hills. In 1908 the family moved to Jaffa (q.v.) where his father was a founder of the Ahuzat Bayit quarter which later became Tel Aviv (q.v.). After high school, Sharett studied law in Constantinople and then volunteered as an officer in the Turkish Army during World War I. In 1920, while studying at the London School of Economics, he joined the British Poalei Zion (q.v.) movement. In 1931 he became Secretary of the Jewish Agency's (q.v.) Political Department, and in 1933, at the 18th Zionist Conference, was elected head of the Political Department after the assassination of Chaim Arlosoroff. On June 29, 1946 Sharett and other leaders of the Jewish Agency were arrested by the British in Palestine and were imprisoned in the Latrun (q.v.) camp for four months. During 1947 he sought approval at the United Nations for the United Nations Special Committee on Palestine (q.v.) Partition Plan (q.v.). Sharett became the state of Israel's first Foreign Minister in 1948. As Foreign Minister, he initially sought a nonaligned status for Israel, but after the Korean War he promoted closer ties with Western democratic countries. He sought contacts with developing nations in Asia and Africa and also signed the Luxembourg Agreement with West Germany's Konrad Adenauer. In January 1954, after Prime Minister David Ben-Gurion (q.v.) temporarily retired from office, Sharett became Prime Minister but retained the Foreign Affairs portfolio. With Ben-Gurion's return as Prime Minister in November 1955 and subsequent disagreement between the two men surfaced, Sharett resigned. In 1960, Sharett was elected Chairman of the Executive of the World Zionist Organization (q.v.) and Jewish Agency (q.v.) and remained active in Mapai (q.v.) party activities. He died in 1965.

SHARIR, AVRAHAM. Born in 1932 in Tel Aviv (q.v.). He studied Law at the Hebrew University (q.v.) of Jerusalem, and became an attorney. He was active in youth and student circles of the General Zionist (q.v.) Organization and served as Parliamentary Secretary of the Liberal Party (q.v.) until 1964 and as its Secretary

General from 1974. From 1964 to 1967 he headed the Jewish Agency (q.v.) Economic Department in the United States and served there as an Economic Consul for Israel from 1970 to 1974. From 1967 to 1970 he was Director General of the Employers' Organization, a member of the High Court for Labour Relations, and a member of the Government Committee on Pensions. Sharir was first elected to the Ninth Knesset (q.v.) in May 1977, after serving as Liberal Party (q.v.) National Elections Manager. On August 5, 1981, following his reelection to the Tenth Knesset, he was sworn in as Minister of Tourism. He served as Minister of Tourism in the Government of National Unity (q.v.) established in 1984.

SHARM EL-SHEIKH. A point on the southern tip of the Sinai Peninsula (q.v.) which allows control of the passage of shipping through the Strait of Tiran (q.v.) between the Red Sea and the Gulf of Aqaba (q.v.). Egypt used this position to prevent shipping to Israel. The United Nations Emergency Force (UNEF) was introduced to that location following Israel's withdrawal from Sinai in 1957 and remained there, guaranteeing freedom of navigation, until May 1967. Israel captured the position during the Six Day War (q.v.) and remained there until after the Egypt-Israel Peace Treaty (q.v.) which guaranteed freedom of passage.

SHARON, ARIEL (NICKNAMED ARIK) (FORMERLY SHEINERMAN). He was born in 1928 in Kfar Malal, a farm village not far from present-day Tel Aviv (q.v.). At the age of 14 he joined the Hagana (q.v.), was wounded during the War of Independence (q.v.) in 1948, and subsequently rose swiftly in the ranks of the Israel Defense Forces (q.v.). In 1952 he established the "101 Unit" for special operations (a special commando force known for its daring operations behind enemy lines), and in 1956, he commanded a paratroop brigade, units of which parachuted into the Mitla Pass to mark the beginning of the Sinai War (q.v.). He then studied at the British Staff College in Camberley and, upon his return, was appointed head of the Israel Defense Forces School of Infantry. In 1962 he became Director of Military Training of the IDF and, that same year, he graduated from the law school of the Hebrew University (q.v.). In the Six Day War (q.v.) of 1967 he commanded an armored division which fought in the Sinai Peninsula (q.v.) and, in 1969, became commanding officer of the Southern Command.

In June 1973 Sharon resigned from the IDF, joined the Liberal Party (q.v.), and was instrumental in bringing about the alignment of Herut (q.v.), the Free Center (q.v.), the State List (q.v.) and the Liberal Party (q.v.) within the framework of the Likud bloc (q.v.). The Yom Kippur War (q.v.) brought him back to active military service as a reserve officer in command of an armored division, units of which were the first to cross the Suez Canal and establish an Israeli bridgehead on the Egyptian side. In December 1973 he stood for election to the Knesset (q.v.), and was elected on behalf of the Liberal Party faction of the Likud bloc. In December 1974 Sharon resigned from the Knesset, in order that his reserve commission with the IDF might be reinstated. In June 1975 he was appointed Adviser to Prime Minister Yitzhak Rabin (q.v.) on Security Affairs and held that position until April 1976, when he resigned to form the Shlomzion Party (q.v.), which gained two seats in the elections to the Ninth Knesset in May 1977. Immediately following the elections, the Shlomzion Party merged with the Herut Party faction of the Likud bloc, and it was on this ticket that he was reelected to the Tenth Knesset on May 30, 1981. He was appointed Minister of Agriculture in June 1977. On August 5, 1981 he was sworn in as Minister of Defense. Sharon was forced from his position as Minister of Defense in February 1983 after the Kahan Commission of Inquiry (q.v.) report concerning the massacre at the Sabra and Shatila (q.v.) refugee camps in Lebanon, but he remained in the Cabinet as Minister Without Portfolio. He later became Minister of Industry and Trade and in December 1988 was reappointed to that position. In June 1990 he became Minister of Construction and Housing. He remains very popular in some sectors of the Likud's constituency and is a potential candidate for Prime Minister.

SHAS see SEPHARDI TORAH GUARDIANS

SHAZAR, SHNEUR ZALMAN (FORMERLY RUBA-SHOV). Born in Mir in the Minsk Province of Russia, on October 6, 1889, he later moved with his family to Stolbtsy, where he received a heder education. Encouraged by his parents' Zionism (q.v.), he entered the Poalei Zion (q.v.) movement in Russia in 1905. During the unsuccessful Russian revolution of 1905, he participated in Jewish self-defense groups. In 1907, he moved to Vilna, where he wrote for Yiddish (q.v.) newspapers in Russia and in the United States. He left for Palestine (q.v.) in 1911 but returned to Russia and then, beginning in 1912, he studied at several German universities. In 1916, he became one of the founders of the Labor Zionist movement in Germany, and the next year helped found Hehalutz in Germany. At the Poalei Zion conference in Vienna in 1920 he gained notice as a prominent spokesman for the right wing. He was responsible for the first conference of the World Hehalutz Organization in 1921. He settled in Palestine in 1924, and became a member of the secretariat of the Histadrut (q.v.) and joined the editorial board of *Davar* (q.v.). In 1949, he was elected to Israel's First Knesset (q.v.) and served as Minister of Education and Culture, in which capacity he was responsible for the 1949 Compulsory Education Law. In 1952, the Soviet government refused to accept him as Israel's ambassador. He became a member of the Executive of the Jewish Agency (q.v.) in 1952 and headed the Department of Information, and after 1954 the Department of Education and Culture in the Diaspora (q.v.). Between 1956 and 1960, he was acting chairman of the Jewish Agency's Jerusalem Executive. Shazar was elected the third President of Israel on May 21, 1963, and reelected in March 1968 and served until 1973. As President, he sponsored the Bible Study Circle and the Circle for the Study of the Diaspora. He has written voluminously on political, social, and historical themes. In January 1964 he was awarded the Bialik Prize for his book on Jewish personalities. He died in Jerusalem (q.v.) on October 5, 1974.

SHELLI (SHALOM LEYISRAEL; PEACE FOR ISRAEL). After the split with the New Communist (q.v.) List in 1965, Maki (q.v.) became more moderate in its opposition to government policies and became primarily Jewish in membership. In 1975, it merged with Moked (q.v.) (Focus), a socialist party, and in 1977, Moked united with other noncommunist groups to form Shelli. The new party was founded by Arie Eliav (q.v.), a former Labor Party (q.v.) Secretary General. The party's platform called for the establishment of a Palestinian Arab state, the withdrawal of Israel to its pre-1967 borders, and political negotiations with the Palestine Liberation Organization (q.v.) on the basis of mutual recognition. Shelli's campaign for the 1977 election secured it two seats—Arie Eliav and Meir Pail the former Moked leader—but the party was unsuccessful in the 1981 election.

SHEMTOV, VICTOR. Born in 1918 in Sofia, Bulgaria, he became involved in socialist Zionism (q.v.) at an early age. He immigrated to Palestine (q.v.) in 1939 and soon became active in the Hagana (q.v.). He entered politics in 1944, joining the Socialist League which later helped to form Mapam (q.v.). He became Secretary General of the party in 1979 and served as a member of the Knesset (q.v.) since 1961. He served as Minister of Health.

SHERTOK, MOSHE see SHARETT, MOSHE

SHILOAH, REUVEN. An intelligence official in the Yishuv (q.v.). He was involved in the Rhodes and Lausanne talks following Israel's War of Independence (q.v.) and in the secret negotiations between Israel and King Abdullah of Jordan in 1949–1950. He was the founder and first director of the Mossad (q.v.) (March 1951 to September 1952). He served as Minister in Israel's Embassy in Washington (1953–1957) and as an adviser to then Foreign Minister Golda Meir (q.v.) (1958-1959). He died in 1959 at age 49.

SHIN BET (SHABAK). Acronym for Sherut Bitahon Klali (General Security Services). The organization responsible for prevention of hostile secret activity in Israel including espionage and sabotage. It was founded in 1948 and headed by Isser Harel (q.v.) until 1954.

SHINUI (CHANGE). In the wake of the Yom Kippur War (q.v.), a small protest group called Shinui was founded by Professor Amnon Rubinstein (q.v.) of Tel Aviv University (q.v.). It sought to effect changes in the Israeli political system and political life and developed a party organization, but did not have a candidate of imposing stature. In 1976, it joined with others to form the Democratic Movement for Change (q.v.) which secured fifteen seats in the 1977 Knesset (q.v.) election. The DMC was constituted under the leadership of archaeology professor Yigael Yadin (q.v.), who served as Deputy Prime Minister under Menachem Begin (q.v.) after the 1977 elections. The party included Shinui, Yadin's own Democratic Movement (q.v.), and individuals and groups from both within and outside the existing political parties. Although composed mostly of elements from the center-left, the party could not be classified in terms of traditional Israeli political ideology. It focused on the need for electoral reform and general improvement in the political life of the country. The DMC's initial success was not enough to make it an indispensable element in the new government, and failing to achieve its major goals, it dissolved itself just prior to the 1981 elections. Shinui again emerged as an independent unit and won two seats in the 1981 elections and joined the Government of National Unity (q.v.) after securing three seats in the 1984 election. It later became part of the Center-Shinui Movement (q.v.).

SHLEMUT HAMOLEDET. The concept of the right of the Jewish people to all of Eretz Israel (q.v.). The Revisionist Party (q.v.), established by Vladimir Jabotinsky (q.v.) in 1925, and his New Zionist Organization (q.v.) supported the principle of Shlemut Hamoledet, and rejected Arab claims for national and political sovereignty in Palestine (q.v.).

SHLOMZION PARTY. A political party formed by Ariel Sharon (q.v.) which contested the 1977 Knesset (q.v.) election and won two seats in parliament. It then joined the Likud (q.v.).

SHOAH see HOLOCAUST

SHOMRON, DAN. Born in 1937 in Ashdot Yaacov, he joined the Israel Defense Forces (q.v.) in 1956. He holds a BA degree in geography from Tel Aviv University (q.v.). He commanded Operation Jonathan (q.v.)

in Entebbe (Entebbe Operation, q.v.) in 1976. He became Chief of Staff of the Israel Defense Forces (q.v.) in 1987 and retained that post until April 1991.

SHOSTAK, ELIEZER. He was born in Poland on December 16, 1911 and emigrated to Palestine (q.v.) in 1935. From 1957 to 1959 he studied Philosophy and Kabala at Hebrew University (q.v.). He was one of the founders of the Herut Party (q.v.), from which he resigned in 1966, and subsequently was a member of the La'am (q.v.) faction of the Likud (q.v.) bloc. First elected on behalf of Herut to the Second Knesset (q.v.) in July 1951, and reelected to all subsequent Knessets, he has served on the Labor, Economics, Public Services and Finance Committees of the Knesset. He has also been Secretary General of the National Federation of Labor and Chairman of the National Health Insurance Fund. He became Minister of Health in June 1977, serving in that post until 1984.

SHOVAL, ZALMAN (ORIGINALLY FINKELSTEIN). He was born in Danzig on April 28, 1930 but left with his family before World War II for Tel Aviv (q.v.). He served in the army and studied economics and international affairs at the University of California at Berkeley and at the Graduate Institute of International Studies in Geneva. He started his career in the Israeli foreign ministry in the 1950s but left to enter a family business. He later entered politics, beginning his affiliation with Rafi (q.v.) under Ben-Gurion (q.v.). He became a member of the Knesset (q.v.) in 1970. The State List (q.v.) later moved to Likud (q.v.) and Shoval shifted as well. He later joined the Knesset on the Likud list. He became Ambassador of Israel to the United States in 1990.

SINAI CAMPAIGN see SINAI WAR

SINAI PENINSULA. The land bridge between Asia and Africa, some 23,000 square miles in size. It has the shape of a triangle bounded by the Gulf of Suez in the West, the Gulf of Aqaba (q.v.) in the East, and the Mediterranean Sea in the North. Its highest point is Jebel Musa (the Biblical Mount Sinai). The peninsula was occupied by Israel in the Sinai War (q.v.) and, after its return to Egypt in 1957 it was captured again in the Six Day War (q.v.). It was evacuated by Israel and returned to Egypt in accordance with the Egypt-Israel Peace Treaty of 1979 (q.v.).

SINAI II ACCORDS (1975). A complex of agreements between Israel and Egypt achieved through the shuttle diplomacy of United States Secretary of State Henry Kissinger. They were signed in Geneva on September 4, 1975 by representatives of Egypt and Israel, and constituted a significant accomplishment. The agreements consisted of a formal agreement between the two parties, an Annex, and a proposal for an American presence in Sinai in connection with an early-warning system. In addition there were memoranda of agreement between the United States and Israel and United States assurances to Israel and Egypt. This was more than a simple disengagement of military forces since they agreed that "the conflict between them and in the Middle East shall not be resolved by military force but by peaceful means." These were the first steps toward increased accommodation between the parties and it moved in the direction of a peace settlement. It was in the Memorandum of Agreement between the United States and Israel regarding the Geneva Peace Conference that the United States pledged that it "will continue to adhere to its present policy with respect to the Palestine Liberation Organization, whereby it will not recognize or negotiate with the Palestine Liberation Organization so long as the Palestine Liberation Organization does not recognize Israel's right to exist and does not accept Security Council Resolutions 242 and 338."

SINAI WAR (1956). The war had its origins in the regional tensions which were common after the Egyptian Revolution of 1952. The arms race was continuing, and tension grew further when the Czechoslovakian-Egyptian arms deal, announced in September 1955, introduced the Soviet Union as a major arms supplier to the Arab-Israeli sector of the Middle East. Palestinian fedayeen (commando) attacks into Israel were on the increase. At the same time Britain and France opposed Egypt's nationalization of the Suez Canal and its support of anti-French rebels in North Africa. Britain and France agreed with Israel that action against the dangers posed by President Gamal Abdul Nasser of Egypt and his policies was essential, and the three powers organized a coordinated operation. Israel moved into the Sinai Peninsula (q.v.) on October 29, 1956, and by the afternoon of the next day, Britain and France issued an ultimatum (as previously agreed) calling on both sides to stop fighting and to withdraw to positions 10 miles (16 kilometers) on either side of the Suez Canal. Israel accepted, but Egypt rejected the proposal. By November 5 Israel had occupied Sharm el-Sheikh (q.v.), and the fighting ended. Israel eventually withdrew from all of the territory its forces had occupied during the conflict under the weight of United Nations resolutions but especially under pressure from the Eisenhower Administration. The United States also provided assurances to Israel concerning freedom of navigation through the Strait of Tiran (q.v.) and in the Gulf of Aqaba (q.v.). The United Nations Emergency Force (UNEF) was created to patrol the Egyptian side of the Egypt-Israel armistice line, which it did until the days immediately preceding the Six Day War (q.v.).

SIX DAY WAR (1967). In mid-May 1967, Egypt proclaimed a state of emergency, mobilized its army, and
moved troops across the Sinai Peninsula (q.v.) toward
the border with Israel. President Gamal Abdul Nasser
requested the removal of the United Nations- Emergency Force (UNEF) from the Egypt-Israel frontier,
and United Nations Secretary General U Thant complied. The UNEF positions were then manned by
contingents of the Egyptian armed forces and of the
Palestine Liberation Organization (q.v.) which had
been established in 1964 at the initiative, and with the
assistance, of the Arab League. Egypt and Israel faced
each other with no buffer, and Nasser announced that
the Strait of Tiran (q.v.) would be closed to Israeli
shipping and to strategic cargoes bound for Israel's port
of Eilat (q.v.). Israel regarded these actions as *causus
belli,* illegal, and aggressive.

On May 30, 1967, Jordan entered into a defense pact
with Syria and Egypt, and Iraqi troops were stationed
along the Israel-Jordan front. The Israeli reaction to
Egyptian mobilization and to the other actions appeared
timid until it became clear that the international system
was not prepared to take any action to support Israel
beyond providing moral support. Israel received no
United States military assistance, and other states
preferred to avoid any involvement in the developing
conflict. Israel then acted on its own. It created a
"wall-to-wall" political coalition (q.v.) (excluding the
Communists) in a Government of National Unity (q.v.),
and Moshe Dayan (q.v.) became the Defense Minister.
On June 5, 1967, Israel launched a preemptive strike
against Egyptian air forces and bases. The war was
broadened after Jordan and Syria joined in the conflict,
initiating their participation by respectively shelling
Israeli positions in Jerusalem (q.v.) and from the Golan
Heights (q.v.). Israel decisively defeated Egypt, Jordan,
Syria, and their allies, and in six days radically trans-

formed the situation in the Middle East: It was in control of territories stretching from the Golan Heights in the north to Sharm el-Sheikh (q.v.) in the Sinai Peninsula, and from the Suez Canal to the Jordan River (q.v.). The territories included the Sinai Peninsula; the Gaza Strip (q.v.); the West Bank, referred to by Israel as Judea and Samaria (q.v.); the Golan Heights; and East Jerusalem.

SMALL CONSTITUTION. Israel's system of government is based on an unwritten constitution. The first legislative act of the Constituent Assembly in February 1949 was to enact a Transition Law, often referred to as the Small Constitution, that became the basis of constitutional life in the state. Administrative and executive procedures were based on a combination of past experience in self-government, elements adapted from the former mandatory structure, and new legislation. According to the Small Constitution, Israel was established as a republic with a weak president (q.v.) and a strong cabinet (q.v.) and parliament (Knesset) (q.v.). It was anticipated that this document would be replaced in due course by a more extensive and permanent one.

SODOM (SDOM). A city on the southern end of the Dead Sea (q.v.) near the Biblical site of Sodom. The Israeli extraction of chemicals from the Dead Sea is headquartered here.

SOLEL BONEH. Literally "paves and builds." A road-building and construction company belonging to the Histadrut (q.v.). During the Arab riots in Palestine (q.v.) from 1936 to 1939, Solel Boneh helped build farm settlements, pave security roads, construct airfields, and erect fortifications. During World War II it helped the British army pave roads and construct airfields, bridges, and army camps. Solel Boneh subsidiaries supply much of the Israeli national demand for stone, gravel, marble, and cement, as well as most of its plumbing and bathroom fittings. The company employs many factory workers in its various enterprises. Its activities have become international and since the 1960s considerable contract work has been carried out in Africa.

SOLOMON (KING OF ISRAEL). The third King of Israel and the son of King David (q.v.) and Bathsheba. He was renowned as a man of wisdom, the builder of the Temple, and as a poet. His reign (965–928 BC) was one of relative peace for Israel.

SOVIET UNION see USSR

SPORTS. Sports began to develop during the early years of immigration to Palestine (q.v.) and in the first decade of the twentieth century a Maccabi sports organization was founded. With the establishment of the British Mandate (q.v.) over Palestine after World War I sports became increasingly popular and football (soccer) became the principal form of popular recreation. Hapoel, the sports organization of the Histadrut (q.v.), was organized in Haifa (q.v.) in 1924 and was composed of sportsmen and women from the unions and the cooperative settlements. The Betar (q.v.) sports organization also was founded in 1924 under the auspices of the Revisionist (q.v.) movement and other organizations were established later.

Israelis became increasingly sports conscious after independence with numerous sports organizations and leagues for many major sports. Physical education classes in schools introduce youngsters to the rudiments of sportsmanship while sports clubs for teenagers, sponsored by the country's various sports organizations, are the training ground for Israel's future athletes. Sports facilities and equipment are provided by the municipalities, regional and local authorities, and by private centers.

Mass sporting events such as the Jerusalem March, the swim across Lake Kinneret (q.v.) (Sea of Galilee), and various marathon runs and walks in different parts of the country are popular for both Israelis and visitors. Soccer, basketball, swimming, tennis, volleyball, track-and-field sports, gymnastics, and sailing are among the most popular sports. League football (soccer), basketball and volleyball teams, organized at local, regional and national levels, play full schedules of games and championship events engendering countrywide excitement.

Israel's major sports organizations are Maccabi, Betar, Hapoel, and Elizur. The Sports Authority of the Ministry of Education and Culture assists in developing sports facilities and programs, sponsors training of instructors and coaches at the Wingate Institute of Physical Education and at teacher training institutions, and coordinates the activities of various sports federations and organizations. Israel has participated in various regional and international sports competitions, including the Olympics in which it participated for the first time in Helsinki in 1952.

The first "Jewish Olympics", the Maccabiah Games, was held in Tel Aviv in 1932 and Jewish athletes from more than twenty countries took part. Games have taken place subsequently, usually every four years.

STATE COMPTROLLER. In May 1949 the Knesset (q.v.) passed the State Comptroller Law of 5709 (1949) which established, under its aegis, the Office of the State Comptroller to supervise the activities of the Government, the ministries, local authorities, government corporations and other bodies, if the Government or the Knesset so desires. The Comptroller is appointed by the President (q.v.) upon recommendation of the Knesset but is independent of the Government and responsible only to the Knesset, a regulation that is strictly interpreted. Its annual report is published and presented to the Knesset. The State Comptroller also serves as an ombudsman, dealing with the public's complaints against any institution of the State. The Comptroller is elected by the Knesset by secret ballot for a five-year term, and may be reelected once.

STATE LIST. Originally founded in 1968 by David Ben-Gurion (q.v.), when he and some of his followers in Rafi (q.v.) refused to join in the new Israel Labor Party (q.v.). The State List won four seats in 1969 when it could still be considered a party of the left. In 1973, sizable remnants of the party joined the Likud (q.v.) alliance, eventually merging with other groups to form La'am (q.v.).

STATE OF ISRAEL BONDS. In 1950 Prime Minister David Ben-Gurion (q.v.) proposed that an Israel bond be floated in the United States as a means of securing urgently needed funds for the new state. He visited the United States in May 1951 to launch the bond drive. The bonds were later sold in other countries as well. An Israel Bonds Organization was created and billions of dollars of bonds were sold.

STATUS QUO AGREEMENT. Israel's religious structure stems partly from a compromise to obviate clashes that took the form of a so-called status quo agreement worked out by David Ben-Gurion (q.v.) on the eve of Israel's independence. It retained the situation as it had existed upon independence: individuals would be free to pursue their religious practices in private as they saw fit while in the public domain there would be no changes in the prevailing situation. This arrangement thus continued the Ottoman Empire's millet system which allowed each religious community to control its own affairs. This allowed preservation of a large system of religious (especially rabbinical) courts and other government-supported religious institutions. The status quo has allowed the Orthodox community to maintain and expand its efforts to assert control over various activities, periodically engendering public conflict and discussion. Although there is a split between the religious and secular approaches to the problem of religion in the Jewish state, there are also differences within the Orthodox religious community as manifest, in part, by the large number of religious parties (q.v.) that have been created over the years. Numerous religious factions, each with their own leadership and agenda, compete with each other to secure loyalty and votes and to achieve goals and political patronage.

STERN (GANG) GROUP. Also known as LEHI (Lohamei Herut Yisrael—Fighters for the Freedom of Israel). The Stern gang was a Jewish underground fighting force in Palestine (q.v.) that was formed by Abraham Stern (Yair) in 1940 after a split in the Irgun Tzvai Leumi (q.v.). At the outbreak of World War II, Vladimir Jabotinsky (q.v.), supreme commander of the Irgun, ordered the cessation of hostile activities against the British Mandatory government in Palestine. Stern, insisting that Great Britain's involvement in the war presented the Jewish national movement with the opportunity to force the British to honor their obligations toward the Jewish people, advocated the intensification of anti-British activities. Lehi's activities were strongly opposed and condemned by the majority of the Yishuv (q.v.), including the Hagana (q.v.), and its policies were in contradiction even to those of the Irgun. In February, 1942, British police officers found Stern and shot him and, subsequently, many leaders and members of the group were arrested. A command composed of Nathan Friedmann-Yellin, Yitzhak Yzer-nitsky (Shamir) (q.v.), and Dr. Israel Scheib (Eldad) took over responsibility for the military and political activities of the organization, which became known as the "Stern gang." Lehi adopted a policy of individual acts of terrorism. In the summer of 1944 the Lehi command decided to extend anti-British hostilities beyond Palestine. In November 1944 Lord Moyne was assassinated in Cairo. Lehi attacked the oil refineries in Haifa (q.v.) and various British military installations, businesses, government offices, British military and police personnel, and army trains and other vehicles, increasingly harassing the administration. Following the United Nations Palestine partition (q.v.) decision of November 1947, Lehi fought the Arab irregulars who attacked the Yishuv. After the Proclamation of Israel's independence, Lehi was disbanded as an independent fighting force, and its units were incorporated into the Israel Defense Forces (q.v.). Friedmann-Yellin was elected on a Lehi slate to the First Knesset (q.v.), but attempts to develop a cohesive political program and to form a political party proved ineffectual.

STRAIT OF TIRAN. Connects the Red Sea and the Gulf of Aqaba (q.v.) (Gulf of Eilat). The Strait is narrow and constricted by islands (Tiran and Sanafir) and reefs. From the Egyptian Sinai Peninsula (q.v.) to Tiran Island the distance is approximately 5 miles. Coral formations constrict the seaway into two navigable channels: Enterprise Passage, which borders the Sinai coast, is 1,300 yards wide, while Grafton Passage, about one mile from the island of Tiran, is about 900 yards wide. Israel has argued that the Gulf of Aqaba should be treated as an international waterway and that no state has the right to deny passage through the Strait of Tiran. The Arab argument is that the Gulf of Aqaba consists of Arab territorial waters and that passage through it and the

Strait of Tiran therefore cannot be undertaken without the consent of the Arab states. Until 1956 Egypt prevented shipping to Israel by military positions along the Sinai shore. These were destroyed by Israel during the Sinai War (q.v.) of 1956. The announcement by President Nasser of Egypt in May 1967 that the Straits were blockaded was a proximate cause of the Six Day War (q.v.). See also GULF OF AQABA; SHARM EL-SHEIKH.

SUEZ CRISIS (1956) see SINAI WAR (1956)

SUPREME COURT. At the top of the judicial hierarchy is the Supreme Court. There is a President or Chief Justice and a number (determined by the Knesset (q.v.)) of associate justices. The Court has original and appellate jurisdiction. It hears appeals from lower courts in civil and criminal matters. It has original jurisdiction in matters seeking relief against administrative decisions that are not within the jurisdiction of any court. In this instance it may restrain or direct government agencies or other public bodies. It also plays a role in certain instances with regard to actions of religious courts. The Supreme Court serves as a guardian of fundamental rights protecting individuals from arbitrary actions by public officials or state bodies or agencies. It does not have the power of judicial review and cannot invalidate the legislation of the Knesset. There is no appeal from court decisions.

SYRIA. Syria is Israel's neighbor to the northeast and has been a major antagonist of Israel since the Jewish state achieved its independence. The two countries have fought in the War of Independence (q.v.); the Six Day War (q.v.), during which Israel captured the Golan Heights (q.v.); the Yom Kippur War (q.v.), in which there were some additional Israeli territorial gains; and the War in Lebanon (q.v.). United States Secretary of State Henry Kissinger brokered a disengagement of forces agreement (q.v.) between the two states in the spring of 1974. No further progress toward peace between the two states has been made and Syria continues to strive for "strategic parity" between the two states. The two states remained in confrontation and no further progress toward peace between them was made until the fall of 1991 when Syria was among the Arab states that met with Israel at the Madrid Peace Conference (q.v.) called by the United States and the Soviet Union to seek an Arab-Israeli settlement.

SYRIA-ISRAEL DISENGAGEMENT OF FORCES AGREEMENT see ISRAEL-SYRIA DISENGAGEMENT OF FORCES AGREEMENT

- T -

TAAS (TAASIYA TZVAIT). Literally "military industry." An enterprise devoted to development and manufacture of weapons and munitions for the Israel Defense Forces (q.v.) and the defense establishment. It was initiated in the aftermath of the anti-Jewish riots of 1921, when the need arose for guns and ammunition to arm the Hagana (q.v.).

TABA. A small (1.2 square kilometer) enclave on the border between Egypt (q.v.) and Israel which remained in dispute when the international boundary was established between the two countries following the Egypt-Israel Peace Treaty (q.v.) of 1979. The matter was put to international arbitration. The arbitrators reported in September 1988 that the area belonged to Egypt. Israel and Egypt signed agreements on February 26, 1989 that turned Taba back to Egypt. Egypt thus regained control of all of the Sinai Peninsula (q.v.) captured by Israel in the Six Day War (q.v.). Israel had retained the area after withdrawing from Sinai in 1982 arguing that the maps showed incorrect lines. After years of fruitless negotiations the issue was submitted to arbitration. Taba itself was an insignificant piece of land, but it became symbolic of a number of difficulties in the Egypt-Israel relationship following the signing of the peace treaty. After the ruling of the arbitration panel, the parties negotiated the specifics of the arrangement which led to the agreements signed in February 1989.

TALMUD. A body of teaching comprising the commentary and discussions of the amoraim (interpreters, sages) on the Mishnah. It is a collection of the ordinances and laws and the beliefs and philosophy of Judaism, and is the product of more than 3,000 sages from various countries over the first 500 years of the Common Era. The Talmud, or the Gemara (Aramaic, "completion"), comprises religious laws, legislative proposals and material from the realms of law, medicine, health, and agriculture, as well as ethical affairs and philosophical treatises on the nature of God and the human soul. The rulings are presented in the form of the deliberations which took place among the sages until they reached a decision. Until the redaction of the Mishnah, the center of talmudic work was Eretz Israel (q.v.) where the Jerusalem Talmud was composed. After some time the center moved to Babylonia, where the Babylonian Talmud, larger in scope than the Jerusalem Talmud, was compiled.

TAMI (TENUAH LEMASSORET ISRAEL; MOVEMENT FOR JEWISH TRADITION). A political party founded in May 1981 by then Religious Affairs Minister Aharon Abuhatzeira (q.v.). The party draws support mainly from Sephardim (q.v.), and claims to seek the elimination of anti-Moroccan sentiment in Israel, but it was created primarily because of Abuhatzeira's personal political ambition and his antipathy toward the National Religious Party (q.v.) leaders, especially Yosef Burg (q.v.). Abuhatzeira left the NRP after receiving what he regarded as insufficient support during his trial on various criminal charges. He accused the NRP leadership of "ethnic discrimination." Tami sought to appeal to followers of the NRP and Agudat Israel (q.v.) by stressing the Moroccan connection, intending thereby to draw voters from Israel's large Moroccan community to fellow Moroccan Abuhatzeira. Abuhatzeira had strong support from Nessim Gaon, a Swiss-Jewish millionaire of Sudanese origin, who had been active in Sephardic causes. He had hoped for a sizable victory which would give him significant bargaining power after the election, but his efforts suffered a number of crucial setbacks, including repudiation by his venerable uncle, Rabbi Yisrael Abuhatzeira, a leader of Moroccan Jews in Israel. In addition, it became clear that he had created a party with a narrow sectarian base—and thus lost any chance for a broader appeal to others, especially Sephardim of non-African origin. The number-two candidate on Tami's original list, Aharon Uzan, was a former agriculture minister in Labor governments, who noted that the party's purpose "is to right the glaring wrongs perpetrated against us North Africans and against the Sephardim in general."

TAMIR, SHMUEL (FORMERLY KATZENELSON). Born in Jerusalem (q.v.) on March 10, 1923, Shmuel Tamir studied in the Government School of Law in Jerusalem and passed his last examinations while a prisoner in an internment camp in Kenya. In his youth he joined the Irgun (q.v.) and was its second in command in the Jerusalem District. He was detained a number of times by the British authorities and the last time was exiled and imprisoned in Kenya. In 1948 he was among the founders of the Herut Party (q.v.), but in the 1950s he retired from it. In 1964 he returned to activities in the Herut Party and was among the founders of Gahal (q.v.). In 1965 he was elected to the Sixth Knesset (q.v.). Tamir, Eliezer Shostak (q.v.), and others formed the Free Center (q.v.). The Free Center joined the Likud (q.v.) when it was established in 1973. In 1976 Tamir and his colleagues of the Free Center terminated the partnership with the Likud after differences of opinion with Menachem Begin (q.v.). When the Democratic Movement for Change (q.v.) was established a few months later, Tamir united with the founders of the DMC in the elections for the Ninth Knesset. He served as Minister of Justice from 1977 to 1980.

TARSHISH. A political party, headed by Moshe Duek, which contested the 1988 Knesset election (q.v.) but failed to gain a seat in parliament.

TCHERNICHOVSKY, SHAUL. A Hebrew (q.v.) poet. Born in 1875 in Mikhailovka, Russia, Tchernichovsky attended Hebrew school where he studied Hebrew and the Bible and at age 10 entered Russian school. When he was 14 years old he was sent to Odessa to further his education. He read poetry, became involved both in Zionist and Hebrew literary circles, and began publishing his poetry in various periodicals. He settled in Palestine (q.v.) in 1931 and in 1936 moved to Jerusalem (q.v.). In 1936 he received the Bialik Prize for his translations from English and Greek to Hebrew. He died in Jerusalem in August 1943. Tchernichovsky made major contributions to Hebrew literature, especially poetry.

TECHNION. The Israel Institute of Technology is located in Haifa (q.v.), and is Israel's leading university in engineering. It is also the oldest institution of higher learning in the country. Construction was begun in 1912, but various factors delayed its formal opening. The first classes were held in 1924. The school grew slowly until the independence of Israel when the significance of science and technology for the development and the security of the new state became apparent. The Technion was envisaged as the institution to provide Israel with the engineers, architects, and research scientists essential for the country's technical advance. It has since become a major and internationally recognized institution in its areas of specialty.

TEHIYA (RENAISSANCE). Founded in 1979, Tehiya is a political party of "true believers" focusing on the Land of Israel with an ideological fervor reminiscent of Israel's political parties in the early years of independence and before. It is composed of both religious and secular elements and appeals strongly to Israel's youth. It has a component from Gush Emunim (q.v.) (Bloc of the Faithful), but various secularists and secular-oriented groupings are also involved.

Tehiya includes old associates of Menachem Begin (q.v.) from the anti-British underground and former Herut (q.v.) Knesset (q.v.) members such as Geula Cohen (q.v.) and Land of Israel Movement (q.v.) personalities have also joined. Included among its prominent members were Moshe Shamir, Aluf Avraham Yoffe, Dr. Zeev Vilnay, and Dr. Israel Eldad. Tehiya's origins are in the Camp David Accords (q.v.), which it wanted to see revised in favor of a more hardline stance; and the Egypt-Israel Peace Treaty (q.v.), which called for total withdrawal from the Sinai Peninsula (q.v.) and commitment to autonomy for the Palestinians.

Tehiya believes that Begin sold out and that the occupied territories (q.v.) must remain in Israel's hands.

The party's head is Professor Yuval Neeman (q.v.), a physicist from Tel Aviv University (q.v.), a leading nuclear scientist with a long-standing role in the defense establishment. In July 1982, Tehiya joined the ruling coalition of Menachem Begin's Likud (q.v.). This move seemed to help ensure Tehiya's future and to help strengthen the opposition in the government to concessions concerning Palestinian autonomy in the West Bank (q.v.). Neeman became Minister of Science and Technology. Rafael Eitan (q.v.), former Chief of Staff of the Israel Defense Forces (q.v.), assumed the leadership of the combined Tehiya-Tsomet (q.v.). Tehiya campaigned in the 1988 election on a platform that called for "peace for peace," without Israel yielding any portion of the Land of Israel, and for increasing settlement in the territories as a guarantee of peace. It supported having Israeli sovereignty applied to Judea (q.v.), Samaria (q.v.), and Gaza (q.v.).

TEL AVIV UNIVERSITY. Established as a small institution in 1956, it has grown into Israel's largest university with its campus centered in Ramat Aviv.

TEL AVIV-YAFO. Tel Aviv-Yafo is the second largest city of Israel and the nation's chief financial, commercial, and industrial center. It is one of the most modern cities in the Middle East and lies on the eastern shore of the Mediterranean Sea. The southwestern section of the city was formerly a separate town called Jaffa (q.v.). Cultural attractions in Tel Aviv-Yafo include the Museum Haaretz and the Tel Aviv Museum. Tel Aviv University (q.v.) is one of the city's several institutions of higher learning. Tel Aviv-Yafo is the center of Israel's primary manufacturing district. About half the nation's business companies are in the area. Their products include building materials, chemicals, clothing, electronic equipment, machine tools, and processed foods.

The city is also the nation's leading center for such activities as banking, publishing, and trade. Israel's political parties have their headquarters in Tel Aviv-Yafo. In 1909, Jewish immigrants from Europe founded Tel Aviv northeast of Jaffa. Tel Aviv was administered as part of Jaffa at first, but it became a separate town in 1921. Tel Aviv grew rapidly as Jewish immigrants arrived mainly from Europe. It became Israel's first capital when the nation was established in 1948. The capital was moved to Jerusalem (q.v.) in 1949, but the Israeli Ministry of Defense and many foreign embassies remained in Tel Aviv. Most government departments maintain offices in Tel Aviv. In 1950, Tel Aviv and Jaffa merged to form Tel Aviv-Yafo.

TELEM. A political party which was formed by Moshe Dayan (q.v.) in the spring of 1981 and contested the Knesset (q.v.) election that summer. The party won two seats in the Knesset. After Dayan's death in October 1981 those two members joined Likud (q.v.) and the party dissolved.

TERRITORIES see OCCUPIED TERRITORIES

THEATER. Israel's theater companies present a wide variety of classical and contemporary plays with Jewish and universal themes, either written in Hebrew (q.v.) or translated from other languages. These companies perform to large audiences, both in their home theaters and in auditoriums throughout Israel. Habimah (q.v.), the National Theater, was founded in Moscow in 1917, under the patronage of Stanislavsky. From its inception, it was linked with Hebrew culture and Zionism, producing plays that depicted the life of the Jewish people throughout the ages. Habimah began performing in Palestine (q.v.) in 1928. Cameri Theater (est. 1944) has been the Tel Aviv municipal theater since 1970. It contributes to the development of Hebrew theater with a lively repertoire. The Haifa Municipal Theater (est. 1961) was the first theater in Israel to be publicly sponsored. It tends toward productions of original Hebrew plays, often on controversial subjects. The Beersheba Municipal Theater (est. 1974) is Israel's newest repertory company and was established to bring theater to the population of the Negev (q.v.). Numerous other theater groups exist and perform for enthusiastic audiences.

TIBERIAS. A city on the western shore of the Sea of Galilee (q.v.). It was founded in the first century and soon thereafter became an important center of Jewish learning. It went through a number of periods of growth and decline and now is mainly a resort and tourist site.

TICHON, DAN. Born in Kiryat Haim on January 5, 1937. A graduate of Hebrew University (q.v.) in economics and international relations. Tichon is a member of the Knesset (q.v.) on the Likud (q.v.) list.

TIRAN, STRAIT OF see STRAIT OF TIRAN

TORAH. The Five Books of Moses. The first five books (the Pentateuch) of the Bible consist of: Genesis (in Hebrew: Bereshit); Exodus (Shemot); Leviticus (Vayikra); Numbers (Bamidbar); and Deuteronomy (Devarim). The Torah is the centerpiece of Judaism; it not only contains the law and a philosophy of religious belief and worship for Jews, but it also serves as a guide for moral conduct and provides a history of the Jewish people.

TORAH FLAG (DEGEL HATORAH) see DEGEL HA-TORAH

TORAH RELIGIOUS FRONT. A joint election list formed by Agudat Israel (q.v.) and Poalei Agudat Israel (q.v.)

to contest the Knesset (q.v.) elections in 1951, 1955, 1959, and 1973. As a result of these elections, it won five, six, six, and five seats, respectively.

TOUBI, TAWFIK. Born on May 11, 1922 in Haifa (q.v.). Toubi is a Christian Arab journalist and has been an active member of the Communist Party (q.v.) since 1940. He has also been a Knesset (q.v.) member since the first Knesset was elected in 1949. He is the Deputy Secretary General of the Israel Communist Party. He retired in July 1990.

TOURISM. Tourism has been and continues to be an important earner of foreign exchange as more than a million visitors come to Israel each year. Israel has built up a substantial tourist industry with impressive facilities designed to attract additional tourists and to lengthen the period of their stay in Israel. These have included ski slopes, beach resorts and archaeological and historical sites in addition to religious and Biblical attractions.

TREATY OF PEACE BETWEEN THE ARAB REPUBLIC OF EGYPT AND THE STATE OF ISRAEL see EGYPT-ISRAEL PEACE TREATY

TRUMPELDOR, JOSEPH. A Zionist pioneer born in Russia in 1880 who settled in Palestine (q.v.) in 1912. He worked in Kibbutz Degania (q.v.) and participated in the defense of Jewish settlements. Trumpeldor helped to organize the Jewish Legion (q.v.) which served with the British Army during World War I. He returned briefly to Russia in 1917, but then returned to Palestine in 1919. Trumpeldor died in 1920 while defending Tel Hai against Arab attackers and this action made him a legendary hero. The Revisionist (q.v.) youth movement and its sports organization are named after him—Betar (q.v.) (acronym for Brit Yosef Trumpeldor).

TSABAN, YAIR. Born in Jerusalem (q.v.) in 1930, Tsaban was a member of the Hagana (q.v.) from 1945 to 1947 and of the Palmah (q.v.) from 1948 to 1949. He helped to found Kibbutz Zorah. He served as a member of Maki (q.v.), helped to found Moked (q.v.) and Shelli (q.v.). Tsaban joined Mapam (q.v.) in 1980 and has represented it in the Knesset since 1981.

TSOMET (TZOMET) (MOVEMENT FOR ZIONIST REVIVAL). Party founded in November 1987 as a breakaway from Tehiya (q.v.) that contested the 1988 Knesset (q.v.) election. Led by former Israel Defense Forces (q.v.) Chief of Staff Rafael (Raful) Eitan (q.v.), the main elements of the party's program include: (1) no land now under Israeli control should be subject to negotiation in peace talks with the Arabs; (2) the solution to the Palestinian problem lies east of the Jordan River; and (3) Israeli law should be applied to the occupied territories (q.v.).

TSUR, YAACOV. Born in 1937 in Haifa (q.v.), Yaacov Tsur graduated from Hebrew University (q.v.). He is a member of Kibbutz Netiv Halamed Heh. He served as Secretary General of Hakibbutz Hameuhad (q.v.) movement. Yaacov Tsur has been a Labor Alignment (q.v.) member of the Knesset (q.v.) since 1981. He served as Minister of Immigrant Absorption until 1988 and became Minister of Health in the government established in December 1988 and remained in that position until the spring of 1990 when Labor left the government.

TSUR, ZVI. Born in Saslav, Russia, on April 17, 1923. Zvi Tsur joined the Israel Defense Forces (q.v.), rising through the ranks to become Chief of Staff from 1961 to 1964. He later served as assistant Minister of Defense and still later served with the senior management of Clal Industries.

TZVAH HAGANA LE YISRAEL see ISRAEL DE-
FENSE FORCES

- U -

UNITED ARAB LIST. An Arab political party that
contested the 1977 Knesset (q.v.) election and won a
single seat in parliament.

UNITED ISRAEL APPEAL (UIA). Successor organization to the United Palestine Appeal (q.v.).

UNITED JEWISH APPEAL (UJA). A fund-raising campaign organization for the development of the Jewish
national home in Palestine (q.v.) and, later, Israel as
well as for Jewish communities and concerns worldwide.
It began to function as a permanent organization in
1938.

UNITED KIBBUTZ MOVEMENT (HATNUA HAKIB-
BUTZIT HAMEUHEDET). In 1979 the national conventions of Ihud Hakvutzot Vehakibbutzim and Hakibbutz Hameuhad (q.v.) decided to merge into the United
Kibbutz Movement.

UNITED KINGDOM see ENGLAND

UNITED NATIONS PALESTINE COMMISSION.
Shortly after the Palestine Partition Plan (q.v.) vote of
November 1947, the United Nations established a
Palestine Commission to effect the transfer from the
mandatory power to the proposed Arab and Jewish
states.

UNITED NATIONS PARTITION PLAN see PALES-
TINE PARTITION PLAN

UNITED NATIONS SECURITY COUNCIL RESOLU-
TION 242. The United Nations Security Council, on
November 22, 1967, adopted a British-sponsored resolution, designed to achieve a solution to the Arab-Israeli
conflict. The resolution was deliberately vague, but
emphasized an exchange of territory for peace. The full
text of the resolution reads as follows:

> The Security Council, Expressing its continuing
> concern with the grave situation in the Middle East.
> Emphasizing the inadmissibility of the acquisition of
> territory by war and the need to work for a just and
> lasting peace in which every State in the area can live
> in security. Emphasizing further that all Member
> States in their acceptance of the Charter of the
> United Nations have undertaken a commitment to
> act in accordance with Article 2 of the Charter. 1.
> Affirms that the fulfillment of Charter principles
> requires the establishment of a just and lasting peace
> in the Middle East which should include the applica-
> tion of both the following principles: (i) Withdrawal
> of Israeli armed forces from territories occupied in
> the recent conflict; (ii) Termination of all claims or
> states of belligerency and respect for and ac-
> knowledgement of the sovereignty, territorial integ-
> rity and political independence of every State in the
> area and their right to live in peace within secure and
> recognized boundaries free from threats or acts of
> force; 2. Affirms further the necessity (a) For
> guaranteeing freedom of navigation through inter-
> national waterways in the area; (b) For achieving a
> just settlement of the refugee problem; (c) For
> guaranteeing the territorial inviolability and politi-
> cal independence of every State in the area, through
> measures including the establishment of demilita-
> rized zones; 3. Requests the Secretary-General to
> designate a Special Representative to proceed to the
> Middle East to establish and maintain contacts with
> the States concerned in order to promote agreement
> and assist efforts to achieve a peaceful and accepted
> settlement in accordance with the provisions and
> principles in this resolution; 4. Requests the Secre-

tary-General to report to the Security Council on the progress of the efforts of the Special Representative as soon as possible.

UNSC Resolution 242 has been the basis of all subsequent peace efforts. Gunnar Jarring (q.v.), then Sweden's Ambassador to Moscow, was appointed by the United Nations Secretary General in November 1967 to implement the resolution, but ultimately he failed to secure meaningful movement toward peace. The resolution remains unimplemented.

UNITED NATIONS SECURITY COUNCIL RESOLUTION 338. On October 22, 1973 the United Nations Security Council adopted Resolution 338, which called for an immediate cease-fire in the Yom Kippur War (q.v.) and the implementation of United Nations Security Council Resolution 242 (q.v.), and explicitly required negotiations "between the parties." The full text reads as follows:

> The Security Council 1. Calls upon all parties to the present fighting to cease all firing and terminate all military activity immediately, no later than 12 hours after the moment of the adoption of this decision, in the positions they now occupy; 2. Calls upon the parties concerned to start immediately after the cease-fire the implementation of Security Council resolution 242 (1967) in all of its parts; 3. Decides that, immediately and concurrently with the cease-fire, negotiations start between the parties concerned under appropriate auspices aimed at establishing a just and durable peace in the Middle East.

The resolution provided the basis for the initial postwar military disengagement negotiations.

UNITED NATIONS SPECIAL COMMITTEE ON PALESTINE (UNSCOP). Unable to satisfy the conflicting views of the Arab and Jewish communities of Palestine (q.v.) and to ensure public safety because of the conflicts between them, and faced with the heavy burden entailed in retaining the Palestine Mandate (British Mandate (q.v.)), which compounded the extensive costs of World War II, the British conceded that the Mandate was unworkable and turned the Palestine problem over to the United Nations in the spring of 1947. The United Nations Special Committee on Palestine (UNSCOP) examined the issues and recommended that the Mandate be terminated and that the independence of Palestine be achieved without delay. However, it was divided on the future of the territory. The majority proposed partition into a Jewish state and an Arab state linked in an economic union, with Jerusalem (q.v.) and its environs established as an international enclave. The minority suggested that Palestine become a single federal state, with Jerusalem as its capital and with Jews and Arabs enjoying automony in their respective areas. The majority proposal was adopted by the United Nations General Assembly on November 29, 1947. See also PALESTINE PARTITION PLAN.

UNITED PALESTINE APPEAL (UPA). An American organization established in 1925 to coordinate the various Zionist fund-raising efforts primarily to support the establishment of Jewish settlements in Palestine (q.v.). In 1950 it was renamed the United Israel Appeal.

UNITED RELIGIOUS FRONT. In the elections to the First Knesset (q.v.) in 1949 the various religious groups—Mizrahi (q.v.), Hapoel Hamizrahi (q.v.), Agudat Israel (q.v.) and Poalei Agudat Israel (q.v.)—all ran on a single electoral list known as the United Religious Front. The Front won sixteen seats in the Knesset but was not sustained and the religious parties ran individually or in smaller combinations in subsequent elections.

UNITED STATES OF AMERICA. The relationship between the United States and Israel antedates the independence of Israel. President Woodrow Wilson endorsed the Balfour Declaration (q.v.) soon after its issuance in 1917 and the United States Congress did so in the 1920s. Despite these and other statements of support for a Jewish state or homeland in Palestine (q.v.) no substantial action took place until after World War II when the status of Palestine became a matter of considerable international attention. The administration of President Harry Truman sought a significant increase in Jewish immigration to Palestine immediately after World War II as a means of providing a refuge for displaced persons. When the British turned the Palestine Mandate (q.v.) over to the United Nations in 1947 the United States supported the concept of partition and lobbied extensively to achieve that objective. After Israel declared its independence in May 1948 the United States was the first state to grant recognition, although it was *de facto* and not *de jure*.

In the decades since Israel's independence the two states developed a diplomatic-political relationship that focused on the need to resolve the Arab-Israeli conflict (q.v.), as well as to maintain the survival and security of Israel. Nevertheless, while they agreed on the general concept, they often differed on the precise means of achieving the desired result. The relationship became especially close after the Six Day War (q.v.), when a congruence of policy prevailed on many of their salient concerns. In the wake of the Yom Kippur War (q.v.) and the peace process which followed, United States economic and military assistance reached very significant levels. In the Reagan administration the relationship took on an added dimension as President Reagan saw Israel as a strategic asset.

The United States and Israel are linked in a complex and multifacted "special relationship" that has focused on the continuing United States support for the survival, security, and well-being of Israel. The relationship revolves around a broadly conceived ideological factor and is based on substantial positive perception and sentiment evidenced in public opinion and other statements. It is also manifest in United States political-diplomatic support as well as substantial military and economic assistance to Israel. United States commitments to Israel's security and defense are not formally enshrined, but there is a general perception that the United States would prevent Israel's destruction. The United States is an indispensable, if not fully dependable, ally. It provides economic, technical, military, political, diplomatic, and moral support and there are broad areas of agreement with Israel on many issues. Divergence on some issues derives from a difference of perspective and from the overall policy environments in which the two states operate.

UNITED WORKERS PARTY see MAPAM

UNSCOP see UNITED NATIONS SPECIAL COMMITTEE ON PALESTINE

USSR (THE SOVIET UNION). The relationship between the Union of Soviet Socialist Republics and Israel has undergone substantial change over the years. The Soviet Union and the Communist Party were opposed to Zionism, but in 1947 the Soviet Union's representative at the United Nations, Andrei Gromyko, supported the Palestine Partition Plan (q.v.) which led to the creation of Israel. In 1948 the Soviet Union became one of the first states to recognize the new state of Israel and was instrumental in assuring arms from the Soviet bloc to Israel during its War of Independence (q.v.).

However, positive relations in the first years soon gave way to a deterioration of the relationship in the early 1950s that culminated in Soviet arms supply to Egypt announced in 1955. A factor in the relationship then, as later, was the relationship between Israel and the Soviet Jewish population. Israel's desire to ensure the well-being internally of the Soviet Jewish population and to ensure the right of emigration for those who wished to leave the USSR led to conflicts with Soviet authorities and Soviet Union's official position. Despite the growing relationship between the Soviet Union and the Arab states in the decade following the Sinai War (q.v.) of 1956, correct if cool relations were retained with Israel. The Soviet Union contributed to the Six Day War (q.v.) of 1967 through circulation of a fallacious rumor concerning Israeli military mobilization. At this time the Soviet Union and its East European allies (except Romania) broke diplomatic relations with Israel. Since the 1967 conflict the Soviet Union has attempted to become a more significant factor in the peace process. At the same time, since the advent of the Gorbachev approach to foreign policy there has been an improvement in the relationship of the two states. Consular contacts and exchanges have taken place, Soviet Jewish emigration has increased substantially, and several East European states have restored diplomatic relations with Israel. Nevertheless, the Soviet Union has maintained the position that it cannot reestablish relations with Israel until such time as there is substantial movement toward peace and the withdrawal of Israel from the occupied territories (q.v.). On October 18, 1991 the USSR and Israel reestablished diplomatic relations. This was part of the process of preparation for the Madrid Peace Conference (q.v.) that

convened at the end of October 1991 to negotiate a
solution to the Arab-Israeli conflict.

- V -

VAAD LEUMI (NATIONAL COUNCIL). Under the
terms of the British Mandate (q.v.), Jewish and Arab
quasi-governments were established in Palestine (q.v.)
in the 1920s. As early as 1920 the Jewish community of
Palestine (Yishuv) (q.v.) elected an Assembly of the
Elected (q.v.) or parliament by secret ballot. Between
sessions its powers were exercised by the National
Council appointed by the Elected Assembly from
among its members. The National Council, in turn,
selected an Executive from among its membership to
exercise administrative executive power over the Jewish
community. Its role was tantamount to that of a cabinet
and its authority was generally accepted in the Yishuv
and was recognized by the Mandate authorities. At first
its jurisdiction was confined essentially to social and
religious matters, but by the 1930s it also functioned in
the fields of education, culture, health, and welfare.
Through administration of the Jewish community's
affairs, the members of the National Council and the
Elected Assembly gained valuable experience in self-
rule. The Council's departments, staffed by members of
the Jewish community, provided a trained core of civil
servants for the post-Mandate period of independence.
Political experience was also gained as political parties
developed to contest the elections for office. When
Israel became independent many of the ministries of the
Provisional Government were transformations of departments and bureaus that had functioned under the
auspices of the National Council. The National Council
formed the basis of Israel's Provisional State Council
(which exercised legislative authority as the predecessor

of Israel's Knesset (q.v.) or parliament) and the Executive of the National Council formed the basis of the Provisional Government or Cabinet (q.v.).

VILNER, MEIR see MEIR WILNER

- W -

WADI SALIB. An Oriental Jewish (q.v.) (primarily North African) slum neighborhood in Haifa (q.v.) in which there were riots in July 1959 in the wake of a rumor that a police officer had killed a local resident. Subsequently other riots in Wadi Salib and elsewhere also drew attention to the poor economic and social conditions in which many Oriental immigrants were living. Wadi Salib became a symbol of Oriental discontent. See also ORIENTAL JEWS.

WAILING WALL (WESTERN WALL). The Wall, located on Mount Moriah, is all that remains of the Temple of Biblical times. The Temple was destroyed and rebuilt several times with the last destruction at the hands of the Romans in 70 AD. The Wall which is some 160 feet long was the western wall of the Temple courtyard. It has been a symbol of Jewish faith. Its alternate name ("Wailing Wall") is derived from the sorrowful prayers said there in mourning for the destruction of the Temple. According to legend the Wall itself weeps over the destruction of the Temple.

WALL-TO-WALL COALITION. During the crisis preceding the Six Day War (q.v.) of 1967, Israel created a "wall-to-wall" political coalition incorporating virtually all of Israel's political parties in a Government of National Unity (q.v.). The Communists (q.v.) were pointedly excluded but, for the first time, Gahal (q.v.)

and Menachem Begin (q.v.) joined Israel's coalition government. Begin and his political allies remained in the government until the summer of 1970 when they withdrew because of opposition to government policy concerning the terms associated with the cease-fire in the War of Attrition (q.v.) that had been arranged by the United States.

WAR IN LEBANON (1982). Also known as Operation Peace for Galilee. On June 6, 1982 Israel began a major military action against the Palestine Liberation Organization (q.v.) in Lebanon. The announced immediate goal was to put the Galilee (q.v.) out of the range of PLO shelling. It sought to remove the PLO military and terrorist threat to Israel and to reduce the PLO's political capability. It was described as a major response to years of PLO terrorist attacks against Israel and its people. The Israeli incursion into Lebanon came suddenly and Israeli forces moved swiftly north of the Israel-Lebanon border, capturing and destroying numerous PLO strongholds and positions. Within a week Israel was in control of much of the southern portion of the country and thousands of PLO fighters were killed or captured. By the middle of June Israel had virtually laid siege to Beirut. The war enjoyed widespread initial support but later occasioned major debate and demonstration, resulted in substantial casualties, and led to Israel's increased international political and diplomatic isolation. It also brought about major political and diplomatic clashes with the United States. An agreement of May 17, 1983, between Israel and Lebanon providing for the withdrawal of Israeli forces from Lebanon noted that "they consider the existing international boundary between Israel and Lebanon inviolable." Although it was signed and ratified by both states, Lebanon abrogated the agreement in March 1984. All Israeli forces were withdrawn from Lebanon, except for a security zone in southern Lebanon along the border with Israel, by 1985.

WAR OF ATTRITION (1969–1970). In the first years after the Six Day War (q.v.) Israel retained control of the occupied territories (q.v.), and despite various efforts, no significant progress was made toward the achievement of peace. The Palestinians became more active—initially gaining publicity and attention through terrorist acts against Israel, some of which were spectacular in nature. However, the most serious threat to Israel came from Egypt, which embarked on the War of Attrition in the spring of 1969 in an effort, as President Gamal Abdul Nasser put it, "to wear down the enemy." But the war soon took on a broader scope as the Egyptians faced mounting losses and minimal successes, and Nasser sought and received assistance from the Soviet Union. The Soviets soon were involved as advisers and combatants, and Israeli aircraft flying over the Suez Canal Zone were challenged by Russian-flown Egyptian planes. The War of Attrition was ended by a United States sponsored cease-fire in August 1970, and talks under Ambassador Gunnar Jarring's (q.v.) auspices were restarted, but no significant progress toward peace followed.

WAR OF INDEPENDENCE (1948–1949). As Israel declared its independence in May 1948, armies of the Arab states entered Palestine (q.v.) and engaged in open warfare with the defense forces of the new state, with the stated goals of preventing the establishment of a Jewish state and of assuring that all of Palestine would be in Arab hands. This first Arab-Israeli war (known in Israel as the War of Independence) involved troops from Egypt, Syria, Jordan, Iraq, and Lebanon, with assistance from other Arab quarters, against Israel. The war was long and costly: Israel lost some 4,000 soldiers and 2,000 civilians, about 1% of the Jewish population, and each side had successes and failures. The war ended in 1949 when Armistice Agreements (q.v.) were signed with the neighboring Arab states. Peace did not follow and additional wars between Israel and the Arabs were fought over the ensuing decades.

"WARS OF THE JEWS" see YOM KIPPUR WAR

WEIZMAN, EZER. A nephew of Chaim Weizmann (q.v.), who spells his name with one "n" to avoid benefitting from the family connection. He was born in 1924 in Tel Aviv (q.v.). He was educated at the Reali School in Haifa (q.v.), and he joined the Hagana (q.v.) in 1939. In 1942 he enlisted in the British Royal Air Force and in 1948 served as a Squadron Commander in the Israel Defense Forces (q.v.) and rose through the ranks. He studied with the British Royal Air Force from 1951 to 1953 and in 1958 he became Commander in Chief of the Israel Air Force. From 1966 to 1969 he served as Chief of the General Staff Branch of the IDF. He resigned from the IDF in December 1969, apparently convinced that he would not be made Chief of Staff, and immediately entered political life. In 1969–70 he served as Minister of Transport in the national unity government led by Golda Meir (q.v.) in one of the six seats allocated to Gahal (q.v.). He served as Minister of Defense (as a Likud (q.v.) member) but resigned in 1980. He was Minister in the Prime Minister's Office (as a Labor Alignment (q.v.) member) in the 1984 National Unity Government (q.v.). He became Minister of Science and Development in the government established in December 1988.

WEIZMANN, CHAIM. Born in Motol, near Pinsk, Russia, on November 27, 1874. The Weizmann family were ardent Zionists and belonged to the Hoveve Zion (q.v.). He was educated in Germany where he received a

Doctor of Science degree from the University of Freiburg in 1900. In 1904 Weizmann moved to England, where he began his career as a faculty member in biochemistry at the University of Manchester. As director of the Admiralty Laboratories during 1916–1919 he discovered a process for producing acetone. Weizmann became the leader of the English Zionist movement and was instrumental in securing the Balfour Declaration (q.v.). In 1918 he became chairman of the Zionist Commission to Palestine (q.v.). Following World War I Weizmann emerged as the leader of the World Zionist Organization (q.v.) and built a home in Palestine near Rehovot. He served as President of the World Zionist Organization from 1920 to 1946, except for the years 1931–1935. He helped found the Jewish Agency (q.v.), the Hebrew University (q.v.) at Jerusalem, and the Sieff Research Institute at Rehovot (now the Weizmann Institute of Science (q.v.)). In 1919 Weizmann headed the Zionist delegation to the Paris Peace Conference and in the Fall of 1947 he addressed the United Nations General Assembly to plead for the establishment of a Jewish State. Weizmann also appealed to United States President Harry Truman for assistance in the effort to secure a Jewish state. When the United States Department of State seemed willing to omit the Negev (q.v.) from the proposed Jewish state, Truman overrode them and the American delegate supported the plan which included the Negev. On the day Israel declared its independence, the United States immediately extended recognition to the new Jewish state. With the declaration of Israel's independence and the establishment of a provisional government in May 1948 Weizmann became President of Israel's provisional government, and in February 1949, the first elected Israeli Knesset (q.v.) selected Weizmann as the first President (q.v.) of Israel. He was reelected in November 1951, but died on November 9, 1952.

WEIZMANN INSTITUTE OF SCIENCE. A major scientific institution located in Rehovot, focusing on fundamental research and higher education in the sciences. It developed out of the Daniel Sieff Research Institute which was founded in 1934. It was conceived in the 1940s and the first building of the Weizmann Institute was dedicated in 1949. It is named after Chaim Weizmann (q.v.).

WEST BANK see JUDEA AND SAMARIA

WESTERN WALL see WAILING WALL

WHO IS A JEW. In 1950 the Knesset (q.v.) passed the Law of Return (q.v.) granting any Jew immigrating to Israel the right to immediate citizenship. The law did not define a Jew and left it to the Minister of Interior to interpret the clause as he saw fit. In 1958, the then-Interior Minister Yisrael Bar Yehuda issued a directive to ministry officials instructing them to register as Jewish any person who sincerely declared himself to be a Jew. The National Religious Party (q.v.) subsequently resigned from the government. In 1970, the Supreme Court (q.v.) ordered the Interior Ministry's registrar in Haifa (q.v.) to record as Jewish nationals the children of Binyamin Shalit, whose wife was not Jewish. The case aroused controversy and led to the amendment of the Law of Return defining a Jew as "a person born of a Jewish mother or who has been converted to Judaism and who does not profess another religion." Agudat Israel (q.v.) demanded that the amendment stipulate that the conversion be "according to halacha" (q.v.)—the formulation the religious parties have been fighting for ever since. Such a stipulation would exclude conversions by other than recognized Orthodox rabbis. Since then, the issue has come up after every parliamentary election in coalition negotiations with the religious parties. In 1974, a compromise formula drafted by Rabbi Shlomo Goren (q.v.), which called for conversion "according to the manner practiced and accepted among the Jewish people from generation to generation" failed to win support among religious and secular parties. Over the years, the religious parties have made numerous attempts to have their proposed amendment approved by the Knesset. All have failed, but the margin of defeat has narrowed. In June 1988 the effort was rejected by 60 votes to 53. During coalition negotiations over the establishment of the December 1988 government, it appeared that the religious parties might finally succeed, provoking an outcry of crisis proportions from world Jewry. When Shas (q.v.) took over the Interior Ministry after the 1984 elections, there were several attempts to circumvent the Law of Return. Under Rabbi Yitzhak Peretz (q.v.), Interior Ministry officials refused to register Shoshana Miller, an American-born Reform convert to Judaism, as Jewish. Miller appealed the case to the Supreme Court and won, prompting Peretz to resign. In the summer of 1989 the Supreme Court ordered the Interior Ministry to accept non-Orthodox converts to Judaism as immigrants according to the Law of Return and register them as Jews. The ruling on the registration of non-Orthodox converts came at a time when the Interior Ministry had begun to reverse its former practice of allowing such converts to come as immigrants, even though it did not register them as Jews. The ministry had excluded them by demanding that all conversion certificates must be validated by the local rabbinical courts, which accepted only Orthodox conversions. Other prominent cases have included the Brother Daniel case (1962); the status of the Falashas (q.v.) of Ethiopia; and the status of the Bnai Israel (q.v.) of India.

WILNER, MEIR. Born in Vilnius on October 23, 1918. Wilner was educated at a Hebrew high school in Vilnius and at Hebrew University (q.v.) in Jerusalem (q.v.).

Wilner was a signer of the Declaration of Independence (q.v.). A journalist by profession, he was a Knesset (q.v.) member beginning with the first Knesset until his resignation in January 1990. At the time he was Secretary General of the Israel Communist Party (q.v.) and a member of the Rakah (q.v.) faction in the parliament.

WIZO see WOMEN'S INTERNATIONAL ZIONIST ORGANIZATION

WOMEN. Israel has had its share of prominent women, such as Golda Meir (q.v.) who was an important political figure in Palestine (q.v.) from the beginning of the British Mandate (q.v.) through the independence of the Jewish state and later served as Foreign Minister and Prime Minister. At the same time feminist movements have argued that because of the extensive role and political power of the religious minority in Israel, as well as because of the traditional nature of the environments from which many of Israel's immigrant population come, women are treated unfairly and unequally in Israel.

Although the traditional status of women in Palestine prior to the establishment of Israel was inferior to that generally identified with modern society, the status of women has been enhanced by law in Israel. Women have equality before the law, including the right to vote and to hold public office. Bigamy is prohibited. Perhaps the most significant change has been the dramatic increase in the number of female students and women in the educational system, which is particularly the case with the Muslim population. Women are a significant portion of the work force, and have the right to work, without discrimination, at equal pay for equal value of work in the same jobs as men as long as they have the physical capacity to perform the job. Jewish women played a prominent part during the Mandate in the work of the pioneers, in settlement on the land, in the Jewish underground defense forces, and in the political effort. The role of women has been particularly prominent in the liberal professions and in all levels of education, in administration, in retailing, and in industries such as food processing, textiles, and electronics, and agriculture (q.v.). Women began to take part in public and communal life early in the twentieth century and women's organizations were established in the yishuv (q.v.). They participated in public debate from the earliest days and enjoyed full legal equality in most of the organizations of the yishuv from the outset; they also voted for the Assembly of the Elected (q.v.) in 1920.

Educational opportunities are today equal, except in religious schools. The number of women in the Knesset (q.v.) has remained small, although there have been women ministers and Golda Meir ultimately became Prime Minister. Women's organizations reflect every point of view and are very much involved in service work. Women are incorporated in the Israel Defense Forces (q.v.) but they do not fight. They tend to be assigned to clerical, medical, administrative, educational, or communications duties.

Israel's Declaration of Independence (q.v.) provides for complete equality of social and political rights to all citizens without regard to, among other things, sex. The Women's Equal Rights Law of 1951 gives women equal legal status with men. The Equal Pay for Equal Work Law of 1964 assures that women will be treated equally in both private and government employment. There remain some restrictions owing to the application of religious law (Jewish, Christian and Muslim) in matters of personal status. While the emancipation of women is legally assured, the implementation in spirit of course depends on tradition and custom as well as on the attitudes and practices of individuals. Women are not as fully equal in the state of Israel in practice as they are proclaimed to be in legal pronouncements and statutes.

WOMEN'S INTERNATIONAL ZIONIST ORGANIZA-TION (WIZO). The Women's International Zionist Organization was founded in July 1920 in London and in 1949 the seat of its Executive moved to Israel. The organization seeks to unite Jewish women to participate actively in the upbuilding and consolidation of Israel through various activities, including education and training of youth and women in agriculture, home economics, and more generally, in other areas relating to social welfare. It also seeks to strengthen the cultural and spiritual links between the Diaspora (q.v.) and Israel.

WORLD ZIONIST CONGRESS. The parliament of the Zionist movement. It was created by Theodor Herzl (q.v.) as a representative political body that meets at various intervals. The Zionist Congresses were held as follows: 1st Congress: Basle, August 29–31, 1897; 2d Congress: Basle, August 28–31, 1898; 3d Congress: Basle, August 15–18, 1899; 4th Congress: London, August 13–16, 1900; 5th Congress: Basle, December 26–30, 1901; 6th Congress: Basle, August 23–28, 1903; 7th Congress: Basle, July 27-August 2, 1905; 8th Congress: The Hague, August 14–21, 1907; 9th Congress: Hamburg, December 26–30, 1909; 10th Congress: Basle, August 9–15, 1911; 11th Congress: Vienna, September 2–9, 1913; 12th Congress: Karlovy Vary (Carlsbad), September 1–14, 1921; 13th Congress: Karlovy Vary, August 6–18, 1923; 14th Congress: Vienna, August 18–31, 1925; 15th Congress: Basle, August 30-September 11, 1927; 16th Congress: Zurich, July 29-August 10, 1929; 17th Congress: Basle, June 30-July 15, 1931; 18th Congress: Prague, August 21-September 4, 1933; 19th Congress: Lucerne, August 20-September 4, 1935; 20th Congress: Zurich, August 3–16, 1937; 21st Congress;

Geneva, August 16–25, 1939; 22d Congress: Basle, December 9-24, 1946; 23d Congress: Jerusalem, August 14–30, 1951; 24th Congress: Jerusalem, April 24-May 7, 1956; 25th Congress: Jerusalem, December 27, 1960-January 11, 1961; 26th Congress: Jerusalem, December 30, 1964-January 11, 1965; 27th Congress: Jerusalem, June 9–19, 1968; 28th Congress: Jerusalem, January 18–28, 1972; 29th Congress: Jerusalem, February 20-March 1, 1978; 30th Congress: Jerusalem, December 7–16, 1982; and 31st Congress Jerusalem, 1987. See also WORLD ZIONIST ORGANIZATION.

WORLD ZIONIST ORGANIZATION (WZO). The official organization of the Zionist movement founded at the initiative of Theodor Herzl (q.v.) at the 1st Zionist Congress in Basle, Switzerland in August 1897. The World Zionist Organization conducted the political, economic and settlement activities leading to the establishment of Israel. The right of membership in the Zionist Organization was accorded to every Jew who subscribed to the Organization's program—the Basle Program (q.v.) and who paid the Shekel. Each Shekel holder who was at least 18 years of age, was entitled to elect delegates to the Zionist Congress, or to be elected to Congress once having had attained the age of 24. Over the years, the center of the Zionist movement was shifted from place to place until it was transferred to Jerusalem (q.v.). Since 1952, the Zionist Organization has functioned in the framework of the Status Law. In 1960, various changes were introduced in its Constitution (which had been in force since 1899). In 1951, the Jerusalem Program was adopted in addition to the Basle Program. This Jerusalem Program was subsequently superseded by the new Jerusalem Program of 1968.

The Zionist Congress is the supreme body of the Zionist Organization. It is the Congress that is empowered to elect the President, the Chairman, the General

Council, and the members of the Zionist Executive, the Congress Attorney, and the Comptroller. The Congress deals with, and determines, all basic matters relating to the activities of the World Zionist Organization. It is composed of delegates elected in all countries, except Israel where the Zionist parties in the country receive their representation in Congress on the basis of elections to the Knesset (q.v.). The Congress receives and discusses reports from the Zionist General Council and the Executive. Originally, the Congress met annually until 1901, when it was resolved to meet every two years. Subsequently, until 1939, it met every other year (except during World War I). According to the Constitution adopted in 1960, the Zionist Congress convenes every four years.

The Zionist General Council, which is elected by the Zionist Congress, functions in the period between Congresses and is empowered to deliberate and decide on all matters affecting the Zionist Organization and its institutions, including the budget, with the exception of matters relegated solely to the authority of Congress. Its composition reflects the relative strength of forces in the Congress. The Zionist General Council supervises the activities of the Zionist Executive by means of its various committees.

The Zionist Executive is the executive arm of the World Zionist Organization, and is elected by Congress for a period of four years. Some of its members are placed in charge of the various Departments of the Executive, others serve as members without portfolio. The Executive reflects the relative strength of forces in the Congress.

The Zionist Executive is composed of 31 members, 20 of whom operate out of Israel and 11 of whom are based in New York. The latter are known as "The American Section".

WZO see WORLD ZIONIST ORGANIZATION

- Y -

YAACOBI, GAD. Born on January 18, 1935 in Kfar Vitkin, Yaacobi graduated from the Faculties of Law and Commerce of Tel Aviv University (q.v.). He has been a Labor Alignment (q.v.) member of the Knesset (q.v.) since 1969. He served as Minister of Transport. Then, in the Government of National Unity (q.v.) established in 1984, Yaacobi served as Minister of Economics and Planning and later would become Minister of Communications in the government established in December 1988.

YAD VASHEM (THE HEROES' AND MARTYRS' AUTHORITY). The official Israeli authority to commemorate the heroes and martyrs who died in the Holocaust (q.v.). The name, meaning monument and memorial, is derived from the Bible. The Authority was created by an act of the Knesset (q.v.) in 1953. It has archives and a library on the Nazi era and publishes on the Holocaust. Among its buildings is a memorial hall, dedicated in 1961, in which there is a memorial flame and on the floor are inscribed the names of the most notorious of the extermination camps.

YADIN, YIGAEL (FORMERLY SUKENIK). He was the son of the noted archaeologist Eliezer Lipa Sukenik. Born in Jerusalem (q.v.) on March 21, 1917, he joined Hagana (q.v.) at age 15. He left Hagana in 1945 to pursue his education at the Hebrew University (q.v.), but returned at the time of preparations for Israel's independence. He became Chief of General Staff Branch of Hagana Headquarters in 1947 and Chief of Operations of the Israel Defense Forces (IDF) (q.v.) General Staff in 1948, a post he held during the War of

Independence (q.v.). In 1949 he became Chief of Staff of the IDF at age 32 and began to develop the foundations for the reorganization of the IDF into a regular army. He served as one of Israel's negotiating team in the armistice negotiations at Rhodes.

Yadin resigned his military post in December 1952 in protest over cuts in the military budget and to resume his research as an archaeologist. He received his PhD in archaeology from the Hebrew University and later became professor of archaeology at that institution. From 1955 to 1958 he directed the excavations at Hazor and from 1960 to 1961 he led explorations of the Judean Desert caves where the Bar Kochba (q.v.) documents were discovered. From 1963 to 1965 he directed the Massada (q.v.) Expedition. He was awarded the Israel Prize (q.v.) in Jewish Studies in 1956 and the Rothschild Science Prize in 1964. He is the author of numerous publications in the field of archaeology.

After the Yom Kippur War (q.v.) he served as one of the members of the Agranat Commission (q.v.) appointed to look into Israel's state of readiness at the time of the outbreak of the war. In 1976 he decided to reenter public life and seek the position of Prime Minister, arguing that Israel urgently needed political and economic reforms. His announcement was greeted with popular enthusiasm since he was not of the group of politicians that Israelis had been forced to choose from for decades and he had not been involved in the scandals which affected public figures. He seemed to appeal to the Israeli public as a trusted and untainted but fresh political face. In 1976 he helped to form a new political party—Democratic Movement for Change (q.v.). The party did well in the 1977 Knesset election and joined the government coalition. Yadin served as Deputy Prime Minister from 1977 to 1981 in the government led by Menachem Begin (q.v.). He died on June 28, 1984.

YAHAD. A party at the center of the political spectrum founded in 1984 and led by Ezer Weizman (q.v.). The party won three seats in the 1984 Knesset (q.v.) election on a platform that advocated a peace settlement with the Arabs and the Palestinians. It joined the Government of National Unity (q.v.) in which Weizman served as Minister in the Prime Minister's office.

YAHAD SHIVTEI YISRAEL see YISHAI

YEDIOT AHRONOT. Hebrew (q.v.) daily afternoon newspaper published in Tel Aviv (q.v.). It was founded in Palestine (q.v.) in 1939.

YEHOSHUA, AVRAHAM B. (A.B. YEHOSHUA). Avraham B. Yehoshua is part of the "young guard" of Israeli writers whose works were published beginning in the late 1950s. He was born in Jerusalem (q.v.) in 1936 to parents native to the city for six generations, was educated there, and eventually graduated from the Hebrew University (q.v.) of Jerusalem where he majored in Philosophy and Hebrew Literature. He lived in Paris for several years as the General Secretary of the World Organization of Jewish Students, but returned to Israel in 1967 to live in Haifa (q.v.). He served as Dean of Students at the Haifa University, and since 1972, he has been on the faculty there as a professor of literature. His first stories were published in 1957, and since then he has published numerous stories in *Keshet Quarterly,* and various literary-supplement sections of newspapers. In 1962, he published his first full-length book, *The Death of an Old Man.* His other books include *In Front of the Forests* (1968), *Nine Stories* (1971), *In Early Summer 1970* (1972), *Until Winter* (1974), *The Lover,* and others. Among his plays are *A Night in May* and *Last Treatment.*

YEMENITE ASSOCIATION OF ISRAEL. A party led by Salah Mansoura that contested the 1988 Knesset (q.v.) election, but failed to secure a mandate.

YEMENITE PARTY. An ethnic political party that won one seat in each of the first two Knesset (q.v.) elections, but was unsuccessful in sustaining or expanding its political base.

YIDDISH. A German-based language written in Hebrew (q.v.) letters which served as the language of everyday communication of Ashkenazi Jews (q.v.) from eastern and central Europe.

YISHAI. Acronym for Yahad Shivtei Yisrael ("The Tribes of Israel Together"). A Sephardic (q.v.) ethnic political party oriented toward the Yemenite community formed by a breakaway group from Shas (q.v.) to contest the 1988 Knesset (q.v.) elections and led by Rabbi Shimon Ben Shlomo. Ben Shlomo had served in the previous Knesset and he formed the new party after he was removed from the Shas electoral list. It failed to secure a seat in parliament.

YISHUV. The Jewish community in Palestine (q.v.) in the period of the British Mandate (q.v.). The term means settlement. The yishuv was an autonomous political body which gained valuable experience in political procedures and self-rule. A political elite developed, civil servants gained experience, and political parties were established and developed procedures for working together. An educational system was established. The Histadrut (q.v.) was founded and became a major political, economic, and social force. A self-defense capability was created and became the basis of the Israel Defense Forces (q.v.). It provided the foundation for the governmental institutions and political processes of Israel after independence.

YOM KIPPUR WAR (1973). On October 6, 1973 (Yom Kippur), Egypt and Syria launched a coordinated attack on Israeli positions on the Suez Canal and Golan Heights (q.v.) fronts. Taking Israel by surprise, the Arab armies crossed the Suez Canal, secured a beachhead in the Sinai Peninsula (q.v.), and advanced into the Golan Heights while—during the first three days of combat—a skeletal Israeli force sought to withstand the invasion until additional troops could be mobilized. Ultimately Israel stopped the Arab forces and reversed the initial Arab successes; it retook the Golan Heights and some additional territory, while Egypt and Israel traded some territory along the Suez Canal following Israel's crossing of the Canal and its advance toward Cairo. The United Nations Security Council adopted Resolution 338 (q.v.), which called for an immediate cease-fire and the implementation of United Nations Security Council Resolution 242 (q.v.) and explicitly required negotiations "between the parties." Subsequently, United States Secretary of State Henry Kissinger negotiated the Israel-Egypt Disengagement of Forces Agreement (q.v.) of 1974 and the Sinai II Accords (q.v.) of 1975 between Egypt and Israel, as well as the Israel-Syria Disengagement of Forces Agreement (q.v.) of 1974. These involved Israeli withdrawals from territory in the Suez Canal Zone in the two agreements with Egypt and in the Golan Heights in the arrangement with Syria.

The Yom Kippur War resulted in an Israeli military victory, but that victory was accompanied by significant political and diplomatic disappointments and by domestic economic, psychological, and political stress. In purely tangible terms the 1973 war had perhaps the most far-reaching effects on Israel of any conflict to that time.

Personnel losses and overall casualty rates were substantial. The mobilization of the largest part of the civilian reserve army of several hundred thousand caused dislocations in agriculture and industry. Tourism and diamond (q.v.) sales fell, and the sea passage to Eilat (q.v.) was blockaded at the Bab el-Mandeb. Numerous other aspects of the war added to the economic costs of the conflict, and austerity was the logical result. At the same time Israel's international position deteriorated. Although it was not the initiator of the war, Israel was condemned, and numerous states (particularly in Africa) broke diplomatic relations. The ruptures with Africa were a disappointment, but a shift in the attitudes and policies of the European states and Japan was perhaps more significant. The war also increased Israel's dependence on the United States. No other country could provide Israel, or was prepared to do so, with the vast quantities of modern and sophisticated arms required for war or the political and moral support necessary to negotiate peace.

The cease-fire of October 22, 1973, was followed by what Israelis often refer to as the "wars of the Jews"—internal political conflicts and disagreements. The initial domestic political effect of the war was to bring about the postponement to December 31 of the elections originally scheduled for October 30 and the suspension of political campaigning and electioneering for the duration of the conflict. The war not only interrupted the campaign for the Knesset elections, it also provided new issues for the opposition to raise, including the conduct of the war and the "mistakes" that preceded it. In November 1973 the government appointed a Commission of Inquiry (q.v.), headed by Chief Justice Shimon Agranat (q.v.) of the Supreme Court (q.v.), to investigate the events leading up to the hostilities (including information concerning the enemy's moves and intentions), the assessments and decisions of military and civilian bodies in regard to this information, and the Israel Defense Forces' deployments, preparedness for battle, and actions in the first phase of the fighting.

YOSEF, RABBI OVADIA. Born in Baghdad in 1920, he was taken to Jerusalem (q.v.) when he was four years old. He was ordained as a Rabbi at the age of 20. In 1945 he was appointed a judge in the Sephardi religious court in Jerusalem. In 1947 he was elected head of the Cairo religious court and deputy Chief Rabbi of Egypt. In 1950 he returned to Israel and was appointed a member of the rabbinical court of Petah Tikva (q.v.) and of Jerusalem. In 1965 he was appointed a member of the Supreme Rabbinical Court of Appeals in Jerusalem and in 1968 became Sephardi Chief Rabbi (q.v.) of Tel Aviv-Yafo (q.v.). He became the Sephardi Chief Rabbi of Israel. In 1970 he was awarded the Israel Prize (q.v.) for Torah Literature.

YOUTH. Israeli youth are involved in a variety of movements, many of which have a long history and generally are associated with the various political, religious, sports, or labor movements or groups. In addition, there is a Scout organization (Hatzofim) founded in 1919. These youth groups are engaged in all forms of activities common to youth movements worldwide, although some meet the particular needs of Israel. In the latter category are such movements as Nahal (q.v.) which provides for combined military and agricultural service.

- Z -

ZAHAL see ISRAEL DEFENSE FORCES

ZEEVI, REHAVAM. A general in the Israel Defense Forces (q.v.). He later entered politics and became leader of the Moledet Party (q.v.). In February 1991 Zeevi entered the cabinet as the representative of the party after it agreed to join the government coalition.

ZION. The term was used by the Hebrew (q.v.) prophets to refer to Jerusalem (q.v.) as a spiritual symbol. As a symbol of the Holy Land it became central in the religious life of Jews outside of Israel and eventually became the basis of Zionism (q.v.).

ZIONISM. A term coined by Nathan Birnbaum in 1890 for the movement seeking the return of the Jewish people to Palestine (q.v.). After 1896 Zionism referred to the political movement founded by Theodor Herzl (q.v.) seeking a Jewish National Home in Palestine. The term is derived from Mount Zion (q.v.), one of the hills of Jerusalem (q.v.). Zion came to symbolize for the Jews their desire to return to their homeland at least as far back as the Babylonian exile in the sixth century BC. Psalm 137 says: "By the waters of Babylon, there we sat down and wept, when we remembered Zion." In the latter part of the 19th century the eastern European movement that promoted settlement in the Land of Israel called itself Hibbat Zion (q.v.) (Love of Zion). The term Zionism was used for the first time in 1890 in a Hebrew periodical. Theodor Herzl adopted it to refer to his political movement which sought the return of the Jews to the Holy Land.

ZIPORI, MORDECHAI. Zipori was born in Tel Aviv (q.v.) in 1924 and was educated in religious schools. In 1939 he joined the Irgun (q.v.) and, in 1945, was deported to Eritrea, where he remained until 1948. From 1948 to 1977 Zipori served in the Israel Defense Forces (q.v.), reaching the rank of Brigadier General and the position of Assistant Chief of Operations in the General Staff. In 1977 Zipori joined the Herut Party (q.v.) and was elected on behalf of that faction of the Likud (q.v.) to the Ninth Knesset (q.v.) in May 1977. He served as Deputy Minister of Defense throughout the duration of the Ninth Knesset, from 1977 to 1981. On August 5, 1981, after having been reelected to the Tenth Knesset, he was sworn in as Minister of Communications and served in that position until 1984.

BIBLIOGRAPHY

Introduction to The Study of Israel

Almost all aspects of Israel have been the subject of extensive writings by scholars, journalists, and observers. Many of Israel's senior political and other public figures have also published their memoirs and/or have written about various aspects of Israeli life and society. The abundance of material both facilitates and hinders the study, research, and analysis of Israel. The amount of material is so vast that the reader is faced with a bewildering choice. Despite the large quantity of material available in numerous languages, some subjects are barely covered while others are the subject of substantial and often contradictory material of varying quality.

Some of Israel's most prominent institutions—such as the kibbutz—have been extensively studied, while others have had only brief examination.

Israel is well known as a center of publishing. The country has one of the highest books per capita publishing levels in the world. These materials, in Hebrew and some in English and other languages, cover a wide range from novels to serious scientific works in virtually every subject area. Some deal with Israel, while others represent the best of Israeli scholarship and literary capability in virtually every subject area.

The government of Israel is a prolific publisher of high quality materials that can be well used by the reader. These include such items published annually as the *Israel Government Year Book* and the *Statistical Abstract of Israel*.

Keeping Up With Developments

Keeping up with developments relating to Israel is facilitated by the extensive coverage in the American and European English and other language media. At the same time, the reader has access to the Israeli English-language daily *Jerusalem Post,* which also publishes a weekly international edition readily available outside of Israel.

The bibliography which follows is restricted to books and monographs, in part because of the volume of literature on the subject and because these are generally more readily available than articles whether in books, journals, or magazines. The listing is not meant to be exhaustive but rather to provide a basic listing in each of the subject areas for further perusal and has been divided into useful categories to facilitate reading and research. See the Contents which follows.

BIBLIOGRAPHY—CONTENTS

GENERAL

General Works About Israel

Baal-Teshuva, Jacob, ed. *The Mission of Israel.* New York: Robert Speller, 1963.

Ben-Gurion, David. *Israel: A Personal History.* New York: Funk and Wagnalls; New York and Tel Aviv: Sabra Books, 1971.

Ben-Meir, Alon. *Israel: The Challenge of the Fourth Decade.* New York and London: Cyrco Press, Inc., 1978.

Bentwich, Norman. *Israel Resurgent.* New York: Praeger, 1960.

Bermant, Chaim. *Israel.* New York: Walker, 1967.

Cameron, James. *The Making of Israel.* London: Secker and Warburg, 1976.

Chafets, Ze'ev. *Heroes and Hustlers, Hard Hats and Holy Men: Inside the New Israel.* New York: Morrow, 1986.

Cooke, Hedley V. *Israel: A Blessing and a Curse.* London: Stevens and Sons Limited, 1960.

Cragg, Kenneth. *This Year in Jerusalem.* London: Darton Longman & Todd, Ltd., 1982.

Crossman, Richard H. S. *A Nation Reborn: The Israel of Weizmann, Bevin, and Ben-Gurion.* London: Hamish Hamilton, 1960.

Davis, Moshe, ed. *Israel: Its Role in Civilization.* New York: Harper & Row, 1956.

DeGaury, Gerald. *The New State of Israel.* New York: Praeger, 1952.

Dunner, Joseph. *Democratic Bulwark in the Middle East: A Review and Analysis of Israel's Social, Economic, and Political Problems During the Period From 1948 to 1953.* Grinnell, IA: Grinnell College Press, 1953.

Ellis, Harry B. *Israel and the Middle East.* New York: Ronald Press, 1957.

Elon, Amos. *The Israelis: Founders and Sons.* New York: Bantam Books, 1972.

Elston, D.R. *No Alternative: Israel Observed.* London: Hutchinson, 1960.

———. *Israel: The Making of a Nation.* Oxford: Oxford University Press, 1963.

Farrell, James T. *It Has Come to Pass.* New York: Herzl, 1958.

Feis, Herbert. *The Birth of Israel: The Tousled Diplomatic Bed.* New York: W.W. Norton, 1969.

Flink, Salomon J. *Israel, Chaos and Challenge: Politics vs. Economics.* Ramat Gan, Israel: Turtledove, 1980.

Frank, Waldo. *Bridgehead: The Drama of Israel.* New York: George Braziller, Inc., 1957.

Frankel, William. *Israel Observed: An Anatomy of the State.* London: Thames & Hudson, 1980.

Freedman, Robert O., ed. *Israel in the Begin Era.* New York: Praeger, 1982.

Frishwasser-Ra'anan, H.F. *The Frontiers of a Nation.* London: Batchworth, 1955.

Garcia-Granados, Jorge. *The Birth of Israel: The Drama as I Saw It.* New York: Alfred Knopf, 1948.

Gavron, Daniel. *Israel After Begin.* Boston: Houghton Mifflin, 1984.

Grose, Peter. *A Changing Israel.* New York: Vintage Books, 1985.

Heschel, Abraham H. *Israel: An Echo of Eternity.* New York: Farrar, Straus, and Giroux, 1969.

Heubner, Theodore and Carl Hermann Voss. *This is Israel.* New York: Philosophical Library, 1956.

Heydemann, Steven, ed. *Issues in Contemporary Israel: The Begin Era.* Boulder, CO: Westview Press, 1984.

Horowitz, David. *State in the Making.* New York: Alfred Knopf, 1953.

Janowsky, Oscar I. *Foundations of Israel: Emergence of a Welfare State.* Princeton, NJ: D. Van Nostrand, 1959.

Kahane, Meir. *Our Challenge: The Chosen Land.* Radnor, PA: Chilton, 1974.

Kraines, Oscar. *Israel: The Emergence of a New Nation.* Washington, DC: Public Affairs Press, 1954.

Lehman-Wilzig, Sam N. and Bernard Susser, eds. *Public Life in Israel and the Diaspora.* Jerusalem: Bar-Ilan University Press, 1981.

Lehrman, Hal. *Israel, The Beginning and Tomorrow.* New York: William Sloane Assoc., 1951.

Marx, Emanuel, ed. *A Composite Portrait of Israel.* London and New York: Academic Press, 1980.

Meyer, Lawrence. *Israel Now: Portrait of a Troubled Land*. New York: Delacorte, 1982.

Naamani, Israel T. *Israel: A Profile*. New York: Praeger, 1972.

————, David Rudavsky and Abraham Katsh, eds. *Israel: Its Politics and Philosophy: An Annotated Reader*. New York: Behrman, 1974.

Nyrop, Richard F. ed. *Israel: A Country Study*. Washington, DC: American University, 1979.

Oz, Amos. *In the Land of Israel*. New York: Harcourt, Brace & Jovanovich, 1983.

Postal, Bernard and Henry W. Levy. *And the Hills Shouted for Joy: The Day Israel was Born*. New York: David McKay, 1973.

Prittie, Terence. *Israel: Miracle in the Desert*. New York: Praeger, 1967.

Rabinovich, Itamar and Jehuda Reinharz, eds. *Israel in the Middle East: Documents and Readings on Society, Politics, and Foreign Relations, 1948-Present*. New York: Oxford University Press, 1984.

Reich, Bernard. *Israel: Land of Tradition and Conflict*. Boulder, CO: Westview Press; London and Sydney: Croom Helm, 1985.

———— and Gershon R. Kieval, eds. *Israel Faces the Future*. New York: Praeger, 1986.

Safran, Nadav. *Israel: The Embattled Ally*. Cambridge, MA: Belknap Press of Harvard University Press, 1981.

Schoenbrun, David, with Robert Szekely, Lucy Szekely. *The New Israelis*. New York: Atheneum, 1973.

Segev, Tom. *1949: The First Israelis.* New York: The Free Press and London: Collier Macmillan, 1986.

Williams, L.F. Rushbrook. *The State of Israel.* New York: Macmillan, 1957.

Travel and Guide Books

Bazak: Guide to Israel, 1988–1989. Jerusalem: Bazak Israel Guidebook Publishers, Ltd., 1988.

Fodor's Israel, 1980. New York: David McKay Co., Inc., 1980.

Vilnay, Zev. *Israel Guide.* 14th rev. ed. Jerusalem: Hamakor Press, 1970.

Atlases

Aharoni, Yohanan and Michael Avi-Yonah, eds., *The Macmillan Bible Atlas.* New York: Macmillan, 1968.

Atlas of Israel. New York: Macmillan, 1985.

Gilbert, Martin. *Jewish History Atlas.* New York: Macmillan, 1960.

————. *Atlas of the Arab-Israeli Conflict.* New York: Macmillan, 1975.

Historical Atlas of Israel. Jerusalem: Carta, 1983.

Meyer, Herrmann M.Z., comp. *Israel: Pocket Atlas and Handbook.* Jerusalem: Universitas Booksellers, 1961.

Vilnay, Zev. *The New Israel Atlas: Bible to Present Day.* New York: McGraw-Hill, 1969.

Directories, Yearbooks, and Encyclopedias

Bank of Israel. *Annual Report.* Jerusalem: 1955– .

Bridger, David and Samuel Wolk, eds. *The New Jewish Encyclopedia.* New York: Behrman, 1976.

Encyclopedia Judaica. 16 vols. Jerusalem: Keter, 1972.

Hill, Helen, ed. *Zionist Year Book.* London: Zionist Federation of Great Britain & Ireland, 1951– .

Israel. Central Bureau of Statistics. *Statistical Abstract of Israel.* Jerusalem: Central Bureau of Statistics, 1949– .

Israel Government Yearbook. Jerusalem: Government Printer, 1950– .

The Israel Yearbook. Tel-Aviv: Israel Yearbook Publishers, 1950– .

Patai, Raphael, ed. *Encyclopedia of Zionism and Israel.* 2 vols. New York: Herzl, McGraw-Hill, 1971.

Roth, Cecil and Geoffrey Wigoder, eds. in chief. *The New Standard Jewish Encyclopedia.* rev. ed. London: Allen, 1970.

Bibliography

Alexander, Yonah. *Israel: Selected, Annotated and Illustrated Bibliography.* Gilbertsville, NY: Victor Buday, 1968.

Alexander, Yonah, Miriam Alexander and Mordecai S. Chertoff. *A Bibliography of Israel.* New York: Herzl, 1981.

Cohen, Iva, comp. *Israel: A Bibliography—A Selected, Annotated Listing of Works on Israel's Past History and Present Structure and Culture.* New York: Anti-Defamation League of B'nai B'rith, 1970.

Emanuel, Muriel, ed. *Israel: A Survey and Bibliography*. New York: St. Martin's Press, 1971.

Mahler, Gregory S. *Bibliography of Israeli Politics*. Boulder, CO: Westview Press, 1985.

Neuberg, Assia. *The State of Israel: An Annotated Bibliography*. Jerusalem: Centre for Public Libraries in Israel, 1977.

Sherman, John, gen. ed. *The Arab-Israeli Conflict, 1945–1971, A Bibliography*. New York: Garland Publishing, 1978.

Silverburg, Sanford R. *The Palestinian Arab-Israeli Conflict: An International Legal Bibliography*. Monticello, IL: Vance, 1982.

Tronik, Ruth. *Israeli Periodicals and Serials in English and Other European Languages: A Classified Bibliography*. Metuchen, NJ: The Scarecrow Press, Inc., 1974.

BIOGRAPHY AND AUTOBIOGRAPHY

Avi-hai, Avraham. *Ben-Gurion: State-Builder: Principles and Pragmatism, 1948–1963*. New York: Wiley, 1974.

Bar-Zohar, Michael. *Ben-Gurion: The Armed Prophet*. Englewood Cliffs, NJ: Prentice Hall, 1966.

———. *Ben Gurion: A Biography*. New York: Delacorte, 1979.

Begin, Menachem. *The Revolt*. New York: Nash, 1981.

Bein, Alex. *Theodor Herzl: A Biography*. Philadelphia: The Jewish Publication Society of America, 1948.

Ben Zvi, Rachel. *Coming Home*. New York: Herzl, 1963.

Ben-Gurion, David. *Rebirth and Destiny of Israel*. New York: Philosophical Library, 1954.

Ben-Gurion Looks Back in Talks with Moshe Pearlman. New York: Simon & Schuster, 1965.

Bentwich, Norman. *For Zion's Sake: A Biography of Judah L. Magnes, First Chancellor and First President of the Hebrew University of Jerusalem*. Philadelphia: Jewish Publication Society, 1954.

Benziman, Uzi. *Sharon: An Israeli Caesar*. New York: Adama Books, 1986.

Berlin, Sir Isaiah. *Chaim Weizmann*. London: Weidenfeld and Nicolson, 1958.

Christman, Henry M., ed. *This Is Our Strength: Selected Papers of Golda Meir*. New York and London: Macmillan, 1962.

Cohen, Israel. *Theodor Herzl: Founder of Political Zionism*. New York: Herzl, 1959.

Dayan, Moshe. *Diary of the Sinai Campaign*. New York: Harper and Row, 1966.

———. *Story of My Life: An Autobiography*. New York: William Morrow, 1976 and London: Weidenfeld & Nicolson, 1976.

Dayan, Samuel. *Pioneers in Israel*. New York: World, 1961.

Eban, Abba. *Voice of Israel*. New York: Horizon, 1957.

———. *The Tide of Nationalism*. New York: Horizon, 1959.

———. *My People: The Story of the Jews*. New York: Behrman; Random House, 1969.

———. *Abba Eban: An Autobiography*. London: Weidenfeld & Nicolson; NY: Random House, 1977.

Edelman, Maurice. *David: The Story of Ben-Gurion*. New York: Putnam, 1965.

Elon, Amos. *Herzl*. New York: Holt, Rinehart and Winston, 1975.

Fineman, Irving. *Woman of Valor: The Life of Henrietta Szold, 1860–1945*. New York: Simon & Schuster, 1961.

Gervasi, Frank. *The Life and Times of Menachem Begin: Rebel to Statesman*. New York: Putnam, 1979.

Golan, Matti. *Shimon Peres: A Biography*. London: Weidenfeld & Nicolson, 1982 and New York: St. Martin's Press, 1982.

Haber, Eitan. *Menachem Begin: The Legend and the Man*. New York: Delacorte, 1978.

Herzl, Theodor. *Complete Diaries*. 5 vols. Edited by Raphael Patai. New York: Herzl, 1960.

Horin, Meir Ben. *Max Nordau*. New York: Herzl, 1956.

Jorman, Pinchas, ed. *Moshe Dayan: A Portrait*. New York: Dodd, Mead, 1969.

Kling, Simcha. *Nachum Sokolow: Servant of His People*. New York: Herzl, 1960.

Kollek, Teddy and Amos Kollek. *For Jerusalem: A Life*. New York: Random House, 1978.

Kurzman, Dan. *Ben-Gurion: Prophet of Fire*. New York: Simon & Schuster, 1983.

Lau-Lavie, Naphtali. *Moshe Dayan: A Biography*. Hartford, CT: Prayer Book Press, 1969.

Lipsky, Louis. *A Gallery of Zionist Profiles*. New York: Farrar, Straus and Cudahy, 1956.

Litvinoff, Barnet. *Ben-Gurion of Israel*. New York: Praeger, 1954.

―――. *Weizmann: Last of the Patriarchs*. New York: Putnam, 1976.

Lowenthal, Marvin, ed. *The Diaries of Theodor Herzl*. New York: Dial, 1956.

Meinertzhagen, Richard. *Middle East Diary: 1917–1956*. New York: Yoseloff, 1960.

Meir, Golda. *A Land of Our Own: An Oral Autobiography*. Edited by Marie Syrkin. New York: Putnam, 1973.

―――. *My Life*. New York: Putnam; London: Weidenfeld & Nicolson, 1975.

Perlmutter, Amos. *The Life and Times of Menachem Begin*. New York: Doubleday, 1987.

Prittie, Terence. *Eshkol: The Man and the Nation*. New York: Pitman, 1969.

Rabin, Yitzhak. *The Rabin Memoirs*. Boston: Little, Brown, 1979.

Reinharz, Jehuda. *Chaim Weizmann: The Making of a Zionist Leader*. New York: Oxford University Press, 1985.

Rose, Norman. *Chaim Weizmann: A Biography*. New York: Elisabeth Sifton Books, Viking, 1986.

St. John, Robert. *Tongue of the Prophets: The Life Story of Eliezer Ben-Yehuda*. New York: Doubleday, 1952.

―――. *Ben Gurion: The Biography of an Extraordinary Man*. Garden City, NY: Doubleday, 1959.

————. *They Came from Everywhere: Twelve Who Helped Mold Modern Israel.* New York: Coward McCann, 1962.

————. *Eban.* New York: Dell, 1972.

Samuel, Edwin. *A Lifetime in Jerusalem: The Memoirs of the Second Viscount Samuel.* Jerusalem: Israel Universities Press, 1970.

Schechtman, Joseph B. *Rebel and Statesman.* New York: Yoseloff, 1956.

————. *Fighter and Prophet.* New York: Yoseloff, 1961.

Sharon, Ariel. *Warrior: The Autobiography of Ariel Sharon.* New York: Simon & Schuster, 1989.

Shihor, Samuel. *Hollow Glory: The Last Days of Chaim Weizmann.* New York: Yoseloff, 1960.

Silver, Eric. *Begin: The Haunted Prophet.* New York: Random House, 1984.

Simon, Merrill. *Moshe Arens: Statesman and Scientist Speaks Out.* Middle Island, NY: Dean Books, 1988.

Slater, Robert. *Rabin of Israel: A Biography.* London: Robson Books, 1977.

Syrkin, Marie. *Way of Valor.* New York: Sharon, 1955.

————. *Golda Meir: Woman With a Cause.* New York: Putnam, 1963.

Temko, Ned. *To Win or to Die: A Personal Portrait of Menachem Begin.* New York: William Morrow, 1987.

Teveth, Shabtai. *Ben-Gurion and the Palestinian Arabs: From Peace to War.* New York: Oxford, 1985.

————. *Ben Gurion: The Burning Ground, 1886–1948.* Boston: Houghton Mifflin, 1987.

————. *Moshe Dayan: The Soldier, The Man, The Legend.* Boston: Houghton Mifflin, 1973.

Weisgal, Meyer W. and Joel Carmichael, eds. *Chaim Weizmann— A Biography by Several Hands.* New York: Atheneum, 1963.

Weizman, Ezer. *On Eagles' Wings.* New York: Macmillan, 1979.

————. *The Battle for Peace.* Toronto, New York, London: Bantam Books, 1981.

Weizmann, Chaim. *Trial and Error: The Autobiography of Chaim Weizmann, First President of Israel.* New York: Harper & Row, 1949.

CULTURE

Literature, Theatre, Dance, and Music

Abramson, Glenda. *Modern Hebrew Drama.* London: Weidenfeld & Nicolson, 1979.

Agnon, Samuel Yosef. *Days of Awe.* New York: Schocken, 1948.

————. *A Guest for the Night.* New York: Herzl, 1967.

Asch, Sholem. *The Prophet.* London: Macdonald, 1956.

Fisch, Harold. *S.Y. Agnon.* New York: Ungar, 1975.

Fuchs, Esther. *Israeli Mythogynies: Women in Contemporary Israeli Ficton.* Albany, NY: State University of New York Press, 1987.

Hochman, Baruch. *The Fiction of S.Y. Agnon.* Ithaca, NY: Cornell University Press, 1970.

Shakow, Zara. *Theatre in Israel.* New York: Herzl, 1963.

Yehoshua, A.B. *Between Right & Right: Israel Problem or Solution?* New York: Doubleday, 1981.

Archaeology

Albright, William Foxwell. *The Archaeology of Palestine: A Survey of the Ancient Peoples and Cultures of the Holy Land.* rev. ed. Harmondsworth, Middlesex, UK: Penguin Books, 1956.

———. *Archaeology and the Religion of Israel.* 5th ed. Garden City, NY: Doubleday, 1969.

———. *The Archaeology of Palestine.* Rev. ed. New York: P. Smith, 1971.

Avi-Yonah, Michael and Ephraim Stern, eds. *Encyclopedia of Archaeological Excavations in the Holy Land.* 4 vols. Jerusalem: Massada, 1975–78.

Burrows, Millar. *The Dead Sea Scrolls.* New York: Viking, 1955.

Glueck, Nelson. *Rivers in the Desert: A History of the Negev.* New York: Grove Press, 1960.

Kenyon, Kathleen M. *Jerusalem: Excavating 3,000 Years of History.* New York: McGraw-Hill, 1968.

———. *Archaeology in the Holy Land.* 3d ed. London: Benn, 1970.

Negev, Abraham, ed. *Archaeological Encyclopedia of the Holy Land.* London: Weidenfeld & Nicolson, 1972.

———. *Archaeology in the Land of the Bible.* Tel Aviv: Sadan, 1977.

Pearlman, Moshe. *Digging up the Bible: The Stories Behind the Great Archaeological Discoveries in the Holy Land.* Jerusalem: Steimatzky, 1980.

Pearlman, Moshe and Yaakov Yannai. *Historical Sites in Israel.* Tel Aviv: PEC Press, 1964. rev. and enl. ed., Jerusalem: Steimatzky, 1979.

Pritchard, James B., ed. *Archaeological Discoveries in the Holy Land.* New York: Crowell, 1967.

Yadin, Yigael. *The Art of Warfare in Biblical Lands in the Light of Archaeological Study.* 2 vols. New York: McGraw-Hill, 1963.

———. *Masada: Herod's Fortress and the Zealots' Last Stand.* New York: Random House, 1966.

———. *Bar-Kokhba: The Rediscovery of the Legendary Hero of the Second Jewish Revolt Against Rome.* London: Weidenfeld & Nicolson, 1971.

DEFENSE AND SECURITY

General Works

Adan, Avraham. *On the Banks of the Suez.* San Rafael, CA: Presidio, 1980.

Allon, Yigal. *Shield of David: The Story of Israel's Armed Forces.* London: Weidenfeld & Nicolson, 1970.

———. *The Making of Israel's Army.* London: Vallentine, Mitchell, 1970 and New York: Bantam Books, 1971.

Alon, Hanan. *Countering Palestinian Terrorism in Israel: Toward a Policy and of Countermeasures.* Santa Monica: Rand, 1980.

Arian, Asher, Ilan Talmud, and Tamar Hermann. *National Security and Public Opinion in Israel*. Jerusalem: *The Jerusalem Post* and Boulder, CO: Westview Press, for the Jaffee Center for Strategic Studies, 1988.

Avner (Pseud.). *Memoirs of an Assassin*. New York: Yoseloff, 1959.

Bar Siman-Tov, Yaacov. *The Israeli-Egyptian War of Attrition 1969–1970: A Case Study of Limited Local War*. New York: Columbia University Press, 1980.

Begin, Menachem. *The Revolt*. New York: Schuman, 1951.

Beit-Hallahmi, Benjamin. *The Israeli Connection: Who Israel Arms and Why*. New York: Pantheon, 1987.

Bell, J. Bowyer. *Terror Out of Zion: Irgun Zvai Leumi, Lehi, Palestine Underground, 1929–1949*. New York: St. Martin's Press, 1977.

Ben Porat, Yeshayahu, Eitan Haber and Ze'ev Schiff. *Entebbe Rescue*. New York: Delacorte Press, 1977.

Ben-Ami, Yitshaq. *Years of Wrath, Days of Glory: Memoirs from the Irgun*. New York: Speller, 1982.

Beres, Louis Rene, ed. *Security or Armageddon: Israel's Nuclear Strategy*. Lexington, MA: Lexington Books, 1985.

Berglas, Eitan. *Defense and the Economy: The Israeli Experience*. Jerusalem: The Maurice Falk Institute for Economic Research, January 1983.

Bowden, Tom. *Army in the Service of the State*. Tel Aviv: University Publishing Projects, 1976.

Clarke, Thurston. *By Blood and Fire: The Attack on the King David Hotel*. New York: Putnam, 1981.

Derogy, Jacques and Hesi Carmel. *The Untold History of Israel.* New York: Grove Press, 1979.

Dupuy, Trevor N. *Elusive Victory: The Arab-Israeli Wars, 1947–1974.* New York: Harper & Row, 1978.

Eshel, D. *Israel's Air Force Today.* Hod Hasharon, Israel: Eshel Dramit Ltd., 1981.

Feldman, Shai. *Israeli Nuclear Deterrence.* New York: Columbia University Press, 1983.

———. *The Raid on Osiraq: A Preliminary Assessment.* Tel Aviv: Center for Strategic Studies, Tel Aviv University, 1981.

Frank, Jerold. *The Deed.* New York: Simon & Schuster, 1963.

Glick, Edward B. *Between Israel and Death.* Harrisburg, PA: Stackpole, 1974.

Handel, Michael J. *Israel's Political-Military Doctrine.* Cambridge, MA: Harvard Center for International Affairs, 1973.

Harkavy, Robert E. *Spectre of a Middle East Holocaust: The Strategic and Diplomatic Implications of the Israeli Nuclear Weapons Program.* Denver, CO: University of Denver, Graduate School of International Studies, 1978.

Herzog, Chaim. *The Arab-Israeli Wars: War and Peace in the Middle East.* London: Arms & Armour Press, 1982.

Inbar, Efraim. *Israeli Strategic Thought in the Post 1973 Period.* Jerusalem: Israel Research Institute of Contemporary Society, September 1982.

Jabber, Fuad. *Israel and Nuclear Weapons: Present Options and Future Strategies.* London: Chatto & Windus, for the International Institute of Strategic Studies, 1971.

Jackson, Robert. *The Israeli Air Force: The Struggle for Middle East Aircraft Supremacy Since 1948.* 2d ed. London: Stacey, 1972.

Katz, Samuel. *Days of Fire: The Secret History of the Irgun Zvai Leumi.* Garden City, NY: Doubleday, 1968.

Klieman, Aaron S. *Israel's Global Reach: Arms Sales as Diplomacy.* McLean, VA: Pergamon-Brassey, 1985.

Lanir, Zvi, ed. *Israeli Security Planning in the 1980s: Its Politics and Economics.* New York: Praeger, 1984.

Laqueur, Walter. *Confrontation: The Middle East and World Politics.* New York: Quadrangle, 1974.

Lorch, Netanel. *One Long War: Arab Versus Jew Since 1920.* Jerusalem: Keter, 1976.

Luttwak, Edward and Dan Horowitz. *The Israeli Army.* New York: Harper & Row, 1975.

Mardor, Munya. *Haganah.* New York: New America Library, 1966.

Meridor, Yaacov. *Long is the Road to Freedom.* New York: United Zionist Revisionists, 1961.

O'Ballance, Edgar. *The Electronic War in the Middle East, 1968–70.* London: Faber, 1974.

Pearlman, Moshe. *The Army of Israel.* New York: Philosophical Lib., 1950.

Peres, Shimon. *David's Sling: The Arming of Israel.* London: Weidenfeld & Nicolson, 1970.

Perlmutter, Amos. *Military and Politics in Israel 1948–1967; Nation-Building and Role Expansion.* London: Cass, 1969.

———. *Politics and the Military in Israel, 1967–1977.* London: Cass, 1978.

Perlmutter, Amos, Michael Handel, Uri Bar-Joseph. *Two Minutes Over Baghdad.* London: Vallentine, Mitchell, 1982.

Reich, Bernard and Gershon R. Kieval, eds. *Israeli National Security Policy: Political Actors and Perspectives.* New York, Westport, CT, and London: Greenwood, 1988.

Reiser, Stewart. *The Israeli Arms Industry: Foreign Policy, Arms Transfers, and Military Doctrine of a Small State.* New York: Holmes & Meier, 1989.

Ribalow, Harold U., ed. *Fighting Heroes of Israel.* New York: New American Library, 1967.

Rifkin, Shepard. *What Ship? Where Bound.* New York: Alfred Knopf, 1961.

Robinson, Donald B. *Under Fire: Israel's 20 Year Struggle for Survival.* New York: W.W. Norton, 1968.

Rothenberg, Gunter E. *Anatomy of the Israeli Army.* London: Batsford, 1979.

Rubinstein, Murray and Richard Goldman. *The Israeli Air Force Story.* London: Arms & Armour Press, 1979.

Schiff, Ze'ev. *A History of the Israeli Army (1870–1974).* New York: Simon & Schuster, 1974.

Shalev, Aryeh. *The West Bank: Line of Defense.* New York: Praeger, for the Jaffee Center for Strategic Studies, Tel Aviv University, 1985.

Shimshoni, Jonathan. *Israel and Conventional Deterrence.* Ithaca, NY: Cornell University Press, 1988.

Sicker, Martin. *Israel's Quest for Security.* New York and Westport, CT: Praeger, 1989.

Slater, Leonard. *The Pledge.* New York: Simon & Schuster, 1970.

Stein, Janice Gross and Raymond Tanter. *Rational Decision-Making: Israel's Security Choices 1967.* Columbus, OH: Ohio State University Press, 1980.

Tamir, Avraham. *A Soldier in Search of Peace: An Inside Look at Israel's Strategy*. New York: Harper & Row, 1988.

Wallach, Jehuda L. *Israeli Military History: A Guide to the Sources*. New York: Garland, 1984.

Williams, Louis, ed. *Military Aspects of the Arab-Israeli Conflict*. Tel Aviv: University Publications Project, 1975.

Yaniv, Avner. *Deterrence Without the Bomb: The Politics of Israeli Strategy*. Lexington, MA: Lexington Books, 1986.

———. *Dilemmas of Security: Politics, Strategy, and the Israeli Experience in Lebanon*. New York: Oxford University Press, 1987.

Arab-Israeli Conflict

Abi-Mershed, Walid. *Israeli Withdrawal From Sinai*. Beirut: The Institute for Palestine Studies, n.d.

Alroy, Gil Carl, ed. *Attitudes Toward Jewish Statehood in the Arab World*. New York: American Academic Association for Peace in the Middle East, 1971.

Aronson, Shlomo. *Conflict and Bargaining in the Middle East: An Israeli Perspective*. Baltimore, MD: Johns Hopkins Press, 1978.

Bar-Siman-Tov, Yaacov. *The Israeli-Egyptian War of Attrition, 1969–1970*. New York: Columbia University Press, 1980.

———. *Israel, The Superpowers, and the War in the Middle East*. New York: Praeger, 1987.

Ben-Gurion, David. Misha Louvish, ed. *My Talks with Arab Leaders*. Jerusalem: Keter, 1972.

Bentwich, N. *Israel and Her Neighbours*. London: Rider, 1955.

Berger, Earl. *The Covenant and the Sword: Arab-Israeli Relations, 1948–56.* London: Routledge and Kegan Paul, 1956.

Bethell, Nicholas. *The Palestine Triangle: The Struggle Between the British, the Jews and the Arabs, 1935–1948.* London: Deutsch, 1979.

Bloomfield, L.M. *Egypt, Israel and the Gulf of Aqaba in International Law.* Toronto: Carswell, 1957.

Brook, David. *Preface to Peace: The United Nations and the Arab-Israel Armistice System.* Washington, DC: Public Affairs Press, 1964.

Bull, General Odd. *War and Peace in the Middle East: The Experience and Views of a U.N. Observer.* London: Cooper, 1976.

Burns, E.L.M. *Between Arab and Israeli.* Beirut: The Institute for Palestine Studies, 1969.

Byford-Jones, W. *Forbidden Frontiers.* London: Robert Hale, 1958.

Cohen, Aharon. *Israel and the Arab World.* New York: Funk & Wagnalls, 1970.

Cohen, Michael J. *The Origins and Evolution of the Arab-Zionist Conflict.* Berkeley and Los Angeles: University of California Press, 1987.

Dayan, Moshe. *Breakthrough: A Personal Account of the Egypt-Israel Peace Negotiations.* New York: Alfred Knopf, 1981.

Elath, Eliahu. *Israel and Her Neighbors.* London: James Barrie, 1956.

Elazar, Daniel, ed. *Judea, Samaria and Gaza: Views on the Present and Future.* Washington, DC: American Enterprise Institute for Public Policy Research, 1982.

Ellis, Harry B. *Israel and the Middle East.* New York: Ronald Press, 1957.

—————. *The Dilemma of Israel.* Washington, DC: American Enterprise Institute for Public Policy Research, 1970.

Epp, Frank H. *Whose Land is Palestine?: The Middle East Problem in Historical Perspective.* Grand Rapids, MI: William B. Eerdmans Publishing Company, 1970.

ESCO Foundation for Palestine. *Palestine: A Study of Jewish, Arab and British Policies.* 2 vols. New Haven: Yale University, 1947.

Fabian, Larry L. and Ze'ev Schiff, eds. *Israelis Speak: About Themselves and the Palestinians.* New York: Carnegie Endowment for International Peace, 1977.

Feinberg, Nathan. *The Arab-Israel Conflict in International Law: A Critical Analysis of the Colloquium of Arab Jurists in Algiers.* Jerusalem: The Magnes Press, 1970.

Flapan, Simha. *The Birth of Israel: Myths and Realities.* New York: Pantheon Books, 1987.

Forsythe, David P. *United Nations Peace-Making: The Conciliation Commission for Palestine.* Baltimore, MD: Johns Hopkins Press, 1972.

Frischwasser-Ra'anan, H.F. *The Frontiers of a Nation.* London: Batchworth, 1955.

Gabbay, Rony E. *A Political Study of the Arab-Jewish Conflict: The Arab Refugee Problem. A Case Study.* Geneva: Librairie E. Droz, 1959.

Gervasi, Frank. *The Case for Israel.* New York: The Viking Press, 1967.

Gilbert, Martin. *The Arab-Israeli Conflict: Its History in Maps.* 3d ed. London: Weidenfeld & Nicolson, 1979.

Glubb, John B. *Peace in the Holy Land: An Historical Analysis of the Palestine Problem.* London: Hodder & Stoughton, 1971.

Goitein, S.D. *Jews and Arabs: Their Contacts Through the Ages.* New York: Schocken, 1964.

Great Britain and Palestine: 1915–1945. 3d ed. London: Royal Institute of International Affairs, 1946.

Halabi, Rafiq. *The West Bank Story.* New York: Harcourt, Brace & Jovanovich, 1982.

Harkabi, Yehoshafat. *Fedayeen Action and Arab Strategy.* London: Institute for Strategic Studies, December 1968. Adelphi Papers No. 53.

———. *Arab Attitudes to Israel.* London: Vallentine, Mitchell; NY: Hart, 1976.

———. *Arab Strategies and Israel's Response.* New York: The Free Press, 1977.

———. *The Palestinian Covenant and its Meaning.* London: Vallentine, Mitchell, 1979.

———. *Israel's Fateful Hour.* New York: Harper & Row, 1988.

Harris, William W. *Taking Root: Israeli Settlement in the West Bank, the Golan and Gaza-Sinai, 1967–1980.* New York: Wiley, 1980.

Kahane, Meir. *They Must Go.* New York: Grosset & Dunlap, 1981.

Katz, Shmuel. *Hollow Peace.* Jerusalem: Dvir, 1981.

Kotker, Norman. *The Earthly Jerusalem.* New York: Scribner, 1969.

Lilienthal, Alfred M. *What Price Israel?* Chicago: Regnery, 1953.

————. *There Goes the Middle East.* New York: Devin-Adair, 1957.

————. *The Other Side of the Coin.* New York: Devin-Adair, 1965.

Lustick, Ian S. *For the Land and the Lord: Jewish Fundamentalism in Israel.* New York: Council on Foreign Relations, 1988.

Ma'oz, Moshe. *Palestinian Leadership in the West Bank: The Changing Role of the Mayors Under Jordan and Israel.* London: Cass, 1984.

Moore, John N., ed. *The Arab-Israeli Conflict: Readings and Documents.* abr. and rev. ed. Princeton, NJ: Princeton University Press, 1977.

Mroz, John E. *Influence in Conflict: The Impact of Third Parties on the Arab-Israeli Dispute Since 1973.* New York: Pergamon, 1983.

Newman, David. *Jewish Settlement in the West Bank: The Role of Gush Emunim.* Durham, UK: University of Durham, 1982.

Nisan, Mordechai. *Israel and the Territories.* Ramat Gan, Israel: Turtledove, 1978.

Parkes, James. *Whose Land? A History of the Peoples of Palestine.* rev. ed. Harmondsworth, Middlesex, UK: Penguin Books, 1970.

Patai, Raphael. *The Seed of Abraham: Jews and Arabs in Contact and Conflict.* Salt Lake City: University of Utah Press, 1986.

Peretz, Don. *Israel and the Palestine Arabs.* Washington: Middle East Institute, 1958.

Polk, William, D. Stamler and E. Asfour. *Backdrop to Tragedy: The Struggle for Palestine.* Boston: Beacon, 1957.

Prittie, Terence and Walter Nelson. *The Economic War Against the Jews.* London: Secker & Warburg, 1978.

Reich, Bernard. *Israel and Occupied Territories.* Washington, DC: U.S. Department of State, 1973.

———. *Quest for Peace: United States-Israel Relations and the Arab-Israeli Conflict.* New Brunswick, NJ: Transaction Books, 1977.

Reisman, Michael. *The Art of the Possible: Diplomatic Alternatives in the Middle East.* Princeton, NJ: Princeton University Press, 1970.

Rodinson, Maxime. *Israel and the Arabs.* rev. ed. Baltimore, MD: Penguin Books, 1970.

Rosenne, Shabtai. *Israel's Armistice Agreements with the Arab States: A Juridical Interpretation.* Tel Aviv: Blumstein's Bookstores, 1951.

Sachar, Howard M. *Egypt and Israel.* New York: Marek, 1981.

Safran, Nadav. *From War to War: The Arab-Israeli Confrontation, 1948–1967.* New York: Pegasus, 1969.

Schnall, David J. *Beyond the Green Line: Jewish Life West of the Jordan.* New York: Praeger, 1985.

Sella, Amnon and Yael Yishai. *Israel: The Peaceful Belligerent, 1967–79.* New York: St. Martin's Press, 1986.

Sheffer, Gabriel, ed. *Dynamics of a Conflict: A Re-examination of the Arab-Israeli Conflict.* Atlantic Highlands, NJ: Humanities Press, 1975.

Shipler, David K. *Arab and Jew: Wounded Spirits in the Promised Land.* New York: Times Books, 1986.

Stevens, Georgiana G. *Jordan River Partition.* Stanford, CA: The Hoover Institution on War, Revolution, and Peace, Stanford University, 1965. Hoover Institution Studies No. 6.

Stock, Ernest. *Israel on the Road to Sinai, 1949–1956.* Ithaca, NY: Cornell University Press, 1967.

Stone, Julius. *Israel and Palestine: Assault on the Law of Nations.* Baltimore, MD: Johns Hopkins Press, 1981.

Voss, Carl Hermann. *Palestine Problem Today: Israel and Its Neighbors.* Boston: Beacon, 1954.

Yishai, Yael. *Land or Peace: Whither Israel?* Stanford, CA: Hoover Institution Press, 1987.

Jerusalem

Bahat, Dan. *The Historical Atlas of Jerusalem: A Brief Illustrated Survey.* New York: Scribner, 1975.

Benvenisti, Meron. *Jerusalem: The Torn City.* Jerusalem: University of Minneapolis Press, 1977.

Bovis, Eugene. *The Jerusalem Question, 1917–1968.* Stanford, CA: Hoover Institution Press, 1971.

Cattan, Henry. *Jerusalem.* London: Croom Helm, 1981.

Cohen, Saul B. *Jerusalem: Bridging the Four Walls: A Geopolitical Perspective.* New York: Herzl, 1977.

Eckardt, Alice L., ed. *Jerusalem: City of the Ages.* New York: American Academic Association for Peace in the Middle East; Lanham, MD: University Press of America, 1987.

Elon, Amos. *Jerusalem: City of Mirrors.* Boston: Little, Brown, 1989.

Feintuch, Yossi. *U.S. Policy on Jerusalem.* Westport, CT: Greenwood, 1987.

Gilbert, Martin. *Jerusalem: Illustrated History Atlas.* New York: Macmillan, 1977.

Joseph, Bernard. *The Faithful City: The Siege of Jerusalem, 1948.* New York: Simon & Schuster, 1960.

Kenyon, Kathleen M. *Digging Up Jerusalem.* London: Benn, 1974.

Kollek, Teddy. *Jerusalem, Sacred City of Mankind: A History of Forty Centuries.* New York: Random House; Jerusalem: Steimatzky, 1968.

Kotker, Norman. *The Earthly Jerusalem.* New York: Scribner, 1969.

Kraemer, Joel L., ed. *Jerusalem: Problems and Prospects.* New York: Praeger, 1980.

Pfaff, Richard H. *Jerusalem: Keystone of an Arab-Israeli Settlement.* Washington, DC: American Enterprise Institute for Public Policy Research, 1969.

Prittie, Terence. *Whose Jerusalem?* London: Muller, 1981.

Rabinovich, Abraham. *Jerusalem on Earth: People, Passions, and Politics in the Holy City.* New York: The Free Press; London: Collier Macmillan, 1988.

U.S. Congress. *Jerusalem: The Future of the Holy City for Three Monotheisms.* Washington, DC: U.S. Congress, Committee on Foreign Affairs, Subcommittee on the Near East, 1971.

Arab-Israeli Wars

War of Independence, 1948–1949

Banks, Lynne Reid. *Torn Country: An Oral History of the Israeli War of Independence.* New York: Franklin Watts, 1982.

Elston, David Roy. *No Alternative: Israel Observed.* London: Hutchinson, 1960.

Kagan, Benjamin. *The Secret Battle for Israel.* Cleveland: World, 1966.

Kimche, Jon and David Kimche. *A Clash of Destinies: The Arab-Jewish War and the Founding of the State of Israel.* New York: Praeger, 1960.

Kurzman, Dan. *Genesis 1948: The First Arab-Israel War.* London: Vallentine, Mitchell, 1970.

Lorch, Netanel. *The Edge of the Sword: Israel's War of Independence, 1947–1949.* New York: Putnam, 1961.

O'Ballance, Edgar. *The Arab-Israeli War, 1948.* London: Faber and Faber, 1956.

Zurayk, Constantine N. *Palestine: The Meaning of the Disaster.* Beirut: Khayat's, 1956.

Suez War, 1956

Barer, Shlomo. *The Weekend War.* New York: Yoseloff, 1960.

Barker, A.J. *Suez: The Seven Day War.* London: Faber and Faber, 1964.

Bowie, Robert R. *Suez, 1956: International Crisis and the Role of Law.* New York: Oxford University Press, 1975.

Bromberger, Merry and Serge Bromberger. *Secrets of Suez.* London: Pan Books and Sidgwick and Jackson, 1957.

Calvocoressi, Peter. *Suez Ten Years Later.* New York: Random House, 1967.

Childers, Erskine B. *The Road to Suez.* London: MacGibbon and Kee, 1962.

Dayan, Moshe. *Diary of the Sinai Campaign.* New York: Harper and Row, 1966.

Eden, Anthony (Lord Avon). *Full Circle.* Boston: Houghton Mifflin, 1960.

―――. *The Suez Crisis of 1956.* Boston, MA: Beacon Press, 1968.

Finer, Herman. *Dulles Over Suez.* Chicago: Quadrangle Books, 1964.

Henriques, Robert. *A Hundred Hours to Suez: An Account of Israel's Campaign in the Sinai Peninsula.* New York: Pyramid Books, 1967.

Johnson, Paul. *The Suez War.* New York: Greenberg, 1957.

Marshall, S.L.A. *Sinai Victory: Command Decisions in History's Shortest War, Israel's Hundred-Hour Conquest of Sinai.* New York: William Morrow, 1958.

Nutting, Anthony. *I Saw for Myself.* New York: Doubleday, 1958.

O'Ballance, Edgar. *The Sinai Campaign.* London: Faber and Faber, 1959.

Stock, Ernest. *Israel on the Road to Sinai: A Small State in a Test for Power.* Ithaca: Cornell University, 1967.

Thomas, Hugh. *Suez.* New York: Harper and Row, 1969.

The June (Six Day) War, 1967

Benson, Alex, ed. *The 48 Hour War.* New York: IN Publishing Corporation, 1967.

Bondy, Ruth, Ohad Zemora and Raphael Bashan, eds. *Mission Survival.* New York: Sabra, 1968.

Churchill, Randolph A. and Winston S. Churchill. *The Six Day War.* London: Heinemann, 1967.

Dayan, David. *Strike First: A Battle History of the Six-Day War.* New York: Pitman, 1967.

Donovan, Robert J. and the Staff of the *Los Angeles Times. Israel's Fight for Survival: Six Days in June: June 5–10, 1967.* New York: New American Library, 1967.

Howard, Michael and Robert Hunter. *Israel and the Arab World: The Crisis of 1967.* London: Institute for Strategic Studies, 1967. Adelphi Papers No. 41.

Keesing's Research Report. *The Arab-Israeli Conflict: The 1967 Campaign.* New York: Scribner, 1968.

Kimche, David and Dan Bawly. *The Six-Day War: Prologue and Aftermath.* New York: Stein and Day, 1971. Originally published as *The Sandstorm.*

Kosut, Hal, ed. *Israel and the Arabs: The June 1967 War.* New York: Facts on File, 1968.

Laqueur, Walter. *The Road to War: The Origin and Aftermath of the Arab-Israeli Conflict 1967–8.* Baltimore, MD: Penguin Books, 1969. Also published as *The Road to Jerusalem.*

Moskin, Robert. *Among Lions: The Battle for Jerusalem, June 5–7, 1967.* New York: Arbor House, 1982.

O'Ballance, Edgar. *The Third Arab-Israeli War.* London: Faber and Faber, 1972.

Pasha, Glubb. *The Middle East Crisis: A Personal Interpretation.* London: Hodder and Stoughton, 1967.

Pry, Peter. *Israel's Nuclear Arsenal.* Boulder, CO: Westview Press, 1984.

Rihkye, Indar J. *The Sinai Blunder: Withdrawal of the Force Leading to the Six Day War.* London: Cass, 1980.

Robinson, Donald B. *Under Fire: Israel's 20 Year Struggle for Survival.* New York: W.W. Norton, 1968.

Rosensaft, Menahem Z. *Not Backward to Belligerency: A Study of*

Events Surrounding the Six-Day War of June 1967. New York: Yoseloff, 1969.

Shapira, Avraham, principal ed. *The Seventh Day: Soldiers' Talk About the Six-Day War*. New York: Scribner, 1970.

Stevenson, William. *Strike Zion!* New York: Bantam Books, 1967.

Yom Kippur War, 1973

Herzog, Chaim. *The War of Atonement: October 1973*. Boston, MA: Little, Brown, 1975.

O'Ballance, Edgar. *No Victor, No Vanquished: The Yom Kippur War*. San Rafael, CA: Presidio, 1978.

Schiff, Ze'ev. *October Earthquake: Yom Kippur 1973*. Tel Aviv: University Publications Project, 1974.

Sherman, Arnold. *When God Judged and Men Died: A Battle Report of the Yom Kippur War*. Toronto, New York, and London: Bantam Books, 1973.

Sobel, Lester A., ed. *Israel and the Arabs: The October 1973 War*. Oxford, UK: Clio, 1974.

Sunday Times. *Insight on the Middle East War*. London: Deutsch, 1974.

War in Lebanon, 1982

Bulloch, John. *Final Conflict: The War in Lebanon*. London: Century, 1983.

Eban, Abba, intro. by. *The Beirut Massacre: The Complete Kahan Commission Report*. New York: Karz-Cohl, 1983.

Evron, Yair. *War and Intervention in Lebanon: The Israeli-Syrian Deterrence Dialogue*. Baltimore: Johns Hopkins, 1987.

Feldman, Shai and Heda Rechnitz-Kijner. *Deception, Consensus and War: Israel in Lebanon.* Paper No. 27. Tel Aviv: Tel Aviv University, Jaffee Center for Strategic Studies, October 1984.

Gabriel, Richard A. *Operation Peace for Galilee: The Israel-PLO War in Lebanon.* New York: Hill & Wang, 1984.

Kahan, Yitzhak, Aharon Barak and Yona Efrat. *Commission of Inquiry into the Events at the Refugee Camps in Beirut. Final Report. Authorized Translation.* Jerusalem: Government Printer, 1983.

Rabinovich, Itamar. *The War for Lebanon 1970–1983.* New York: Cornell University Press, 1984.

Schiff, Ze'ev and Ehud Ya'ari. *Israel's Lebanon War.* New York: Simon & Schuster, 1984.

Timmerman, Jacobo. *The Longest War: Israel in Lebanon.* New York: Alfred Knopf, 1982.

Intelligence Service

Aldouby, Zwy and Jerrold Ballinger. *The Shattered Silence: The Eli Cohen Affair.* New York: Coward, McCann & Geoghegan, 1971.

Bar-Zohar, Michael. *Spies in the Promised Land: Isar Harel and the Israeli Secret Service.* Boston: Houghton Mifflin, 1972.

Ben-Hanan, Eli. *Our Man in Damascus.* Tel Aviv: A.D.M. Publishing House, 1967.

Blumberg, Stanley and Gwinn Owens. *The Survival Factor: Israeli Intelligence from World War I to the Present.* New York: Putnam, 1981.

Deacon, Richard. *The Israeli Secret Service.* New York: Taplinger, 1978.

Dekel (Krasner), Ephraim. *Shai: Historical Exploits of Haganah Intelligence.* New York: Yoseloff, 1959.

Eisenberg, Dennis. *The Mossad: Israel's Secret Intelligence Service: Inside Stories.* London: Paddington, 1978.

Harel, Isser. *The House on Garibaldi Street: The First Full Account of the Capture of Adolf Eichmann, Told by the Former Head of Israel's Secret Service.* New York: Viking, 1975.

Lotz, Wolfgang. *The Champagne Spy: Israel's Master Spy Tells His Story.* New York: St. Martin's Press, 1972.

Ninio, Marcelle, Victor Levy, Robert Dassa and Philip Natanson. *Operation Susannah.* New York: Harper & Row, 1978.

Posner, Steve. *Israel Undercover: The Secret Warfare and Hidden Diplomacy in the Middle East.* Syracuse: Syracuse University Press, 1987.

Steven, Stewart. *The Spymasters of Israel.* New York: Macmillan, 1980.

ECONOMY

General

Bautista, Romeo M., et al. *Capital Utilization in Manufacturing in Developing Countries: A Case Study of Colombia, Israel, Malaysia, and the Philippines.* London: Oxford University Press, 1982.

Ben-Porat, Yoram, ed. *The Israeli Economy: Maturing Through Crisis.* Cambridge, MA: Harvard University Press, 1986.

Berglas, Eitan. *Defense and the Economy: The Israeli Experience.*

Discussion Paper No. 83.01. Jerusalem: The Maurice Falk Institute for Economic Research in Israel, 1983.

Boxer, Baruch. *Israeli Shipping and Foreign Trade.* Chicago: University of Chicago, 1957.

Chill, Dan S. *The Arab Boycott of Israel: Economic Aggression and World Reaction.* New York: Praeger, 1976.

Combatting Inflation in Israel: A Conversation with Dr. Ezra Sadan. Washington, DC: American Enterprise Institute for Public Policy Research, 1981.

Dagan, Peretz. *Pillars of Israel's Economy.* Tel Aviv: I. Lipschitz, 1955.

Daniel, Abraham. *Labor Enterprises in Israel.* Vol. 1, *The Cooperative Economy,* and Vol. 2, *The Institutional Economy.* New Brunswick, NJ: Transaction Books, 1976.

Fischer, Stanley. *The Economy of Israel.* Working Paper No. 1190. Washington, DC: National Bureau for Economic Research, August 1983.

Ginor, Fanny. *Socio-Economic Disparities in Israel.* Tel Aviv: David Horowitz Institute for the Research of Developing Countries, Tel Aviv University, 1979.

Granott, A. *Agrarian Reform and the Record of Israel.* London: Eyre & Spottiswoode, 1956.

Greenwald, Carol. *Recession as a Policy Instrument: Israel 1965–1969.* Rutherford, NJ: Fairleigh Dickinson University Press, 1973.

Halevi, Nadav and Ruth Klinov-Malul. *The Economic Development of Israel.* New York: Praeger, 1968.

Horowitz, David. *The Economics of Israel.* Oxford: Pergamon Press, 1967.

————. *The Enigma of Economic Growth: A Case Study of Israel.* New York: Praeger, 1972.

Kimmerling, Baruch. *Zionism and Economy.* Cambridge, MA: Schenkman, 1983.

Kurland, Samuel. *Cooperative Palestine: The Story of Histadrut.* New York: Sharon Books for the National Committee for Labor of Palestine, 1947.

Lerner, Abba and Haim Ben-Shahar. *The Economics of Efficiency and Growth.* Cambridge, MA: Ballinger Publishing, 1975.

Malkosh, Noah. *Cooperation in Israel.* Tel Aviv: Histadrut, 1958.

————. *Histadrut in Israel: Its Aims and Achievements.* Tel Aviv: Histadrut, 1961.

Metzer, Jacob. *The Slowdown of Economic Growth in Israel: A Passing Phase or the End of the Big Spurt.* Report No. 83.03. Jerusalem: The Maurice Falk Institute for Economic Research in Israel, April 1983.

Michaely, Michael. *Foreign Trade Regimes and Economic Development: Israel.* New York: Columbia University Press, 1975.

————. *Israel.* New York: National Bureau of Economic Research, 1975.

Ofer, Gur. *The Service Industries in a Developing Economy: Israel as a Case Study.* New York: Praeger, 1967.

Pack, Howard. *Structural Change and Economic Policy in Israel.* New Haven, CT: Yale University Press, 1971.

Pomfret, Richard and Benjamin Toren. *Israel and the European Common Market: An Appraisal of the 1975 Free Trade Agreement.* Tubingen, Germany: Mohr, 1980.

Rubner, Alex. *The Economy of Israel: A Critical Account of the First Ten Years.* New York: Praeger, 1960.

Sarna, Aaron J. *Boycott and Blacklist: A History of Arab Economic Warfare Against Israel.* Totowa, NJ: Rowman and Littlefield, 1986.

Schaafhauysen, Irma. *Development Through Mobilization of Own Resources Exemplified by Israel.* Hamburg: Hamburg Archives of World Economy, 1964.

U.S. Senate Committee on Foreign Relations. *The Economic Crisis in Israel.* A Staff Report. 98th Congress, 2d Session. Washington, DC: U.S. Government Printing Office, 1984.

Agriculture and Irrigation

Bein, Alex. *The Return to the Soil.* Jerusalem: Zionist Organization, 1952.

Darin-Drabkin, H. *Patterns of Cooperative Agriculture in Israel.* Tel Aviv: Israel Institute for Books, 1962.

Lowdermilk, Walter Clay. *Palestine: Land of Promise.* New York: Harper & Row, 1944.

Morris, Yaakov. *Masters of the Desert.* New York: Putnam, 1961.

GEOGRAPHY

General

Aharoni, Yohanan. *The Land of the Bible: A Historical Geography.* 2d rev. and amended ed. London: Burns & Oates, 1979.

Fisher, William Bayne. *The Middle East: A Physical, Social and Regional Geography.* London: Methuen, 1964.

Karmon, Yehuda. *Israel: A Regional Geography*. London: Wiley, 1971.

Orni, Ephraim and Elisha Efrat. *Geography of Israel*. 3d rev. ed. Jerusalem: Keter, 1971.

Smith, George A. *The Historical Geography of the Holy Land*. 26th ed. London: Hodder & Stoughton, 1935.

Flora and Fauna

Alon, Azariah. *The Natural History of the Land of the Bible*. Garden City, NY: Doubleday, 1978.

Bodenheimer, F.S. *Animal Life in Palestine*. Jerusalem: L. Mayer, 1935.

Zohary, Michael. *Plant Life of Palestine: Israel and Jordan*. New York: Ronald Press, 1962.

——— and Naomi Feinbrun-Dothan. *Flora Palaestina*. 4 vols. Jerusalem: Israel Academy of Sciences, 1966.

GOVERNMENT AND POLITICS

Akzin, Benjamin, and Yehezkel Dror. *Israel: High-Pressure Planning*. Syracuse: Syracuse University, 1966.

Arian, Alan. *The Choosing People: Voting Behavior in Israel*. Cleveland and London: Case Western Reserve University Press, 1973.

———, ed. *The Elections in Israel: 1969*. Israel: Jerusalem Academic Press, 1972.

————, ed. *The Elections in Israel: 1973.* New Brunswick, NJ: Transaction Books, 1975.

————, ed. *The Elections in Israel: 1977.* New Brunswick, NJ: Transaction Books, 1980.

————, ed. *The Elections in Israel: 1981.* New Brunswick, NJ: Transaction Books, 1984.

————, ed. *Politics in Israel: The Second Generation.* Chatham, NJ: Chatham House, 1985.

Arian, Alan and Michael Shamir, eds. *The Elections in Israel: 1984.* New Brunswick, NJ: Transaction Books, 1986.

Arian, Asher (Alan). *Ideological Change in Israel.* Cleveland: Case Western Reserve Press, 1968.

Aronoff, Myron J. *Frontiertown: The Politics of Community Building in Israel.* Manchester, UK: Manchester University Press, 1974.

————. *Power and Ritual in the Israel Labor Party: A Study in Political Anthropology.* Assen/Amsterdam: Van Gorcum, 1977.

Badi, Joseph. *The Government of the State of Israel: A Critical Account of Its Parliament, Executive and Judiciary.* New York: Twayne, 1963.

————, ed. *Fundamental Laws of the State of Israel.* New York: Twayne, 1961.

Baker, Henry E. *The Legal System of Israel.* Jerusalem: Israel Universities Press, 1968.

Bayne, E.A. *Four Ways of Politics: State and Nation in Italy, Somalia, Israel, Iran.* New York: American Universities Field Staff, 1965.

Bernstein, Marver H. *The Politics of Israel: The First Decade of Statehood.* Princeton: Princeton University Press, 1957.

Bilinsksi, R., et al. *Can Planning Replace Politics? The Israeli Experience.* The Hague: Martinus Nijhoff, 1980.

Bradley, C. Paul. *Electoral Politics in Israel.* Grantham, NH: Tompson & Rutter, 1981.

Caiden, Gerald E. *Israel's Administrative Culture.* Berkeley, CA: Institute of Governmental Studies, University of California, 1970.

Caspi, Dan, Abraham Diskin and Emanuel Gutmann, eds. *The Roots of Begin's Success: The 1981 Israeli Elections.* London and Canberra: Croom Helm and New York: St. Martin's Press, 1984.

Czudnowski, Moshe M. and Jacob M. Landau. *The Israeli Communist Party and the Elections for the Fifth Knesset, 1961.* Stanford: The Hoover Institution on War, Revolution, and Peace, Stanford University, 1965.

Deshen, Shlomo. *Immigrant Voters in Israel.* Manchester, UK: Manchester University Press, 1970.

Dror, Yehezkel and Emanuel Gutmann, eds. *The Government of Israel.* Jerusalem: The Eliezer Kaplan School of Economics and Social Sciences, The Hebrew University, 1961.

Elizur, Yuval and Eliahu Salpeter. *Who Rules Israel?* New York: Harper & Row, 1973.

Etzioni-Halevy, Eva, with Rina Shapira. *Political Culture in Israel: Cleavage and Integration Among Israel's Jews.* New York: Praeger, 1977.

Fein, Leonard J. *Israel: Politics and People.* Boston: Little, Brown, 1968.

Freudenheim, Yehoshua. *Government in Israel.* Dobbs Ferry, NY: Oceana, 1967.

Gerson, Allan. *Israel, the West Bank and International Law.* Totowa, NJ: Cass, 1978.

Harkabi, Yehoshafat. *The Bar-Kokhba Syndrome: Risks and Realism in International Politics.* Chappaqua, NY: Rossel, 1983.

Horowitz, Dan and Moshe Lissak. *The Origins of the Israeli Polity.* Chicago: University of Chicago Press, 1978.

————. *Trouble in Utopia: The Overburdened Polity of Israel.* Albany: State University of New York Press, 1989.

Horowitz, David. *State in the Making.* New York: Alfred Knopf, 1953.

Isaac, Rael Jean. *Israel Divided: Ideological Parties in the Jewish State.* Baltimore, MD: Johns Hopkins Press, 1976.

————. *Party and Politics in Israel: Three Visions of a Jewish State.* New York: Longman, 1981.

Israel. Ministry of Justice. *Laws of the State of Israel: Authorized Translation.* Jerusalem: Government Printer, 1948–.

Kahane, Rabbi Meir. *They Must Go.* New York: Grosset and Dunlap, 1981.

Kieval, Gershon R. *Party Politics in Israel and the Occupied Territories.* Westport, CT: Greenwood, 1983.

Kimmerling, Baruch. *Zionism and Territory: The Socio-Territorial Dimension of Zionist Politics.* Berkeley, CA: Institute of International Studies, 1983.

Kraines, Oscar. *Government and Politics in Israel.* Boston: Houghton Mifflin, 1961.

Liebman, Charles S. and Eliezer Don-Yehiya. *Religion and Politics in Israel*. Bloomington, IN: Indiana University Press, 1984.

Likhovski, Eliahu. *Israel's Parliament: The Law of the Knesset*. Oxford, UK: Clarendon Press, 1971.

Mahler, Gregory S. *The Knesset: Parliament in the Israeli Political System*. Rutherford, NJ: Fairleigh Dickinson University Press, 1981.

———. *Readings on the Israeli Political System: Structures and Processes*. Washington, DC: University Press of America, 1982.

Mars, Leonard. *The Village and the State: Administration, Ethnicity and Politics in an Israeli Cooperative Village*. Westmead, UK: Gower, 1980.

Medding, Peter Y. *Mapai in Israel: Political Organization and Government in a New Society*. Cambridge, MA: Harvard University Press, 1978.

Merhav, Peretz. *The Israeli Left: History, Problems, Documents*. Cranbury, NJ: A.S. Barnes, 1980.

Nahas, Dunia H. *The Israeli Communist Party*. London: Croom Helm and New York: St. Martin's Press, 1976.

Newman, David, ed. *Gush Emunim: Political Inspiration and Settlement Objectives*. New York: St. Martin's Press, 1984.

Penniman, Howard R. and Daniel Elazar, eds. *Israel at the Polls, 1981*. Washington, DC: American Enterprise Institute for Public Policy Research, 1986.

Peretz, Don. *The Government and Politics of Israel*. 2d ed. Boulder, CO: Westview Press, 1979.

Peri, Yoram. *Between Battles and Ballots: Israeli Military in Politics*. Cambridge, UK: Cambridge University Press, 1983.

Perlmutter, Amos. *Anatomy of Political Institutionalization: The Case of Israel and Some Comparative Analyses.* Cambridge, MA: Center for International Affairs, Harvard University, 1970.

———. *Israel: The Partitioned State.* New York: Scribner, 1985.

Rackman, Emmanuel. *Israel's Emerging Constitution, 1948–51.* New York: Columbia University, 1955.

Rubenstein, Sondra Miller. *The Communist Movement in Palestine and Israel, 1919–1984.* Boulder, CO, and London: Westview Press, 1985.

Rubinstein, Amnon. *The Zionist Dream Revisited: From Herzl to Gush Emunim and Back.* New York: Schocken, 1984.

Sager, Samuel. *The Parliamentary System of Israel.* Syracuse: Syracuse University Press, 1985.

Samuel, Edwin. *Problems of Government in the State of Israel.* Jerusalem: Rubin Mass, 1956.

Schnall, David J. *Radical Dissent in Contemporary Israeli Politics: Cracks in the Wall.* New York: Praeger, 1979.

Seligman, Lester G. *Leadership in a New Nation: Political Development in Israel.* New York: Atherton, 1964.

Shapiro, Yonathan. *The Formative Years of the Israeli Labour Party.* London: Sage, 1976.

Sharef, Zeev. *Three Days.* Garden City NY: Doubleday, 1962.

Sharkansky, Ira. *The Political Economy of Israel.* New Brunswick, NJ: Transaction Books, 1987.

———. *What Makes Israel Tick? How Domestic Policy-Makers Cope with Constraints.* Chicago: Nelson-Hall, 1985.

———. *Wither the State? Politics and Public Enterprise in Three Countries.* Chatham, NJ: Chatham House Publishers, 1979.

Shimshoni, Daniel. *Israel Democracy: The Middle of the Journey.* New York: Free Press, 1982.

Spiegel, Erika. *New Towns in Israel: Urban and Regional Planning and Development.* New York: Praeger, 1968.

Sprinzak, Ehud. *Gush Emunim: The Politics of Zionist Fundamentalism in Israel.* New York: American Jewish Committee, 1986.

————. *Kach and Meir Kahane: The Emergence of Jewish Quasi-Fascism.* New York: American Jewish Committee, 1985.

Vlavianos, Basil J. and Feliks Gross, eds. *Struggle for Tomorrow: Modern Political Ideologies of the Jewish People.* New York: Arts, 1954.

Wolfsfeld, Gadi. *The Politics of Provocation: Participation and Protest in Israel.* Albany, NY: State University of New York Press, 1988.

Yaacobi, Gad. *The Government of Israel.* New York: Praeger, 1982.

Yanai, Nathan. *Party Leadership in Israel.* Philadelphia: Turtledove, 1981.

Zidon, Asher. *Knesset: The Parliament of Israel.* New York: Herzl, 1967.

Zohar, David M. *Political Parties in Israel: The Evolution of Israeli Democracy.* New York: Praeger, 1974.

HISTORY

History of Israel and Palestine

Barbour, Neville. *Palestine, Star or Crescent?* New York: Odyssey, 1947.

Bauer, Yehuda. *From Diplomacy to Resistance: A History of Jewish Palestine, 1939–1945*. Philadelphia: Jewish Publication Society, 1970.

Ben-Gurion, David. *Israel: Years of Challenge*. New York: Holt, Rinehart and Winston, 1963.

———. *The Jews in Their Land*. Garden City, NY: Doubleday, 1966.

Bentwich, Norman and Helen Bentwich. *Mandate Memories, 1918-1948*. London: Hogarth, 1965.

Benvenisti, Meron. *The Crusaders in the Holy Land*. Jerusalem: Israel Universities Press, 1970.

Buber, Martin. *Israel and Palestine*. New York: Farrar, Straus and Young, 1952.

Cohen, Amnon. *Palestine in the 18th Century: Patterns of Government and Administration*. Jerusalem: Magnes, 1973.

Crossman, Richard H.S. *A Nation Reborn*. New York: Atheneum, 1960.

Dunner, Joseph. *Republic of Israel: Its History and Its Promise*. New York: McGraw-Hill, 1950.

Garcia-Granados, Jorge. *The Birth of Israel, The Drama As I Saw It*. New York: Alfred Knopf, 1948.

Horowitz, Dan and Moshe Lissak. *Origins of the Israeli Polity: Palestine Under the Mandate*. Chicago: Chicago University Press, 1978.

Hurewitz, Jacob C. *The Struggle for Palestine*. New York: W.W. Norton, 1950.

Jones, Philip, comp. *Britain and Palestine 1914–1948: Archival Sources for the History of the British Mandate*. London: Oxford University Press, 1979.

Katznelson, Rachel Shazar. *The Plough Woman: Memoirs of the Pioneer Women of Palestine.* 2d ed. New York: Herzl, 1975.

Kimche, Jon and David Kimche. *Both Sides of the Hill.* London: Secker and Warburg, 1960.

Koestler, Arthur. *Promise and Fulfillment: Palestine 1917–1949.* New York: Macmillan, 1949.

Lowdermilk, W.C. *Palestine: Land of Promise.* New York: Harper & Row, 1944.

Lucas, Noah. *The Modern History of Israel.* New York and Washington, DC: Praeger, 1975.

Maoz, Moshe, ed. *Studies on Palestine During the Ottoman Period.* Jerusalem: Magnes, 1975.

Marlowe, John. *The Seat of Pilate: An Account of the Palestine Mandate.* London: The Cresset Press, 1959.

Nathan, Robert, Oscar Gass and Daniel Craemer. *Palestine: Problem and Promise.* Washington, DC: Public Affairs Press, 1946.

Parkes, James. *A History of Palestine from 135 A.D. to Modern Times.* Oxford: Clarendon, 1949.

Sachar, Howard M. *A History of Israel: From the Rise of Zionism to Our Time.* New York: Alfred Knopf, 1976.

———. *A History of Israel. Volume II: From the Aftermath of the Yom Kippur War.* New York: Oxford, 1987.

Sacher, Harry. *Israel: The Establishment of a State.* London: Weidenfeld & Nicolson, 1952.

Samuel, Maurice. *Harvest in the Desert.* Philadelphia: Jewish Publication Society, 1944.

———. *Level Sunlight.* New York: Alfred Knopf, 1953.

Sanders, Ronald. *The High Walls of Jerusalem: A History of the Balfour Declaration. The Birth of the British Mandate for Palestine.* New York: Holt, Rinehart and Winston, 1984.

Sanger, Richard H. *Where the Jordan Flows.* Washington, DC: Middle East Institute, 1963.

Stein, Leonard. *The Balfour Declaration.* New York: Simon & Schuster, 1961.

Sykes, Christopher. *Crossroads to Israel.* Cleveland and New York: World Publishing, 1965.

Tuchman, Barbara W. *Bible and Sword: England and Palestine from the Bronze Age to Balfour.* New York: Minerva Press, 1968.

Jewish History

Bamberger, Bernard J. *The Story of Judaism.* New York: Schocken, 1964.

Baron, Salo W. *A Social and Religious History of the Jews.* 9 vols. New York: Columbia University, 1952, 1957, 1960, 1966.

Bauer, Yehuda. *A History of the Holocaust.* New York: Franklin Watts, 1982.

Ben Zvi, Itzhak. *The Exiled and the Redeemed.* Philadelphia: Jewish Publication Society, 1957.

Bentwich, Norman. *The Jews in Our Time.* Baltimore, MD: Penguin Books, 1960.

Chouraqui, Andre. *A History of Judaism.* New York: Walker, 1963.

Finkelstein, Louis, ed. *The Jews: Their History, Culture and Religion.* New York: Harper & Row, 1950.

Graetz, Heinrich. *History of the Jews.* 6 vols. Philadelphia: Jewish Publication Society, 1891–1898.

Grayzel, Solomon. *A History of the Jews.* Philadelphia: Jewish Publication Society, 1947.

————. *A History of the Contemporary Jews from 1900 to the Present.* New York and Philadelphia: Meridian Books and Jewish Publication Society of America, 1960.

Margolis, Max and Alexander Marx. *A History of the Jewish People.* Cleveland and New York and Philadelphia: World Publishing Company and The Jewish Publication Society of America, 1958.

Parkes, James. *A History of the Jewish People.* rev ed. Baltimore, MD: Penguin Books, 1964.

Roth, Cecil. *A History of the Jews: From Earliest Times Through the Six Day War.* rev. ed. New York: Schocken, 1970.

Sachar, Abram Leon. *A History of the Jews.* 5th ed., rev. and enl. New York: Alfred Knopf, 1965.

Sachar, Howard Morley. *The Course of Modern Jewish History.* New York: Dell, 1958.

Eichmann Trial

Arendt, Hannah. *Eichmann in Jerusalem: A Report on the Banality of Evil.* rev. and enl. ed. New York: The Viking Press, 1964.

Friedman, Tuviah. *The Hunter.* Edited and translated by David C. Gross. New York: Macfadden Books, 1961.

Hausner, Gideon. *Justice in Jerusalem.* New York: Harper & Row, 1966; Schocken, 1968.

Linze, Dewey W. *The Trial of Adolf Eichmann.* Los Angeles, CA: Holloway House Publishing Company, 1961.

Perlman, M. *The Capture and Trial of Adolf Eichmann.* New York: Simon & Schuster, 1963.

Zeiger, Henry A., ed. *The Case Against Adolf Eichmann.* New York: New American Library, 1960.

INTERNATIONAL RELATIONS

General

Amir, Shimeon. *Israel's Development Cooperation with Africa, Asia and Latin America.* New York: Praeger, 1974.

Argov, Shlomo. *An Ambassador Speaks Out.* London: Weidenfeld & Nicolson, with the Van Leer Institute, 1983.

Aron, Raymond. *DeGaulle, Israel and the Jews.* New York: Praeger, 1969.

Balabkins, Nicholas. *West German Reparations to Israel.* New Brunswick, NJ: Rutgers University Press, 1971.

Bialer, Uri. *Mapai and Israel's Foreign Policy, 1947–1952.* Jerusalem: Hebrew University, 1981.

Brecher, Michael. *The Foreign Policy System of Israel: Setting, Images, Process.* New Haven: Yale University Press, 1972.

———. *Israel, The Korean War, and China.* New Brunswick, NJ: Transaction Books, 1974.

———. *Decisions in Israel's Foreign Policy.* New Haven: Yale University Press, 1975.

Brecher, Michael with Benjamin Geist. *Decisions in Crisis: Israel, 1967 and 1973.* Berkeley, CA: University of California Press, 1980.

Crosbie, Sylvia K. *A Tacit Alliance: France and Israel from Suez to the Six Day War.* Princeton, NJ: Princeton University Press, 1974.

Curtis, Michael R. and Susan Aurelia Gitelson, eds. *Israel in the Third World.* New Brunswick, NJ: Transaction Books, 1976.

Deutschkron, Inge. *Bonn and Jerusalem: The Strange Coalition.* Philadelphia: Chilton, 1970.

Draper, Theodore. *Israel and World Politics: Roots of the Third Arab-Israeli War.* New York: The Viking Press, 1968.

Eban, Abba. *Voice of Israel.* New York: Horizon, 1957.

Eytan, Walter. *The First Ten Years: A Diplomatic History of Israel.* New York: Simon & Schuster, 1958.

Feldman, Lily Gardner. *The Special Relationship Between West Germany and Israel.* Winchester, MA: Allen and Unwin, 1984.

Glick, Edward B. *Latin America and the Palestine Problem.* New York: Theodor Herzl Foundation, 1958.

Golan, Galia. *Yom Kippur and After.* Cambridge, UK: Cambridge University Press, 1977.

Grossmann, Kurt R. *Germany's Moral Debt: The German-Israel Agreement.* Washington, DC: Public Affairs Press, 1954.

Heller, Mark A. *A Palestinian State: The Implications for Israel.* Cambridge, MA: Harvard University Press, 1983.

Herzog, Chaim. *Who Stands Accused? Israel Answers Its Critics.* New York: Random House, 1978.

Hillel, Shlomo. *Operation Babylon.* New York: Doubleday, 1987.

Joseph, Benjamin M. *Besieged Bedfellows: Israel and the Land of Apartheid.* Westport, CT: Greenwood, 1988.

Kaufman, Edy, Yoram Shapira, Joel Barromi. *Israel-Latin American Relations*. New Brunswick, NJ: Transaction Books, 1979.

Klieman, Aaron. *Israel's Global Reach: Arms Sales as Diplomacy*. Elmsford, NY: Pergamon-Brassey's International Defense Publishers, 1985.

Kreinin, Mordechai. *Israel and Africa: A Study in Technical Cooperation*. New York: Praeger, 1964.

Laufer, Leopold. *Israel and the Developing Countries: New Approaches to Cooperation*. New York: Twentieth Century Fund, 1967.

Liebman, Charles. *Pressure Without Sanctions: The Influence of World Jewry on Israeli Policy*. Rutherford, NJ: Fairleigh Dickinson, 1977.

Medzini, Meron, ed. *Israel's Foreign Relations: Selected Documents, 1947–1979*. 5 vols. Jerusalem: Ministry of Foreign Affairs, 1976–1981.

Peleg, Ilan. *Begin's Foreign Policy, 1977–1983: Israel's Move to the Right*. Westport, CT: Greenwood, 1987.

Raphael, Gideon. *Destination Peace: Three Decades of Israeli Foreign Policy*. New York: Stein and Day, 1981.

Roberts, Samuel J. *Survival or Hegemony? The Foundations of Israeli Foreign Policy*. Baltimore and London: The Johns Hopkins University Press, 1973.

Romberg, Otto R. and George Schwinghammer, eds. *Twenty Years of Diplomatic Relations Between the Federal Republic of Germany and Israel*. Frankfurt-am-Main: Tribune Books, 1985.

Sagi, Nana. *German Reparations: A History of the Negotiations*. Jerusalem: Magnes, 1980.

Slater, Robert. *Israel's Aid to Developing Nations*. New York: Friendly House Publishers, 1973.

Tekoah, Yosef. *In the Face of Nations: Israel's Struggle for Peace.* New York: Simon & Schuster, 1976.

Vogel, Rolf, ed. *The German Path to Israel, A Documentation.* London: Oswald Wolff, 1969.

Wilson, Harold. *The Chariot of Israel: Britain, America and the State of Israel.* London: Weidenfeld & Nicolson, 1981.

Israel and the United Nations

Azcarate, Pablo de. *Mission in Palestine 1948–1952.* Washington, DC: Middle East Institute.

Beker, Avi. *The United Nations and Israel: From Recognition to Reprehension.* Lexington, MA: Lexington Books, 1988.

Bernadotte, Folke. *To Jerusalem.* London: Hodder and Stoughton, 1951.

Burns, E.L.M. *Between Arab and Israeli.* New York: Obolensky, 1963.

Hutchison, E.H. *Violent Truce.* New York: Devin-Adair, 1956.

Israel and the United Nations. Report of a Study Group Set Up by the Hebrew University of Jerusalem. New York: Manhattan Publishing Company, 1956.

Israel and the United States

Blitzer, Wolf. *Between Washington and Jerusalem: A Reporter's Notebook.* New York: Oxford University Press, 1985.

———. *The Exclusive Story of Jonathan Jay Pollard: The American Who Spied on His Country for Israel and How He Was Betrayed.* New York: Harper & Row, 1989.

Ganin, Zvi. *Truman, American Jewry and Israel, 1945–1948.* New York: Holmes & Meier, 1979.

Glick, Edward B. *The Triangular Connection: America, Israel and American Jews.* London: Allen & Unwin, 1982.

Grose, Peter. *Israel in the Mind of America.* New York: Alfred Knopf, 1983.

Kenen, I.L. *Israel's Defense Line: Her Friends and Foes in Washington.* Buffalo, NY: Prometheus, 1981.

MacDonald, James G. *My Mission in Israel, 1948–1951.* New York: Simon & Schuster, 1951.

Nachmias, Mitza. *Transfer of Arms, Leverage, and Peace in the Middle East.* New York; Westport, CT; London: Greenwood, 1988.

Reich, Bernard. *The United States and Israel: Influence in the Special Relationship.* New York: Praeger, 1984.

Safran, Nadav. *The United States and Israel.* Cambridge, MA: Harvard University, 1963.

Schechtman, Joseph B. *The United States and the Jewish State Movement: The Crucial Decade, 1939–1949.* New York: Herzl and Yoseloff, 1966.

Snetsinger, John. *Truman, the Jewish Vote and the Creation of Israel.* Stanford, CA: Hoover Institution Press, 1974.

Wilson, Evan M. *Decision in Palestine: How the United States Came to Recognize Israel.* Stanford, CA: Hoover Institution Press, 1979.

Israel and the Soviet Union

Dagan, Avigdor. *Moscow and Jerusalem: Twenty Years of Relations Between Israel and the Soviet Union.* London: Abelard-Schuman, 1970.

Hazan, Baruch A. *Soviet Propaganda: A Case Study of the Middle East Conflict.* New York: Wiley, 1976.

Ivanov, K. and Z. Sheinis. *The State of Israel: Its Position and Policies.* Moscow: State Publications of Political Literature, 1958.

Klinghoffer, Arthur Jay with Judith Apter. *Israel and the Soviet Union: Alienation or Reconciliation?* Boulder, CO: Westview Press, 1985.

Krammer, Arnold P. *The Forgotten Friendship: Israel and the Soviet Bloc, 1947–53.* Urbana, IL: University of Illinois Press, 1974.

Magil, Abraham. *Israel in Crisis.* New York: International, 1950.

Ro'i, Yaacov. *Soviet Decision Making in Practice: The USSR and Israel, 1947–1954.* New Brunswick, NJ: Transaction Books, 1980.

————, ed. *The Limits to Power: Soviet Policy in the Middle East.* London: Croom Helm, 1979.

Sella, Amnon. *Soviet Policy and Military Conduct in the Middle East.* London: Macmillan, 1981.

SOCIETY

General

Arian, Asher, ed. *Israel: A Developing Society.* Assen, The Netherlands: Van Gorcum, 1980.

Bachi, Roberto. *The Population of Israel.* Jerusalem: Institute of Contemporary Jewry, Hebrew University, 1977.

Ben-Rafael, Eliezer. *The Emergence of Ethnicity: Cultural Groups and Social Conflict in Israel.* Westport, CT: Greenwood, 1982.

Ben Zvi, Itzhak. *The Exiled and the Redeemed.* Philadelphia: Jewish Publication Society, 1961.

Berler, Alexander. *New Towns in Israel.* Jerusalem: Israel Universities Press, 1970.

Curtis, Michael and Mordechai S. Chertoff, eds. *Israel: Social Structure and Change.* New Brunswick, NJ: Transaction Books, 1973.

Eisenstadt, Samuel N. *Israeli Society.* New York: Praeger, 1967.

————. *The Transformation of Israeli Society.* London: Weidenfeld and Nicolson, 1985.

Friedlander, Dov and Calvin Goldscheider. *The Population of Israel.* New York: Columbia University Press, 1979.

Hazleton, Lesley. *Israeli Woman: The Reality Behind the Myth.* New York: Simon & Schuster, 1977.

Isaacs, Harold R. *American Jews in Israel.* New York: John Day Co., 1967.

Matras, Judah. *Social Change in Israel.* Chicago: Aldine Publishing Co., 1965.

Patai, Raphael. *Israel Between East and West: A Study in Human Relations.* Philadelphia: Jewish Publication Society, 1953.

Roumani, Maurice M. *From Immigrant to Citizen: The Contribution of the Army to National Integration in Israel.* The Hague: Foundation for the Studies of Plural Societies, 1979.

Russcol, Herbert and Margalit Banai. *The First Million Sabras: A Portrait of the Native-Born Israelis.* New York: Dodd, Mead, 1970.

Sachar, Howard Morley. *Aliyah: The Peoples of Israel.* Cleveland and New York: World Publishing Co., 1961.

————. *From the Ends of the Earth: The Peoples of Israel.* Cleveland: World, 1964.

Samuel, Edwin. *The Structure of Society in Israel.* New York: Random House, 1969.

Schoenbrun, David. *The New Israelis: A Report on the First Generation Born in Israel.* New York: Atheneum, 1973.

Segre, Dan V. *Israel: A Society in Transition.* London: Oxford University Press, 1971.

Shokeid, Moshe and Shlomo Deshen. *Distant Relations: Ethnicity and Politics Among Arabs and North African Jews in Israel.* South Hadley, MA: J.F. Bergin Publishers, 1982.

Simon, Rita J. *Continuity and Change: A Study of Two Ethnic Communities in Israel.* New York: Cambridge University Press, 1978.

Smooha, Sammy. *Israel: Pluralism and Conflict.* London: Routledge & Kegan Paul, 1978.

Stock, Ernest. *From Conflict to Understanding: Relations Between Jews and Arabs in Israel Since 1948.* New York: The American Jewish Committee, 1968.

Stone, Russell A. (with the collaboration of Louis Guttman and Shlomit Levy). *Social Change in Israel: Attitudes and Events, 1967–79.* New York: Praeger, 1982.

Weingrod, Alex. *Israel: Group Relations in a New Society.* New York: Frederick A. Praeger Publishers for the Institute of Race Relations, 1965.

————. *Reluctant Pioneers—Village Development in Israel.* Ithaca, NY: Cornell University Press, 1966.

————. *Studies in Israeli Ethnicity: After the Ingathering.* New York: Gordon and Breach, 1985.

Education

Ben-Baruch, E. and Y. Newmann, eds. *Educational Administration and Policy Making: The Case of Israel.* Beer-Sheva, Israel: Ben-Gurion University, 1982.

Bentwich, Joseph S. *Education in Israel.* London: Routledge & Kegan Paul, 1965.

Braham, Randolph L. *Israel: A Modern Education System.* Washington, DC: United States Government Printing Office, 1966.

Mar'i, Sami K. *Arab Education in Israel.* New York: Syracuse University Press, 1978.

Religion

Abramov, S. Zalman. *Perpetual Dilemma: Jewish Religion in the Jewish State.* Rutherford, NJ: Fairleigh Dickinson University Press, 1979.

Aviad, Janet. *Return to Judaism: Religious Renewal in Israel.* Chicago: University of Chicago Press, 1983.

Badi, Joseph. *Religion in Israel Today: The Relationship Between State and Religion.* New York: Bookman Associates, 1959.

Ben-Dor, Gabriel. *The Druzes in Israel: A Political Study: Political Innovation and Integration in a Middle Eastern Minority.* Jerusalem: Magnes, 1979.

Birnbaum, Ervin. *The Politics of Compromise: State and Religion in Israel.* Rutherford, NJ: Fairleigh Dickinson University Press, 1970.

Buber, Martin. *Israel and the World: Essays in a Time of Crisis.* 2d ed. New York: Schocken, 1963.

Dana, Nissim. *The Druze: A Religious Community in Transition.* Jerusalem: Turtledove, 1980.

Don-Yehiya, Eliezer. "The Politics of Religious Parties," in *Public Life in Israel and the Diaspora.* Edited by Sam N. Lehman-Wilzig and Bernard Susser. Jerusalem: Bar-Ilan University Press, 1981.

Hitti, Philip K. *The Origins of the Druze People and Religion, with Extracts from their Sacred Writings.* New York: AMS Press, 1969.

Kraines, Oscar. *The Impossible Dilemma: Who Is a Jew in the State of Israel.* New York: Bloch, 1976.

Leslie, Samuel C. *The Rift in Israel: Religious Authority and Secular Democracy.* New York: Schocken, 1971.

Liebman, Charles S. and Eliezer Don-Yehiya. *Civil Religion in Israel: Traditional Judaism and Political Culture in the Jewish State.* Berkeley, Los Angeles, London: University of California Press, 1983.

Makerem, Sami N. *The Druze Faith.* New York: Caravan, 1974.

Marmorstein, Emile. *Heaven at Bay: The Jewish Kulturkampf in the Holy Land.* London: Oxford University Press, 1969.

Miller, William M. *The Baha'i Faith: Its History and Teachings.* South Pasadena, CA: W. Carey Library, 1974.

Rabinowicz, Harry M. *Hasidism and the State of Israel.* Rutherford, NJ: Fairleigh Dickinson University Press, 1982.

Reiser, Stewart. *The Politics of Leverage: The National Religious Party of Israel and Its Influence on Foreign Policy.* Harvard Middle East Papers, Modern Series, No. 2. Cambridge, MA: Center for Middle Eastern Studies, Harvard University, 1984.

Roth, Cecil and Geoffrey Wigoder, eds. in chief. *The New Standard Jewish Encyclopedia.* rev. ed. London: Allen, 1970.

Schiff, Gary S. *Tradition and Politics: The Religious Parties of Israel.* Detroit: Wayne State University Press, 1977.

Steinsalz, Adin. *The Essential Talmud.* New York: Basic Books, 1976.

Weiner, Herbert. *The Wild Goats of Ein Gedi: A Journal of Religious Encounters in the Holy Land.* Cleveland and New York and Philadelphia: World Publishing Company and Jewish Publication Society of America, 1963.

Zucker, Norman L. *The Coming Crisis in Israel: Private Faith and Public Policy.* Cambridge: MIT Press, 1973.

Arabs in Israel

Cohen, Abner. *Arab Border Villages in Israel: A Study of Continuity and Change in Social Organization.* Manchester, UK: Manchester University Press, 1972.

Ginat, Joseph. *Blood Disputes Among Bedouin and Rural Arabs in Israel: Revenge, Mediation, Outcasting, and Family Honor.* Pittsburgh: University of Pittsburgh Press, 1987.

Jiryis, Sabri. *The Arabs in Israel.* New York and London: Monthly Review Press, 1976.

Landau, Jacob M. *The Arabs in Israel: A Political Study.* London: Oxford University Press, 1969.

Lustick, Ian. *Arabs in the Jewish State: Israel's Control of a National Minority.* Austin, TX: University of Texas Press, 1980.

Marx, Emanuel. *Bedouin of the Negev.* New York: Praeger, 1968.

Schwartz, Walter. *The Arabs in Israel.* London: Faber and Faber, 1959.

Smooha, Sammy. *Social Research on Arabs in Israel, 1948–1977: Trends and an Annotated Bibliography*. Ramat Gan, Israel: Turtledove, 1978.

———. *The Orientation and Politicization of the Arab Minority in Israel*. Haifa, Israel: University of Haifa, 1981.

Zureik, Elia T. *The Palestinians in Israel: A Study of Internal Colonization*. London: Routledge, 1979.

The Kibbutz

Baratz, Joseph. *A Village by the Jordan: The Story of Degania*. New York: Sharon, 1957.

Ben-Yosef, Avraham C. *The Purest Democracy in the World*. New York: Herzl and Yoseloff, 1963.

Bettelheim, Bruno. *The Children of the Dream*. London: Macmillan, 1969.

Darin-Drabkin, H. *The Other Society: The Kibbutzim of Israel*. New York: Harcourt, 1963.

Fishman, Aryeh, ed. *The Religious Kibbutz Movement*. Jerusalem: 1957.

Kanovsky, Eilyahu. *The Economy of the Israeli Kibbutz*. Cambridge, MA: Harvard University, Center for Middle East Studies, 1966.

Krausz, Ernest, ed. *Sociology of the Kibbutz*. New Brunswick, NJ: Transaction Books, 1983.

Leon, Dan. *The Kibbutz: A New Way of Life*. Oxford, UK: Pergamon Press, 1969.

———. *The Kibbutz: A Portrait from Within*. Tel Aviv: Israel Horizons, 1964.

Mittelberg, David. *Strangers in Paradise: The Israeli Kibbutz Experience.* New Brunswick, NJ: Transaction Books, 1988.

Rabin, Albert I. *Growing up in the Kibbutz.* New York: Springer, 1965.

Shur, Shimon, et al. *The Kibbutz: A Bibliography of Scientific and Professional Publications in English.* Darby, PA: Norwood, 1981.

Spiro, Melford E. *Children of the Kibbutz.* Cambridge, MA: Harvard University, 1958.

———. *Gender and Culture: Kibbutz Women Revisited.* Durham, NC: Duke University Press, 1979.

———. *Kibbutz: Venture in Utopia.* aug. ed. Cambridge, MA: Harvard University Press, 1979.

Stern, Boris. *The Kibbutz That Was.* Washington, DC: Public Affairs Press, 1965.

Tiger, Lionel and Joseph Shepher. *Woman in the Kibbutz.* New York: Harcourt, Brace, Jovanovich, 1975.

Weingarten, Murray. *Life in a Kibbutz.* New York: The Reconstructionist Press, 1955.

The Moshav

Abarbanel, Jay S. *The Cooperative Farmer and the Welfare State: Economic Change in an Israeli Moshav.* Manchester, UK: Manchester University Press, 1974.

Klayman, Maxwell I. *The Moshav in Israel: A Case Study of Institution-Building for Agricultural Development.* New York: Praeger, 1970.

Viteles, Harry. *A History of the Co-Operative Movement in Israel: A Source Book.* 7 vols. London: Vallentine, Mitchell, 1966–68.

Immigration

Avriel, Ehud. *Open the Gates! A Personal Story of "Illegal" Immigration to Israel.* New York: Atheneum, 1975.

Barer, Shlomo. *The Magic Carpet.* London: Secker & Warburg, 1952.

Bauer, Yehuda. *Flight and Rescue: Brichah.* New York: Random House, 1970.

Dekel, Ephraim. *B'riha: Flight to the Homeland.* New York: Herzl, 1973.

Deshen, Shlomo and Moshe Shokeid. *The Predicament of Homecoming: Cultural and Social Life of North African Immigrants in Israel.* Ithaca, NY: Cornell University Press, 1974.

Eisenstadt, Samuel N. *The Absorption of Immigrants.* Glencoe, IL: Free Press, 1955; Greenwood Reprint, 1975.

Gitelman, Zvi. *Becoming Israelis: Political Resocialization of Soviet and American Immigrants.* New York: Praeger, 1982.

Gruber, Ruth. *Rescue: The Exodus of the Ethiopian Jews.* New York: Atheneum, 1988.

Isaacs, Harold R. *American Jews in Israel.* New York: J. Day, 1966.

Kimche, Jon and David Kimche. *The Secret Roads.* New York: Farrar, Straus, and Cudahy, 1955.

Sachar, Howard Morley. *Aliyah: The Peoples of Israel.* Cleveland: World, 1961.

Shama, Avraham and Mark Iris. *Immigration Without Integration: Third World Jews in Israel.* Cambridge, MA: Schenkman, 1977.

Shuval, Judith T. *Immigrants on the Threshold.* New York: Atherton, 1963.

Weingrod, Alex. *Reluctant Pioneers: Village Development in Israel.* Ithaca, NY: Cornell University Press, 1966.

Weintraub, Dov, et al. *Immigration and Social Change: Agricultural Settlement of New Immigrants in Israel.* Jerusalem: Israel University Press, 1971.

ZIONISM AND ANTI-ZIONISM

Avineri, Shlomo. *The Making of Modern Zionism: The Intellectual Origins of the Jewish State.* New York: Basic Books, 1981.

Berger, Elmer. *A Partisan History of Judaism.* New York: Praeger, 1951.

———. *Who Knows Better Must Say So.* New York: Bookmailer, 1955.

Buber, Martin. *Israel and Palestine: The History of an Idea.* London: East and West Library, 1952.

Cohen, Israel. *A Short History of Zionism.* London: Muller, 1951.

Gal, Allon. *Socialist Zionist Theory and Issues in Contemporary Jewish Nationalism.* Cambridge: Schenkman Publishing Company, 1973.

Gilbert, Martin. *Exile and Return.* Philadelphia: Lippincott, 1978.

Gonen, Jay Y. *A Psychohistory of Zionism.* New York: Mason/Charter, 1975.

Ha'am, Ahad. *Selected Essays.* Cleveland and New York and Philadelphia: World Publishing Company and The Jewish Publication Society of America, 1962.

Halkin, Abraham S., ed. *Zion in Jewish Literature.* New York: Herzl, 1961.

Halpern, Ben. *The Idea of the Jewish State.* 2d ed. Cambridge, MA: Harvard University Press, 1970.

Heller, Joseph. *The Zionist Idea.* New York: Schocken, 1949.

Hertzberg, Arthur, ed. *The Zionist Idea: An Historical Analysis and Reader.* New York: Doubleday, 1959.

Herzl, Theodor. *The Jewish State: An Attempt at a Modern Solution of the Jewish Question.* London: R. Searl, 1934.

———. *Old New Land.* New York: Herzl, 1960.

Hess, Moses. *Rome and Jerusalem.* New York: Bloch, 1945.

Laqueur, Walter. *A History of Zionism.* London: Weidenfeld and Nicolson, 1972.

Learsi, Rufus. *Fulfillment: The Epic Story of Zionism.* New York: World, 1951.

Litvinoff, Barnet. *The Road to Jerusalem: Zionism's Imprint on History.* London: Weidenfeld and Nicolson, 1965. Also published as *To the House of Their Fathers.*

Petuchowski, Jacob J. *Zion Reconsidered.* New York: Twayne, 1966.

Rabinowicz, Oskar K. *Fifty Years of Zionism: A Historical Analysis of Dr. Weizmann's "Trial and Error".* London: Robert Anscombe, 1950.

Schechtman, Joseph and Yehuda Benari. *History of the Revisionist Movement.* Tel Aviv: Hadar Publishing House, 1970.

Segre, Dan V. *A Crisis of Identity: Israel and Zionism.* Oxford, UK: Oxford University Press, 1980.

Shavit, Yaacov. *Revisionism in Zionism.* Tel Aviv: Yariv, 1978.

Smith, Gary V., ed. *Zionism the Dream and the Reality: A Jewish Critique.* Newton Abbot, UK: David and Charles, 1974.

Sokolow, Nahum. *Hibbath Zion (The Love of Zion).* Jerusalem: Rubin Mass, 1941.

———. *History of Zionism, 1600–1918.* New York: Ktav, 1969.

Taylor, Alan R. *Prelude to Israel: An Analysis of Zionist Diplomacy 1897–1947.* rev. ed. Beirut: The Institute for Palestine Studies, 1970.

Vital, David. *The Origins of Zionism.* Oxford, UK: Oxford University Press, 1975.

———. *Zionism: The Formative Years.* New York: Oxford University Press, 1982.

ABOUT THE AUTHOR

BERNARD REICH is Professor of Political Science and International Affairs and Former Chairman of the Department of Political Science at George Washington University in Washington, DC. He also is Chairman of Advanced Area Studies—Fertile Crescent at the Department of State's Foreign Service Institute and a member of the adjunct faculty of the Defense Intelligence College. He serves as a consultant to various United States government agencies and to international business on Middle Eastern affairs. He has lived in the Middle East on Fulbright and National Science Foundation Fellowships and has visited there often.

Among other works, Professor Reich is the author of *Quest for Peace: United States-Israel Relations and the Arab-Israeli Conflict; The United States and Israel: Influence in the Special Relationship; Israel: Land of Tradition and Conflict;* coauthor of *The United States and the Israel-Arab Conflict;* editor and coauthor of *Political Leaders of the Contemporary Middle East and North Africa: A Biographical Dictionary;* coeditor and coauthor of *Government and Politics of the Middle East and North Africa* (two editions), of *Israel Faces the Future,* of *Israeli National Security Policy: Political Actors and Perspectives,* and of *Israeli Politics in the 1990s: Key Domestic and Foreign Policy Factors;* as well as the author of numerous articles, book chapters and monographs on Israeli politics and foreign policy, on other aspects of Middle East politics, and on United States foreign policy.

Dr. Reich received his B.A. with Special Honors from the City College of New York in 1961 where he was elected to Phi Beta Kappa. He secured his M.A. (1963) and his Ph.D. (1964) from the University of Virginia.